THE ACTOR'S ENCYCLOPEDIA OF CASTING DIRECTORS

CONVERSATIONS WITH OVER 100 CASTING DIRECTORS ON HOW TO GET THE JOB

KAREN KONDAZIAN
with EDDIE SHAPIRO

Foreword by Richard Dreyfuss

lone eagle
PUBLISHING COMPANY
Los Angeles

THE ACTOR'S ENCYCLOPEDIA OF CASTING DIRECTORS

Copyright © 2000 by Karen Kondazian

LONE EAGLE PUBLISHING COMPANY
2301 Westwood Boulevard
Los Angeles, CA 90064
Tel: 800-FILMBKS • Toll Free Fax: 888-FILMBKS
www.loneeagle.com and www.eaglei.com

Printed in the United States of America

Cover design by ADVANTAGE, London, T: +44 20 7613 3933
Book design by Carla Green
Edited by Lauren Rossini

Library of Congress Cataloging-in-Publication Data

Kondazian, Karen.
    The actors encyclopedia of casting directors / Karen Kondazian with
    Eddie Shapiro.
        p.   cm.
    Includes filmographies.
    ISBN 1-58065-013-9
    1. Acting—Vocational guidance. 2. Casting directors Interviews.
    I. Shapiro, Eddie.
    PN2055.C66   1999
    792' .028'029—dc21   99-39868
                                                            CIP

Photo Credits:

Pages xiii, 1, 9, 13, 19, 23, 29, 33, 45, 49, 57, 61, 65, 71, 75, 79, 83, 95, 99, 111, 117, 133, 139, 147, 151, 157, 167, 183, 197, 217, 221, 225, 233, 253, 265, 271, 275, 285, 289, 301, 305, 309, 325, 329, 333, 343, 351, 357, 365, 369, 377, 385, 389, 393, 397, 405, 413, 417, 421, 425, 431 and 437 by Ed Krieger

Page 243 by Dale MacDiarmid

Pages 37, 187, and 191 by Edward Shapiro

Page 201 by Alisha Tamburri

Page 455 by Stephen Vaughn

Page 443 by Merie W. Wallace

Page 87 by Alan Weissman

All other photos are provided courtesy of the author.

Lone Eagle books may be purchased in bulk at special discounts for promotional or educational purposes. Special editions can be created to specifications. Inquiries for sales and distribution, textbook adoption, foreign language translation, editorial, and rights and permissions inquiries should be addressed to: Jeff Black, Lone Eagle Publishing, 2337 Roscomare Road, Suite Nine, Los Angeles, CA 90077 or send e-mail to: info@loneeagle.com

Distributed to the trade by National Book Network, 800-462-6420

Lone Eagle Publishing Company is a registered trademark.

To my parents
Lillian Marie Paul
and Varnum Paul
who, with their constant love and support,
have taught me that anything is possible.... Anything.

—Karen Kondazian

Contents

FROM ANOTHER P.O.V.

ABOUT THE AUTHORS
    AND PHOTOGRAPHER

FOREWORD BY RICHARD DREYFUSS

In 1976 or '77, I taught a class for ten weeks called "How to be an Unemployed Actor in Los Angeles." I interviewed casting directors and agents and I taught the kids how to schmooze people, what the relationships are. I taught them that on an interview, your job is two-fold: to either get the job or to be remembered. I told them that I never brought a picture or a résumé because I figured that if I couldn't get casting directors to remember me from my presence in the room, nothing I wrote down on a piece of paper was going to make a bit of difference. I would be provocative and charming and funny. You want to get agents and casting directors to the point where they wake up at three o'clock in the morning and say, "I wish I could get Richard a job today." Acting is based on the showing of a personality. It's not just whether or not you can be the character. Can this vivid person show me this character through their own vivid personality?

Sometimes, during a conversation with a casting director on an audition, you can feel the audition slipping away. They might be asking you questions about yourself and you can actually start to feel their indifference. That's when I would say, "Excuse me, let me read this scene for you because that's what I do best. I'm the best actor you're going to see today so I might as well read it." And then I'd read it. Even if I wasn't the best one, they're going to remember I said that. And I'd do that often. My father once said, "Don't you ever apologize for who you are! EVER!" I never, ever walked in saying, "Oh God, you're so great for seeing me."

My primary ambition at a very early age was to be a great actor. I knew fame was part of that and I wanted it, but I didn't want that first. So, if I was going to write my life story, I would have said the Academy Award was a goal that was best kept in front of me. I liked the pursuit more than the arrival. What I loved in those days—and still love—was to watch as many of the films as I could. I would watch films over and over and over again. There were films shown thirteen times a week on Channel 9 and Channel 13. I would watch Spencer Tracy, Charles Laughton, Jimmy Stewart, Cary Grant or whoever it was over and over. And I made no bones about the fact that I was imitating some of them. I would incorporate their stuff. I did that all the time. I was addicted to my ambition and to my love of theatre and acting. It was ferocious. I'm much better when I'm hungry for something and trying to get it than I am having attained it and being there.

Concerning great screen acting, I believe that there is something mysterious that occurs between a camera, film and an audience. There's a magic involved. I think part of it has to do with a willingness to be known emotionally . . . you know, kids these days seem to think that the moments when they're working are all that there is . . . then where is the rest of your life? I would say this—you've gotta learn patience; you've gotta learn enjoyment. Try to parse your ambition so it doesn't swallow up the rest of your life. And finally, if you want to be an actor, act. It's really simple. The more you act, the better you get. Go to classes. Go to workshops. Act more hours of the day than not. Act for free. If you're lucky, every once in awhile, you'll get paid. Think of the early years of your life as an apprenticeship. Don't think you're going to be handed your stardom. But do consider what you're going to do if you get it.

—Richard Dreyfuss

How to Use this Book

You have at your fingertips an invaluable resource which can serve you in any number of ways. Read cover to cover, it can provide vital information to help you create or maintain a career. As a reference guide, the book can serve you every time you have an audition. Called in for *Frasier*? Look up Jeff Greenberg and see what he has to say. Meeting with John Levey on *ER*? Go right to the source. Learn what they like and what they don't so you can go into your audition knowing what to expect. You'll be that much more armed and prepared. You'll also see that, while many casting directors feel the same about a lot of issues (they all like training and preparation and hate phone calls), they contradict each other left and right over others (memorization, props). The reality is that there is no singular, right answer. There are, however, opinions from industry professionals in this book and by reading them and seeing what makes the most sense for you, you can choose your own path wisely.

It is also important to remember that casting directors are a nomadic bunch (which is why a series may go through several different casting directors during its run). They move from project to project and therefore may no longer be where they were when this book went to press. So while their wisdom is timeless, their addresses may be fleeting. If you're having trouble finding a particular casting director, the best source is *The C.D. Directory*, a quarterly address book available through Breakdown Services, Ltd. (In Los Angeles: 1120 S. Robertson, Third Floor, Los Angeles, CA 90035; (310) 276-9166. In New York: (212) 869-2003). The Casting Society of America (CSA) also keeps track. Though not all casting directors are members, the majority are and can be found via the CSA, located at 606 North Larchmont Blvd., Suite 4B; Los Angeles, CA 90004.

While reading this book, bear in mind that though we've covered a large cross-section of casting directors, there are many more who we couldn't include without this book out-weighing your car. The exclusion of any casting director is by no means indicative of their status or talent. But if you tell all of your friends to buy this book, we'll be able to do a second volume and include everyone!

You may also notice that some interviews are significantly longer than others. Since all of the interviews were initially published in either *Drama-Logue* or *Back Stage West*, their length is wholly dependent on the space we were allowed. Again, brevity or length is no indication of the subjects' status or talent.

Most importantly, this book exists to empower you. Far too much within this business is out of your control. Hopefully, with this book, you can feel stronger. It's your destiny. So own it.

And good luck to you!

Acknowledgments

Though we'd like to pretend that we did it all ourselves, we have to thank the following individuals, without whom, things would have been a whole lot tougher. First came Faye Bordy, the editor at *Drama-Logue* who, in 1994, decided that the column "Sculpting Your Career" would make a good addition to her newspaper. She provided the forum for these interviews to take shape and the pressure to churn them out weekly. We are deeply indebted.

In 1997, Rob Kendt, editor of *Back Stage West*, allowed us the space and opportunity to expand the column, renaming it "The Actor's Way." His help, encouragement and inspiration have been invaluable, and his patience (we're not always easy) would make several saints blush. He also gave us the rights to the columns and many photographs, making this book possible. Thanks also to the attentive *Back Stage West/ Drama-Logue* staff, including Scott Proudfit, Rebecca Clerc, Jamie Painter and especially to Steve Minard, who tirelessly put all the photographs on disc. We would like to especially thank Rob Kendt and Scott Proudfit for their respective biographical introductions to the James Cameron and John Woo interviews.

Our heartfelt thanks to Joan Singleton and Jeff Black at Lone Eagle Publishing who took us to the next level by agreeing to publish this book. And we thank our editor, Lauren Rossini, for being undaunted by a manuscript the size of Rhode Island.

In the transcribing of the *Drama-Logue* columns, Leon Fermanian and Teresa Cook, who each spent time assisting, deserve many thanks.

Thanks to Barbara Keegan who, as we raced to deadline, came on to help us update addresses and credits.

Thanks to Ed Krieger for his photographs. Sometimes they said just as much as the actual interviews!

Thanks to casting director Ellie Kanner, who connected us with Lone Eagle Publishing, the publisher of her own book, *NEXT: An Actor's Guide to Auditioning*.

Thanks to Shirley and Larry of the Casting Society of America (CSA), and also to Breakdown Services for helping us locate lost subjects.

We would like to thank Cathy Leslie for her "connections," that allowed us to set up our fascinating interview with James Cameron.

Likewise, thank you to Gregory and Laurence Walsh for their assistance in arranging our meeting with the wonderful John Woo.

A grateful thanks to Gary Grossman for his assistance in facilitating the interview with Milton Katselas.

And of course, a very special and grateful thanks to all of the interview subjects. They shared their wisdom, their time and sometimes, their lunch. Without their generosity, there would be no book.

We both thank our parents who've always supported us and gave us the education which enabled us to write. They also listened as we complained about each other.

There have been friends whose support and inspiration have meant more than they know. Karen thanks Loreen Arbus, Tara Boles, Nicole David, Jason Evers, The Fountain Theatre, Julie Garfield, Margie Haber, Jack Heller, the Stephen Jizmagian family, Paul Jordan, Milton Katselas, Cathy Leslie, Lyle Leverich, Simon Levy, Terry Liebling, Ron Link, Lucille Maross, Lee Melville, Richardson Morse, H. David Moss, Paul Ryan, Lee Strasberg, Clyde Ventura and Polly Warfield.

Eddie thanks Elizabeth Bauman, Melinda Berk, Scott Cameron, Jeffrey Dersh, Donna Ekholdt, Jeffrey Epstein, Gregory Gettas, David Giella, Charles Hunt, Jennifer Keller, Joe Quenqua, Gregg Rainwater, Chris Toth, Tom Young, and David Wolf.

And finally, we want to acknowledge each other. Neither one of us would be in a position to write these acknowledgments without the other. So thanks, K.K. Thanks, Eddie.

Introduction: Why Do You Want to Be an Actor?

Dr. Robert Maurer, Clinical Psychologist

Dr. Robert Maurer is the director of Behavioral Sciences for the Family Practice Residency program at Santa Monica UCLA Medical Center, and serves as a faculty member with the UCLA School of Medicine. He also travels extensively, presenting seminars and consultations on a broad spectrum of issues facing people and organizations today. Particularly relevant to performers are his lectures on success, creativity, and fear. Maurer has appeared on ABC's *20/20* and been profiled by *The Los Angeles Times*.

Did you ever pursue the arts yourself?
Well, I was cast as Hansel in *Hansel and Gretel* in the third grade. I was hailed by the school paper as the definitive Hansel, so my acting career peaked rather young.

Twelve or fourteen years ago, I was researching people who were successful in their jobs, health, and relationships, and I had the opportunity to interview highly creative people in the entertainment industry. At that time, I was also offered the opportunity to give a guest lecture to a writing class at UCLA. Researching for that class, in the course of looking at interviews with very successful writers talking about how they created their characters and their stories, I realized the paths of the artist and of the scientist were the same. We are both interested in understanding truth and understanding the human condition. The only difference is the vehicle used to communicate those understandings. Successful artists are visionaries. They intuitively and through other magic see what we scientists need instruments and machines to see. So I saw the opportunity to learn at the feet of actors and writers that which science had not yet found the tools to discover. That was how I became interested in working with actors.

Some of the most pivotal changes in my life were not in a therapist's office, but sitting in a theatre watching a play and being transformed by the experience. I feel a debt of gratitude no price of admission can ever pay. When I've lectured to theatre companies, I've never taken a penny as a way of repaying the gifts that I've received from the theatre. And everything I say applies as much to film as theatre.

What do you suppose drives actors into the profession?
Art has played a powerful and unrecognized role in the history of the world. I think the major motivation for people to be artists, and it can sometimes get complicated and/or corrupted, is this powerful need to express their spirits. There is a passionate need to be creative, to be expressive, to be seen and heard; you see children play-acting from the time they have words and the ability to move. They begin fantasizing, playing, imagining and creating. To me, that is the essence of the human spirit—the ability to imagine and create. What the actor does is refuse to let go of that most human of all our drives. Most of us get corrupted in that pursuit and go after other things such as money, power, possessions. But acting, in its true sense, is the essence of the human spirit. Now what has happened with acting, as it has with most other aspects of human life, is that we get distracted by the need to survive and the need to make money and the need to make things commercial.

George Wolfe said that theatre is people sitting in the dark watching people in the light talking about what it means to be human. It's true. That's why people spend all this money to go to theatre and movies and ballet and to read books— to bring something into their lives that they cannot create on their own; actors make them laugh, make them cry and make them re-examine their lives. Even some of the most commercial of vehicles give people access to emotions that, in their personal lives, they don't have the ability to access. Actors take us to the depths and the heights and give us a feeling of being alive. If we can't do it in our relationships and our work, or in the way we move our bodies, we'll do it in the darkness of a theatre. What's so hard for actors is, given the absolute misery of the process—the auditions, so many classes, the rejections, some of the people you have to work with, all the things that make it painful—that dreams can easily get crushed and people can forget why they began.

For some people, money then becomes their measure of success.
Yes, and it all boils down to how you define success. Most people get trapped by defining success as what they acquire in life: their possessions, how much money they earn, their titles and their credits. I think it's even more problematic for an actor because, unlike any other profession I know, the more success you have the more you have a momentum that continues unabated. As a psychologist, for example, you just assume that once you have established a reputation or competence, even though you will continue to grow and work, basically your future is ordained. That's true for most professions. In acting, one success is no guarantee that you'll get another job, let alone continued success.

There was a twenty-year study of painters in Chicago; they looked at people beginning in their graduate training in art, through their training, to what happened to them. They looked at one thing: those who loved school, who just enjoyed painting and the process, and those who were tolerating school and making the best of a difficult situation in the hopes that they would someday paint in a way that would be recognized with fame and fortune. The only people still painting twenty years later were those who loved painting and the process. Painting, like acting or writing or dancing, is such a difficult task. The rewards are infrequent. When they come, when you win the prize, when you get the acclaim, it can be very intense; but those moments are still few and far between, given the number of hours, weeks and months of work there is between those epic events. The people who love their craft and see themselves as artists, and carry that identity through and study each day, who use walking down the street as a place to study and observe, who absorb every person they meet because they don't know when that person might show up in an artistic endeavor, those are the people who thrive. To me, that's the only definition of success that matters. Successful people are able to sustain their identity as separate from their profession and what's happening to them. That's particularly important in the arts where what happens to you bears only faint correlation to your talent. Unless you take joy in the pursuit of it, you're better off doing something else.

An actor's life can be so miserable with all of its obstacles. But as an actor or a mother or a toll booth operator it's the same challenge: how do I learn to take joy in this moment? Most of us are convinced that if we could only have something outside ourselves, we'd be happy. We want the right relationship, the right job, enough money. It's the same tragic error that we all make and actors have a harder time overcoming it because the environment is so punishing, even for working actors. Once you make a project, you're at the mercy of everyone. I heard a review of a movie on the radio this morning and it trashed an actor for two minutes. Most of us don't have to deal with that. My mistakes are made within the privacy of an office.

What's your advice to actors who put the rest of their lives "on hold" in pursuit of their careers?

The only reason we want to be successful and on a series making a lot of money is we think that that's what's going to make us happy. We're all striving to be happy. What we lose along the way is the realization that we can all create that happiness, even in the face of all of these adversities. Human beings are capable of it. That's why we are amazed by the Mother Theresas and Christopher Reeves and Nelson Mandelas of the world; they can live amidst pain, poverty, imprisonment and still find a way to create their own beauty. They are, if you will, artists. They create their own beauty in an environment where it otherwise might not exist. They make their own stages. The actor has simply made that his or her life's work, which is the most grand thing a human can do; but the grandeur of it can easily get lost when one's trying to pay the rent or the car insurance.

Do you favor any techniques to help people focus on the moment?

One thing we recommend is to do volunteer work with people who are struggling. One of the tragedies of the human mind is that we forget how lucky we are. Even an unemployed actor has at least found his life's dream, is living in a democracy and probably has his health. No matter how miserable our lives are during periods of rejection and bleakness, by comparison we are wealthy beyond means. We have so much to be grateful for; unfortunately, we're just not wired for gratitude. The experience of helping others is to remind yourself how lucky you are to have found your craft and to have the freedom to pursue it—even if that pursuit can be painful. A second technique is having someone ask you, "What do you have to be grateful about right now? What are you enjoying right now?" One of the things we've discovered about the human brain is that it doesn't store everything that's happened to you, it stores what it uses. If you go through the day saying, "What's wrong with me? Why can't I get a break? Why can't I lose weight?" the brain doesn't have the capacity to say, "Hey, that's not fair. Those are ugly questions and I refuse to listen to you talk to me that way." Instead, the brain is forced to start looking for answers and will start storing columns of cells about every weakness, flaw or mistake it can remember. It's got all of that stuff stored whereas all of the positive stuff gets no storage because you don't go around saying, "What am I happy about? What's great about today? What do I love about being an actor?" Those questions may sound kind of sappy but you want to practice saying them out loud so the brain gets used to storing information that relates to what you're grateful for and happy about. Christopher Reeve, when he was interviewed by Barbara Walters, acknowledged all the pain and suffering he went through but he also said that he realized how lucky he was. We are all capable, even in the face of adversity, of celebrating how lucky we are. Reeve focuses his mind and knows that he has the potential to control and shift the emotional experience, no matter the circumstances. That's what art is all about—the ability to shift one's perceptions of things.

Do you have any final tips for the actor?

I've worked with people in countless different professions. The most heroic of life's paths is that of the creative artist. There is nothing that fulfills the human experience more. There are other animals that work together, that use tools, that have language. The only thing that anthropologists have found that separates humans from other animals is our ability to create our own beauty. No art has been discovered among any other species. The only thing worthwhile in having an animal as complicated, difficult, and potentially destructive to itself and the planet as the human being is, is it's potential to create art. The only people on the planet risking that path, attempting to fulfill the God-given gifts of being human are the artists.

As far as I'm concerned, there are two tragedies in the artist's life. First, the artist doesn't appreciate how grand and heroic the path is. He or she takes the most difficult and gallant road on the planet and then feels bad if it's not commercially successful. The second is how artists are treated in the world. It's not recognized that they are essentially our spiritual leaders. They are providing what religion attempts to provide. We dearly hope that they will entertain us and give us light and show us the way.

John A. Aiello, csa

John A. Aiello began his career in New York as an actor and producer. When a production of *On Tina Tuna Walk*, which he cast in New York, was to be mounted in Los Angeles, he relocated to co-produce and cast it. *Tuna Walk* and the play he cast the following year, *The Ten Percent Review,* earned a total of fifteen Drama-Logue Awards. Soon after, Aiello moved on to television as a casting assistant to Junie Lowry-Johnson. He subsequently worked as an associate to Lowry-Johnson on

the television series *Civil Wars, NYPD Blue* and *Murder One* and the feature, *The Hand that Rocks the Cradle*. Aiello went independent in 1995 and cast *The Nutty Professor*. Other recent work includes *Sliders, The Burning Zone, Dellaventura* and *Fast Track*. Currently he casts the series *Nash Bridges* and *Martial Law*.

During callbacks, the auditioning actor faces a great number of people in the room. To whom should he address his questions?
Though in most cases in television it is the producer who makes the final decisions, it's best to address the director, because it is he or she who will direct the actor. But this dynamic varies from show to show and even from episode to episode, depending on the producer/director relationship.

What do you think can empower the actor during the audition process?
Professionalism is the key empowerment. Come in, do the scene, say "Thank you," and leave. Many actors expend a great deal of energy trying to make an impression with their presence through a lot of chitchat. That can prevent the director and producer from seeing you as the character.

I don't recommend that the actor ask if they want to see the scene done in another way. Though you may think you gave a bad reading, the director may have thought you were brilliant. If they want to see anything different, they'll ask.

It's also really important to be on time. Having been an actor and producer myself, I am a stickler for punctuality. I hate to keep actors waiting to go in or producers waiting between actors. Waiting zaps energy. I try to balance the schedule so nobody on either side waits longer than ten minutes.

What are some tips that you think can enhance an actor's career?
Believe in yourself, then go along and do all the other things that are necessary to keep your talent up to date. Most people in other walks of life work at least forty hours per week. If an actor is not spending at least forty hours a week honing his craft in some way, then acting is just a hobby. A career needs constant attention. The actor has to spend his time taking classes, doing workshops, going to the theatre, watching all the television shows that he hasn't seen before, and doing everything else possible to promote his career. Being an actor is not just picking up the sides and auditioning.

Are you open to unsolicited submissions?
Though everything that comes into the office crosses my desk, I don't recommend actors send their headshots and résumés unsolicited. Because even when I find you interesting, if I don't have anything for you at that time, I have to recycle them. On the other hand, when we get submissions for a specific show, we divide them by character first, then go through them and decide who to bring in for a pre-read, who to take to the producers directly, and who to put on a list for generals in the future. Sometimes I may not have anything for an actor, but if they have a great look, I may bring them in for a general during slow weeks. But a general for me is not chitchat and monologue. Instead, I send the actor sides from actual scripts and ask them to prepare like a real audition. Then they come in and read it with me.

How do you keep in touch with new talent? Do you go to the theatre?
Yes, I do, but only when I know someone involved in the production, when a title intrigues me, or when a show gets great reviews. We also keep in touch with

the work of actors by watching films and television. When my assistants see someone they like, they research them and bring them to my attention. Both my assistants want to be casting directors in the future and are very aggressive.

Should an invitation to the theatre include a picture and résumé, or do you prefer postcards?

Postcards are more economical and ecological. It's the picture itself that sells me on somebody, not necessarily their résumé. Many résumés exaggerate and mislead. I've seen résumés where the actor mentions work on shows I worked on, and know for a fact they didn't do. Or maybe they were an extra. But if you list it, you have to mention it was extra work. Not that being an extra during your early career is wrong; you have to start somewhere. As an extra, you have a chance on the set to learn the lingo, as opposed to wasting your time talking to the other extras and hanging out around the craft service table. Watch and learn about camera angles, observe how actors get direction, see how a performance changes from take to take. Eventually, your observations may pay off and you may move up from being an extra to doing under-fives, then to co-starring roles and even higher.

What advice do you have for veteran actors who don't book as much as they should?

It seems that every five years, there is a great turnover of writers, directors and producers. Yet many veteran actors reach a point where—though they are available—they refuse to audition for the new directors and producers. They want the part offered to them. While I can understand it, I feel that this attitude is detrimental. You never know who you are reading for; the director you read for today may end up directing a major feature in six months. You should never turn down an opportunity to audition and show your talent to as many people as possible.

What do you enjoy most about casting?

I love actors. I live vicariously through them. I like to encourage people to be what they want to be. If they want to be actors, I encourage them and help them to be better at it. I didn't get that nourishment when I was an actor. Today, nothing gives me a bigger thrill than finding an exciting talent, bringing them to the producers, and seeing them book the role. Or, if they don't get it, but do such a good job that everybody likes them, I am thrilled because I can bring them back again for other roles. It gives me a great feeling to be able to say, "Look who I found for you!"

Do you have any other thoughts you want to share with actors?

I wish actors would prepare better for their auditions. Many don't prepare at all. They come in without knowing who they are reading for, what the role is, what the style of the show demands. They pick up the sides right before they walk in the door and say, "I'm sorry, I just got these sides a couple of minutes ago." It just doesn't work for me. My big thing is thorough research and detailed homework. If, for example, you are asked to read for a television show you have never seen, you should be able to go to your own video library, which should have at least one copy of every show that is on television right now, pop in the tape and study it. If, for example, your sides feature a character named John, you will know that he is a series regular and is played by so and so. Now you will know how to play the scene because you will know how he acts and reacts. The same scene, read opposite a Drew Carey, is entirely different when it is played opposite a Sean Connery. So, know what your role is, know who you will play against, know the style of the show. Then prepare the best you can, come in, do it, leave and try to forget all about it. Go out instead and take charge of doing forty hours a week for your career.

Do you have any suggestions about how to cope with the constant rejections that actors have to deal with?

Do what I did; find a therapist with a sliding scale.

. . . .

John A. Aiello
c/o *Martial Law*
7850 Ruffner Ave.
Van Nuys, CA 91406
. . . .

JULIE ASHTON

Julie Ashton got her entry into show business early on as a professional dancer and teacher. During her training at Arizona State University, she entered an actor's talent search and won. She was flown to Los Angeles and met with many of the same people she associates with now. One of the contest's judges, veteran casting director Caro Jones, took Ashton under her wing and hired her on as a reader. While she continued acting for a bit, she ultimately decided to stay in

casting. After interning with Jones, Ashton worked as an assistant to Cody Ewell before moving to the office of Mike Fenton and Judy Taylor. There, she worked as an assistant before she was promoted to casting director and added *Bad Girls, Operation Dumbo Drop* and *Lightning Jack,* among others, to her credits. While still with Mike Fenton, she independently cast *Flipper, Leviation, Anarchy TV* and *The Killing Jar* before moving on to the position of director of casting at Saban Entertainment. Her work there has included the pilot for the hugely successful *Mighty Morphin Power Rangers*, the series *Breaker High*, and several television films including *Addams Family Reunion* and *The Christmas List*. In 1997, she was promoted to vice president of casting for Saban Entertainment.

In a sense, you started your casting career as a reader. Can you talk about how this kind of experience might be beneficial to an actor?

Being a reader was invaluable. You get to see what the casting directors and directors are looking for. You get to observe the whole process. And when the actor leaves, you get to hear the casting director, the director and the producer discuss what they liked and didn't like. You see through their eyes how someone comes in and either blows an audition or gets it. And what makes them get it. It might not be because they were the greatest actor in the world. It might be because they had the right look or because they were really prepared and professional. It actually happens all the time that an actor blows me away but one person in the room doesn't agree, and the actor doesn't even get a call-back. Of course, if I'm in a position where if I feel strongly, I can say, "Look, I'm gonna fight for this person. They're worth seeing again." But it's not like I can do that every time with every actor or I'd lose my credibility.

After working with Caro Jones you moved on to the late Cody Ewell and then to Mike Fenton and Judy Taylor. Are there any special things they've taught you?

Collectively, every one of them liked actors and showed a lot of respect and compassion for them. That's why they've become the successes that they are and that's what they taught me. We need actors. We want actors to be as good as they possibly can. They always tried to make actors feel comfortable so the actor was relaxed and the best performance could come out. Negativity in any way hurts the actor, their performance, and ultimately, you, the casting director.

What's your advice to a young actor who has no SAG card and little experience?

Study, study, study. Even if you have natural talent and even if you're beautiful, you must know how to audition and know the business. The most important thing when auditioning is being prepared. There just isn't any reason not to be. And it makes us look good. We want everyone to be great. We want the producer to have so many choices he doesn't know what to do. That's why we always give the actors time with sides. We give an average of forty-eight hours notice for an audition and, at the very least, twenty-four.

Recently, at a call-back, I had people who had been given literally a week and a half notice. Still, half came in and asked for sides. HALF! They hadn't bothered to get the sides and prepare. It's either laziness or they really don't care. They think they can come in and grab the sides and do it. I'm here to tell you that it doesn't happen that way. Consistently, the ones who prepare and make choices land the job. And don't think that I won't remember those who come in unprepared.

Another part of preparing is asking important questions beforehand. For example, some actors like props. There are casting directors who won't even look at you if you come in with a prop. So ask in advance. Call the assistant and find out what the casting director likes or if they mind. Likewise, the use of an accent. Call. Or have your agent call. But do the research. The more information you're armed with, the better the scene will be. It's all about preparation!

Are there people who come in and don't have that charisma until they read?
I've had a few actors walk into a room and disappoint me with the way they look and then they'll read and turn me right around. And it may not be because they're not the most beautiful or anything else; it might be because they didn't match my vision of the character or what my producer and director are looking for. Then they'll go into this reading and completely blow me away and I'll have to say, "You have completely changed my original concept of who you were from when you walked in the door." Of course, the opposite has happened, too. A person can come in and you think, "You're it! You're it!" and then they open their mouth and you think, "You're not! You're not!" You can often tell within the first two sentences of the audition.

> *A person can come in and you think, "You're it! You're it!" and then they open their mouth and you think, "You're not! You're not!"*

Any final words of wisdom?
Everyone should study. Study and empower yourself with as much information as you can. There are actors out there making millions of dollars who still take classes. You should never stop learning. You should never reach a point where you say, I've learned everything there is to know about being an actor. If you do, you'll never fulfill your potential. Keep active. Get into a play. Time and time again I hear actors saying, "I'm not working, my agent never sends me out." Well, what are you doing to get work? I hit that point, too, as an actress, and I had to reinvent myself and move on. I'm not telling actors to move on but rather then sitting in a chair, you have to do something. You are always going to be your own best agent. A lot of actors I know, and that I'm a fan of, have not necessarily come to me through agents. I see them in a play or at a workshop or showcase. It's the actor you see over and over again, popping up around town that makes you think, "He really wants this." And that means something to us as casting directors. Those actors are not sitting at home saying,

"I don't know anybody in this town," and feeling sorry for themselves. Everyone wants to have a decent agent. Preferably a great agent. But only you can control your own destiny.

I know a lot of people who generate their own work in this town. It's really important that you do as much as possible. Don't stop. That goes for all of us. Even though I've been blessed with the situation I'm in, I can't just stop and say, "Okay, I know every actor in town." There are tons of actors out there I don't know yet and more people come to town every day. It took a lot of work to get here. It wasn't just luck. I had to take steps and pay my dues like in any other business. Intern. Assistant. Assistant at a bigger company. Casting director. Head of casting. And that's the way it goes whether you're an attorney, or a journalist or whatever. You have to work hard at it. I believe that if an actor really, really works hard and they put as much as they possibly can into their careers and, if they have talent, they're gonna make it. Whether it's just getting by and making a living as an actor or becoming a huge star, you'll reach your own personal level of success.

. . . .
Julie Ashton
VP of Casting
Saban Entertainment
10850 Wilshire Blvd., Suite 1010
Los Angeles, CA 90024
. . . .

ANTHONY BARNAO

The multi-faceted Anthony Barnao came to the world of casting after having been an actor, teacher and agent. As an actor he appeared in the off-Broadway revival of *Fortune and Men's Eyes* and *The Sign in Sidney Brustein's Window* opposite Mary McDonnell.

He served as head of casting at Empire Pictures in Los Angeles and Rome from 1984-87, as resident casting director of the L.A. Stage Company from 1984-85, and as director of casting for movies and mini-series for CBS from 1989 to 1990.

His work on pilots and series includes *Crazy Love, Kane,* and *Boy Meets Girl.* He also cast such movies of the week (MOW) as *Breaking the Surface: The Greg Louganis Story, Roseanne: Portrait of a Domestic Goddess, Conviction: The Kitty Dodd Story,* and *Face of a Stranger* for which Gena Rowlands won a Best Actress Emmy.

On the feature film front, he's worked on *Sinking of the Rainbow Warrior, Doomsday Man, Re-Animator, Tracers* and *Prison* directed by Renny Harlin.

His stage credits include *Bermuda Avenue Triangle, Rue Merchants of Chaos* and, for the La Jolla Playhouse, in association with Reuben Cannon, *War Babies, As You Like It* and *Big River,* which moved to Broadway and won multiple Tony

Awards. He is the founder and artistic director of the Blue Sphere Alliance Theatre Company in Hollywood.

Barnao has also directed the feature *Annie's Garden* and the play *Bull Pen*. Currently, he casts the NBC series *The Profiler*.

Which do you prefer: casting or directing?

Though I really love and enjoy casting, it's not always a totally creative process. You can't really see your creative input followed through all the way. Producers and directors edit your ideas. In contrast, as a director, I am responsible for the vision from beginning to end, and that's very exciting to me.

Why do you think some talented actors succeed and others don't?

Successful people are no different from anyone else except they are more focused, driven and work harder. They zero in on what they want and stick to it until they get it. They don't just talk about it. They do it.

Dreaming is fine but it's nothing without continuous practice and action. You can't compete for the Olympics and be a phenomenal athlete unless you have been training all year round. Yet some actors think they can be good without constant practice. Ironically, a lot of the great stars still go back and get coaching, while many out-of-work actors stop their classes and workshops because they feel they don't need any more training.

What advice do you have for actors who choke when they are taken to network?

The keys to overcoming the pressures of going to network are relaxation and concentration. If your instrument is relaxed, your emotions will be accessible. Your body will feel safe and allow itself to express. But if there is tension in you, it will stop your artistic process. Tension chokes the actor by stopping the emotions from coming out. Concentrating on the person you are reading with is another helpful tool. It can turn you into a person who is in the moment, as opposed to an actor who is just reading in a room.

It is also helpful to know that everyone in that room is behind you. Even the network president wants you to be good. They don't sit there with folded arms and say "impress me." They are happily anticipating that you will be the one who is going to do well for them. You may also make the mental adjustment that everyone in that room is just a human being, like you are, and not a person who has power over your life.

Can you talk about what the different mediums require from the actor?
For the stage, it's all about craft, while television has an incredible need for likeability. Film demands faces that you can't stop looking at. These are faces that can't hide the inner life. Some of the best film actors are not the best actors in the world, but they have this attractive chemistry or charisma.

Do you think that charisma can be taught?
I believe that it can be developed. You can help yourself become more charismatic by learning to become more aware of who you are. The primary thing that the actor has to offer is his essence and his truth. What better gift can you offer to an audience than your true self? So tap into your unique truth and emotions and express them. Even if it is rage and anger. Look at Al Pacino; he's a master screen actor who uses his anger and power and turns them into pure charisma. Powerful actors are comfortable with their emotions and paint with them in their work.

Can you talk about where this reservoir of emotions resides and how to access it?
Your thoughts have a home in your body and that is in your mind. I believe that emotions reside in the center of your body. For example, when your heart is broken, you feel a heaviness in the chest; when you get nervous, you get butterflies in your stomach—also the home of ulcers, etc. In order to open your center wide, however, your instrument has to feel relaxed and safe. Cherish what you have inside. All the experiences that you have lived through are your assets, power that you can bring to your work.

Do you have any antidotes for alleviating the pain of constant rejections?
You can't make your career your whole life. If you do that, you put your whole fate in other people's hands. And of course, as a result, you feel depressed. Instead, have varied interests that you value, and over which you have some control. In other words, try to live a balanced life.

It also helps to be clearly aware that a career in acting is a very long race. Therefore, know that you may have to persevere for a long time before anything breaks through for you. If you can't do that, there is nothing wrong with getting out of it and doing something else you love instead. You will not be a failure for having done that; just the opposite.

Any final career-sculpting advice?
I feel that, during the audition process, actors give away too much of their power. Make the ten minutes you have in the room *your* ten minutes. You have invested

hours preparing for this moment. We are there to serve you by watching your work. Be confident and be yourself. Don't try too hard to get a conversation going, or try to be a nice person. It's not necessary. But again, be professional and courteous. Also, don't ask if you can do it this way or that way. Just do it. Don't give your power away by asking permission. Yet be respectful of the person and their office at all times.

When you prepare for an audition, put a stamp on your work by playing an aspect of yourself. Anchor the character in yourself, then dress it up, alter it or mask it to fit the role. It has never made sense to me that actors want to lose themselves in a role. As brilliant as Brando is, have you ever seen one of his movies where he wasn't himself? You can't lie to the camera. It looks right into your soul.

. . . .

Anthony Barnao
6760 Lexington Ave.
Los Angeles, CA 90038

. . . .

DEBORAH BARYLSKI, CSA

Deborah Barylski got her start in casting working with Eileen Knight on the series *Lou Grant*. As a casting assistant and then associate at MTM Television, she also worked on *St. Elsewhere, Newhart* and *Remington Steele*. Barylski has done many series and pilots since then but is best known for her eight year stint casting *Home Improvement*, including the pilot episode in 1991. In 1997, she added the pilot and series of the NBC hit, *Just Shoot Me* to her plate.

A few years ago, an actor who did feature films would never think about doing television. Now it happens all the time—*Just Shoot Me's* George Segal and Laura San Giacomo being prime examples. Do you think that the television versus feature chasm has closed completely?

People are discovering that doing television does not necessarily ostracize them from working in features. Or vice versa. It's a much more open system than it was a few years ago. I think one of the reasons a lot of people have gone from film to television is that they've discovered that the half-hour format allows for an incredibly livable life, especially if they have small children. The actors are at work Monday through Friday from ten until six and in town instead of on location somewhere. They can send their kids off to school, go home and have dinner with their family, have the kids on the set. Really, there is only one late night a week, the taping night.

What does the schedule of a sitcom work week look like for the actor?

Day One is the table read. It's usually the first time that the producers, writers, director and company have heard the script out loud. The network is sometimes there as well. That takes about half an hour. Then, depending on the show, you might be released for the day or have a short rehearsal. The producers take the script and do rewrites that evening. On Day Two, you come in and there are new pages. You read through it again. Then you rehearse it as if you were doing a play. Some simple blocking. You try not to set it too much. Then you show the producers and writers a roughly blocked run-through so that they can see what needs to be changed. At the end of Day Two, the writers do the major rewrite. You sometimes come back to the table on the third day with a brand new script.

During those blocking rehearsals, do the actors get to contribute their suggestions?

That depends on the director. But basically the blocking for half hour sitcoms is very simple. It's entrances, exits, and a few setups so the camera can help tell the story.

Some actors new to sitcoms say that they have problems playing to the camera and to a live audience at the same time. Do you have any advice?

They have to play to the camera. There are microphones above the actors and monitors for the audience so the actor doesn't have to worry that the audience is going to be left out. The audience can and does feed the actor. But actors can't act as if they're playing to the last row in a theatre. Anyway, on Day Three you show up on the stage and usually there is another read-through since the writers have made the biggest changes in the script the night before. Then you rehearse and adjust the blocking. At this point, there are still no cameras on the set. It's like rehearsing a play.

At what point do actors start to memorize their scripts?

Starting to memorize any time before the second day is not beneficial because so much changes. But most everyone is off-book (has memorized their lines) by end of the third day or beginning of the fourth.

As the director is blocking, he's also got the camera angles in mind. He knows that if someone goes two steps too far, they're going to be out of frame. On the third day, the director sits with the associate director to plan all of the shots. Day Four, cameras come in. It's called camera blocking day. The camera operators are given the "choreography" that the director has worked up the night before. Then there is another run-through, sort of like a final tech dress rehearsal. They're adjusting positions as they go along, seeing what works and what doesn't on camera. The fifth day is opening night.

Home Improvement tries to shoot as much as they can during the day. They try to get a whole show in the can without an audience there, then they take a break and do it just once with the audience present. *Just Shoot Me* does some pre-shooting but the bulk of the filming is done in the evening in front of the audience. If there are big wardrobe, makeup or set changes they try to shoot those scenes on Day Four or on the morning of Day Five so they're not holding up the audience for three or four hours for major shifts in wardrobe or set. After you shoot the show on the fifth night, your week is done.

Is it stop and go during shooting or do the scenes play straight through?
They try to play the scenes all the way through and they do each scene a few times.

What happens if an actor goes up on lines?
Then they have to start over. But the rule of thumb for actors is that you never stop until the word "cut" is yelled because they can always do pickups. A series regular might be able to say, "You know what, I have to stop and do that again," but not a guest player. A guest player is a hired hand. You go in there and do what you're told. Don't stop the action. There might be something in the reaction of the people around you that could be perfect and if you stop it, you've ruined something that could've been used. So you never stop. If you go up, try to recover and keep going and let the director decide if he or she wants to stop.

So, do you think improvisation skills are important to actors?
Absolutely. Taking improv classes stimulates the creative process and helps keep you inventive. But some great actors are really bad at improv. And not all people who are good at improv are good actors. There are some improv people who are hysterical with their own material but can't seem to make the transition into making someone else's words funny. There are actors who I think are doomed forever to be what I call sketch actors: they're funny, clever and witty . . . but shallow. But improv training is always going to be a great acting and learning tool to open up the heart and soul and get the juices going.

What are some things that you don't like actors to do at auditions?
I hate it when actors come in and aren't prepared. Also, people who are late for appointments piss me off. An actor has a lot of jobs to do. One of them is to be well trained, to take classes and do plays to keep the instrument in tune. That's

the artistic side, the part many people love. But then there is the business side and that involves getting enough sleep before an audition, finding out its location ahead of time, being on time and coming prepared. That's the business side of it. You have to be good at both sides. There are thousands of actors in Los Angeles. If you do not handle yourself in a professional manner, I may not call you in again. There are many other actors who could come in and fill that slot.

Do you think that there are good actors who are not particularly good at auditioning?
I know some people who have that problem. There are people I love on stage but every time I bring them in, it's just like a flatline. They're not being real or they're wooden or theatrical. Even with adjustments, they still can't seem to nail it. I eventually stop calling those people in because I can only give someone so many chances over a period of time. I'll try them again after a year or two but if they're not delivering two or three times in a row, I'm not going to be able to call them back in.

No matter how gifted they are?
No; because television is essentially about time. Producers want to audition someone, plug them in and have them be as low maintenance and as low profile as possible. In and out, no rocking the boat. They can't risk putting the technical crew into Golden Time (double their hourly wage) because they're waiting for the performance that you haven't given them yet.

What do you mean by low profile?
When you come in on the set you have to realize that it's not about you. You're a guest star or a co-star or a featured player on the show—you might even have the biggest part—but it's not about you. It's about the series regulars, it's about the producers, it's about getting out of there at a certain time because they've got to do publicity pictures. It's about everything but you. That's why, if you cannot come into an audition and nail it, you're not going to get cast. That's why producers really want to see the performance in the room. They want to make sure that you can get there by yourself just in case the person directing can't help you. There might be refinements but basically, they want to see what they're going to see on film. We don't have four weeks for you to rehearse it and get it in shape.

Finally, what are your tips for actors?
Get out of yourself. If you find yourself with extra time, instead of going to the beach, volunteer at a retirement home. Keep yourself well rounded. Acting is

what you do, not who you are! Enlarge your perspective as a person so acting is not the only thing that gives you joy. Figure out something else you can do that feeds you, something you can do while you're waiting for the phone to ring. Whether or not you have success, you must figure out why you're in this business. If you're in it because you must act, then you're going to get pleasure from acting classes and auditioning. You're going to get pleasure every time you do it. If you're in it because you want fame or attention, you're going to have a lot harder time. You have to decide if acting is your career or your avocation. If you're in it for the long haul, you have to look at the arc of your career. But define yourself by who you are, not by your career alone.

. . . .

Deborah Barylski
Disney Studios
500 S. Buena Vista St.,
New R-1, Rm. 5
Burbank, CA 91521

. . . .

LISA BEACH, CSA

Lisa Beach received her Bachelor's Degree in English from Harvard University, then worked as a researcher, before coming to the world of casting as an assistant to David Rubin. Her work for Rubin includes the features *War of the Roses, Men Don't Leave, Scrooged, Less Than Zero* and others. She went on to become an independent casting director as well as a casting executive. As vice president of casting at HBO (1992-1994), she supervised the casting of such features as *The Burning Season, Tyson, Witch Hunt* and one of her favorites, . . . *and the Band Played On* which won both an Emmy and Artios Award for casting in 1994. As director of casting for Hollywood Pictures at Disney, she oversaw the casting of the features *Arachnophobia, The Marrying Man,* and *Taking Care of Business,* among others.

Her work for television includes the MOWs *The People Next Door, Christmas Box, Out on the Edge,* and the series *Dirty Dancing.* Her features include *Bad Influence, School Ties*—for which she was nominated for an Artios in 1993—*Citizen Ruth, Richard III* and the mega-hits *Scream* and *Scream 2.*

What are some of the things you learned while working with casting director David Rubin?

He taught me everything I know about casting. Not only the logistics of office management and list making, but also the more subtle intangibles. I worked with him for about two years and learned how to be with an actor in a room and get the best out of them. I also learned to quickly put faces to roles in the scripts I read. David honed my abilities and focused my vision. He taught me that this is as much a business as an art form. An actor can be 99 percent talent, but without a business sense, he or she will suffer.

What, to you, is business sense?

I see so many talented actors who don't realize that every audition is a job interview. It is a part of the business of being an actor. If you conduct your professional life with even a modicum of business sense, you will see results. I suggest that after you see a casting director, you write down in a journal or card file everything about the meeting: the day you came in, the part you read for, the name of the casting director, what the result was, who ended up getting the part, and what you think you did right or wrong during the audition. Write your own critique of the audition, and improve on it the next time.

An actress friend of mine took that kind of systematic approach to her career. She doggedly pursued and got an agent. She did countless waiver productions, she studied very hard and constantly networked with other actors about what was going on in town. As a result, she finally landed a role as a series-regular. She never allowed herself to feel helpless. She worked to empower herself all the time.

> *I suggest that after you see a casting director, you write down in a journal or card file everything about the meeting . . . Write your own critique of the audition, and improve on it the next time.*

Do you prefer being a casting executive or an independent casting director?

My experience as vice president of casting at HBO was terrific. I wouldn't have missed it for the world. But while there, I missed the hands-on experience that independent casting offers. On balance, I much prefer to be in a room with actors. I love looking into an actor's eyes and seeing what's going on in there. It's like watching a play all day long, and it's fascinating.

What are some of the things you like to see actors do during auditions, and what are some of the things that you dislike?

I love to see that the actor has worked on the part. I don't like it when I perceive that they didn't care enough to work on it thoroughly, or that they're trying to wing it. Preparing well, however, does not mean that the actor needs to be off-book. Somehow, it looks too studied to do that. In most cases, when you don't have the support of the sides in your hand, you will blow it. Furthermore, when you're off the sides, the auditors, whether it's producer, director or casting director, unconsciously expect a full and final performance from the actor. So unless you are doing a screen test, don't worry about having sides in your hand.

I also like eye contact with the actor. But I dislike being fondled during love scenes. It has happened many times—even with women. It is very uncomfortable for me. For the most part it is best not to touch casting directors as you never know what their limits are.

More than all of that, I love actors who use their intelligence. I can't think of any actor of great repute who isn't smart about what he does. They think through the role and know that less is better than more. On the other hand, you have actors who are all external with nothing going on inside.

Should the actor come in as the character?

I don't mind that. As soon as an actor walks in, I can usually get a sense whether they are already in character or whether they want to chat a little. Similarly, the good actors come in and gauge my mood accurately. The audition process starts as a dance between the casting director and the actor, and culminates as a solo when the reading begins.

Can actors submit to you?

Yes they can; I look at every picture that comes in. But they better have a great headshot. Your headshot is your calling card. If I see a headshot that arrests my attention longer than a second, I flip to the back to read the résumé. If you have a great headshot, I may bring you in even if you don't have great theatre or film credits.

A good headshot is well-lit and captures the essence of who you are. There are so many shots out there that don't tell me who the actor is. They are mostly shoulder shots against a neutral background, with badly combed hair. A good photo, even if you lose or gain fifty pounds, still reflects the essence of where you are in your head at that minute. When taking those shots, find a way to feel good about the world in your head and feel confident about what you are doing.

Do you search for talent by going to the theatre?

I'd rather see an actor in my office than see them in a play that isn't well produced. If I were an actor, I'd rather have an agent than a casting director come to the play. As a casting director, if I have a working relationship with an agent I respect, I will gladly take the time to meet with an actor they recommend.

Approximately how many actors do you bring in for each role?

To cast three or four roles, I go through maybe 1,000 submissions. I bring in twenty to thirty for each role. For the director, I bring in five or six. The hardest parts to cast are the smaller roles of three or four lines. The actor has got to come in after preparing well and just do it for what it is. Don't drag it out, don't ham it up, don't emote too much. Make it simple. Don't think that this is going to be your star-making role, or that it's your one and only chance to impress everybody. Those smaller roles are not really about you. Just find a little back story to get yourself into that place, than give it just enough weight. But nothing more than that.

Any parting comments?

I am passionately committed to what I do. And an actor can show me respect by loving what they do as much as I love doing what I do. So when you come in, don't be nervous. I am here to help you. Just come in as prepared as you can be, be respectful of the material and your craft and really show that you want to do the role well. I have great respect for actors who are dedicated and committed. To me, getting the right cast is one of the most important aspects of the movie making process. That's why I have no interest in becoming a producer or director. I want to be a casting director for the rest of my life.

. . . .

Lisa Beach
Sony Pictures
10202 W. Washington Blvd.
Myrna Loy Building, Room 12
Los Angeles, CA 90232
. . . .

TERRY BERLAND

Independent commercial casting director Terry Berland got her start as a casting assistant at New York advertising agencies. It wasn't long before she was casting for major agencies including Young & Rubicam, J. Walter Thompson and eventually, BBDO where she was head of casting. Her résumé reads like a veritable commercial Who's Who with every conceivable product type represented. Among her most recognizable current campaigns are the Taco Bell  talking Chihuahua ads, the Baskin and Robbins pink spoon spots and the Round-Up Killer Weed ads. Berland also teaches commercial classes. Her comprehensive book, *Breaking Into Commercials,* is available through Plume Publishing.

Having worked at ad agencies, you must have a whole different perspective on the clients' issues concerning actors.
Yes, and that's what I try to teach actors. For so many years I basically lived with ad people. I reviewed audition tapes all the time with the creative team so I got to know their likes, their dislikes, how they think and what they're looking for.

Are those the people who watch callbacks?
Some of them. The callbacks are usually attended by the director, the producer,

the art director and the writer. They stay after the callback and sort through all the people that came in. And usually, then and there, they pick who they want to show to the creative directors, the creative supervisors, and then finally the client.

Do you have any audition tips for actors from an agency's point of view?

The bottom line is that in commercial auditions there are so many personalities involved in the selection process that you can't guess who will like what. There are at least ten people who have to agree on the final conclusion. So you just have to know your commercial technique, be very good at what you do and let your personality shine. The commercial itself sells the product so the actor really doesn't have to go in there and figure out how to sell it. They have to figure out how to let out their personality.

Do you think there is a specific technique unique to commercials?

Well, it is different from theatre, film, or sitcom. They all have different energies but the trick in commercials is to know how to convey your message in half a minute. It's a thirty second scene with a beginning, middle and end, and you have to convey information, not just with words, but by using the camera. The same preparation has to go into this as any other scene. If the actor creates a history for their character and knows exactly what the environment of the scene is, it creates a texture. They're not standing in a void.

Let's talk a little about voice-overs. How does an actor get into that?

Well, you need to have your calling card. For on-camera work, it's a picture and résumé. For voice-overs, it's a demo tape. Tapes shouldn't be more than two and a half minutes long and should sound finished and professional. That means you go to a demo tape production company where they can put together a tape of spots with music and sound effects. The spots need to sound real. And you have to work with someone to discover what sort of style of commercial suits you best because you only want to have the very, very best on your tape. The competition is so stiff that it has to sound professional. A casting director will turn a tape off within the first six words if it doesn't sound up to par. But even before an actor makes a tape, they should take a workshop that puts them in front of a microphone in a studio type situation. With current technologies, there are people who can make a tape sound really good. That doesn't mean that the actor is good. You don't want to have a good tape and not be able to perform well when you're actually at an audition. You need the time in front of the microphone to practice and get comfortable. It would be like having a picture that doesn't look like you. If you're not ready to live up to the recording, a good tape doesn't really help you.

Especially since, when you're recording an actual spot, they want you to be right on the money. They don't want you to do too many takes, do they?
Actually, for voice-overs, doing twenty to thirty takes doesn't mean you're not doing well. They want lots of choices because for television, they have to choose the voice to go with the picture and they need to find the attitude that's going to best match the image. So it's not unusual for them to have you do thirty or more takes. There could be five creative people, sitting behind the glass, whispering to each other and directing you to try it a little warmer, a little faster, a little colder, a little brighter. Then they have all of those choices to work with.

When you cast a commercial like the wonderful Taco Bell spot you did with the Chihuahua, what kind of information do they give you to start with?
They told me about the dog's personality and that he should sound real. I'm known for my casting of voices that are not animated.

How do you define an "animated voice?"
An animated voice is a carton character voice. The actor will change their voice so it doesn't sound human. I'm always called in to cast a real voice that will go with one of these objects and to me, that's more fun because most of the animated voices all end up sounding the same. It was hard for the actors at the Taco Bell auditions because they would see this cute little dog and they'd tend to put on an animated voice. I had to keep directing actors away from their own instincts. That takes a lot of trust on the actor's part. The actor who got it kind of fought me at first and resisted the direction because he had prepared something else. He had his own idea of how to make this dog come alive and I think it's very difficult to come in and have the casting director tell you to do it a different way. I can appreciate that it's hard to let go when your choices are taken away.

Do you give actors time to go out and re-think their choices?
The caliber of actor I work with doesn't need that. They're very quick. But certainly if someone asked me for time, that wouldn't be a problem.

Would improv work be good training for that kind of quick thinking?
Absolutely. Improv can be very important. It really prepares you to think quickly on your feet. I just cast an on-camera Kodak spot—and only actors with a comedic and improv background could do this particular spot. That background, by the

way, should be on their résumé. I've had agents try to convince me that their actor is really funny but I look at their résumé and there's nothing that tells me that. And I love actors who have theatre on their résumés. When I'm working on a huge campaign and I have two days to cast it and can only see sixty people, I'm going to bring in the strongest actors with the best training for the job. Résumés are really important. Many times I find that commercial actors do not come in with their résumé. If I don't know the actor, I look at their résumé so I can have a conversation with them and start getting to know them. And many times, my clients look at the résumés. So it's a big mistake for an actor to say, "Oh, it's only a commercial," and not bring a résumé. Furthermore, they don't know what else I'm casting or what else the directors are working on. We all cross over all of the time.

I never list my commercial work on my résumé, just my theatrical credits. Is that the proper thing to do?
Yes. The proper thing to do is to write "commercials upon request" because you don't want to indicate any conflicts. Let's say you did a big Pepsi campaign but you're not under contract for that anymore. My clients don't know that and if I'm casting for Coke and they see Pepsi on your résumé, they'll stay clear of you. So you want to avoid that.

Once an actor has gotten some training and made a voice-over tape, what's their next step?
Now you want to find agent representation, although I should mention that before you do, there are ways to get work by yourself. With some research, you can find production companies who are making industrials or local radio spots. You can also find work outside of the immediate Los Angeles area.

Can actors submit unsolicited voice-over tapes to you?
They can, but the unfortunate reality is that we get bombarded with tapes that end up in a big box. I just don't have time to listen to all of those tapes. I am busy casting. After a spot is cast, I'm dealing with clients, ad agencies, production companies and tying up loose ends from the job that just finished. So the harsh reality is that there is very little time to listen to tapes.

So how can an actor without an agent get you to listen to their tape?
Timing and luck. I've had people bring me their tapes with balloons and cakes attached. Sometimes it works; sometimes it doesn't. I recently had some down time before a session and decided to try to make a dent in my tape box. The first tape I pulled out was of an English man who was really good. I was actually going

to call him in for the spot I was working on because I needed an English accent but the spot got canceled. Luck and timing. To be an actor is a business now. And part of marketing yourself is getting out your materials so that luck can happen. It's a crap shoot, but perhaps someone will pick up your tape. Actors should also have their demos packaged well. The tape is packaged with what's called the "J" card—the piece of paper that goes inside the cassette box. There are people who design "J" cards to draw attention. Having your name just typed on your case will not be as eye-catching as someone who has a professionally designed "J."

Do people put pictures on their "J" cards?
No. You don't want to include a picture of yourself because you don't want perceptions about your appearance to influence the response to your voice. It doesn't matter what your age is or what you look like. You could be fifty and have a thirty-year-old voice. So you don't want your picture on it. But the image on your "J" card should give some sense of your vocal essence. The casting director will gravitate toward the more professional looking tape box.

Do you perceive voice-over as tougher to break into than on camera work?
People say that voice-over is a closed field. It isn't. We're always looking for new voices. It is hard to get into but we are always looking for the new voice. If you're really good, the cream rises to the top. Even for announcer work, real voices are the trend now. And it helps to be a good actor because in voice-over, you only have your voice with which to convey your message. There is no body language, no eyes, just your voice to support the message you're carrying. It helps to know people in the field who can introduce you to their agents. Referrals are really the best way to meet an agent.

Any final tips for actors?
Remember that the buzz word for commercials is playful; try to have fun on commercial auditions. You can get to the point where you can really play when you're confident in your technique and you know what you're doing. Even announcers in announcer spots usually need some kind of twinkle in their voice.

. . . .

Terry Berland
Terry Berland Casting
c/o Westside Casting Studios
2050 South Bundy Drive
Los Angeles, CA 90025
. . . .

Sharon Bialy, csa

Sharon Bialy is a native New Yorker who grew up immersed in the theatre. Her first foray into casting in Los Angeles was as assistant to Rick Pagano, who promoted Bialy to associate, and later, to partner, with Debi Manwiller and himself. The partnership of Pagano/Manwiller/Bialy has cast over a dozen features including *Bound by Honor, Drugstore Cowboy, The Three Musketeers* and the series *Crime Story* and *The Young Riders*. In 1994, Bialy amicably separated from her partners and began a  career as a solo casting director. Since then Bialy has worked for the esteemed Guthrie Theatre and cast the films *Mr. Holland's Opus, Race the Sun* and *Santa Fe,* which she also co-produced.

Does it make any difference which agent represents a talented actor?
It would be a lie to say it doesn't. Agents develop relationships and reputations based on their aesthetics. Some agents have superb taste. Certain agents conduct their business better than others, but that's a very hard thing for the actor to find out. For example, when we had a casting office in Hollywood, there were two agents in the same building. They never came up to introduce themselves to us. When your agent hasn't bothered to meet the casting directors in the same

building, that's a clue that they don't know how to conduct business. Agents must establish a web of relationships.

What is your opinion of acting classes?
The hardest thing about the acting profession is the fact that somebody else has to give you permission to do it. Somebody has to grant you a job. It's different for painters and writers who can just sit at home and create whenever they want. So every opportunity you get to act, you should do it. And acting classes offer that opportunity.

Auditions are also opportunities to act. And so they should be joyful experiences. As a casting director, I love auditions, because during the readings, I get to act with some of the greatest actors around.

Is there any difference in quality between actors who have theatrical training and those who don't?
It depends on the medium. There is a difference. There are certain actors who innately understand the camera and don't need a theatrical background. However, I have usually found that it is the actors with solid theatrical backgrounds who have depth in their work, color in their choices, and an inborn understanding of life and emotions that comes across clearly.

Can you talk a bit about film technique?
There is a difference between auditioning for the theatre and auditioning for film. The simplest explanation would be large and small. For film and television, the camera is so close it captures everything you do. You can't lie. Your choices are minute, but they are still choices. The actor should display his emotions in a smaller fashion and draw the viewer into him. While for the stage, the actor has to reach out. That's why, when I cast theatre actors for film, I tell them, "Just be aware that the camera is right up to your nose. That is the only thing you have to remember."

What impresses you about an actor during the audition process?
It's important for the actor to come in confident. I know that's very hard to do because everyone is so needy. But as soon as you project that desperation and neediness, it gets in the way of getting the part. The producer and the director want to hire actors who make them feel confident and secure. As soon as they see the insecurities, it makes them nervous. The best thing to do is to walk in, be friendly and courteous, do the part and leave. Don't stand there and say, "I can do this part in a lot of ways." If you're good, they know that you can do it in a lot of different ways.

However, an actor should restart his reading if he feels it's not going in the right direction. I think you can break any rule if you are good. If you mess up, you just better be damn good the second time.

I think actors need to be receptive about what's going on in the audition room. If the director gives them a direction, it means that they're interested so actors should make sure to adjust exactly, according to the director's instructions. Unfortunately, actors often do not respond to the new directions and give the same reading.

It's also important not to change your performance during your callback. The reason you are being called back is because I liked what you did in the first place, so show the same choices to the producer.

Some actors don't like to over-prepare for an audition. They just like to walk in and go with their instincts. What is your opinion on that?

Some people can do that. I have seen people who haven't read the script before an audition get the part anyway. But I don't think that's the norm. For a big part, it is better to do your homework. It is very hard to compete against people who have studied the script and who know the arc of a character. If the character grows within the story and the actor is familiar with the journey the character will take, then he will know exactly where the scene he is reading for the director fits within the sequence of the whole. But if you just walk in cold and don't know anything about the whole script, it's going to be tough for you to compete. Generally, I think people need to work harder. Most people don't work hard enough. You get ahead in this town by luck, by talent and by hard work. And hard work counts for a lot.

What suggestions do you have for actors who were once mid-level stars, but who now can't get any work?

I would strongly suggest that they get involved in the world of independent film. They should inform their agents—and yes, the agent works for you, not the other way around—that they are willing to work for scale on independent films. A lot of these films are directed by young people who will be the next wave. Some of these movies are shown at festivals such as Sundance, and every executive in the business attends. Plus, these new directors who are doing their first films will be thrilled to be working with those older actors. Money should not be a deterrent to those senior actors. I did *Crossing the Bridge*, Mike Binder's first film, and I remember a particular actor turned a role down because it only paid scale plus 10 percent. It was a beautiful role and the person who ended up doing it revived his career.

Do you have any closing advice for actors?

Some brilliant actors are shy in interviews. So if you know you are shy and really love the work, then just concentrate on the work. Don't go into a room and try to be the life of the party. On the other hand, if you are a personality, enjoy it. Actors need to seize the moment. When a great theatre director comes to town and offers you a small role in a play, take it. It will shape the kind of actor you will become. A lot of actors do ninety-nine seat waiver theatre in Los Angeles to be seen, as opposed to doing good work. The truth is, if you do it to do good work, you'll probably be seen anyway. The motivation has to be the work itself.

Throughout my career agents have asked me, "Why are you still doing theatre casting? You don't need it anymore." But nothing compares to the experience of going into a room with great actors and directors and putting together the casting of a great play. It inspires you; it shapes your whole aesthetic. It also makes you a better casting director.

Similarly, actors should realize that the quality of doing two lines in a film by a great director is more integral, more important to their career arc, than doing a bigger part with better pay in something else. Sure, they could make $1,200 a week or more in a sitcom, but what does that mean in the span of their career versus a body of really great work with talented, inspiring people?

I feel that the best actors are fiercely intelligent. It's a combination of work ethic and brains. There is a difference in people who strive to be great and those who just do it. Those who strive to be great accomplish things in life and are better actors who make better choices.

. . . .

Sharon Bialy
P.O. Box 570308
Tarzana, CA 91356
. . . .

TAMMY BILLIK, CSA

While attending UCLA, Tammy Billik interned for Fenton-Feinberg Casting and enjoyed working on the projects *Raiders of the Lost Ark* and *E. T.* so much that she decided to pursue casting as a career. After working as an assistant to casting directors Judith Holstra, Marcia Ross, the late Elizabeth Leustig, Meg Lieberman and Marc Hirschfeld, she took over casting on Fox TV's *Married . . . with Children*. Other credits include *Unhappily Ever After, One of the Boys, Honey, I Shrunk the Kids* (the series), and *Ellen* as well as several pilots and films. In addition to her casting talents, Billik graduated from Loyola Law School and passed the bar exam in 1992.

Does being a lawyer help you in casting?
It helps me when I negotiate with agents and people take me more seriously in general. Other than that, it has given me a broader overview of the whole business. I have a greater understanding of how society and the legal system interact. It has also given me the opportunity to volunteer my legal services to groups like AIDS Project Los Angeles.

Can actors without representation submit to you?

We are open to submissions, even from actors without representation. Generally, if it's a non-represented actor, they're not going to have a wide body of film and television credits, so I look at their theatre credits: where they've studied, what they've done, who they've studied with. I like to see people who take their work seriously. I definitely like to meet new people and when a face jumps out at me from a headshot, I bring them in for a specific role or for generals.

Do you go out to look for new talent, and how do you choose where to go?

Our policy here is that everybody in the office has to see at least one thing a week and report to the rest of us. When they see somebody they find interesting, we often bring them in when a part becomes available. It's important to keep your finger on the pulse. Actors who are doing comedy work can send us notes or faxes. In addition, every six months we have a Casting Society of America Night at the Improv, where we get casting directors out to see comedians.

Can you offer us some dos and don'ts regarding sitcom auditions?

Preparation is very important. You don't have to memorize the lines, but the more familiar you are with them, the more into the role you will be. It's very frustrating for me when an actor comes in and is just reading off the page, not familiar with the role at all. Know the texture of the show. For example, there is a big difference between *Ellen* and *Married . . . with Children*. So an actor coming in to create a character for *Ellen* should know that he can't be too broad and on the ceiling. I suggest that an actor coming in to read for a sitcom make himself extremely relaxed and comfortable. If you are uptight, it's going to wreak havoc on your ability to make the lines work. It's all got to jell easily and naturally.

Another thing we appreciate here is when an actor comes in with a strong choice. Take a stab at it, and if you fail, I'll point you in the right direction. In general, when doing comedy, don't underplay it too much. You have to keep your feet on the ground in order to be real, but you also have to realize that you are dealing with heightened reality.

How would you define "making a strong choice?"

Making a strong choice does not mean being loud or broad. It means knowing exactly what you want to do, focusing in on it and committing to that choice. Even when your choice of who the character is and how he behaves doesn't jell with certain sections of the script, don't waffle. Stay committed to it. I like to see people make creative choices. Give me something I'm not expecting. If I've seen the same part read the same way thirty times and somebody comes in and inventively brings out hidden aspects of the subtext, then they definitely are going to catch my attention.

Any suggestions on how actors can control their audition anxiety?

Auditioning is a very stressful situation: you come in, you desperately want the job, and you put unbearable pressure on yourself. You have to let go of that pressure, and not just for the time you are in the office, but even before and after the audition. Just try to forget about getting the job, and instead focus on performing the work that you know you can do well. I always try to find out what I have in common with the actor, so that we get to a place of comfort before we begin the audition process. A short chat seems to take some of the pressure off.

Someone said that doing comedy is like playing a good game of tennis. Do you agree?

The analogy with tennis is misleading because it implies that you should just throw your line, reposition yourself and then throw it back again. Comedy needs more than that. You have to be completely present for that person's line, allow it to sink in as it applies to your character, and then respond to it creatively. This means you have to pay very close attention to what the other actor is doing and saying. You can't just be waiting to deliver your next line no matter what they say or do. Your response has to come from the impulses of the other actors. All good acting should.

How should the actor prepare for a callback?

If you came to my office and did your audition in a way that got you a callback, stick to what you did and don't make any radical changes. One of the most frustrating things for us is to see an actor do something completely different in the callback because they are trying to make it better. They work on it so hard that they lose what was there in the first audition If you want to make radical changes, it is better to call and discuss it first with the casting director.

Any further advice for actors?

Don't give up. I really believe that actors are the most dedicated, the most hard working people in the business. That's why I strongly feel that the casting director should be the actor's best friend. When the actor has any questions about something, he should be able to talk to a casting director without hesitation. It is in our own best interest to give the actor all of the information that he needs. In our office, we know that we are nothing without good performances. We welcome open dialogue with actors, because we want them to give the best possible performance they can.

. . . .

Tammy Billik
Disney Studios
500 S. Buena Vista St.
Building R-1
Mail code 7764
Burbank, CA 91521
. . . .

Mark Brandon

Mark Brandon is an associate at Binder Casting, one of New York's busiest theatrical casting offices. Initially, the Chicago born Brandon worked as an actor with a musical background but a need for more stability eventually led him to casting. Shirley Rich, the casting director of several Jerome Robbins projects, brought him to Jay Binder. He began as a part-time assistant at Binder during pilot season and six months later became an associate. His responsibilities there encompass the Disney stage projects, including the smash hits *Beauty and the Beast* and multi-Tony Award winning *The Lion King*. Next up for him is the premiere of the new Elton John, Tim Rice musical, *Elaborate Lives: The Legend of Aida*.

What made you give up acting?
I was tired of traveling and living out of a suitcase. I never really felt like I was in control and I wanted to do something where my career wasn't in other people's hands. It's just such a difficult business. I needed to have something where I felt I had a creative outlet. The casting director is part of the creative team. I have a background in acting, I have a music degree from the University of Illinois, I studied piano for twelve years and I wanted to find something that utilized all of those things for me. This ended up being the perfect job for me.

Can you talk a bit about casting *The Lion King*?

The Lion King is a very, very specific, very difficult show to cast. There are thirteen principles in a cast of fifty and everyone is so different. Julie [director Julie Taymor] has done an incredible job of taking her unique vision of the show and transferring it to the stage. Not only does the show rely on really true actors, it requires performers unlike most Broadway performers.

How do you define the difference?

The sensibilities might be a little different and a little earthier—this just has a more contemporary feeling. A good portion of the ensemble cast has never done a Broadway show before. Most of the dancers come from the world of concert dance because Garth Fagan's wonderful choreography comes from modern dance. So the Broadway dancer doesn't always connect to that world. The technique is different, the training is different. And since we try very hard to maintain the African sound, again a lot of the Broadway singers aren't really appropriate because they don't necessarily respond to that sort of style. It's a very specific vocal quality. It's a very chant-like sound without a lot of vibrato. Americans and a lot of Broadway singers are used to singing with that vibrato. When we audition people and ask them to take the vibrato out of their voices they find it's not an easy thing for them to do.

It must have been a very difficult process to cast the show originally.

We looked for almost two years. We had to do a lot more searching than just putting out breakdowns and letting the submissions come in.

Did you find any actors through submissions?

We found people primarily through open calls and searching the country. Little by little, as word got out as to what we were looking for, it became easier. Now, with the popularity of the show, people are coming out of the woodwork. But casting it is still an arduous process because of the vocal and physical demands of the show.

Plus, you had to find a child who was so talented!

The boy playing Simba has to be ten to twelve years old and essentially carry the first act. He has to have a huge presence and really be able to sing, dance and act. There aren't too many ten-year-olds out there who can stand on the stage and make you believe that their father just died. The child who we just put in actually came to me from an unsolicited picture that came across my desk. I thought, "This kid has a great look." But he'd never been involved in a Broadway show or even auditioned for one before. He came in and was totally natural. He'd never done any professional acting in his life. So it just goes to show—you never know. Do I look at pictures and résumés that come across my desk? Yes. Do I open all my mail? Yes. This kid didn't even have a résumé. Just a school snapshot. Casting the girl to play Nala is a really big challenge too. It's a very specific look and, like the boy, they have to be able to sing, dance and act. We're also challenged because at that age, the kids get too big in about twelve seconds.

The kids you cast were so likable. They have so much charisma.
They have to be stars. And that's not something you can learn how to do. It's something that's innate.

There are so many wonderful, young, fearless actors who get shy as they grow up.
People always want to get back to that freedom. The point of being a child is that you're basically fearless. Life hasn't happened to you yet and there's still that childlike abandon. The boy in the show now is not overwhelmed by being in a Broadway show, he's just having a great time.

It seems that in New York theatre, casting directors will work with people at auditions to get what they want. In Los Angeles, particularly in the film and TV world, there's very little of that.
We do work with people in this office because we want them to succeed. My first statement to actors is that I'm on their side. If they look good, I look good. I will spend twenty minutes with an actor I'm really interested in. We'll go through the music, I'll tell them the musical director's approach. I will take them through the scenes, tell them what's happening, and lead them in the right direction. Then I send them away and bring them in for the creative staff. I will spend that twenty minutes with an actor and work with them so their audition can be that much better. We're constantly doing that because that's what it's all about.

Is there anything that you've always wanted to say to actors?
To me, if you're a musical actor, you're an actor first. You're not a singer, then an actor. I respond first to the actor inside of people when we're looking for musical actors. Hitting the notes and having the range is important but ultimately, the reason we're all here is to communicate the emotion. So if you're just singing the notes, who's going to care if you're not putting across a message? I respond to people who are prepared for auditions, who really spend time to pick apart their material, who make the choices and put it all back together.

You have to have all that technical background before you walk in the door. Then you walk in and all that technical background needs to go out the window. It should just be innate and all your concentration is on the words. The words are always the most important part. It's taking that material, picking it apart, spending time with it, thinking about it all beforehand so that in the audition the only thing you do is tell the story. That's why you study. Actors sometimes think that they can get away with not taking classes. Singing is a muscle. If you don't keep singing, if you don't keep studying, eventually all that stuff will deteriorate. Acting is the same way.

Any final tips?

The minute the actor walks in the door, the actor is the one who should be control of their audition. The minute the actor lets someone else take charge is the minute the audition becomes a failure. You need to be in charge and you need to walk in saying to yourself, "I'm gonna do my best, I'm prepared." And enjoy it when you walk in the door. You can't let every audition be a life or death situation. So many actors obsess about why they did not book a job. Stop wasting your energy and your time. Stop second guessing because there could be any of three thousand reasons. If it's meant to happen it's gonna happen. And you've got to love what you do. If you don't, if you're not totally in passion and in love with what you do, go do something else.

. . . .

Mark Brandon
Jay Binder Casting
321 West 44th Street, Suite 606
New York, NY 10036

. . . .

Jaki Brown-Karman

Jaki Brown-Karman worked as an agent for the Henderson-Hogan Agency in New York, and then for Jack Fields in Los Angeles before branching out into casting and working on such features as *Waiting to Exhale, Once Upon a Time . . . When We Were Colored, Boyz N the Hood, Hollywood Shuffle, Stand and Deliver* and many others.

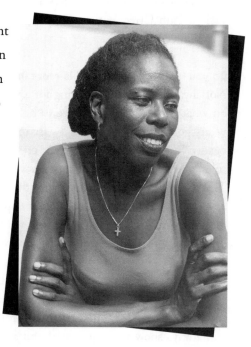

For HBO, she cast the movies *Strapped, Deadly Voyage*, and *Miss Evers' Boys* for which she received an Emmy nomination. For PBS she co-produced the American Playhouse project *A Raisin in the Sun* starring Danny Glover. For the networks she cast such MOWs as *Gathering of Old Men* and *Terror At London Bridge* and such pilots and series as *In the House, The New Odd Couple, Sirens, South Central* and *Chicago Hope.*

How did you shift from being an agent to casting?
By volunteering to cast a second year AFI film project based on Joseph Conrad's *Heart of Darkness.* The piece was so good that all the actors were willing to get involved in it without pay. When the film was ready for viewing, I sent invitations to the industry. People from Paramount Studios came and saw it and offered me the job to cast the pilot for *The New Odd Couple.*

You have already cast a definitive women's film—*Waiting to Exhale*. Do you feel that Hollywood will wake up and start to produce more minority or female-driven films?

In terms of women, the industry has regressed in some ways. In the old Hollywood days, there were great stories with female star protagonists. Today, we have created a new genre of the super-hero, action-adventure stuff, with guys who can do everything. If you were to suggest to somebody that they make a woman the lead in one of those movies, they'd start laughing. Yet in the seventies, actresses such as Pam Grier, Vonetta McGee and Angie Dickinson successfully played action-adventure leads.

Do you feel that Hollywood is more interested in looks than talent?

Not always. When I am casting for a writer-director who has strict parameters on what he wants, then I have to be specific about putting my net out. If he wants gorgeous "tens," then I cast in the traditional Hollywood standard of beauty. But when I am given some creative room, I may bring in for the leading roles, talented, "charactery" actresses who may not be as traditionally beautiful. That's why I love independent films; they give me a lot more flexibility. Directors and writers in that world are far more open to making the people in their films look the way people look in the real world. These small films also give me the opportunity to meet new faces that are represented by smaller agencies.

Do you have any pet peeves during auditions?

My biggest pet peeve is that, though my office makes absolutely sure that the material is available more than twenty-four hours in advance for the actors, one will always show up unprepared and say, "I just got the material." It gets me every time. If you are an actor, what are your priorities, if not getting a job? You have to stay awake all night if need be to prepare for an audition. Don't come in and ask for a few more minutes or say, "This is going to be rough, because I just got the material." I have no sympathy for someone who is unprepared. And 90 percent of the time it shows.

Similarly, if you had the opportunity to get the script as well as the sides, please don't come in and tell me that you didn't have a chance to read the whole thing. An audition is like a school test—if you've done your homework, there is no reason for you not to get a decent grade.

I think that nervous anxiety often makes actors lose 20 percent of their I.Q.

Then you have to find a way to control your fears, and to come in prepared and as relaxed as you can be. If you are nervous and yet give a fabulous audition, that's fine. But usually if you're nervous and don't give a good audition, it's over. If you are a hyperactive person, one way to control your nerves is to go pace around awhile, relax, then come in and have a seat. Or go sit down alone somewhere to calm yourself instead of gossiping non-stop in the waiting room. This incessant chatting with other actors also dissipates the energy you should bring into the room. Don't waste your energy outside. Gossiping often gets so out of hand, that on many occasions we have had to stop readings in order to go out and silence the waiting actors. It's good to reconnect with old friends, but your main purpose should be getting the job.

There are also other disadvantages regarding waiting room chatter. Some actors have the tendency to psych other actors out by announcing to all: "I know the director; he hired me for his last two films," and the like. For a newcomer, hearing this can be devastating news. It can ruin his concentration and confidence. Another sabotage technique used is this: when I walk out to take the next actor in, an actor who knows me jumps up and hugs me to show all the others that he has a relationship with me. This offends me, though I go through the motions.

Do you go to the theatre?

It's my favorite thing. My associate, Robyn Mitchell, and I have gone to many "off-off-Cahuenga" theatres to stay on top of the pulse of the theatre in Los Angeles. But we can't go to every play. Unfortunately actors aren't the most objective people when it comes to their own work in a play. They invite casting directors even when the play gets bad reviews. Also, it doesn't help to be the best thing in a bad production. We respond best when the entire ensemble gets positive reviews.

Unfortunately actors aren't always the most objective people when it comes to their own work in a play. They invite casting directors even when the play gets bad reviews. Also, it doesn't help to be the best thing in a bad production. We respond best when the entire ensemble gets positive reviews.

What thoughts can you offer regarding forging ahead in spite of rejections?

Though acting is a noble profession, if a person does not have a strong sense of who and what they are, it can also be one of the most frustrating. It's not always the most talented actor who gets chosen. I try to discourage people from becoming actors as gently as I can. But if you have a great passion for it, then go for it. You have to absolutely, positively follow your heart and totally go for your dream. But just know that you might be really poor and may never make decent money. Remember, only 5 percent of the SAG membership works regularly and makes a living wage.

Know that you may have to wait for a long time before anything breaks through for you. You may not make it as an ingenue, but you can make it even in your forties and fifties as a character person. In fact it's tougher to make it when you are young. There is so much competition. There's always somebody coming out of high school who wants to be an actor. That pool is constantly replenished, but the pool of older actors dissipates as many drop out of it and pursue other avenues. Can you afford to hang out, knowing that you have the talent to finally make it happen? Actors have to ask these questions to themselves constantly.

If you stick around, dreams may come through. I know many actors who were facing eviction and were totally broke when their agent called and said something like, "The producers of the television series that you auditioned for want you for a series-regular role. You'll be making at least one hundred thousand dollars next year!"

Jaki Brown-Karman
Voice mail: (323) 856- 6155

MARY V. BUCK, CSA AND
SUSAN EDELMAN, CSA

Mary V. Buck and Susan Edelman of
Buck/Edelman Casting have, over the
past fifteen years, cast more than one
hundred and fifty projects including
films, series, pilots and movies-of-the
week. Their diverse body of work
includes the MOWs *Noah, The
Tempest, No Greater Love, A Father
for Charlie, Against the Wall, A
Dangerous Affair* and *Enemy
Within*; the mini-series *In The Best
of Families* and *Favorite Son*; the
pilots for *Cupid, Ask Harriet,*

**Mary V. Buck (l) and
Susan Edelman (r)**

House Rules, Party of Five, All American Girl, The Wonder Years and *Melrose Place*;
and the features *Star Trek II* and *The Little Mermaid*. Buck and Edelman have
both worked as casting consultants for the Fox Broadcasting Co., and have been
nominated for ten Artios Awards, winning twice.

Why did you choose to become partners?
EDELMAN: We have a very similar approach to our work. We have similar
tastes and laugh a lot together.
BUCK: The thing that attracted me to Susan and why I wanted so much to
work with her was her sense of humor. The pressure during the casting season is

so intense that if you are not working in an environment where you can stop, take a minute and find the laughter and joy in the job, you could easily turn into a neurotic person. What people in other areas of film and television don't sometimes realize is that casting directors answer to a lot of people. We have to treat actors well and make sure that they come in to the audition well prepared; we have to make sure that our producers are happy which, on a pilot, could consist of six or seven people; we have to keep the director, the production people, the studios, the networks, the agents and managers all happy. In the midst of all this, we are expected to be creative, come up with new ideas and treat everybody with kid gloves. So, it is essential to be able to laugh amidst all the pressure.

How can actors develop this healthy attitude?

EDELMAN: By developing an attitude of not taking it all so personally. It is worth remembering that many, many factors go into an actor getting a role. It's not just about your talent. You may look too similar to someone else in the film, you may not be the right age or they may want a name. Also, it is important for actors to know that their career may span fifty years, and through these years they will go through many ups and downs. Therefore, in order to remain sane and happy, they have to think of the long term, they have to hold on to their passion, and should never allow an audition to debilitate them. If it does, they won't last more than a year.

BUCK: I also want to add that I believe that every actor needs to go into some kind of therapy. I don't think you can be a good actor if you haven't explored yourself thoroughly. Finding out who you are, what makes you tick, what buttons can be pushed and learning how to deal with those buttons, will help you tremendously to deal with this process. All the knowledge you gain about yourself will help you to get into the audition room with a little more confidence.

> *It is worth remembering that many, many factors go into an actor getting a role. It's not just about your talent.*

When an actor finally gets into the audition room, what qualities make you take notice?

BUCK: It's an instinctive thing. Often, someone brings something into the room that makes them much more special than anybody else. If it is followed up with talent and they can make the role come to life, that's even better. There are people who just have "it" naturally. We've been known to sit here for days, reading actors who are merely okay. Then all of a sudden someone walks in and you say, "Yes!" There's a palpable energy that enters the room with them. Of course, sometimes they're disappointments, because when they start the audition, nothing happens. On the flip side, often a person walks in who looks like everybody else, but as soon as they begin, four seconds into the piece, you realize that they are really special. Other times, the actor who walks in is so close to the role that the two are just born for each other. Or the actor is so appealing that the writer and producer will gear that role to bring up the unique characteristics of the actor.

EDELMAN: All of this stuff is, perhaps, the wrong information to be giving actors, because if you are trying to figure out what the casting director or producer or director wants, you are not doing the work. You can't try to be what we want you to be. You can't think, "I need to be appealing." You can't worry about any of that. If you come in well prepared and do a good job, even if you are not right for a role, our note will say, "Remember for other things." Actors should not be obsessed with trying to figure out what we're looking for in a particular role. Because whoever you are, we may have the perfect role for you in two months. Worry only about your work and not about anything else.

What audition behaviors leave a positive or negative impression on you?

BUCK: We respond well to actors who have done their homework. That is, they have picked up the material, worked their sides, made a choice, come in and delivered the audition. Just try to have a good time and then leave. You don't need to schmooze. If you are right for the role, you'll go further. If you're not, you won't. If you do a good job, we will remember you for other parts. But what we will remember more than a good audition is a really bad one. It sticks in the mind.

EDELMAN: We all hate it when actors are ill prepared. Some actors don't prepare so that later they can use the false alibi of, "I didn't get the job because I didn't have the time to prepare for it, not because I was not good or right." They do that to protect their heart. But you can't do that. The audition process is part of this business. You must separate from it emotionally and recognize that a career can last for fifty years. Think of the long haul.

Casting directors work closely with directors. Do you have any favorite collaborations?

BUCK: In twenty years of casting, working with John Frankenheimer on HBO's *Against the Wall* was probably one of the best experiences I've had. He lets you do your process as a casting director if he trusts you. We were already on the project before he came in. He is an imposing man. There is something very special about him, and he has an incredible background. We met him and showed him pictures and résumés of who we thought would be right for the movie, and he responded very quickly to our proposals. We immediately knew that we were all on the same page and it made the experience a fulfilling one. He also stated that he wanted to see only two or three actors for each role. Agents hate to hear this, but it's great for the casting director. It was also a terrific experience because he's great with actors. If he feels that an actor is not in the room and present, or is just kind of walking through it, he will push to get the best out of them.

Any final advice on how to best sculpt one's career?
BUCK: You have to make your own decisions about how you want to do that. Read everything, listen to everyone's opinion, but then mold them into what you think you should do. Always make sure to do the practical, professional things well. Get the script in advance, prepare thoroughly, make strong choices, treat the receptionist well, etc. And after an audition, whether you get the job or not, have the power to get in your car and drive away from it knowing you tried to do your best. Also, make a firm decision about who you are, and bring that into the room. Look in the mirror realistically. And as I said before, if you can, get some therapy and explore your depths. If you have no money, there are groups you can go to for ten bucks a week. You can also do this through meditation and other techniques. And you can get friends of your age group together and discuss what's going on honestly. Don't do it in terms of the business alone. Talk about who you are, how you see yourself, how others see you. Be truthful and realistic. I know that this can be painful and risky but you have to do it. Acting is the riskiest career in the world. Belief in yourself may be the ticket that keeps you going.

. . . .
Mary V. Buck and Susan Edelman
Buck/Edelman Casting
4045 Radford Avenue, Suite B
Studio City, CA 91604
. . . .

Victoria Burrows

Victoria Burrows started her career as an associate casting director with Barbara Claman and Mark Schwartz on such television series as *Dynasty* and *The Colbys*. After debuting as a solo casting director on an afternoon special directed by Randa Haines, she moved to Steven J. Cannell Television to cast the series *The A-Team* and *21 Jump Street*. She subsequently cast the pilot and series for *Wiseguy* and has worked on approximately sixteen different television shows, including

Werewolf, MacGyver, Walker, Texas Ranger, Tales from the Crypt and *Diagnosis Murder*. Her television movie and miniseries credits include *And the Sea Will Tell, Stephen King's It, Harvest of Lies, The Patty Duke Reunion* and *Beyond Possession*. More recently, she cast the features *Contact, The Frighteners, For Richer or Poorer* and *The Muse*. Coming up are the Tom Hanks film *Castaway;* the Julie Andrews and James Garner MOW *Winter Visitor* and the feature film trilogy *Lord of the Rings*.

You've worked a lot with Director Robert Zemeckis. Can you talk about what the audition process is like with him?
On the six projects that I have done for him, Bob Zemeckis has always been open to the casting director's vision. To him, casting is a team effort and he's

really interested to see what the actor brings to the piece. During pre-reads, I tape all the auditions, then review them and show him what I think he's looking for. He either likes them, or says, "Let's look some more." After he reviews the taped readings, I bring in the people he liked. When you come in, he makes you feel at ease and then we read. If he wants your reading to go in another direction, he'll ask for it—and the actor better be ready to change their stuff right on a dime.

All directors want to be sure the actor can spontaneously adjust to new situations. Sometimes they will give a new direction just to see how the actor handles it. So when a new adjustment is asked for by the director and the actor says, "I am not ready, can I just have a little more time?" directors get nervous. What happens on the set if an actor cannot easily adapt to changes?

Are you open to bringing in actors who don't have many credits?
We don't worry much about a person's credits, as long as they bring truth and reality to the material. I recently flew out an actor from New York who has very few credits but I think perhaps he has a real shot at doing a role.

How did you locate him?
A friend recommended him, so I called New York and asked him to put himself on tape. He did, and it was amazingly creative. Often actors lose the emotional reality of the character during the "dialogueless" parts of a scene, but not this actor. He created a character who was alive both during the dialogue and between the lines.

Do you tape all your sessions?
I always videotape. So when you come in to audition for me, please don't wear white shirts, it drains away the color from your face. Black and dark denim are the best, they make your face stand out more.

I also recommend that the actor be really, really familiar with the material. But always hold the sides in your hand because even if you memorize it, you may forget a line and bring the whole process to a stop. It's also a good idea to ask the casting director whether it is crucial to be writer-conscious. That is, whether the actor should stick to the words verbatim or if he has the freedom to improvise. If the writer, producer and director need to hear the words as written, the casting director can tell the actor that.

Are you open to unsolicited submissions?
Yes, I look at everything. If their face inspires me for something I am doing at that time, I will ask them to come in. But if the picture does not inspire me for

a current project, it gets tossed out. That's the risk you take whenever you mail out unsolicited submissions.

Can actors submit unsolicited tapes to you?

If you do, don't expect them back for a long time. Each month I have to look at forty or fifty tapes I have asked for, which doesn't leave much time to look at the unsolicited ones.

There is a creative solution to this problem, however. Some actors mail a postcard with their picture on it and ask you to respond by checking one of the options they have printed on it. They are: 1) Would you like to set up an interview? 2) Would you like to see a tape of my work? 3) Would you like me to check back in two or three months? The casting director then mails the self-addressed/stamped card with the option that suits them best. I think this is a very good business approach.

> *When you come in to audition for me, please don't wear white shirts, it drains away the color from your face. Black and dark denim are the best, they make your face stand out more.*

What type of pictures grab your attention?

We first look at the pictures, then turn them over and read the résumés. That's why I tell actors that their picture is their first agent. The quality of the picture is so important that I recommend the actor invest all they can in it. I prefer glossies or pearlized photos and not the lithographs. They seem too flat.

When we are sitting there with stacks of pictures, we connect only with those that convey a clear sensibility and have eyes that are full of life.

Should an actor inform you when he is about to appear in a good scene on television? If so, how should he let you know?

If you are going to be on a show where you have a big scene in the last half-hour, for example, call and tell the assistant. Postcards are not a good idea however, because we don't go through our mail every day, and we may miss your show. Either way, it's hit and miss. It's best to call on the day or the day before the show is on. But when you do, don't ask for the casting director, give that information to the casting assistant.

What behavior should actors avoid when coming in to see you?

When you are preparing your character, direct yourself in such a way that you imply or give the illusion of the physical contact written in the script. I was once thrown against the wall by an actor. I thought I could handle it and continued, but when he threw me against the next wall, I had to stop it. Another actor knelt in front of me and pushed his hand up my skirt, yet another wanted to kiss me. It's best to discuss all the physical stuff you have prepared with the casting director first!

Any final comments?

Don't sabotage yourself. When preparing for an audition, some actors read the script and convince themselves that they are not right for the role. When you doubt our choice, it tells us you don't trust our process. I may have called you in because I believe that you can actually make it happen. This past week, I watched numerous actors come in for a major role and lose it because they did not believe themselves as the character.

Trust our creative choices. I love actors because they have the power to disappear into a character and create a new reality. Casting directors love to receive this gift of art from actors. We want to get the jazz, as much as you want the job.

. . . .
Victoria Burrows
11811 Olympic Blvd., Suite 105
Los Angeles, CA 90064
. . . .

REUBEN CANNON, CSA

Reuben Cannon has cast such features as *What's Love Got to Do with It*, *Who Framed Roger Rabbit* and *The Color Purple*. His MOWs and telefilms include *The Josephine Baker Story*, *Roots: The Next Generations* and *The Winds of War*. On the episodic front, he has cast *Matlock*, *The Rockford Files* and *Moonlighting*, among others. Cannon received Artios Award nominations for both *What's Love Got to Do with It* and the MOW, *David's Mother*. Recent work has included *Get On the Bus*, *Fly Away Home* and *Eddie*.

How can actors deal with the frustration of not getting to read for casting directors?

The frustration lies more in not using their gifts and talents than not being able to get an appointment with a casting director. I tell actors, "You have a gift and what you want to do is share it." That working towards mastery will make you feel more like an actor because you are performing. That will help reduce an actor's anxiety of not being able to see a casting director.

If we are really honest, we have to ask actors, "Why are you feeling frustrated? Is it because you are not working or because you are not using your craft?" I always tell young people to question themselves as to why they want to become actors. Are you doing it to become famous or because life is not worth living unless you can express what it is you're feeling?

What do you think of casting director workshops as a way for actors to meet casting people?

Someone at SAG came up with the idea of Town Hall meetings and the various other SAG seminars that allow casting directors to come in, answer questions and address actors' concerns, many of whom feel disconnected from the industry. I like to take part in those as opposed to some of the paid workshops because I don't believe an actor should be required to pay to learn what I know. I can encourage actors and tell them there is no great mystery to becoming a successful actor. It is the investment and the time you put into it. There is no substitute for experience, training and for the process that comes forth with training. Your destiny does not lie in the hands of a casting director. Your destiny lies in your own hands. There are many roads to Hollywood outside Hollywood. We cast all over the world. One need not be here.

What advice can you give actors to aid them in preparing for auditions?

When we cast *The Rockford Files* MOW, we had to put a call out at 2:30 P.M. for actresses to come in and read at five o'clock the same day, meaning they had no time to read the script. We read several actresses. A few didn't give a good reading because they did not understand the context of the character and where the character was at that moment. Then an actress came in and her talent shined through immediately. Her uniqueness, her skill, her commitment to the truth came through. Actors cannot afford to ever let a single day go by in which they don't do something to invest in and to improve their craft. They can't afford not to. The demands placed upon you, in television especially, require you to be at peak performance level at all times, twenty-four hours a day.

The way to stay at peak level is to do theatre. When you study the master actors, you find that they all have a solid background in the theatre. I am always impressed when I ask an actor about current projects they are doing, and they mention not the recent film or television work, but a theatre piece. That tells me a great deal about the character of the artist, and their commitment to excellence. If I decided to stop casting and pursue an acting career tomorrow, knowing everything I have learned in the past twenty-five years of casting, what would I do? I would join a theatre company of experienced and dedicated actors and I would do as many plays as possible. I would not allow my instrument, my craft, to become dull.

So, first and foremost, actors have to invest in themselves, invest in their craft, invest in doing the work, and trust that the rest will all be provided. The rate of success is in direct proportion to his or her commitment. The other thing is not to second guess yourself. Be aware of the work that you do in an audition. Don't ever give less than you can. Don't hold back on your creative expression. Give more, even if it is too much. When you're coming from truth, they'll appreciate it. The great thing about casting is the discovery of how many ways a piece of material can be interpreted. There is both the way you read it and the way we hear it. And then someone comes in and gives something completely different and unanticipated. It's true and real, and it's coming from a wonderful place. That's why doing too much is not the problem. The problem is doing too much that is not really you, and giving a performance you don't believe in. Don't be afraid of being original. There is a voice inside all of us that is unique. Getting in touch with that voice and using it to interpret the material makes it distinct and beautiful. Don't deny yourself and don't let yourself be afraid.

In your opinion, what is the difference between merely good acting and great acting?
I think great acting comes from the depth of the soul; a combination of craft, personality and a sense of magic. Great actors also have a certain emotional availability. It is their humanistic side that we respond to—or their deranged side. I maintain that the camera loves a certain schizophrenia. The camera absolutely loves borderline craziness, and so does the viewer. We love it when we see a non-conformist. The camera magnifies a great performance and also a flawed one. That's why you cannot afford to show anything but truth. When you are performing, you really have to be committed to the moment.

You have been on of top your profession for the past twenty-five years and still have a sterling reputation as a wonderful human being. To what do you credit this balanced success?
I live my life from a perspective of God, family, and career in descending order. When I take care of the spiritual and family aspects, the career side seems to take care of itself. I cannot say I have been successful in finding the perfect balance yet, because there have been times when I have spent long hours, even on the weekends, at work. Yet I usually find time for myself in the early morning for my prayers and meditation.

How can actors bring this kind spirituality to their craft?
Alice Walker once said something that I truly subscribe to. She said "When an artist or anybody does something from the heart, it leaves a heart-print." When an actor is performing from a base of an inner truth, that's where the spiritual

aspect comes from. When you really work from within, from the inside out, you are going to impact people. You are going to move them and elicit a response. When I watch actors, I'm always asking myself, "Where is their work coming from? Is it cerebral? Is it emotional? Does the actor believe it?"

Everybody has talent. It is the time and energy you have taken to invest in, to develop and to investigate the art that makes the difference. It is a very courageous thing to become an actor, because you are exploring parts of yourself that most human beings would never dare do. When you take that inner reality, use it to interpret a piece of work and then perform it, you rivet the viewers; you intrigue and fascinate them. It is that inner spiritual working and interpretation that I look for—whether it's a guy playing Cop No. 1, or whether he's playing the lead. Ralph Winters, the man who trained me, gave me one bit of casting advice that I have used as my basic guiding principle. He said, "Reuben, always hire actors who are superior to the roles that they have to play." And that's exactly what I have done. That way, the material is always elevated.

As a casting director, I always seek to elevate and enhance that which is presented as a script. I approach my work by thinking, "What can I do as a casting director to elevate the material? Which actors can I bring to this project who are going to enhance it?" Eighty percent of good filmmaking is good writing and good casting.

Is there anything else you would like to add?

I really understand the angst of the actor from an experiential level as well as from an observational level. A lot of that stress and depression can be relieved if the energy and effort are spent exploring your craft and having a dedicated commitment to becoming an excellent actor as opposed to becoming a personality.

Every four years I take class so I can be among actors. I go through the same process. I sing, perform, I'm judged. It's invigorating and stimulating. We all need an outlet for creative expression. I really believe that the more people create positive outlets to express themselves, the quicker we will have a saner society. I sing for my sanity.

. . . .

Reuben Cannon
5225 Wilshire Blvd., Suite 526
Los Angeles, CA 90036
. . . .

ALICE CASSIDY, CSA

After casting the series *The Fall Guy*, Alice Cassidy went to Lorimar Pictures and worked on such MOWs as *I Know My First Name Is Steven*, and *Burning Bridges*. Her work on pilots there includes *Nearly Departed, Half and Half, Prince Street* and *The World According to Straw*. She also cast the series *The People Next Door, The Hogan Family, Full House* and others.

As an independent, she cast the series *Over the Top, Between Brothers*, three seasons of *Doogie Howser, M.D.,* the MOWs *Monster Smasher, Safety Patrol, The Price of Love, The War for Baby Jessica, The O.J. Simpson Story, Confessions* and the animation special *Eek, the Cat* for which she won an Artios in 1994.

How do you find new talent?
I constantly go to the theatre and movies, and I watch television. A casting director has to be aware of everything that is going on. Otherwise an agent may call and talk about someone and you won't know who that person is. I am more likely to go to plays with large casts, but I can't go to all of them. We get so many flyers.

How should an actor prepare for a reading?

By making strong choices. A wrong choice is better than no choice. Try to read the whole script beforehand. If you can't get hold of one, get your agent to tell you about the overall story. Figure out, within the context of the whole piece, what sense your character makes in it. And if you have questions, ask them.

In the pre-read, if you are not happy after you read the first time, ask to read again. It's your room while you are in there. But don't bring in props. The pre-read is all about seeing how smart you are and what choices you make.

Another thing we look for is your ability to listen while the other person is reading. The best actors in the world are the best listeners. The best way to listen is *not* to be thinking about what you are going to say next. Be in the scene and the moment, because only after you hear what the other person is saying can you respond appropriately. Your responses have to feel like they are being created for the first time. Don't anticipate what's going to happen next.

Are there any practical no-nos during readings?

Wear something that gives the feeling of the character. But no costumes, please. It's very off-putting. When you arrive in costume, you are telling me where your energy went. You rented a nurse's uniform, instead of coming here the day before to read the script. Trust me, we have enough imagination to see past what you're wearing. Don't wear jewelry that jingles. It's distracting. And don't wear too much perfume. I recently had a producer in the room who was allergic to perfume and his coughing and sneezing was all we could hear. The most important thing for you to concentrate on is what the scene is about and what your character wants.

Also, in my opinion you do yourself a terrible disservice when you come into the room and you are completely wrong for the role. An actor will say to his agent or manager, "I heard about this role, you have a relationship with this casting director, I want to get in on this part." Believe me, it's better that we meet during a general. Look into the mirror. Don't force yourself into things you are not right for. It ruins your credibility. Let's face it, actors and casting directors need each other. We need to trust each other. We respect certain agents who send only the right actors. Especially when an emergency arises and a new actor is needed overnight to fill a role.

Any suggestions on callback etiquette?

Come in, say hello, and get comfortable in the room quickly. Telling one anecdote is okay, but three or four is way too many. I understand actors do that to control their nerves, but the people in the room have a million other things on their minds. They are in there to get the work done, not socialize.

What advice would you give to a young actor just starting out?
Study hard with a fine teacher and get involved with an existing theatre group that does good work. You can learn by watching other actors and you will be exposed to people who may be able to recommend you to agents or casting directors. You shouldn't isolate yourself. This is a terribly hard town. You have to become part of a network. Actors in a group can be generous and provide enormous support.

Remember that good looks aren't enough. You have to study. I had a few projects that needed really great-looking people. But most of the people who came in were not studying. There is a left-over myth from old Hollywood that all you have to be is good-looking. On many occasions during auditions, somebody walks in and there is a collective "Aah, thank you, God!" Then they start to read, and it's, "Never mind." There's always an image in the director's head of who the character is,

> *On many occasions during auditions, somebody walks in and there is a collective "Aah, thank you, God!" Then they start to read, and it's, "Never mind."*

and if you walk in and fit that image, they will pray that you can act. But if you can't, no matter how good looking you are, it's, "Next!"

Do you find that it gets easier for older actors to land roles because most of the competition drops out after a while?
I think competition is still as strong, but as you get older, you get more comfortable with yourself. Your acting choices become clearer. Hopefully, you also become more established after a while. This means that the casting community knows who you are.

Do you think that it helps the actor to package himself as a type?
Why limit yourself to one type? Instead, target the casting people and directors who do the type of work you are good at. For example, maybe you should focus on comedy if you are comfortable in that, for example. If there is a darkness in you, then maybe focus on drama. This will still give you a wide enough range that includes a variety of roles.

We casting directors have to work on this area also. It's easy to see actors as types. But it's our responsibility not to have these barriers, these categories. Actors are capable of a lot more than we assume.

What tips can you give to actors who read for the under-five roles?

Those are hard roles to do because you usually don't have enough to work with. There is no back story. It's best to be simple in your choices. Create your own back story, so that it is a complete person saying those few lines.

Suppose you are reading for a nosy neighbor. If you make it a little more interesting by adding another dimension to it, you have an advantage over the others. Even if you make a wrong choice, you made a strong decision. Even if you don't get that role, you have indicated to me that you are a hard-working, interesting actor. I'll make a note to bring you in again.

Any advice on dealing with rejection?

There are so many factors as to why you might be rejected that it is not worth worrying about. Sometimes we can't even articulate the reasons. The agent calls and we can't offer clear feedback. Other times the reasons are specific. Or it's a matter of the director wanting someone who looks like his uncle. Or an actor is completely opposite to what they are looking for, but gave such an interesting reading that they changed their minds.

So it's best to only focus on being yourself and to come in with strong choices. What are your feelings about what makes the character interesting? Don't come in to act a character. Come in being the person.

. . . .

Alice Cassidy
c/o CSA
606 N. Larchmont Blvd., Suite 4B
Los Angeles, CA 90004
. . . .

LINDSAY CHAG

Asked what she looks for most when an actor comes in to audition, Lindsay Chag says, "I look to see how really alive they are, and whether they love not only what they do, but how they do it."

Lindsay Chag came to Los Angeles after majoring in Drama and Psychology at Stanford. She interned at a casting office for eight months before becoming an associate on such features as *Naked Gun, Troop Beverly Hills* and *Pet Sematary*.

As a casting director, her work includes the pilots *I'm Home, Doogie Howser, M.D.* and the Carrie Fisher penned *Esme's Little Nap*; the MOWs *Exile*, and *Lady in a Corner*; the series *Anything but Love, Stand by Your Man, Babylon 5* (in conjunction with Fern Champion/Mark Paladini) and *Relativity*; and the features *Dracula: Dead and Loving It, Robin Hood: Men in Tights, Hangman* and *Stained Glass*, among others.

What types of actors most interest you?

I use all types but what I look for most, hands down, is extensive theatre training. Theatrically trained actors usually have an innate understanding of characterization, of how to communicate the intricacies of human reality. They usually work organically from moment to moment. That kind of work is compelling and purely magical.

You love theatre, yet many actors in town think that casting directors don't go to the theatre looking for new talent.

Casting can be demanding—it can take a lot out of you. So sometimes, after a long day's work, you would prefer to go home. But we have a distinct responsibility to our directors and producers to bring them a high quality and volume of available talent. We can only do this well by seeking out talent—by going to the theatre, showcases and screenings, and watching films and television. Discovering talent and being able to circulate it is exhilarating. That doesn't feel like work to me.

I also believe that if an actor has talent and is willing to discipline himself and respects his craft enough to become trained and learn professional etiquette, he will not go unnoticed. He will be found. Trust that. Simply do your work and believe in yourself. The rest will fall into place.

Perhaps actors complain too much instead of focusing on the work?

Complaining keeps you stuck. Progress is then impossible. It is far more productive to take an active responsibility for your career and your life. We are too easily distracted. We fear, we doubt, we worry, we complain. It's a familiar and disastrous routine. We are also too easily dismayed. Although being hopeful and inspired is a more difficult choice than giving up or complaining, it is far more rewarding. In reality, there are more than enough jobs, success and money to go around for all of us. Relax. Give yourself and others a break. Slow down. Be kind and generous. Strive to improve yourself, your art, your profession, your community. This will transform you instantaneously.

Let's say your agent is not sending you out enough. Is it only that they are not doing their job? Can you do something about it? Ninety-nine percent of the time, the answer is, yes, you can do something to assist your agent and your career. But then comes the fear: "What if I do take responsibility and do go out, and still fail?" Don't worry about that. If you have talent and there is a positive energy about you, you will succeed because others will notice you, want to be around you and want to work with you.

What actions can help the actor free himself from unnecessary negativity?

Be of service to someone or something. Volunteer for Project Angel Food one hour a week and I guarantee you'll become a more gentle and more real human being. And a far better actor. Another practical step actors can take is to volunteer to be a reader with a casting director—either at a pre-read or a producer's session. This sort of experience can show you what key mistakes are made as well as what great things other actors do, and you may hear how each actor is discussed by the producers and directors after they leave the room. You then can carry this knowledge to your next audition and avoid those pitfalls. I also recommend that actors be spontaneous and adventurous in their lives. This helps one's spirits soar. For example, I highly recommend sky diving. It is the ultimate leap of faith. It is one of the most exhilarating, freeing experiences you can have. I mean, after you jump out of a plane, auditioning will not feel so difficult. In fact, nothing does. Once you've done it you've got a great sense of freedom. You feel like you can do anything!

What sort of an attitude can help the actor when they're preparing to enter the auditioning room?

Actors often enter a casting office tentatively. But if your spirit is small, so then will be your legacy. You must know your worth and value. We not only want you to do well—we need your talent as much as you think you need the job! Come in fully knowing that it is your time and opportunity. If you truly, truly love acting then the audition process and everything that goes along with it should be joyful. But you have to love both the highs and the lows of your profession. There are always going to be difficult situations. So don't rely on somebody else to make the experience a good one for you. Try to respect, love and enjoy your profession. Come from a spiritual base and your career can take flight.

Can you elaborate further on coming from a spiritual base?

Many of us are enthralled with self-gratification. "What and who will reward me quickly?" is our constant question. I think the purpose of life is to stand for something, to contribute, to be responsible, useful and compassionate. You have to adjust your attitude away from, "Me, me, me," and towards, "We're all in this together." The ironic thing is that, if you do, you will find what you truly seek. If your essence is positive than so will be your reality.

What is star quality? What defines sex appeal? What creates magnetism? All derive from a state of being truly alive. When your own unique soul is revealed, when its energy is released, people want to be around you. It infuses your work with something profound. The beauty and the magic of all of this is that you as an actor do have power over your ultimate destiny. By living a life of high integrity and purpose and by enjoying the ride, you can imagine greatness and become it thoroughly. Be kind. Be humble. Laugh a lot. Miracles will find you.

Any parting observations on how best to sculpt an acting career?
You have to take care of the fundamental and essential aspects of your profession. That is, you have to constantly work on your craft and technique. You have to be professional in your conduct. You have to always be prepared when you go in to audition. You also have to have business acumen. These basics will not guarantee success, but they will enable you to take pride in how you pursue it—and they will better your chances of achieving it and of handling it when it happens.

But more importantly, you have to educate your artistic and spiritual sides. Anything that is artistic is innately generous. Art does not belong to any one person. It is to be shared. Live with that mentality and you will rejoice at other peoples' success. And you'll realize there is an

> *Just love the experience of the audition. It's merely an experience within your life, it doesn't define your life. Be moment oriented, not result oriented.*

abundance of everything, that there is no scarcity. I see too many actors who come from desperation and fear. The audition is reduced to, "If this doesn't happen, if this one shot doesn't come through, I've failed and I may not get another shot." That thinking is so untrue. There is more work available now than anytime in the history of the profession. Film, cable, the Internet—it's all constantly expanding. Just love the experience of the audition. It's merely an experience within your life, it doesn't define your life. Be moment oriented, not result oriented.

I believe that the only way to stand out as an actor is to enrich yourself as a human being. When you do, you will shine and I guarantee that I'm going to remember you. I will know that I met SOMEBODY! In a larger sense, live a life that counts—make the difference that says you have lived here.

. . . .
Lindsay Chag
Living Dreams Productions
11684 Ventura Blvd., Suite 803
Studio City, CA 91604
. . . .

Denise Chamian, csa

Denise Chamian cut her casting teeth at Jane Jenkins and Janet Hirshenson's highly respected The Casting Company before striking out on her own. Several projects followed including a score of independent features and television series. While working on the HBO film *Chameleon*, for Rysher Entertainment, she strongly impressed producers Dave Alan Johnson and Mike Pavone. When they went over to Dreamworks they encouraged Steven Spielberg to hire Chamian as the casting  director for his series *High Incident*. He was so pleased with Chamian's work on that show that he hired her for the next Dreamworks feature, *Mousehunt*. A few other features (including *Small Soldiers* and some of the U.S. casting for Stanley Kubrick's *Eyes Wide Shut* with Tom Cruise and Nicole Kidman) followed before Spielberg asked her to cast his epic, Academy Award winning World War II drama, *Saving Private Ryan*. More recently, Chamian cast the features *Mission to Mars, Rules of Engagement, Blast from the Past* and *Dudley Do-Right* with Brendan Fraser, Sarah Jessica Parker, and Alfred Molina.

You have a great look; have you ever considered acting?
(laughing) I took acting in high school and I was terrible. I never consciously thought I'd be in show business. I was looking for something creative to do which would utilize aspects of my personality and wasn't too structured or normal. Casting was perfect for me, although when I became a casting director, I made a concerted effort to learn how to read with actors and to become a better actor myself. A huge complaint that I hear from actors is that so many casting directors are terrible to read with, so that's why I made the effort. I went to friends of mine who are actors and made them practice with me. I think I've gotten pretty good at it. But it sometimes depends on the actor. When I read with an actor who's not very good, my reading can be affected. And when I'm reading with someone who's really special and really talented, it can elevate my reading as well. I can read the same part with ten different actors and I read it ten different ways depending on what they are giving to me. Everybody's rhythm and interpretation are different.

That's what the best casting directors do. They listen to the actors and help facilitate their reading instead of just reading the words a hundred miles an hour.
You try to. When you're reading with so many people and you have three and four-hour sessions each day, it's hard to keep that energy going for every person. But it's fun to read with actors and it's exciting. Especially when you have a director in the room and you want all the actors to be the best they can be. Then you have to be all that you can be. I've had the benefit of learning how to do that from some really excellent people that I've worked for like Jackie Briskey and Jane Jenkins—both of whom are excellent readers. Those ladies taught me what to give to an actor. A lot of casting directors don't learn that.

Let's talk about *Saving Private Ryan*. How many speaking roles were there in that film?
About sixty. We took twenty or so actors from here and found the rest in London. Priscilla John, a wonderful casting director there, put everyone on tape for us. I went through those tapes and chose whom I thought Steven should see.

The leads didn't go through that process, did they?
Actually, except for Tom Hanks and Ed Burns, they did. When I was working with Steven on *High Incident*, I learned that he likes a lot of reality. On that show, he didn't want to see the same faces he'd seen on television. He wanted me to go out and find people who were different. We put everyone on tape and he

was working with me. He has an amazing ability to pick certain people out. Basically, that was the process we used during *Saving Private Ryan*.

When we started doing this project, Tom Hanks was the only actor attached. We wanted to find new faces, because we didn't want audiences coming with any preconceived notions about who these actors were. We didn't want any baggage. I went through a lot of pictures and résumés with him. From the beginning, we had a very nice working relationship where we could just sit down and go through stuff. Steven likes to see everyone on tape first and that gives me a tremendous amount of freedom. I can experiment, I can see a bunch of people and decide who I think he should see. Once he decided who he wanted, he would have a little meeting with them. In the case of Adam Goldberg and Vin Diesel, there were no parts for these guys but he saw them, fell in love with them and had the writers write parts for them. He loved their faces and their acting and felt that we needed to have them in the movie. That's what I love about Steven. He's not locked into exactly what's in the script. He's very open and very collaborative and that allows him to paint a much deeper landscape. All of those guys have a heart and soul about them and they all have their own unique personality. We did a really careful job of picking those people but I could bring the same actors to another director who wouldn't have chosen them. So really, it's Steven's ability to look at someone. He can watch someone read three or four lines of something and know that that's who he wants.

What is it like for the actors to finally meet with Spielberg?
He's wonderful. I really have such strong feelings for Steven, because he's given me such wonderful opportunities. I think he's like that with a lot of people. He loves the process of film making so much, whether it's casting or cinematography or designing the set—all of it excites him. He's like a playful kid and his enthusiasm washes over an actor. When he walks into a room to meet an actor who he's loved on tape, he's genuinely excited to meet them, because they've done such wonderful work. I think he tries to put the actors at ease, because it's daunting to meet him for the first time. The minute he walks into a room, he has this way about him that's very accessible and very genuine.

Does he ever direct the actors during those meetings?
They don't read in front of him. He has done that only on very few occasions. He doesn't like to do that because he realizes that it makes actors nervous. So for the most part, if he's seen somebody on tape, he just wants to talk to them.

Do you have any suggestions for actors about taped auditions?

I know that a lot of actors don't like them. There's certainly something to be said about meeting with a director and communicating with him about what he wants. That's a wonderful and very exciting process. But there are a lot of directors who work off tape these days and it's something actors are going to have to get used to. It gives casting directors the ability to see more people and to choose the best version of a reading. That's how I work. There were people who read a scene from *Saving Private Ryan* four times before I said, "Okay, this is the one I want to send over." I think that is helpful. Things are very different in an audition room than they are on tape. That's one thing I saw on *High Incident*. You'd see something on tape and think, "Oh, that doesn't work even though it worked in the room." Or you'd see something you didn't see. Something that you might not have thought looked good in the room, actually looks great on tape. It's a tool, like anything else.

What are some of your likes and dislikes at auditions?

I like it when people have questions about the material that they want to have answered. I think it's important to have all the information that you can as an actor, and I enjoy giving people that information. Part of my job is making the actor feel comfortable when they come in. I'm the hostess, basically, and I have to nurture actors. In return, I like them to come in with a good, positive attitude and not have a chip on their shoulders. Just do a good job and trust that if they do, I will recognize that. Plus, I can see beyond this one part that they're presenting to me. It's all about preparation and doing the best job that you can. Nobody who walks into my office can ultimately know what it is that I'm looking for. You just have to give it your best shot. That's all that you can do as an actor.

Do you have any tips to help the actor build up audition confidence?

That's hard to do. I think people have really unfair expectations about what actors should always be prepared to come to the table with. I think they have to allow actors to be human beings and express their fear, express their doubt. The actors need to take responsibility for having their questions answered so there's less doubt. It's up to the casting director to make the actors feel comfortable enough to do that. It's hard. Sometimes you're working with producers and directors who don't particularly like the casting process. It's something they have to get through to get the movie made and they don't create an atmosphere in the room that allows the actor to do their best work. As the casting director, a lot of times you have to get beyond the fear in the room. You have to turn that energy around.

Do you have any final tips?

I really appreciate it when people are prepared, open, and receptive. I know it's hard to deal with the depression and rejection. I get that too, when I don't get something that I've gone out on. It stays with me for days. It's tough and you're human and you have to know that something else is gonna come along and it's gonna be the right thing. It'll happen. I am the classic example of what can happen to you after many years of hard work. It just takes one person to recognize that you have talent and give you a shot and then everything changes. Of course, it's so much luck. It's so many of those kinds of things; that's why I never take for granted where I am. I know that I got to this place because of a series of lucky events. Now it's my job to stay here by working hard and keeping up the faith people have in my work. It's the same for an actor. It can happen at any time. You just have to be ready for it when it does.

Denise Chamian
c/o CSA
606 N. Larchmont Blvd., Suite 4B
Los Angeles, CA 90004

FERN CHAMPION, CSA AND MARK PALADINI, CSA

Both Fern Champion and Mark Paladini started out in New York as actors before making the shift to casting. Champion, after casting day players for *Saturday Night Fever*, was brought to Los Angeles by producer Robert Stigwood to cast the large ensemble for the film *Sergeant Pepper's Lonely Hearts Club Band*. She and former partner Pamela Basker subsequently cast *The Naked Gun*, five *Police Academy* films, three *Friday the 13th* films

Fern Champion (l) and Mark Paladini (r)

and three *Cheech and Chong* films. They also cast the thirty hour mini-series *War and Remembrance*.

Paladini came to Los Angeles in 1989 after having freelanced as an assistant to various casting directors in New York. He met Champion, worked as her assistant, moved up to become an associate and is now a full partner.

Together Champion and Paladini have cast numerous television and film projects including *Crusade, Beverly Hills 90210, Babylon 5, Legend, The New WKRP in Cincinnati, The Simple Life, The Mask, Spy Hard* and two *Mortal Kombat* features.

Have you ever brought newcomers into the business?

PALADINI: We brought Cameron Diaz, who was a model and hadn't acted before, into the female lead role in *The Mask*. After searching high and low and putting her through audition hell, she finally got it. Chuck Russell, the director, was totally open to people who had never acted before but who had the instinct for it. Some others might have said, "That person has never acted, so don't even bother."

CHAMPION: I love and admire beauty, yet for a role like that, the men had to take the front row seat in making the final decision. Men, better than I, know what is sexy. But as a female, the thing that was most appealing to me was Cameron's accessibility. She was also fabulous to look at, had an incredible body, yet she was not one of those walking robots. She was real. So I knew that female audiences would like her, too. Then I looked at Chuck and Mark and I knew they loved her. She had all the right stuff that made her more than a one-dimensional centerpiece.

What do you look for during an audition?

PALADINI: You have to come into the audition and bring the role to life. You have to take it off the page and make it into a living, breathing, person. When you do that, all of a sudden we say, "So that's what makes it work!" As casting directors, we know to a certain degree what the ingredients of a role are. But it is seeing actors skillfully blend aspects of themselves into a role without losing the essence of the character that makes a special audition.

How can actors get to meet you?

CHAMPION: Don't send us a picture on a general basis. Submit only when we are working on a project that has a particular role you may be right for. We open up every submission. Even if an actor doesn't have a long list of credits but has an interesting face, we take them under consideration.

What type of photo grabs you?

CHAMPION: It has to be representative of who you are and what you are. A good picture is 50 percent of what gets you through the door. It's amazing how many pictures you can pass by without even bothering to turn them over to read the résumé. They are airbrushed, bland, or include the actors' dog or parrot. Don't do that. Make them straight, dead-on, looking right at the viewer. Let the photo be just you.

What are some of your audition dos and don'ts?

CHAMPION: Agents can be manipulative to a fault because they want the actor to get out and they want them to meet the casting people. Sometimes they send actors in for roles they shouldn't be out for. When that happens and the actors just can't see themselves playing the role, they become very arch in their reading. When an actor faces this situation, he should either come in and tell us he is not comfortable with the role, or should cancel the appointment. You can smell it if an actor doesn't want to be in on a certain part. You can sense it in their body language.

Similarly, we don't want to hear you come in and say, "I am not ready. I didn't have time to prepare because my car broke down, or my dog is in the hospital, or there was too much traffic on the freeway." If you're not ready, ask to re-schedule.

I think actors sometimes use excuses to hedge their bets: "I didn't get the part because I wasn't prepared, not because I was not good enough."

CHAMPION: Don't do that, it's a bore.

PALADINI: I hear actors doing it all the time. It's hard to respect that. Excuses don't belong here. You have to be professional.

CHAMPION: You wouldn't expect a surgeon to come in and say, "I had a late night; it may not be a straight incision."

Do you ever offer feedback to actors immediately after a reading?

CHAMPION: Nobody wants to wait long for test results. That's why we very often give actors the callback right there and then, or tell them, "You were terrific but it's not going to work for this part. You probably are not going to come back." We enjoy being the first to call the actors on the phone and say, "You got the part!"

Any advice on how to best deal with rejection?

PALADINI: There are so many factors that come into play when decisions are being made as to who gets what part that it makes absolutely no sense for actors to judge themselves harshly.

CHAMPION: Casting people go through the same stuff actors do. Often, they'll feel that they'll never work in this town again. No one should live like that. You've got to say, "Let me get on with life. Let me go to the museum, let me live." You need to have other interests. You can't just sit with a bunch of unemployed actors and discuss how hard it is, how depressing it is, and bitch and moan and be so upset and strung out that when you do get that audition, you try so hard that you fall on your face. Have positive passion; don't be a victim.

Any final thoughts?

PALADINI: Trust yourself and trust that you alone are right for the part. In the long run, that is what is going to get you the part. You shouldn't have a limited view of who you are, either. Some people just say, "This is me, and that's how I am." They typecast themselves, as opposed to seeing all their different facets. The actor has to absolutely trust their specialness which they then can freely bring to every part that they read for. Ultimately, as I said, it is one's uniqueness that makes one right for a role.

CHAMPION: Let me once again talk about Cameron and about Robin Shu, another newcomer that we put in *Mortal Kombat*. The truth and uniqueness that these two fresh performers brought to their roles was beautiful because they were not tainted by various techniques that coaches can inculcate in performers. They were childlike and pliable, which made them receptive to directions that the casting people and the director gave them. When I say childlike, I don't mean it in a negative sense. A child listens openly, without any preconceived notions. It is extremely important for actors to develop discrimination and to carefully pick and choose which teachers they study with.

In terms of insecurity, it's normal. You chose this career, give it time. But also know when that time becomes overextended.

Fern Champion and Mark Paladini
Champion/Paladini Casting
5757 Wilshire Blvd., Suite 670.
Los Angeles, CA 90036

Brian Chavanne, csa

Brian Chavanne started as an actor and stage/production manager in New York before becoming a casting associate at the New York Shakespeare Festival in 1985. For the past fourteen years, he has worked as an independent casting director for theatre, television and film in New York and on the West Coast. In addition to his work with the New York Shakespeare Festival he has cast for Broadway, The Hartford Stage Company, The WPA and La Jolla Playhouse. He was the casting director for *The*  *Who's Tommy, The Cherry Orchard, Macbeth, A Funny Thing Happened on the Way to the Forum* and many other productions. For television he cast the MOW, *Lockerbie: The Tragedy of Flight 103* and several pilots and series including *Hardball, The Good Life* and *Circus*. His films include *Tales from the Darkside: The Movie, Strictly Business, Avalon* (in conjunction with Ellen Chenoweth) and *James and the Giant Peach*. He was honored with Artios Awards for his work on the films *Pocahontas, The Lion King,* and *Anastasia*. Currently he is the vice president of television casting for Walt Disney/Touchstone Television.

Why did you quit acting?

I quit acting when I realized what was required of a good actor and knew that I did not have it. The best actors manage to convince you that they are in the moment, that they *are* the character they're playing. You never see the wheels turning. There is, of course, another type of actor, who is so skillful that though you see the wheels turning, you have great fun watching them. The great actors like Jack Nicholson and Julie Harris can do both. Good, magical acting is not something you can teach anyone. You can be ten years in Julliard and never learn how to do that. You are born with it. It's a structural thing in your psychological makeup. That's why I have a passion for good acting. I think a lot of casting directors who have artistic sensibilities deeply appreciate good acting.

As a casting executive, are you involved in on-line casting?

My key duty here is to interface with people on different levels—from talent to business affairs to on-line casting directors to agents—so that we put together first rate talent in the studio's television projects. And even though I do go to the auditions, the actor primarily reads for the on-line casting directors.

The animated features that you cast—*The Lion King, Pocahontas, Anastasia* and *James and the Giant Peach* have stars doing the voices. Why is it necessary to use stars even for animated features?

The studio wants well-known people for marketing purposes. They also want great vocal performances. Some people don't take these performances seriously but we go through the same casting process as on any big budget feature except, of course, we don't care about the actor's look and age, only his voice. Then there is the added consideration of whether the person has a distinctive voice that in some way matches the image that they are supposed to fill. And finally, we have really good actors doing the voices in these movies because we want them to be real. Whenever an agent calls and says, "I have an actor who does cartoon voices," I want to slam the phone down. How dare they treat this as if it's a Saturday morning thing. These are stories. It's all about acting, about playing a role. It's not about doing a voice. The audience is engaged because you have great actors telling a story.

Can you tell us about the process of casting for animated films?

We tape the readings of the actors and subsequently play them again and again as we look at the animated images. When somehow a voice jumps out of the tape machine into the image and the character on the screen comes to life, we know that we've found the right actor. Other times the reverse may take place.

That is, when we greatly love a voice, images are then created to match it. Casting for animation features is an intricate process. The filmmakers agonize over everything and it takes a long time for a decision to be made.

Do you have any actor pet peeves?
I am not enamored of actors who are only interested in instant fame and fortune. There are a number of twenty-two-year-old actors who have been in the business for only ten minutes but who actually turn down parts! I can understand when an actor passes on a role because it is racist, sexist, or too violent. But to pass on a role just because it's not the lead is bad policy. Obviously these young actors have no idea how hard it is for most people. And nobody is as good as they think they are. So get over it. Otherwise, what may happen is that when people pass on projects long enough, the casting directors move on and don't call that talent anymore. Don't be a victim of your own hype. It's narcissistic and self-destructive.

Do you think that acting success is possible for people who have had no training?
It is easier for people who have gone to school because they do get seen. Certainly in New York, the graduates from the main drama schools are seen in showcases. But if you are just off the bus from Iowa and have no experience, I don't think you're going to get to the studio level very soon. The only exception is if you are incredibly beautiful and don't mind doing a show like *Baywatch*. I am not denigrating *Baywatch*, mind you. I think it's okay, because television is all about what people want to see and how to take the audience out of themselves and their daily routines. If I wanted to see my mother in a house-frock, I wouldn't need to watch television or movies to do that. So I don't find any reason to condemn that part of the business.

But if you want to take acting more seriously, watch and study the great actors. And train and do theatre as much as you can. But do theatre because you want to improve your craft, not because you want casting directors to come and see you. You also have to be savvy about the business side of it. There are many resources that teach and explain how the business works. Read books that tell you how the relationship between casting directors, agents and producers works.

Is it okay for actors to ask casting directors to help them find agents?
I don't know about other casting directors but if I meet an actor I believe in, I will help them find an agent. I've done it many times. I recently saw three talented actors in a play and, when one of them asked me to find an agent for him, I helped out and he was signed. I admire talented people and strongly feel that they need to be nurtured. I don't like it when actors are treated like one more

piece of meat coming through the door. When I was an on-line casting director, I did my best to keep that from happening. But I find that for the most part, the people I have worked with respect actors.

Do you feel that casting directors are appreciated enough by actors?
I often ask actors, "Who was the casting director on that project you worked on?" and they won't even know the person's name. That's a big shame because it was the casting person who got you into the room and who told the producer, "You have to go with him, he's great!" Casting directors fight for you. Don't forget that. Agents need to be appreciated, too. Do you know how many times agents passionately plead for their actors? And a lot of times, they do get their way with me because I trust many of them. None of us gets anywhere on our own. We need to acknowledge those who help us on the way.

Many older actors who were once stars can no longer get roles. Why do you think this happens?
It's not that people purposely persecute these actors. It's just that perhaps they don't fit in now. Some actors lose their edge as they age. And don't forget, television is mostly geared toward the young. You are selling to people with disposable income. And they like to watch people their own age. But if you can tell the truth as an actor at twenty-one, you can tell the truth at sixty. You don't lose that.

Any final words to the actor?
It is important to remember that when you don't give a great audition, perhaps because you are having a bad day, it does not mean that we think you are bad all the time. We do call you back. People do get better. There are actors that I now admire who at one time were terrible. But they kept working and improving. Sometimes it's just a matter of a certain kind of confidence that makes all the difference. If you are driven and are in the business for the right reasons then hang in there because it may pay off. But if you are much older and haven't had the success you dreamed of in your twenties, I guess you have to say, as a mature adult, "That's life and it's time to move on."

. . . .

Brian Chavanne
Disney/Touchstone Television
VP of TV Casting
500 South Buena Vista St.
Team Disney Building 418-B
Burbank, CA 91521

. . . .

Barbara Claman, csa

Barbara Claman was one of the first freelance commercial casting directors in New York and is also known for putting many actors in their first starring roles, including Richard Gere, Holly Hunter, Sigourney Weaver, Darryl Hannah and a multitude of others. Throughout a steady career on both coasts, she has cast over thirty feature films, including *Defending Your Life, Modern Romance* and *Iron Eagle*; more than fifty movies for television including *The Ties that Bind, Holy*  *Joe, Dial M for Murder, Burden of Proof* (Artios nomination), *April Morning*, and over thirty television pilots and series including *Wolf, Renegade, Silk Stalkings, Sliders, Pensacola, The Watcher* and *Equal Justice* (Artios nomination). For her five years on the daytime drama, *Santa Barbara*, Claman received yet another Artios nomination.

How can an actor who is new in town and without an agent get to you?

In the first place, he shouldn't have come to town without an agent. I get worried about an actor who comes from New York and hasn't had an agent there. But if he was really good and got himself an agent in New York or Chicago, he'll get an agent here.

What's happening now is that more and more people are coming to Los Angeles before they are ready. They don't have a portfolio, they don't have a background in off-Broadway or off-off-Broadway. They come to Los Angeles to become stars and they don't have any experience. The cream will always rise to the top, but if you are not ready, you can't just come here on your Harley-Davidson and announce, "I have arrived." Actors have to have a lot of theatrical background. It isn't easy to do eight pages a day on episodic television. I want to see people who can work really hard six days a week. Also, don't lie on your résumé. It's very embarrassing when I've done the show and you haven't.

Do you direct actors during audition sessions?
Yes, I do, during the pre-screening process. But in casting sessions for television I have never seen a director direct an actor. They want the actor to come in with a finished product, because they're going to do eight to ten pages a day, and they can't afford to have long discussions with actors. When you audition for film, however, you need to give only a suggestion of the character you're going to play. The director needs to have something he can mold, so if you give a performance during the audition, the director might say, "Could you do that again without performing it? Can you just be?" A really good actor knows the difference. He knows how to craft a reading for television and how to craft one for film. After all, you've got three months to build a character on film. In contrast, I've done the kind of television shows where, in the last act, the character goes absolutely crazy. Sometimes that ends up being the first thing that is shot. So as a performer you are required to shoot that last climactic thing immediately. That doesn't allow you much time for growth. A lot of good film actors will not do television because the time constraints are such that they can't build a character.

Do you prefer actors to memorize their lines before a reading with you?
You better memorize it! Know your lines, come in, and hold your script in your hands so if you do forget your lines, you can look down. Actors can pick up a script the day before and have the time overnight to study it. If you haven't memorized it, if you don't have it in your insides, then you haven't crafted that scene. How are you going to get the job? Television is so instantaneous! In sum, it's better to memorize, do, and be. When that actor comes in and reads with me and meets me eye to eye, they can lean over the desk and do whatever they want because everyone is riveted on them. Those who do that are the ones that usually get the jobs.

What is your secret to successful casting?

One secret of casting is organization. The minute my breakdown goes out, we start getting submissions. I have people here who open up every package that gets sent in, and file them in folders. From the very beginning I can see what agents have sent what and immediately know what I am still lacking. If, let's say, William Morris hasn't submitted, I begin to hound them to get the people I want. In the meantime, I have read the complete script and have made my list knowing which actors do episodic and which don't. Agents are no help in episodic television simply because they don't have the time to read the scripts. They read only the breakdowns, which are really too general to give you the nuances of the character and often have no clear idea of what the casting director is looking for.

In your opinion, what is the secret that turns certain actors into stars while totally pushing others into oblivion?

I like to tell the story of what happened when I went to see *Dames at Sea*, an off-Broadway musical, many years ago. There were three young actresses in it who were at the starting gate together. All three of them were equally charming, terrific and were written about glowingly. Two of them you've never heard of since; the third one was Bernadette Peters. Now, why does this happen? Is it just talent? Is it luck? Is it drive? Of course it's all of the above, plus a strong stomach in response to continuous rejection. To have your self-esteem cut into ribbons every single day of your life and yet to optimistically continue is a unique talent. This is such an unkind business that you have to have the toughest hide in the world.

Do you have any final advice to actors?

Always be armed with good pictures, résumé and tape. Always be passionate about the type of work you love to do. If an actor feels happiest doing *Richard III* in repertory, then he must go and do that and leave Hollywood and the rat race behind. That way, his passion for the business will continue to grow. An actor has got to nourish himself, because nobody's going to do it for him. The moment the passion is gone, get out of the business.

Age is also a problem in this business. Unfortunately, for women, forty-nine is considered old. I suggest that actresses of a certain age develop a lot of hobbies because not a lot of people are likely to come knocking on their door.

A healthy attitude to have is to be detached after giving an audition. Once you've come in and done it, forget about it. Either you got the part or didn't get the part. Don't kill yourself over how you think you should have done it or could have done it.

A lot of people leave the business because they haven't made it, and damn if three or four years later they don't show up again. It's in their blood. If this is your bliss, follow it and don't give up!

. . . .

Barbara Claman
c/o CSA
666 N. Larchmont Blvd., Suite 4B
Los Angeles, CA 90004

. . . .

ANDREA COHEN, CSA

According to Andrea Cohen, actors should clearly understand that casting directors are their partners and safety net. "When actors come in to read for me," she explains, "they should feel free to ask questions and discuss the part. They should feel they can do this without fear. I am there to help you get the job."

Cohen began as a secretary with ICM before joining MTM as a casting coordinator on *Hill Street Blues*. She advanced to Casting Associate on *Newhart*. As an independent, she cast over a dozen pilots and series including *Alright Already, Love and War, Head of the Class, Home Court, Townies* and, for ten seasons, *Murphy Brown* for which she received six Artios Award nominations, winning twice, in 1989 and 1990.

Other than talent, what do you look for in an audition?
I am borrowing from a colleague here, but casting is about falling in love—and I don't mean romantically. It's about getting excited about somebody who walks into a room. Recently, I got a script in the morning and we had to cast fifteen characters overnight. An agent mentioned an actress for one of the roles and I thought, "That's the girl I saw on television the other night. I've

been dying to meet her." I got her in here and she had this incredible energy. She was smart, she was vibrant, she was different. You can't help but fall in love with a talent like that.

When deciding who to bring in for a pre-read, I mostly look for either really good regional theatre credits, or actors who have done half-hour shows. I look for good theatre background because acting in sitcoms is very similar to doing plays. We rehearse for four days then shoot in front of a live audience on the fifth day.

Yet, often training alone is not enough. Knowing how to do comedy without pushing it is something that has to be intuitive with the actor. It's almost like having a sixth sense. I don't think anybody had to teach the great actors on *Murphy Brown* or any top sitcom how to be funny. Acting for sitcoms is an art that some learn immediately, others eventually, and still others, never.

Do you go to the theatre in search of talent?
Yes I do. I also go to the movies and watch tremendous amounts of television. It's often very hard to do all this viewing and yet keep up with social and familial commitments.

How do you decide which plays to see?
Sometimes I look at who is in the cast, and if I know one actor I trust, I'll go. Other times, I make my decision based on the good track record of the theatre. Or I go because the play sounds intriguing.

Are you open to receive cards and flyers about stage productions?
Yes, I am. I look at every piece of mail that crosses my desk. It's also great when actors send me cards to let me know when they'll be on TV or in a feature film. Being aware of the actors' work is extremely important. Right now I'm watching a lot of television because lately there have been so many new, exciting actors.

Are you open to unsolicited submissions?
Yes, and I look at all of them. But if you don't have regional theatre credits, great training, an interesting quality that I may be looking for, or a couple of sitcom credits, a submission may not yield results.

What audition behaviors endear actors to you?
I love it when actors come in well prepared. Whenever we have time, we fax the sides to them so they have ample time to prepare. But I don't believe in

memorization. I have seen too many actors trip up by forgetting lines, while facing the pressure of performing in front of a producer and director.

I also have this personal comfort zone that I request actors to respect. I put the chair of the actor a little distance from me so that I can see more than a talking head. So please do the reading from where the chair is placed. It's just one of my little quirks. Similarly, I don't advise actors to liberally pick up objects from my desk and use them as props.

The most important thing, however, is how good your audition is. All these small considerations can be overcome if you blow us away.

Do you have any other pet peeves?

If you get a callback, don't change your audition. Other than that, I don't think I have any real pet peeves.

I consider actors as partners. I understand that for many actors, a guest shot on a top-rated sitcom is a big break because it may snowball to other things. But just because you may have gotten the job through me, you don't have to feel indebted to me. No gifts. You have already given me a gift by solving my puzzle. Also, not only should actors not be afraid of casting directors, they should also realize that we are people too. We may have bad days. And how much time we spend with you is dictated by how many people I have to see in a given day, by how many parts I am casting and by how large the role is. All of these things come into play.

Any suggestions on how to cope with the constant rejection?

Before choosing acting as a career, know that you will face a lot of disappointment. So somehow develop a tough skin and at the same time, find something else that you are good at. And if that something can also bring you income, all the better. When you have other interests, you will be a happier person and the audition process will be fun as opposed to a life and death situation. Value who you are as a person in addition to who you are as an actor.

Some casting directors recommend that an actor should quit if, after many years, their career is not taking off. Do you agree?

Once you decide to become an actor, no one has the right to tell you when or whether to quit. There are many people out there who should be doing other things because they will never become great actors. But they have to make that decision themselves.

If something comes your way that isn't what you always dreamed of, but it's something interesting, then it would be foolhardy to ignore it. I know many exactors who are extremely successful writers, executive producers, directors, casting directors, or have some career not even related to the business.

There are also many actors who come late into the game. I know of a doctor who became an actor after he retired and he books all the time. I truly believe that if you have the right combination of charisma, luck and skill, you will make it. But there has to be something compelling enough about you that people are going to want to watch. In order to finally succeed, you have to have guts and a strong sense of perseverance. It takes an amazing amount of fortitude to become an actor. It takes courage to continue being an actor. And it takes a great deal of courage to quit acting when you realize that it's not happening. Yet, even if you quit for awhile, it's not the end of your dreams. You can always come back.

· · · · · · · · · · · · · · · · · · ·

Andrea Cohen
4053 Radford Avenue, Suite B
Studio City, CA 91604

· · · · · · · · · · · · · · · · · · ·

BILLY DaMOTA, CSA

Maverick casting director Billy DaMota came to Los Angeles from San Francisco to play guitar on a record a friend of his was recording. After meandering through a variety of jobs, he gravitated to casting by serving as an assistant casting director on such films as *The Running Man* and *Three Amigos*. After four years, he became an associate casting director on the film *Colors*. His first film as a full-fledged casting director was *Miracle Mile*. Although he enjoyed casting the studio feature

Above the Law, he now prefers to cast independent films. Never having left his passion for music behind, he still plays guitar with the group, "Shelly O'Neill and the Big Way."

Will you accept unsolicited pictures and résumés from actors, even if they have no agent and are non-union?

I see a lot of people without agents or union affiliations. I think it's stupid for a casting director not to look at unsolicited material. They are only cutting off an area that can be a source of great talent. You don't want to be the one who did not discover a major talent just because you didn't want to open your mail. I want to know who's out there. I've Taft-Hartleyed over two hundred people in my career. And the reason I get involved with so many people is because I want to cast the best person for the role.

What I don't like though, is when an actor sends me a picture and résumé without a cover letter. Write something like, "I understand you're working on a project I might be right for," or, "I just moved from Chicago and I would like to do a scene for you," or, "I'm in a play at the Tiffany, could you come and see me on Friday night?" Those are the people whose pictures I'll keep and who I'll call at a later date, when they are right for something. Tell me what you want. Take some initiative.

What do you specifically look for in actors?
I look for actors who have a lot of training and lots of theatre experience. I would rather see those actors than a so-called name or an actor who has been doing soaps for five years. Actors who have made a name for themselves in some nighttime show or soap can fall into some bad acting habits and become talking heads. I don't think soaps make bad actors, but actors can get lazy.

When actors come in to audition for you, do you direct them?
Absolutely. If I see potential in a reading, I'll do anything I can to work with that actor to bring out what I believe the director is looking for, and not let somebody just slip through my fingers. And I never assume that the actor I am reading at the moment is either the worst or the best there is until I have seen everybody. Sometimes I see a person who is great, then another comes along and blows them away. And sometimes the best actor of the day is not necessarily great at first, but I will work with them. Why see twenty actors when you can see three really good ones who just need a little direction?

Many actors are told, "Don't act, just react, be yourself," when they go in to read.
The auditors are referring to the general nature of the personality of the actor. What we all buy is the essence of who that person is. But that person is also hired to do a good job of creating a character. Their essence still has to radiate through that character.

So when actors get the material early and find out what the project is about and how the scene they are reading fits within the context of the script, they can more easily come up with genuine inner connections between themselves and the characters they are going to read. This gives them an edge over probably 90 percent of the other actors.

What do you think about actors who prefer to instinctively "wing it" with their auditions?

Those are the actors who usually don't know how to do the work and allow it to be fresh every time. There is a way you can study a part without driving it into the ground, without making it stale. The more information you have, the more power you have to create a better character. To me the most important thing to see in a reading is whether an actor really understands the character.

Do you think it works against the actor if they stop in the middle of a reading that is not going as well as it should and ask to begin again?

No. But I recommend that the actor stop the audition before they finish it—even if they are being taped. Once you get through it, they're not going to let you do it again. You can't just say, "I don't really think I nailed it, can I do it again?" They will say, "No, thank you, that was very, very good. Goodbye. Next." Actors have rights. We as casting directors depend on you the actors to keep us working. We want you to be as good as you can. So when you come into the office and you don't think you're on the right track, tell us you'd like to start all over again. Apply your rights.

Why do you prefer to work on independent films?

When you work for the big studios you realize how much of a secretary you can be turned into. There are so many cooks that your creative visions get lost in the mix and you wind up having no control over the final process at all. But on independent films, you work with first time directors who are very open to new and young talent. That is to say, actors who have not necessarily achieved any track record or don't have any name value yet. Therefore, I don't have to worry about satisfying the Marketing Department, but rather the director who wants to put together the best cast he can.

Another reason is the fact that, as an independent contractor, I'm not on staff and I have the freedom to do whatever I want to do and go wherever I want to go.

How can actors find out about all the independent movies being cast?

If you look at the breakdowns, almost any day, you'll see that most of the films being released are independent films. They only pay scale plus ten, but they are incredible opportunities for unknown actors who haven't yet had the opportunity to appear in a studio picture. But an actor has to depend on a good agent who understands that a lot of times, when an independent film comes out in the breakdowns, their clients, who are not necessarily star names, might be right for the leads.

Do you have any final advice for actors?

In the old days, when you came to Los Angeles, your agents and your managers groomed you and gave you the tools and vehicles to become a star. There is no "studio system" to groom you any longer. As a result, nowadays actors are just wandering around out there, aimlessly. They are waiting for something to happen without doing the work and without laying the foundation. Ninety percent of actors come in to their audition unprepared. They pick up sides five minutes before they come in for a major supporting character. They have made no choices, have no direction, haven't come up with any character. They ask me, "How do you want to see this character?" I want to see what you have created for me. If you're not there with your teeth sunk into a character, then you aren't ready to read for me. It's the other 10 percent of actors who know what they are doing, who are excited about the project and who understand the character that get the parts. I want every actor who comes in to see me to be excited that they're doing this for a living. I want everybody, from the smallest day player to the leads, to be excited that they are there. If they're not excited, they shouldn't be there.

Everybody has a dream—whether they want to be the best garbage man or the best actor. Everybody has a goal they set up in their life about places they want to go. But actors often get so involved with the business side of their career that they forget why they got into the business in the first place. And I see this in actors' eyes—they become dead. They become uninspired. When an actor walks into my office, what I look for is that glow in their eyes that says they still have that dream. The day they lose the fire for what they want is the day they have to get out of the business.

When an actor has that fire in their eyes and that passion in their soul, then nothing can stop them. The credo by which I live is this: "Whatever the mind of a human can conceive and believe in, it can achieve."

Billy DaMota
Ensemble Entertainment
P.O. Box 4635
Glendale, CA 91222

JOANNE DeNAUT

Joanne DeNaut began her casting career in theatre when she joined the staff of Costa Mesa's prestigious South Coast Repertory (SCR) in the fall of 1979. Initially, she assisted South Coast's artistic directors (David Emmes and Martin Benson), assuming the casting duties there until 1985. She then returned to New York and assisted an independent casting director for films. In 1990 she returned to South Coast as artistic associate, company manager. She has been SCR's casting director  there four seasons now. DeNaut has a Bachelor of Arts with a major in social ecology from the University of California, Irvine.

It seems that many casting directors start out as actors. Did you?
No, I come from a very different background. But I think casting was kind of instinctual for me because as a kid I read a lot and everything I read, I cast in my head. It never occurred to me that casting was a viable, paid position. My first love was environmental planning and that's what I had intended to do after school but I came to realize that planning meant a lot of red tape.

How can actors get to meet you? Do you do generals?
I would encourage people to send their pictures and résumés to me and request

a general. I open every single envelope. I only have generals once or twice a year but I also do the Equity lottery auditions in May. I see a lot of people that way. But I don't pre-audition for individual shows, so I'm particular about who I bring in because they're going straight to the director. And sometimes, if I get a picture of someone with great credits and I think they might be right for something specific in the season, they go into my folder for that show so I don't forget them.

What do you like to see on a résumé?
Training is a big plus. And you don't have to be from Yale, Julliard or NYU—but if you are, that's an even bigger plus. There are a few people without training who have great credits and it's clear that they've worked in good places so I'll see them. If they've only done television, it can be harder. You can't really tell the range of someone's work from a sitcom but if you see them on *Law and Order, The Practice* or *NYPD Blue*, for example, you can tell.

Would you bring somebody in who had done a lot of TV and film but no stage work?
Probably not. I don't think they would be comfortable on stage if they've never had that experience. They should do some Equity waiver theatre and they'll either find out that they love it and can't live without it or that it's not for them.

What about wonderful actors who just don't audition well?
That does happen. And there are actors who won't read for that reason. Then there are actors who audition really well but don't go any further. They don't go on to an exciting level of theatre. The audition that got them the role is as far as they go.

Do you have any particular likes and dislikes when people come in to audition?
I feel that people should stay on the page. Don't try to be off-book. It's a read. Come in and read. Nobody expects you to be off-book. They end up concentrating so much on memorizing that they tend to paraphrase and it throws the work off. Since we do new plays, in many cases the playwright is there, so paraphrasing is *not* a good idea. No one is going to think any more of you if you've memorized.

Also, at generals, don't come in and do a Shakespearean monologue. Do something contemporary. A contemporary monologue is going to give me a better sense of who you are and what you could really play. If you've done classical, it's on your résumé and we know you can do it and if we do a classical piece, we'll call you in on the basis of that résumé. But if you've got two minutes to impress me, do something that shows me you! And keep it fresh. There are people who come in and you get the sense that their material is the same monologue they did in high school. Get another one. It's work but it's worth it. There are so many great plays with wonderful contemporary language.

The other thing that bothers me is people coming in who are just not prepared. They don't even really know why they're here but they come in because their agents send them. They don't bother to find out who the director or the writer is and sometimes that writer is sitting right there. It's ridiculous. And sometimes people want to take a long time in the audition and you can't do that. There just isn't enough time.

Other times auditions don't go well because the material is just not suited to certain actors. I mean, you could be a fabulous actor but not right for a certain kind of comedy. You have to know what your limitations are and what you can do. Actors think that, because they're actors, they can play all of these different roles but the best thing to do is what you do best. And you need to know what that is. That's what will show you in the best light and that's what is going to get you the roles. It goes back to choice—picking your material and your monologue carefully. You need to get something that really frames you and is unique. Something that's you and is going to make people notice you. That's the whole point. Otherwise, why do this at all?

A lot of actors complain about the time it takes to travel to Costa Mesa to audition at SCR. Do you ever audition in Los Angeles?
No. If people are serious about working here, they need to know what the drive is.

Let's talk a little about South Coast Repertory. The theatre was awarded with the 1988 Tony for outstanding regional theatre. It's clearly an extraordinary place. You develop new talent and you have a conservatory.
Yes, we have several. We have a professional conservatory run by Karen Hensel that runs for eight intensive weeks in the summer. That's by audition only. Karen also runs an adult conservatory year-round. Finally, we have the young people's conservatory for children age seven through eighteen. We have a great faculty of professionals and there are all kinds of classes going on throughout the week.

Any final words of advice?
Obviously, if you're in this business it's because you have to be, because it's a passion and nothing else will do. And that's admirable. But having something

else in your life to do when you're not acting is so important. It can make the angst a little less intense. But continue on your craft. Find monologues, take classes, write if you feel compelled to, go to the movies, see lots of theatre.

What was it that Neil Simon recently said about SCR?
He said something to the effect that if he were to do a play someplace other than New York, he'd choose South Coast Repertory. It's our reputation. I talk to a lot of people and I know a lot of playwrights, directors and actors and everybody who's ever worked here only has kind things to say about the experience. And we owe that to David Emmes and Martin Benson, the artistic directors. These two guys built this placed and they're still here. They still care and they sweat blood and tears in this place and it's infectious. That's why I came back. I had severe withdrawal and to be asked back was an honor.

. . . .
Joanne DeNaut
South Coast Repertory Theatre
P.O. Box 2197
Costa Mesa, CA 92628
. . . .

LESLEE DENNIS, CSA

Leslee Dennis was born in Queens and grew up in New York. Married at nineteen and the mother of two daughters by twenty-two; she spent several years as a Long Island housewife before a divorce, a move to Los Angeles, and a second marriage to an actor who got her involved in show business. What began as a fascination with actors and their craft blossomed into a career in casting that has included over a dozen films for Showtime, four Academy Award nominees  and one winner, *Leiberman in Love* directed by Christine Lahti. Other directors she's worked with include JoBeth Williams, Griffin Dunne, Jeff Goldblum, Danny Glover, Kathleen Turner, Treat Williams and Peter Weller. Most recently, Dennis cast the series *Nash Bridges*, *Michael Hayes*, and *Buddy Farrow*.

Tell us a little about your background and how you got into casting.
Well, I always had a curiosity about acting but I never had the need or the guts to try it myself. I did do some dancing in community theatre and thought that was a lot of fun. But I had this need to know more about acting. Every time I saw a really fine performance I'd say, "How did they do that?" I would just marvel at the performances.

I had a friend who was an actor and was very involved with Lee Strasberg at the Actors' Studio. Whenever Lee would talk, I would go and listen. I was getting the answers to my questions about acting from a master. I felt blessed to be in that place at that time. I still didn't know what I was going to do with it, I just loved it. And Lee loved me because I didn't ask him things or bother him at all. He just knew that I was listening.

My exposure to Lee gave me a need to work with actors and help them get to those deep performance levels. Somewhere in my head, I decided I wanted to try casting. I just couldn't get a job. Most of the business seemed practically half my age and it was very hard to convince these younger casting directors that I could work for them. It was very closed.

Around that time I ran into a casting director, Kathleen Letterie, and she told me that a friend of hers was looking for an assistant. That person was [the late] Marsha Kleinman and she was willing to give me a chance. I was lucky to apprentice with the best. I would never dare come to work each week without having gone to a play or two, without having watched everything on TV and without going to a movie. Every day I came in and told her about the actors I had seen. I don't think that kind of training really exists as much these days and younger casting directors often suffer for it.

Casting is my form of creative expression. I have an incredible passion for it. It's very serious to me. I work very hard to make sure that it feels, in my heart, that a person is the right person for a role. I need to be able to hear an actor saying the role. Marsha would ask me if I was able to hear the actor saying the lines of the character and if I believed it. That has to do with an actor's quality, an actor's essence and it's nothing we can change. Some things you can change, some you can't. Marsha taught me that.

She also taught me that good taste in actors and good taste in casting are two different things. You can have wonderful taste in actors but if you put them in the wrong roles, they're not going to shine. That's bad casting. But if an actor has talent, it's just a matter of finding the right part for them. Often, you have to really convince the producers or directors of that concept because they think they can fit a name actor into any role. And they can't—unless we're talking about Meryl Streep or someone like Jessica Lange. The thing I love about Lange is that she's not afraid to go to those deep, dark places and summon them out to play ugly, crazy, or whatever it is that she has to be. She just goes to the edge, says, "I'll take a chance" and then jumps. So many people get to that point and then freeze.

Sometimes in auditions, when actors go to those places, particularly for television, they can be accused of being too "big."
If you're really true and simple, and you don't think about it as a performance, it'll happen. I find it much more powerful if something is just underneath the surface. You know it's there, just boiling underneath. If you have a full inner life

going on, that's the most powerful thing you can bring. Lange, for example, is a smoldering actor. She doesn't have to say a word but you can see everything.

I'll never forget when Strasberg told an actor to try a scene just sitting in a chair. He couldn't do it. Lee said, "See, it's easy for you to do a lot physically and create a lot of business but the hardest thing for you to do is just sit there, experiencing what's going on and doing nothing."

How can actors get to meet you?

People can submit. I look at all of my mail. I may not look at it every single day but I do eventually look at everything. If an invitation to a show looks interesting and I don't have time to go, I'll send one of my assistants. I'll tell them that if they see anybody they like, they should bring them in to meet me. I do generals when I have the time but working on episodic television is very fast paced. Most of the time, I'm too busy casting to do generals. But I always love to be able to meet new people. Particularly when I have a challenge for a specific role. I like it when I can find new people and give them a chance and a start.

Are there any particular likes and dislikes you have in audition situations?

The thing I hate the most is when I see someone in a pre-read and I say, "That's perfect, I'm going to bring you back for the director," and they go home and proceed to work on it and change the whole thing. They come in the next day and ruin their audition and embarrass me. If you're getting a callback, just trust that we want to see what you did before. Don't change it unless you're asked to. You won't get the job, you will only embarrass yourself and you'll embarrass the casting director who probably won't call you in again.

I also don't like it when an actor does not know how to leave the room. Some actors like to get chatty and that's fine when we're alone and if time allows. I want them to feel comfortable when they come into the room, because I'm not going to get anything from an uncomfortable actor. But in a producer session, I've seen actors start talking just talk and schmooze. They'll stay in the room as if they're waiting for some kind of sign or feedback from us. We don't have time. I try to space my auditions so people aren't in a crowd out there. So when an actor just talks and talks about other stuff, it can throw off the whole schedule and it upsets me tremendously to keep actors waiting.

Showing up on time for your appointments is also really important to me. I try to space my auditions so they run like clockwork. Sometimes I've had jam ups but not regularly. I try to get actors their appointments at least two days in advance so they have enough time to get the script and to prepare. So it upsets me when they wait until the last minute to pass or to change the appointment. Sometimes it's the fault of the agent, but it's really annoying. What I do like is when you come in, you're prepared, you're pleasant, you make a choice, you make a commitment to your choice, you do it and you're out of there.

After the actor finishes reading is it okay to offer an alternate reading?

I think it depends on the situation; I wouldn't want to generalize. However, if actors get off to a rocky start, I always encourage them to stop and do it again. If you don't stop yourself and adjust, you're never going to get your legs back. You're going to be self-conscious and it just gets worse. By the time you've finished, people aren't going to be willing to sit through it again so you have to stop yourself early in the audition. Seize the room. Take control. It's your time. You have our attention.

What are your thoughts on pictures?

Pictures are very important. They're your calling card. If I don't know who you are, your pictures are going to make the difference between my calling you in, your picture going into my files or my not seeing you at all. What's very hard is, if you don't look like your picture, I think I'm bringing one person in and someone else walks into the room. It becomes a waste of both of our time. So you must invest in a picture that shows you in the most honest way. Otherwise it's misrepresentation and you only succeed in irritating the casting director.

Any final tips?

One of the most important things that an actor needs to know is that we're not the enemy. When an actor comes in and does well, I could get up and kiss them. And often I do. I can't be happier than when someone does well. It makes my job easier and it means that there are fewer people I need to see. And my hiring you makes me look like I know what I'm doing. So just remember that we're on your side. Sometimes it may not seem that way but remember—you don't know what kind of a day we've been having before you came in. Someone may have just yelled at us. Actors also really need to take responsibility for their own auditions. They have to try not to take things personally, although I understand why they do. The business is the business and there's no way you can change what is. What you can do is go in and do the best that you can. Then let it go. After that, it's up to the universe.

. . . .

Leslee Dennis
c/o CSA
606 N. Larchmont Blvd., Suite 4B
Los Angeles, CA 90004

. . . .

LOUIS DIGIAIMO

Louis DiGiaimo studied accounting at Fairleigh Dickinson University and briefly worked as an accountant before joining a commercial advertising firm as a casting director. In the '60s, when New York City opened an office to facilitate filming in the five boroughs, DiGiaimo saw this as an opportunity to pursue a career in casting. He managed to meet with director Martin Ritt, who was planning to shoot a New York film, *The Brotherhood*, about the Mafia. DiGiaimo not only

tracked some good actors who might be right for the film, he roamed the docks of New York and photographed non-actors who could fit into the look of the film. Impressed with his ingenuity and thoroughness and because he did this extraordinary work on spec, Ritt hired DiGiaimo, thereby helping to launch a powerful career. DiGiaimo has cast over one hundred major projects, among them the award winning *The French Connection, The Godfather, Thelma and Louise; Good Morning, Vietnam; Rain Man* and the critically acclaimed NBC television series *Homicide*.

More recently, DiGiaimo cast *Sleepers*, with Brad Pitt, Dustin Hoffman and Robert De Niro, *G.I. Jane* with Demi Moore and *The Brave* for debuting director Johnny Depp. He both produced and cast *Donnie Brasco* starring Al Pacino and Johnny Depp.

What was it like to produce after all of those years of casting?
It's very tough to produce. It took me five years to get *Donnie Brasco* together. I first found the book and then a screenwriter to adapt it. Barry Levinson and Mark Johnson helped me develop it. I enjoyed the process and I'll do it again if the opportunity comes up. But I still love casting. I love to put the puzzle together, and then move on to the next project.

How do you begin this process of putting the puzzle together?
As I read the script six or seven times, images of actors begin to come to me. Then I start making lists, thinking of various combinations of actors that might work well together, listening to suggestions from agencies. All of that happens on a gut level for me. After all these years, the choices I make are instinctive. I know actors and I can sense whether they will work out in a particular movie. Finally, I bring my choices to the director, and quickly the offers go out to those the director falls in love with.

How did Brad Pitt, a relative unknown at the time, end up in *Thelma and Louise*?
The character of J.D. was the kind of part that doesn't come by often. It was such a showy part that, if played well, it would make the actor into a star. We initially had Billy Baldwin for the role, but he got offered a lead in *Backdraft* and had to drop out of his commitment to us. So we started a new search in Los Angeles. The movie began to shoot before we cast that part. I saw over three hundred actors. George Clooney was one of the finalists. Ridley Scott, the director, liked Brad, but thought he was too young. I thought Brad had what we needed. He was an actor who would set her sparks off. We brought him back in to read with Geena Davis and the magic worked. He got the part.

Do you often give new actors a chance?
It depends. For example, director Ridley Scott always tells me, "Surprise me; bring me people I haven't seen before." He wanted to work with me because he'd enjoyed seeing new faces and interesting casting choices in the Barry Levinson films I had cast. In general, I go down the list of actors whose work I know. Then, if time permits, I start to explore new ways. There are always new actors in town.

Do you fight for actors you believe in, when the director rejects them?

I think that a casting director should have strong opinions and fight for actors they feel are right for particular roles. When I was casting *Good Morning, Vietnam*, I immediately thought of Forest Whitaker, whose work I loved in *The Color of Money*. Barry Levinson, the director, didn't think he was physically right for the role. But I insisted and Forest came in to read for us. He did great. Then, when he found out he was going to read with Robin Williams for the callback, he suddenly got very nervous and the second reading was flat. Lucky for us, Robin Williams was out of town the day of the callback, and when we postponed the reading, Whitaker relaxed into the situation, gave a great reading and landed the part.

The other day, a writer friend of mine told me that a big producer in Hollywood told him, "DiGiaimo is better than the casting director I use, but he has strong opinions." I take that as a compliment.

How many actors do you bring in for each role?

Not too many. Anybody can make a long list of potential actors for each role. I prefer to narrow down the numbers. Some directors, such as Barry Levinson, like to see a great number of actors. In contrast, William Friedkin likes a very small number. This also depends on whether I am casting a comedy or a straight story. Comedy acting needs special techniques, and while some actors are funny in the first reading, they can lose it when they have to deal with the whole script. In those cases, sometimes we bring in many people for each role.

How do you track new actors?

I go to the theatre in New York. People also send me pictures. But I would only call someone from a picture if they were a perfect fit for something I was casting at that time. I don't like generals. You can't hire somebody just on personality. If I don't see you in a play, I have friends who go to the theatre all the time, and they tell me when they see somebody exciting. Get out there and work! Even if casting directors don't come to see you, there is always a next time. If we don't see you today, we may do so next year. It takes a long time to build a career. Keep plugging and don't despair. But don't hassle people. They may turn against you.

What would you do if you were a young actor?

I'd never leave New York City. You have to live life before you can begin to act. And there is something about living in New York that can give you such an education. Twenty years ago, I would see fifty-year-old successful actors who preferred to stay and work in New York. But a couple of years ago, there was a mass exodus from New York to Los Angeles. Everyone wants to be in movies or get a series. They want to get rich so they'll have the power to do anything they want. But lately, these actors are returning to New York to do theatre.

Do you have any pet peeves regarding the conduct of actors during auditions?
It's annoying when the actor comes into the room and says he just got the script and didn't have time to look it over. If that's the case, don't come at all. When you come in, you have to give the best you can without any excuses. And I don't care if you goof and forget your lines. As long as your attitude is right and you understand what's going on in the scene, that's fine with me. If you fumble a line, don't worry, and don't make a big deal about it. Just forge ahead.

How much does having good connections help an actor land important roles?
Some actors, and even stars, think it's all about who you know and that's just not true. Knowing people may get you in through the door, but it's talent that gets you a role. Once the actor enters the room, friendships don't mean anything anymore. No one is going to put their reputation on the line and cast an incompetent actor just because a friend recommended him. And don't look at each audition as a life and death situation. Some actors think that they are always auditioning for the one part that is going to kick their career into high gear. I'll never forget this girl who had to audition for a one line role—she stayed up all night, worrying about it. Don't do that. If you're really good, eventually it's going to happen.

. . . .
Louis DiGiaimo
214 Sullivan Street, #2C
New York, NY 10012
. . . .

KAREN AND BARBARA DIVISEK

Karen Divisek and her younger sister, Barbara, have spent the last twenty-two years running what they describe as a family business. Karen, who studied constitutional law at Berkeley, first got involved with

Karen Divisek **Barbara Divisek**

casting when she went to work with the late casting director Marsha Kleinman. When Kleinman was offered a position at Paramount shortly thereafter, she entrusted the commercial end of her business to Karen and eventually gave it to her. After graduating from high school, Barbara joined her sister and a partnership ultimately evolved. Now, after more than two decades and a massive list of credits to their names, the sisters Divisek have worked on just about every conceivable product, in every conceivable location, using the talents of celebrities, union, non-union, real people, athletes, kids and various barn-yard animals. They number James Ivory and the Coen Brothers among the many directors with whom they've worked. Last year alone the company worked on over 225 jobs.

Do you serve different functions as casting directors in the office?
BARBARA DIVISEK: I attempt to keep the ship sailing straight with organization. Karen provides the creative support. Nobody can give more to actors than Karen can. I think Karen is unbelievable at taking an actor and

telling them how to turn something into their own words. She's brilliant at it. I'm too busy thinking about administrative stuff. That's our balance.

KAREN DIVISEK: Barbara also looks at every picture that comes into the office. She makes the first cut of weeding out. Then I'll weed, then she'll re-weed. Sometimes we disagree but we do it together. Our brother works with us too. He's one of our main session directors.

BARBARA DIVISEK: And my husband keeps the place running from an equipment standpoint. He's also the one who got us to start teaching commercial acting. He said that we had a lot to offer and we'd get more back from teaching. He's right; teaching is enormously gratifying.

Do you have anything you want to say about pictures?

BARBARA DIVISEK: If someone comes into a session looking dramatically different from their picture, Karen and I want to know about it so we can talk to the agent. But beyond that it's not important if a picture has a shiny or matte finish, or if it's three quarter or head-shot. That doesn't matter as long as it's a true representation of the person walking in that door. It makes us crazy when it's not!

KAREN DIVISEK: Current photos help an actor's credibility. If you're shopping for a house and you see a picture and then you get there and the house doesn't look anything like the picture, you're gonna be a little bit bummed. It's the same thing. You see an actor's picture and you're all excited; you can't wait to meet this guy—and then what walks in is completely different. You call the agent and they haven't even seen the actor for awhile themselves; they don't know what you're talking about. It's an actor's responsibility to stay current with their agents. If a photograph isn't representative, then the actor is seeing themselves as vastly different from what they really are. And then, when I read the résumé, I wonder how much is really true.

Any advice on auditioning and slating?

KAREN DIVISEK: A slate should be reflective of you as a human being. Not, as some actors think, of the character, but as the real you. Never slate as the character because they may change the character. As an example, we were auditioning beautiful women for a fragrance and they wanted them to be really mean and bitchy. Almost nasty. So a couple of the girls chose to take on that attitude when they slated. We absolutely loved the way one actress looked. She was perfect— but the clients wouldn't give her a callback because they thought she was so nasty in her slate and in her reading that she had nothing else to offer. After the first day of auditions, when the client watched the tape, the mean thing scared him to death. He realized he wanted something else. But that woman had already taken herself out of the running. Casting often is a learning process. It tells the client what they don't want as much as it tells them what they do.

BARBARA DIVISEK: And also, sometimes tapes are passed around to other people. For instance, we just did a job for an ad agency and two weeks later, we got a call from a production company saying, "We're unhappy with our casting tape so we are looking at the casting tapes you did for that ad agency. You were casting for the same age range and types we are looking for, so we viewed your tapes and found two people we now want to book." We'll also do a day of auditions and then suddenly the clients decide they're adding another type so they'll review the tapes again, looking for that type. If someone has pigeon-holed themselves, they're stuck.

KAREN DIVISEK: The slate is your five seconds to show them who is going to show up on the set. I've heard directors and agency people talking and they'll love three actors so it will come down to, "Yeah, but who do we want to hang out with all day?" Oh, and never slate using your agency. What if the ad agency doesn't have a good relationship with your agent? They shouldn't be distracted with information they don't need.

Do you only see people through agents?

KAREN DIVISEK: As I mentioned, every submission that comes through this office is looked at. Barbara goes through every single picture.

BARBARA DIVISEK: I feel that if someone spent the money to get a picture here, the least we can do is look at it.

KAREN DIVISEK: We can't keep them all, but we do look. We'd need a building the size of Costco if we kept them all!

BARBARA DIVISEK: It's bad enough to see all the job files in my garage. We do keep files on specialty acts, athletes and real people. But we don't keep general submissions. For one thing, actors move on and they're not always available for commercial work.

KAREN DIVISEK: When we Taft-Hartleyed Michael J. Fox for his McDonald's commercial, he was already being brought in to audition for *Family Ties*. Although we had hired him, a week and a half later when we wanted him, he had been signed to the series and that was the end of that.

What do you think makes someone commercially successful?

KAREN DIVISEK: There are people who can make magic, who can go through that lens and make three dimensions out of two. You can tell. There is something about the way they are with the camera and the way it translates. Some beautiful people don't translate well to the screen. Part of it is relaxation and part of it is being able to silence the little voice inside of your head that critiques.

Also, the people who are successful in our business are the people who are always working on their craft.

BARBARA DIVISEK: Actors can also do research by just being current with what's out there. They should look and see what commercials they think they're right for and to know what their market is.

KAREN DIVISEK: And what are the people wearing in those commercials? Those are the kinds of clothes they should have in their wardrobes for auditioning. It's interesting because theatrically it's not really appropriate to dress the part for an audition but commercially, it is.

BARBARA DIVISEK: Of course, if we're seeing people to play nurses we don't want everyone to run out and buy uniforms. But my husband is an actor and he has a doctor's lab coat that he uses quite often. He also has a photographer's vest so that he can look like a safari guy. It's not a requirement but it can help to give the flavor.

How do you think the business has changed over the years?

KAREN DIVISEK: When I started in this business, twenty people was a cattle call. Now it's not unusual to have sixty people at a callback! Also, more people are making decisions in terms of casting. When I started, the director normally got his way and worked in close conjunction with the agency/producer. They had a game plan. The director shot the commercial, cut the commercial, and the first time the client was shown anything was the finished cut. Now the client is involved with pre-production and casting and it's much more complex.

Any final words of advice?

KAREN DIVISEK: When an actor comes in to audition, he is being asked to act. He is not being asked to write, to direct, to prop or give opinions. He is being asked to come in and fulfill what is on the page and to make the translation into a performance. Common sense and knowing that this is a business are the most important tools. But there is nothing better than having fun in this business!

. . . .
Karen and Barbara Divisek
Divisek Casting - Commercials
6420 Wilshire Blvd.
Lower Lobby, #100
Los Angeles, CA 90048
. . . .

CHRISTY DOOLEY

For the past fourteen years, Christy Dooley has been head of casting for *The Bold and the Beautiful*, the CBS daytime drama watched by over eighty million people daily. She began her career as a theatre major at San Diego State and worked as a theatre actor and director in Northern California. In Los Angeles, she split her time between working with theatre groups and at various behind-the-scene jobs. Dooley has worked within the industry as a casting coordinator, production assistant and as an assistant to the director of business affairs at Telepictures.

> *You can be the most talented actor in the world, but if you don't know how to get out there and sell yourself, nobody is going to find out what you're capable of.*

What made you move from acting to casting?

Though I loved acting, I realized that I wasn't very good at selling myself. You can be the most talented actor in the world, but if you don't know how to get out there and sell yourself, nobody is going to find out what you're capable of. When I realized that I was frustrated as an actor, I began to ask myself, "What else can I do that will combine all my skills?" The answer was casting. I am a much better buyer than a seller. And I love the feeling of being able to help actors rather than competing with them.

Is there any room for newcomers on *The Bold and the Beautiful* and how can actors get to you?

I look at every submission that comes across my desk. When a face captures me, I turn the picture over and look at the résumé. If the résumé captures me also, I'll bring the actor in, regardless of whether or not they have an agent.

I file submissions according to the level of the actor's camera experience. If, for instance, they have no camera experience but I see that they are seriously working on their craft, I might give their picture to my assistant to consider them for extra work. If the person has a little bit of camera experience, I might consider reading them for under fives. If they have more experience, I put them in the files for principal or recurring roles.

Then, of course, you have the negotiated roles for series-regulars. For that you do need an agent or lawyer who will negotiate on your behalf with our Business Affairs Department.

Why would it be beneficial for an inexperienced actor to do extra work on your show?
Daytime is a three camera medium requiring technical skills beyond acting. That's why I tell people to do extra work first. That way, they can get on the set and watch how the contract players hit their marks, perform for the right camera, hold their moments before each fade, etc. An inexperienced actor would be lost on the set. As a result, we would have to stop production and explain the basic technical necessities to them. That costs the company extra time and money; a luxury they can't afford.

Other than technical considerations, how is acting for daytime different from acting in features or night-time episodic?
Acting is acting, truth is truth. In essence, the actor's approach should be similar in every medium. However, there are some differences. In daytime, you're shooting a complete show every day, five days a week. So your memory muscles better be in great shape. Also, since you are taping scenes that are relatively similar, you have to learn to find those small nuances that will add dimension to the role.

Another difference worth being aware of is this: Daytime revolves around the contract player. That's who the audience tunes in to see every day. Therefore, when you come onto the show as a day player, you are there to service the contract player. It can be difficult for an actor to come in and not make the scene about his character, when he naturally wants to do so. The day player has a responsibility to create real people and to make them interesting, without taking the focus away from the contract player.

What is the auditioning process that an actor would go through to become a regular on your show?
I can read up to about two hundred people and narrow that down to about twenty-five through callbacks with me. I work with them, and give them direction

to see if they can make adjustments. Then, I take seven or eight of them to the producers. They either hire them or we go to screen tests.

The screen test is like the real thing. You rehearse with the director, you go to wardrobe and makeup and you work on the set with one of the contract actors. Finally, they either decide to hire you based on the test, or we go back to the drawing board.

What, to you, is a good headshot?

A good picture is one that actually looks like you and captures the life in your eyes. A picture like that stops you and makes you look. Your headshot is your business card. Save your money and have professional pictures taken. Don't go to a friend who has a camera. When I go through a stack of pictures and see some that don't look professional, I may not even turn them over to see what credits the actor has.

Similarly, we call in people based on their glamorous pictures, but sometimes when they walk in, they don't look anything like the headshot. So don't hire makeup and hair people before a shoot unless you are able to duplicate that look again.

Do you have any actor pet peeves?

I am not into gimmicks. I can't tell you how many bars of soap I have received with a note saying, "I want to be on a soap." I have also been mailed dinner rolls with a note, "I want a role." I've even gotten tennis shoes with notes saying, "Trying to get my foot in the door." Everybody thinks they are being original. Actors should not waste their money like that. I look at every submission that crosses my desk, and I give everybody equal consideration. Also, don't spend your money sending me flowers. A thank-you note is fine. Finally, do not call me and ask for a role because you want to make your insurance. I am not a social worker. Becoming an actor is a choice you made.

Instead of gimmicks, focus on getting yourself out there to be seen. By that I don't mean stopping by a casting director's office or phoning them constantly. That becomes intrusive. Be constructive. Get into a play and send me a flyer. I will try to see as many as I can. But I am choosy and I get about ten fliers a day. It's best to send me a note and the reviews. Even if I don't come and see you in the play, if the reviews are great, I may ask you to come in.

Any final thoughts?

Actors have to absolutely realize why they are acting. Search and find your motives in pursuing a career in acting. Once you are committed, find out what it is that you have that is different from everybody else, and focus on selling that. So many people come in and they are so mainstream. They just offer middle of the road interpretations so they don't offend anybody. If you do that, you are not special. You are just like 85 percent of the people who come in.

Then you have the other 15 percent. Those are the actors who take the words and make them jump off the page in truthful and unusual ways. They paint such convincing mental pictures for you that you can't help but hire them. Every actor should strive to belong to that special 15 percent.

. . . .

Christy Dooley
CBS/The Bold and the Beautiful
7800 Beverly Blvd., Suite 3371
Los Angeles, CA 90036.
. . . .

MICK DOWD

Mick Dowd's background in entertainment began as a singer. He appeared on the shows of Merv Griffin and Johnny Carson, among others. He also performed on stage before switching to production. He produced commercials for about five years before becoming an agent. Two years later, he moved into casting commercials and in 1993, formed Dowd-Reudy Casting with his partner, Tom Reudy. Their most recent clients have included Ford, 7-Up, California Cheese, Nissan, AT&T, Nike, American Airlines and two Japanese commercials, one featuring Brad Pitt and one with Leonardo DiCaprio. After more than a decade in casting, Dowd seems to have happily settled there.

There are some people in this industry who really don't like actors very much. They think that they're either neurotic or childish. What's your take on that?
I've always had an affinity for actors, and yes, they can be children but I've always loved talent. I know that there are a lot of casting people who don't like actors, but I'm just the opposite. I really like them.

A lot of actors think that commercial casting is all about the look.
A lot of it does have to do with the look. Which is why, often when people

think they did horribly at an audition, they may still book the spot. They may not have had their best reading but there was something that the client liked. That's why, when actors have bad scene partners and ask to do the reading again, I tell them it makes no difference. I've had so many people get jobs despite bad partners. It's the look. You don't have to be brilliant with these things. Yes, there are brilliant people, but the bottom line is whether you have the right look and if your personality is appealing. The thing I have to tell actors all the time is, especially in an initial audition, the producers are only going to look at the first few seconds of tape.

Does that start with slating- "Hello my name is . . . "?
Yes. They watch the slate and decide if they like the look. If it's right, they'll watch a few words to make sure you can read. They're not going to watch you for thirty seconds worth of dialogue because there are so many people to watch. At that point, they're deciding whether or not to call you back and fast forwarding to the next person.

They wind up just seeing if there's something about you they like. That's all they need to see. The bottom line is that it isn't that tough in commercials. Doing a minute commercial shouldn't be tough for an actor, if the actor and the director are good. In auditions the director just wants to see the quality of who the actor is inside, as opposed to somebody acting things. So, while they know they can probably get what they need acting-wise in the end, they want to see what comes across from the actor in their eyes, who they are.

The thing we all forget about is that the camera photographs your thoughts as much as your features. It really does and that's a lesson for actors to really remember. Even though you may think you're not doing anything, your thoughts subtly register on your face and your face changes. That's really the beauty of acting, especially when you have such a limited time on camera. It's just a few seconds. If you just can think it, that's really all you need.

Knowing what you know, if you were going in on a commercial audition, what are some of the things you would and wouldn't do?
I would absolutely be myself. I wouldn't be forcibly funny, but I'd certainly have personality. I would hope that when I came in I would be exactly who I am with maybe a little extra energy. Just really be me. I would also be willing to take some chances to make some mistakes; to stretch something just a little further than other people might be doing, but not in a way that looked like I was intentionally trying to show off or be too cute. Not contrived. I don't like it when actors try to put a little button on the end of what they say, or try to have a cute little slate. It

shows right away when somebody's phony. I've seen whole rooms turn off to people in a callback for that reason. If you're phony, it really comes across on camera. I think that's the main thing.

Do actors ever ask to see their take after an audition?
Yes and I show it to them if I have the time. It never hurts to ask anything. When you walk into a room, if you have any questions about what's going on, just ask.

Do you ever erase people from your tape?
Oh, absolutely, sure. I try a lot of new people who I haven't met before. They come in from their pictures and a lot of times people look nothing like their photos. So, I have no qualms about erasing people if they were really not who I thought they were going to be when I called them in. If they are not what we are looking for, there's no reason to keep them on the tape. But I would never tell the actor. I'd let them go through the thing.

For actors without agents, is it okay to just send a picture to your office or drop it off?
Actors do it all the time and, yes, I look at all the pictures. I do. I don't call all that many unsolicited people in because I've been burned so many times by people who do not look like their photographs. Sometimes, you'll only have one chance with a casting director so you want to be exactly who you represented yourself to be in that picture. It doesn't matter if you're beautiful or not so beautiful, but whatever you look like, be sure it matches your headshot.

I think everybody's always trying to be beautiful. Both men and women. But sometimes being beautiful can actually get in your way, right?
It can. People just don't realize that there are so many beautiful men and women in this city. People will come from all over this country and they've probably been told by their friends and neighbors how beautiful they are and that they should go to Hollywood and be famous. They get here and one is handsomer and one is more beautiful than the next and there are hundreds of them. The interesting thing, actually, is that I think so many of these beautiful people have been so catered to for most of their lives that they really haven't developed a whole lot of personality. They're just totally about their look. When somebody beautiful comes in who has a personality, a sense of humor and some energy, they're like a piece of gold and those are the people who become stars. They're the ones who know that they have to be something other than just a great face and a great body.

Having worked with a lot of those people who went on to become stars, do you think you can recognize the "it" thing about them? Even in primitive form?
Yes, but I also think that that "it" thing is really different in the different mediums. I think there are certain people who have "it" on stage, but it doesn't translate to film. You don't get that same thing when they're on camera. There have been so many times that I've had people come in and I'll be standing and talking to them while they are on camera and when I look at the monitor, it is not the same person. The camera picks up something totally different from what you're seeing face to face and, a lot of times, what the camera picks up is really magical. It's not always there in person but it's what the camera sees that makes them a star.

I've also seen people who are totally wonderful on camera who never become stars. Some talented and wonderful people pop out and some don't because the opportunity or the luck was not there. They weren't in the right place at the right time. Michelle Pfeiffer was discovered in the supermarket. If she hadn't been there . . . who knows? The whole thing is like stepping on a ladder. If you miss a step, maybe that's the last step you take. There may be another chance, and endurance and sticking with it can bring you success, but sometimes you miss it. You chose the wrong pilot or did the wrong thing or missed whatever it was. That's the business.

Is there anything else that you want to say to actors?
There really is no secret to commercials. It's really one of those things where everybody does have a chance. That's the nice thing about them. There are very few people I've seen that I'd tell, "Oh there's just no hope for you." In commercials, there really is something for everybody. Maybe it's a one-shot deal, once in your life you might get a commercial and other people might get fifteen in a month, but it would be stupid to say to somebody, "Don't even think about this because you'll never be able to do it."

Do you think that the people you see over and over again in commercials have anything in common?
Yes and no. Generally, those people have moved into the right period of their lives. They look like a certain type so, while maybe when they were younger they didn't work as much, they've grown into something else and now they work all the time. They'll grow out of that period, too. And of course, those are the people who know their craft. Sometimes though, I think it's something that can't be taught.

What does it mean to renew a commercial?

A commercial can only run for twenty-one months. After that, the client has to renew contracts if they want to keep it running. If it's a successful commercial, it will probably be cheaper for them to renew than to shoot a whole new spot. It's a fine line for the agents. They have to up your price enough to make it a good deal for you, but not so much that the client decides that it's a better deal to just do a new commercial.

Do you think actors should memorize the copy for a commercial audition?

I think it is very important for an actor to learn the first line. Then it doesn't matter if you read the thing; just know the first line because a lot of times that's all they're going to see. Remember I was talking about that fast forwarding? They'll just look at somebody to see if they like them. So make sure you get that first line. It gives you that initial contact and the focus that is what they're going to remember.

Another thing about auditions is that you have to ask for what you need. If the cue card isn't where you can read it, have it moved. If you can't read the card, you're not going to be good. If you're uncomfortable, you're not going to be good. Sometimes you'll need a second to focus on the cue card. You'll look at your script outside and then come in and look at the cue card and, even though the same words are printed, it looks like Chinese. So ask to take a second. Why wouldn't I let you? I want you to be good.

Actors sometimes get paranoid about taking up too much time.

It's a few seconds you're taking up. It may seem like you're taking up hours, but you're really not. You're taking up ten seconds of looking at that cue card. You're not wasting anything. It's your life. It's your job. I want you to be good. They want you to be good. You want to be good.

. . . .

Mick Dowd
Dowd/Reudy Casting – Commercials
c/o The Casting Studios
5724 West 3rd Street, #508
Los Angeles, CA 90036

. . . .

DONNA EKHOLDT, CSA

Like many casting directors, Donna Ekholdt worked as an actor before she went into casting. Where she differs from other casting directors lies in the fact that she doesn't consider herself to be someone who gave up acting but as "an actor who has shifted focus." After training extensively as an actor, Ekholdt suffered from back problems which led to surgery. During her recovery, she interned with Liberman/Hirschfeld thereby beginning her career in casting. Later, she moved on to working

with Tammy Billik, Gary Zuckerbrod and Karen Rea where her work as an associate included the films *Far and Away* and *Death Becomes Her*. With Susan Bluestein, a colleague Ekholdt still considers her mentor, she cast the mini-series *Children of the Dust* and *The Oldest Confederate Widow Tells All*, both Artios Award nominees. She considers herself fortunate to have been included with Bluestein, Alexa Fogel and Junie Lowry-Johnson for their Emmy win for *NYPD Blue*'s second season. Ekholdt spent the subsequent year as manager of casting at NBC where she was responsible for overseeing a number of series and MOWs with a specialty in comedy. She then moved to 20th Century Fox where she and Randy Stone (senior vice president of talent and casting) headed the entire roster of 20th Century Fox TV projects including *The X-Files, Millennium, Chicago Hope, Ally McBeal* and *The Practice*. Ekholdt left Fox in 1998 and recently cast the MOW *The Beat Goes On: The Sonny and Cher Story*. She is also currently working on a practical handbook for actors.

Can you talk about your acting training?
I trained at USC and with Stella Adler, Bill Ball—a remarkable man who made the A.C.T. program famous—Guy Stockwell and Mark York who changed the way I saw acting, mostly because of his [Sanford] Meisner background and the fact that he offered me so many different approaches. The changing moment for me in my work and the way I perceived what it is an actor needs to accomplish was the day we were doing a conflict improv and I became furious with the other actor. I realized that it was no longer about pretending to be in a situation and pretending to feel, it was about pretending to be in a situation and really feeling in your soul. It changed my life.

As an actor I live, I just *live* for the moment when there is a connection, when that thing happens and you know that what's being exchanged is honest and real and emotionally stirring. And now, I live for that moment as a casting director. It's the reason I don't use readers for the most part and never have. I keep doing this for that moment that we hope for as actors. It's that moment we're waiting for, that moment that is the addiction of doing this. When it happens, you think, "That's it! It happened!" and it takes your breath away. Working on *NYPD Blue*, for instance, was an amazing experience. I've never worked physically harder in my life. But having David Milch's words to say and having that exchange occur was very fulfilling to me.

Do you get to experience that "moment" a lot?
It doesn't happen as often as I would like. I work very hard at making myself available in the hopes that it will happen. And it doesn't necessarily only have to happen with me. If I feel as if there are two actors in the room and it happens to them, it moves through the room. We all feel it. But it doesn't happen often enough. I think many actors spend their auditions trying to make every moment 100 percent. If an actor could understand that if there were only two or three moments in a whole audition that hit that thing, that nail it, that's enough. The rest just has to be honest talking.

Should an actor stop an audition if they feel that it's not going well?
Absolutely. I'm always surprised by actors not wanting to start over when the

train is going someplace they don't want to be going or not taking charge of their audition. We've got fifteen minutes invested in them before they walk in the door. My assistant's time is my time and between the two of us we had to go through the pictures, set up a drive-on, pull sides, copy the sides, get on the phone and schmooze with your agents, send you the sides or make them available or fax them, whatever. All that is time. So we've already invested fifteen or twenty minutes in you before you ever walk in the door. Why wouldn't I give you two more to get what I hoped for when you walked in? Many casting directors will hate that I say this—but we are creative employment agencies and I emphasize the word *creative*. I am being paid to find someone who fits a position. So each person who walks through the door and comes up with the goods is one more choice for the director and five fewer I have to see. Not that we don't love meeting actors. We love them but the fact of the matter is, I have to do the job. That's what I'm getting paid for. So if I have to come up with five choices per role (and in episodic you're doing anywhere from twelve to twenty-two roles per week), do the math. How badly do you think I want you to get the role? So yes, if you need to, take command and start over. Own your audition. Of course, you better have something to offer when you start over, particularly if you've done the whole scene. But if you see that train going somewhere you don't want to be, stop it. Without a big apology.

Another tip on auditions: no props, no staging, just sit down and work. If an actor is a trained actor, I will assume that they can walk, talk, hold a glass, hold a phone or any other prop I hand them. I will assume all of those things without question until they show me otherwise. The problem is actor after actor who's only had an evening with the sides cannot invest their body in the objective because the objective hasn't been around that long. It is not imbedded in them yet. They're working off material they've only had for an evening and they will walk in and want to physically act out the whole scene or they'll want to stand because some school of acting teachers has told them, "You will have more energy." My belief is, if you are invested in an objective with life or death stakes, why would standing make a difference? You will have energy because something is at stake. All the time, I get actors walking in and standing when they're not physically comfortable that way. Walk in, shake hands or whatever you need to do, sit down in a chair and make it about the close-up. That's what the audition is anyway. Unless you're talking physical comedy it's all in the close-up. Some actors do better work when they move, some are propelled by that, but I don't think there are a lot of them out there. You do what you need to do and do what the scene is about. The scene is never about the physical contact, it's never about the phone, the glass or the prop. The scene is never about anything except the conflict:

what's going on between two people and how hard are they fighting for it. Andre Braugher, a really wonderful actor said, and I'm paraphrasing, "Nothing is as powerful as stillness so I don't move unless I can improve on that. Nothing is as powerful as silence so I don't speak unless I have a chance on improving on that." I think that says it all.

Any other advice you'd like to impart to actors?
Remember that if you're not getting better, you're getting worse. I see actor after actor and I ask them, "Are you in class?" And they say, "Oh no, I'm taking some time off." My response is always, "How will you make up for the lost time?" There is no retaining and staying the same. We must be like dancers and musicians. If a ballerina doesn't dance for two weeks, she cannot do what she did two weeks ago. Why would an actor believe that the accessibility to the most fragile muscle in the body, his soul, would remain ready to operate at full voice or full speed? Physical trainers say, "Use it or lose it," and that absolutely applies to acting. Use it or lose it.

When I was teaching, I used to ask my students to keep logs, diaries of the hours that they spent working on their careers—working on monologues, working on scenes, sending out pictures, reading scripts—I didn't count movies or TV because even though those are required, for most people they are pleasure. One week I asked people to pull out their journals and I just went around asking, "How many hours?" and this one girl stood up proudly and said nineteen hours. "Nineteen hours," I said, "not even a part-time job for what you told me was your dream." She was totally taken off guard and she said, "Well, I have a job and I have to make money." I said, "You're wearing boots right now which must have cost $150. Now, couldn't you be wearing something that cost less? Because those hours on your boots translate into hours working which translate into hours missed as an actor." So it's being fiscally responsible about your career, and it's not that I don't understand not having money. I come from a family that struggled for money and I've mopped floors to pay for classes. But if you're wearing Armani suits (excluding one or two audition outfits), if you're overspending the money anywhere else, those are hours subtracted from the pursuit of your goal.

Any thoughts on actors marketing themselves?
Make sure that your picture represents what you're selling. We all know that there are roughly fifteen stock characters types. You better know which ones you are and what you're selling. I say, put the label on the can. If I get a picture that says you're peas, and carrots show up, I'm angry. I'm probably pressed for time

and I'm not looking for carrots today. I'll call you when I need carrots. If your picture doesn't represent you, you're not gonna get called in for something you could conceivably get and you'll get called in for all of the things you're not right for and won't get. I recommend that actors figure out what character types they do best—the three types they can sell. And you're gonna want to ask as many people as you can for an objective opinion. Once you know what your three types are, what characters are your best, spend three weeks reading every single script you can get your hands on, watching every moment of TV you can manage. Go to every film you can see and count how many times each one of those types shows up. The character you're best at may not be the one with the most opportunities to cast you. It may be your second type and if it's number two then that's what you sell and you sell big. Your picture reflects it, your résumé, your presentation. Sell yourself in that package. Market yourself that way. Then, after the casting directors have gotten into the habit of putting you on their list every time that part shows up, it is not that hard to convince us to see a good actor for something a little bit different—one of your other characters. Then you start marketing that second character. You get student films showing you in that part, you look for that role. Then you show your agent: look how well I do this, too. Remember, your agent is not responsible for packaging you—you're responsible for packaging you. After all, the agent gets 10 percent. Are you doing the remaining 90 percent? I know very few actors who can honestly say, "Yes."

> *I say, put the label on the can. If I get a picture that says you're peas, and carrots show up, I'm angry. I'm probably pressed for time and I'm not looking for carrots today. I'll call you when I need carrots.*

. . . .
Donna Ekholdt
137 N. Larchmont Blvd., Suite 495
Los Angeles, CA 90004
. . . .

Judy Elkins

According to commercial casting director Judy Elkins, "Right now, real people are in. Everybody in commercials today has to look not like an actor, but like somebody you may know."

Elkins started her career as a receptionist for a production company but was soon promoted to casting voice-overs and she hasn't stopped since. Over the past twenty years she has cast thousands of commercials.

How have commercials changed in the last twenty years?
When I first became a casting director, we would bring in only ten to twenty people for a role and they were all commercial, white bread, all-American, Rock Hudson and Doris Day types. The only ethnic types acceptable were black commercial actors. Now, we bring in thousands of people from all backgrounds. I often see one hundred to two hundred people a day. What many clients now require are theatrical actors who are a little offbeat and who have some edge and character.

There also seem to be a lot more celebrities doing commercials.
Today the commercial business is a status thing. It wasn't so before. Before, only actors whose careers were down-and-out did commercials. Now everybody wants to do commercials, even stars who work all the time.

What techniques should the auditioning actor know in order to succeed in commercials?

They must know how to relate to the camera. They should observe themselves on video in order to find out what they are doing right and wrong. And then they must learn how to adjust and improve themselves.

When an actor comes in, I often interview them on camera. Therefore, it is important that they know how to be relaxed when they talk to the camera. If I say to an actor, "Tell us your name and something interesting about yourself," they can't just nervously say, "My name is such and such, and you want me to say something about myself?" Don't repeat the question. Just get on with telling the camera who you are, and be prepared to tell an interesting story.

Another question may be, "If you were casting yourself in a role, who would you be?" Have an answer, be creative. Don't just stammer or mumble. Say something interesting. Most of the kid actors—and some of the adult ones—have no idea how to relate to the camera. Commercials are tough. You have thirty seconds to sell yourself, to sell the product and to be liked. It's much harder than going into a theatrical interview where you have time to develop a character.

Actors should take every class they possibly can, especially classes that are videotaped. At the end of the class, you'll know how you look, what colors look good on you, what color lipstick suits you best, etc. Even actors who have already made it need to continuously study. The biggest mistake people make in commercials is that they think it is easy. They think, "Hey, I'll make commercials and make a lot of money so that I can do real work in the theatre."

Also, I see many actors who come in totally unprepared. They don't look at the script, they ask for cue cards. SAG says I have to have cue cards, but when actors come in and depend on the cards alone, then I know they are just here to make money. It is far better to come in half an hour early, take the sides, go out for coffee and study the lines. I respect those who do that. Unfortunately, most actors just come in, glance at the sides, socialize, and that's it. The actors who study their sides and know what they are doing are the ones who will inevitably book. I have come to the conclusion that sometimes actors deliberately sabotage themselves. They feel that they aren't going to get the role anyway, so they don't bother trying. That way they protect their egos and can say to themselves, "Well, I wasn't really trying."

What are the best types of photos for commercials?

Composite photos are absolutely out. In the old days, actors would have a commercial composite, with a smiling pose on one side and four images on the other side, showing them in a suit, in casual clothes, with glasses, etc. We don't want that anymore. That's out. What we need is an up-to-date photo that looks like you. You can't walk in and look three or four years older than your picture, with your hair a different length or your nose pierced.

What behavior during auditions annoys you?

Sometimes, winning the lottery is easier than getting a commercial. The competition is that intense. But most actors walk into the interview with an attitude that says, "I don't really care about this interview." I sometimes have people assist me during auditions and when they see the "I don't care" attitude of some actors, they tell me, "I just don't believe it! They were called in on this and they just threw it away! How can they? Don't they know what the odds are to just get in the door?!"

Many come in and say things like, "Oh, I didn't think it was necessary to bring pictures." Or, "I have a picture in the car, shall I get it?" Please, approach this business with the utmost professionalism.

> *Even if you are paired with people who don't know what they're doing, do the best job you can and you will inevitably stand out in the room.*

During an audition, how can an actor overcome being paired with another actor who is not up to par?

Even if you are paired with people who don't know what they're doing, do the best job you can and you will inevitably stand out in the room. Don't worry about the others. Be yourself and your performance will still shine through.

What practical advice can you give commercial actors?

Both men and women should have a look that is up-to-date. If long hair is out, their hair should be shorter. I have some actresses coming in who have the same look they had ten years ago. They have the same hairdo and even the same style of wardrobe. It doesn't work. You have to continuously keep yourself up-to-date. Same thing for men. Though men have it easier, they still have to pay attention to what looks are fashionable.

Today's clients don't want a Los Angeles Look. They want an Anywhere, USA Look. They don't want a trendy look. So don't come in with a deep suntan. Nobody wants to see that. If you want to be a working actor in commercials, get out of the sun! Currently, nobody is looking for surfer types.

Any final thoughts?

People who work in this business are very fortunate. What a great way to make a living! You are treated well, commercial directors are great, the union protects you and if you get lucky, you also make a wonderful living.

. . . .

Judy Elkins
Chelsea Studios
4605 Lankershim Blvd., Suite 500
North Hollywood, CA 91602

. . . .

MIKE FENTON, CSA

If there were superstars among casting directors, Mike Fenton would be among them, with credits that include *E.T.*, *Beaches*, *Raiders of the Lost Ark*, the *Back to the Future* series, *Aliens*, *Shampoo*, *Chinatown*, *One Flew over the Cuckoo's Nest* and, more recently, *Dante's Peak* and *Lost in Space*.

Fenton studied cinema at UCLA and formed his casting company, Roos-Fenton Casting, in 1971 with Fred Roos. When Roos went on to produce films, Fenton brought in Jane Feinberg and created Fenton-Feinberg casting. The two worked together for sixteen years before Feinberg retired. Fenton is currently partnered with Allison Cowitt under the name of Fenton-Cowitt Casting. Recent credits include the Hallmark television films *Arabian Nights* and *Cleopatra* and the feature *Muppets in Space*.

What advice do you have for actors just starting out?
If I were going to guide a young person in terms of what to do to have a career, the first question is: Do you love acting? Because if you do not love acting, the heartache and the rejection in this business are so powerful that they can destroy a person's life.

Once you get past that step, I would recommend finishing high school and college and doing every play you can possibly do while you are in school. After graduation, the artist, if they have the means, should go to either New York or London to study. In New York, do as much as you can—Broadway, off-Broadway—get a background. Do some soap operas, do some commercials, put a reel together. At that point, having made this investment in your career, you must make the decision about where to go. Do you really want a career in smoggy Los Angeles, or do you want to raise a family and go to someplace like Orlando or New Orleans? Pick someplace in the United States where there is theatre that pays money, where they make commercials, where they make industrials and every once in a while, a television movie or film comes through. Find a place that gives you the quality of life you are seeking. Or chuck all of that, come to Los Angeles, get a job, start studying with a local acting teacher and do everything you can to get an agent.

Those are two avenues you can follow, but that doesn't mean actors will pay any attention to my advice. Most actors will just show up in Los Angeles without a great deal of training and they'll do this ridiculous thing of going out and getting into showcases because they've been told by somebody that casting directors will come and make them stars. That is nonsense. I don't think casting directors spend their time going to showcases looking for actors. The showcases I have gone to have been dreadful and I no longer go to showcases. The quality of the performer is usually just godawful. For the most part, it seems to me to be a waste of time.

There are plenty of dedicated people who have followed your advice and still don't work regularly. Isn't there's a lot of luck involved?
Yes, and I think luck is also connected with looks. I think that when we talk about people who are successful in the business, for the most part we speak about young people who have "the look." For the most part, the people who get movies made are people who have a look—Matt Damon, Leonardo DiCaprio, Uma Thurman, Julia Roberts. Of course, there are others, but it's a very small group of people.

And it's always a crapshoot. When Sylvester Stallone did *Rocky*, I would venture to guess there were a number of studio heads who said, "We're not going to do this movie at this budget with an unknown actor." When Matt Damon and Ben Affleck wanted to do their picture, there must have been a number of studios who turned them down, who didn't believe in them. When young people create projects and then hope to star in them, they obviously need additional elements to make the project. If they can get a Robin Williams to work in their movie for ten days and not only be the glue that holds it all together but the sales tool as well, then it can happen.

But believe me, there are many attractive people who are skilled actors with terrific projects that they cannot get launched. Luck is something we can't measure, and we can't say when or if it's going to happen.

So what do you say to someone who has done all of the things you've advised and comes here to Los Angeles?
More than anything, what an actor needs is an agent who can open doors. That is the key to a career. An actor is very lucky if he or she scores an agent who believes in them, who lives, eats, sleeps that actor, fights for that actor, gets the actor out. And there are agents who do that. Of course, when the actor becomes successful, the bigger agencies swoop down and take them away from that same agent. That's the nature of the beast. But anyone coming to Los Angeles must realize that the agent is the key to their career.

Would getting a good manager help to get a good agent?
It could. A manager can help you get an agent, but the bottom line is that the manager is there for hand-holding and guidance, the agent is there to make it all happen.

Can you talk about some of the people you've discovered?
I don't think casting directors really discover people. Many, many years ago we used Jim Carrey on a motion picture called *Finders Keepers*. Did I know when I put Jim Carrey in that film that he would be who he is today? Absolutely not. He got the film because his agent, Joe Funicello, suggested him to me, and showed me a piece of tape that I showed to the director. That was an agent making an opportunity for an actor, and it happens all the time. Most agents are smart enough that they do their job and they step back. They don't say, "I created this person," any more than I think it's fair for a casting director to say that. It's a system that does it. A casting director would probably not even be aware of an artist if an agent they trusted hadn't opened the door and sent the individual to them. That's why I think the agent makes careers. Not only do I think that, I'm convinced of it.

But you discovered people like Ethan Hawke, Richard Dreyfuss, Kevin Costner...
Not really. I was made aware of those people by agents. Now, granted, I saw Richard Dreyfuss at Beverly Hills High School a hundred years ago, but that didn't matter. His agent kept hitting me over the head and saying, "You've seen him perform, now you've got to find something for him." Agents make careers.

Is there anything, besides being gifted and trained, that you love when an actor comes in to audition for you, and anything that bothers you?

Well, actors who are late are out of my book. There are no excuses, there are no reasons. It is unprofessional. You cannot be late. It's bad enough to be late to meet me, but boy, if you have an appointment to meet a director, there is no excuse short of being dead. None. Period. And I see it over and over again. Young people can be so cavalier about time, it is unreal. I make a mental note when somebody has been late for a director—they just don't come in on an interview with me again. It's very simple.

Do you have any tips for readings with you?

We don't usually read actors at auditions. Sometimes we put them on tape when our director is out of the city, but generally we just interview them. It's nice to sit and chat with actors who have reasonable résumés.

> *You cannot be late. It's bad enough to be late to meet me, but boy, if you have an appointment to meet a director, there is no excuse short of being dead. None. Period.*

A reasonable résumé?

A reasonable résumé is one that doesn't have too many little white lies on it.

How can an actor have the opportunity to sit and chat with you if they don't know you?

Through their agent.

What if they don't have an agent?

Then it's impossible.

So if they send a picture and a résumé to you, what happens to that picture and résumé?

We have them recycled. I don't kid actors, and I won't kid you: There are not enough hours in a day and there are so many agents sending us clients who fit into the system. And that's what we're looking for—actors who fit into the system. I can't see actors without agents because I'm too busy and I have an obligation to my producers and directors. I can only see you when you are represented by an agent who opens the door for you.

What if they send a tape to you?
We'll look at the tape. As long as it's been professionally assembled and has professional work on it. That work can be student films, commercials, soap opera and, of course, television and motion picture tests—but not taped stage work, and not something you paid somebody to film.

Do you have any advice for actors auditioning for directors?
Any director would probably be very pleased if an artist coming in to read was off-book. That is your obligation as a professional actor—to be off-book —but don't let the director know it, because you don't want the director to think he or she is seeing a finished performance. You should be off-book because it gives you so much more freedom, particularly if you're asked to improvise.

You've worked with some great directors. I've heard that one or two of them are a bit eccentric when they work with actors at auditions.
All directors are eccentric. That's why they're directors, and God bless them all.

Actors, too?
Yes, of course actors are eccentric. But I think that one of the nice things about actors today is, for the most part, they are very educated and well read. Acting is a profession. One should carry oneself as a professional. One should act like a professional. If one cares to have a grunge look, at least make damned sure your clothes are clean. Make sure you've had a shower in the last month. Show yourself as a professional. Believe me, it helps.

· ·
Mike Fenton
Fenton-Cowitt Casting
16311 Ventura Blvd., Suite 1255
Encino, CA 91436
· ·

Eddie Foy III and Jerry Franks, csa

Eddie Foy III and Jerry Franks are true veterans of Hollywood casting. With over seventy-five years of combined casting experience, the two joined forces in 1998 to work on the Fox series *Beyond Belief*. Foy began his casting career over thirty years ago and worked on such notable shows as *The Donna Reed Show*, the *Planet of the Apes* films, *Barney Miller*, the landmark *Roots* and *Masada*. More recently he's been casting network specials and mini-series including *Super Bloopers, Deep Family Secrets, When Stars Were Kids* and, most significantly, the annual Jerry Lewis telethons.

Franks began casting on *Barney Miller* and went on to work on such series as *The Fall Guy, Fame*, the daytime series *Capitol* and several features, including *Bagdad Cafe* for which he, along with his former partner, Al Onorato, won an Artios Award. Additionally, Franks, who has three Emmy nominations for television films, has held several executive casting positions (executive in charge of talent and casting, 20th Century Fox; daytime consultant at ABC, CBS and NBC) and has twice been elected to serve as president of the Casting Society of

America. Like Foy, Franks is very involved in fund-raising for charitable causes and is particularly proud of the work he's done for Cedars-Sinai Thalians Mental Health Unit.

Since this interview, the two have amicably dissolved their partnership. Both continue to cast independently.

Let's start with your background. Eddie, you, of course, started out as an actor from a very famous family.
FOY: Yes, my grandfather was Eddie Foy and, of the Seven Little Foys, my father was sixth. He's the one that stayed in the business and then I started acting on Broadway at the age of ten or eleven. Anyway, in 19—(laughing)

You don't have to give dates.
FOY: What do I care; I'll give a date. I'm sixty-three. Some people call me old-fashioned—I say it's experience. Anyway, acting became secondary because I realized that what I really wanted to be was the middleweight boxing champion of the world. So for years my life was boxing. Theatre had little or nothing to do with it. To this day, I'm on the board of directors for the World Boxing Hall of Fame. Theatre and casting are my hobbies. If they weren't, I wouldn't be doing it.

You've been in casting for a long time.
FOY: Since 1961. I actually quit for awhile and moved to Vegas with my daughter. I was the entertainment director at the Sahara until I was lured back ten years ago.

What about you, Jerry?
FRANKS: I was never an actor. I started out at Universal as a casting assistant in the '70s. I hopped around until 1981 when I joined Al Onorato—one of the most honorable human beings in Hollywood—from '81 to '91. Al, like Eddie and myself, just loves actors and we closed our company so he could work with them more closely as a manager. I continued casting.

What are some of the things you guys have done that you're most proud of?
FOY: Of everything that I've done, the one thing that sticks in my mind more than anything else is *The Jerry Lewis Easter Seal Telethon*. I do that every year. I do it for the kids. They make me believe in life. I'm involved with three things very seriously: muscular dystrophy, cancer research and my family.

FRANKS: And I'm very involved with mental health care and AIDS research. It's very interesting because Eddie is doing his fund raising on one end of the office and I'm doing mine on the other! We kind of swap ideas because it's very, very hard work trying to get celebrities to appear for nothing. They're asked twenty times a day to give their time and there is only so much they can give.

What are you working on now?
FRANKS: Well I've only been here since April of 1998. I'm assisting Eddie on an episodic show called *Beyond Belief* airing on Fridays on Fox. We've had great success with it. The audiences and the numbers keep rising and it's a fun show to do. We use mostly unknown actors.

That's great news for unknown actors! Do you look at pictures and résumés that are submitted through the mail?
FOY: Every single one.

So when you open an envelope, what makes you call someone in?
FOY: The first thing that I look at is the background. I look for training. I look to see where their college education has taken them. I look to see the directors they have worked with. Finally, when I'm done with that, I will turn the résumé over and look at the picture. The agent is the last thing I look at. I'm not interested in all of the actor baggage.

Like what?
FOY: I call all of the "stuff" that actors carry outside of their talent "baggage." They're worried about whether or not they should have a manager, if their agent is any good, are they dressed right, are they in the right workshop, etc. They have so much stuff going on that they forget that all we care about is seeing them act and do their work.
FRANKS: Within the last five to ten years we seem to be dealing with more and more actors who are less serious about their profession. This is not a hobby, it's a profession, just like being an attorney or a physician. Actors who are serious about the profession have got to learn their craft.
FRANKS: I've been quoted before as saying that I prefer New York actors to Los Angeles actors because in New York, actors learn their craft. They're always in classes, be it acting, dance or voice, and they're always honing their gifts. Many actors in Los Angeles don't seem to do that.

Is it true that you don't do auditions?

FOY: I hate auditions.

FRANKS: This is the first time I've ever worked off tape without having first met the actor. Eddie has taught me a whole new way of casting.

FOY: I started working this way after a conversation with Ron Stevenson who told me about how he cast *Murder, She Wrote*. He used tape, which I found interesting. About three months later I was working on a film directed by and starring Beau Bridges. I tried the method of ordering tape instead of reading tons of actors. I would make selections for Beau to watch and then we'd call in a few people for him to meet and that was it. I also used that method for another Dick Clark show, *Trial By Jury*, where we just didn't have time to read people. Casting directors are merely the conduit to bringing talent to the producers and the director. If we can't sit in an office and sense, by an actor's background and tape, if a particular performer is qualified, we shouldn't be doing what we do. Any casting director who has to sit in an office and pre-read and pre-read to pick one person to take to a director, really should be working at McDonalds.

What happens when you come across a well-trained actor who is too new to have tape?

FRANKS: Then we bring them in. We've actually been reading actors for the last several weeks because we've been looking at some younger roles.

If an actor doesn't have tape, would you tell them to make tapes at home and send them to you?

FRANKS: No, those are the worst. The material isn't right; the quality isn't right. It's amateurish and a disservice to the actor.

What about the places where actors can pay to have a tape made?

FRANKS: That's a good point to mention. Actors must be very, very judicious and very careful about the ads they answer because there are so many scams out there. As a matter of fact, as a former president of CSA, I should mention that CSA has always been proactive about breaking up the scams in this town. There are so many scam artists out there. So many of those tapes are worthless.

On a professional tape, actors should always have their best work first, correct?

FOY: Your most recent work should be the first thing on the tape.

If someone has done some really good work on older series, should they include those clips on the tape?

FOY: At the end. It's okay to include them but first let us see what you look like now, not what you looked like twenty years ago.

FRANKS: It's the same for a résumé. Your most recent credits should come first. But that doesn't mean your older credits shouldn't be there if they're credits that are prominent and you're proud of them. What's sad is that many casting directors have no relationship to the past. The newer casting directors don't know the actors or shows of yesterday and it makes it very difficult.

FOY: Often, the younger actors don't know anything either. It's pretty scary that they don't know anything about the foundation, the history of what show business is all about.

I think they assume it's useless information that won't help them get a job.

FOY: They're wrong. If you're going in to meet Jerry Franks or Eddie Foy, you sure as hell better know what Eddie Foy and what Jerry Franks have cast separately and together. If you're going in to met Mike Fenton, you better know what he likes and dislikes. If you're going up to meet a producer or a director you better know what that director or producer has done. You better do some research. Find out who and what we are. That's your job. Be a professional. There are actors who walk in here and they're not clean, they haven't shaved, they haven't washed their clothes and they work off a thing called sides—I mean what happened to a script? People used to come pick up scripts. Now they read from faxes and have no idea what the script is all about. That's professional?

> *There is nothing more exciting, nothing that makes your heart pound faster, then when an actor opens his mouth and knows what he's doing. It's such a rush.*

FRANKS: Not to mention that we do not support the practice of actors having to pay to get material faxed from a service. That's wrong. We are responsible for providing the actor with the material. SAG rules say that actors, if they request it, must be provided with a script twenty-four hours before they go into an office.

FOY: Actors have got to learn how to act and stop being politicians. All they seem to want to do is network. They should work harder at getting into plays. I don't care if you've got to go out to a place in Thousand Oaks and read in a twenty seat theatre, get in a play. And get into a class. But the actor has to be very careful about who their acting coach is. Too many acting teachers and coaches are bad actors who can't get work, so they teach the actor bad habits. Make sure you research your acting teacher and can be confident in their skills.

FRANKS:. From the casting director side, there is nothing more exciting, nothing that makes your heart pound faster, then when an actor opens his mouth and knows what he's doing. It's such a rush. It must be the same kind of rush that an actor gets when they know they've given a good performance. It's an inexplicable high. Someone has taken these words and transformed them into a living thing.

· ·

Eddie Foy III
Dick Clark Productions
2920 W. Olive Ave., Suite 106
Burbank, CA 91505

Jerry Franks
c/o CSA
606 N. Larchmont Blvd., Suite 4B
Los Angeles, CA 90004
· ·

RISA BRAMON GARCIA, CSA

Risa Bramon Garcia has brought
together some of the most memorable
ensemble casts of the last decade. In
conjunction with New York casting
director Billy Hopkins, she has cast
*JFK, Born on the Fourth of July, Wall
Street, The Doors, Talk Radio, Heaven
and Earth* and *Natural Born Killers*,
acting as associate producer on the
latter two films. She also cast the
pilot for *Roseanne*, and such
landmark feature films as *Speed,
The Joy Luck Club, Fatal
Attraction, Something Wild,
Desperately Seeking Susan, Jacob's Ladder, Sneakers, How to Make an American
Quilt, Flirting with Disaster* and *The Peacemaker*.

Garcia also produces and directs theatre in the Los Angeles area, but of late has
been concentrating on a film directing career, doing projects for such cable
networks as HBO, Lifetime and Comedy Central. Garcia made her feature film
directorial debut with *200 Cigarettes*.

How did you get into casting?
Theatre has always been my first love. I got into casting while working on a play
marathon at the Ensemble Studio Theatre (E.S.T.) in New York in 1978, and I
just never left. I became partners with Billy Hopkins and we cast and produced

shows all over New York (including the landmark Lincoln Center productions of *Six Degrees of Separation* and *Speed the Plow*). I directed at E.S.T. at night and worked at HBO, scouting comics, by day. There were a couple of casting directors who liked our work and would call us for a list of actors when they were stuck. I always did it as a favor because I loved doing it. One of those casting directors eventually recommended us for a movie they had turned down and we got the job. It was *Desperately Seeking Susan* which turned out to be a career changing opportunity and the doors flew open. The casting got all this incredible attention. People were saying, "Where'd they find these actors—Laurie Metcalf, Steven Wright, Madonna and John Turturro? How'd they do it?"

I stayed in New York until 1989 and continued to cast, direct and produce, but decided to move to Los Angeles when I realized that I wasn't interested in the regional theatre directing offers I was getting.

Since you moved to Los Angeles, have you continued to direct and produce, or have you limited yourself to strictly casting?
I continue to flex my muscles in the theatre, but in New York it was different. I was a director who also cast. After I moved to Los Angeles, theatre directing was not as significant in people's eyes. I became a casting director who wanted to direct, or who had directed theatre in the past. Casting to me is like my waitressing job. It's the thing I do to make money, and I am good enough at it that I can focus on other things as well and still do a good job at casting. My first love is directing.

Besides theatre, I have associate produced a couple of films for Oliver Stone, *Heaven and Earth* and *Natural Born Killers,* but I am now working towards a career in film directing.

How did you begin your relationship casting for Oliver Stone?
Billy Hopkins and I had just cast *Something Wild, Angel Heart* and *Fatal Attraction* when Oliver Stone came to New York looking for a casting director for *Wall Street*. At that time, we were considered hot, new, young New York casting directors. During our first meeting, Stone scared me, but I came to realize later that he was testing us. He was really pushing us to see if we were up to the kind of rigorous work that he was going to require. For him, the work was always intense. He works so fast. It's like being in the trenches in the war zone. When you work for him, you have to be prepared, ready and willing to totally enter a whole world. After eight years and eight films with him, I decided to move on to other things. With mutual respect, we parted.

Can you talk a little about Oliver Stone's casting process?
Mainly he looks at actor's tapes, but when he does see an actor in person, he is different from most directors because he doesn't like to sit and chat for fifteen minutes with each actor during the audition. He's not cruel to them, but he is dismissive. I've learned over time to educate actors so they understand that what they really have to do when they audition for him is to just go in, do their work and leave. Don't expect anything, don't expect to be taken care of, coddled, handled or stroked. He doesn't do that. What he does is really do the work. He wants to see what you're about. He wants to see what you can bring to the part. He wants people to disagree with him. He wants people to bring him ideas.

What are your thoughts about training and classes?
For me, training comes from working, not so much from taking classes. Performing in a theatre is absolutely the best training ground. Every actor should spend some time in the theatre. I know there are people who become really famous and don't go back to it, but there is nothing more powerful than working in theatre. That's how you can keep your instrument tuned. It's such an extensive, intensive training ground.

Do you prefer actors to come in to an audition with their lines memorized?
Yes, I do. The actors who always get the jobs are the ones who make the commitment to the work, and come in and do the audition with specific choices. For example, Saul Rubinek gets almost everything he auditions for. He learns the role, comes in and gives a performance. People are so worried about giving a performance during an audition. People who come in with confidence and perform get the parts much more readily than people who come in with a million excuses. The producers and directors ultimately want results. They need to see that you can do exactly what they want.

Many casting directors say, "Don't memorize the script, but if you do, hold it in your hand as you audition."
It's fine to glance down and look at your pages, but you still have to be in the scene. I don't think you can really play the scene if you don't know what you're doing. Memorizing can also take you out of yourself and into the character. You must walk out of that room knowing you gave the best possible interpretation of that scene, that role, in that moment. Most of the time you aren't going to get a reader like me in the room with you. I make eye contact and I will act the scene with the actor. But it's not always going to be like that. You're usually going to get some tired person who just gives you the words. You really have to be ready

and able to do the scene. You don't have to have it memorized to the point where you don't need the paper, but you've got to know what you're doing, make a really committed choice and go with that. I am astonished at how many actors come in unprepared. To come in unprepared in order to be spontaneous is a notion that needs to be broken.

Why do you think some actors get parts when they just instinctively "wing" their audition, rather than preparing?

I think that works for small parts, but rarely have I seen people get substantial parts that way. The more you prepare, the better your chances become. But sometimes I see actors come in with a strong choice and when the director says, "That's very interesting, can you try it another way?" they can't adjust. Even when you get on a movie set there are some directors who will say, "Let's try it a completely different way." Scorsese does that, Levinson does that, Oliver Stone does that.

Do you have any final comments you'd like to make to actors?

Al Pacino once said, "The audition is the work." It's not about getting the part so much as it is about acting—and you're acting when you are auditioning. So when you go into a room and you do your audition, come out of there and say, "I acted today." That's really important. The audition is your chance to act; let that be the reward in itself.

We all have to sculpt our careers and do what we have to do until we get there. I feel that there are a lot of actors out there who are not in control of their careers and they don't know why, how, or where. A lot of actors who don't come from the theatre don't understand what acting is all about when I talk about committing yourself to the work. It's making choices and working on the audition as a real piece of acting. A lot of actors lose sight of that. I suggest that actors take firm control of their careers, have their vision and not allow anybody to keep them from it.

. . . .

Risa Bramon Garcia
c/o CSA
606 N. Larchmont Blvd., Suite 4B
Los Angeles, CA 90004

. . . .

MELINDA GARTZMAN, CSA

Melinda Gartzman studied history and economics at Stanford University and worked in the advertising department at the New York Times before becoming a casting director. Her credits include the TV movies and miniseries *Deadly Family Secrets, The Margaret Mitchell Story, The Deliberate Stranger, Amy Fisher: My Story* and pilots and series *Family Matters, Maybe this Time, Misery Loves Company* and *Falcon Crest.* Gartzman won the Artios Award for Outstanding Achievement in

Pilot Casting for *I'll Fly Away* and has recently completed casting two MOWs: *Going Home* with Jason Robards and *Silk Hope* with Farrah Fawcett.

What goes on inside the audition room during callbacks after one actor exits and before another one comes in?

Before an actor comes in, the casting director might say a few words to the producer and director such as, "This actor is a little green but I see potential there." But what is more important for the actor to know is what is said after they leave the room. I suggest that actors walk away very slowly from the audition place. Don't get out of the building too fast, because you may be asked to come in again. There are usually several people auditioning the actor, and one of them may have seen something that the others didn't. Or one person might say, "I wish he'd done it another way." Then the casting director says, "The actor made a choice. If you want to see something different, we can ask him back right now."

Why wouldn't the producer or director ask for an adjustment while the actor is in the room?

In most cases they do, but on some occasions, it takes a little while to decide whether they are interested in an actor or not. When actors come in and dazzle you, the choice is easy. But when the actor's choice is subtle or varies from what we might have had in mind, then it takes a little longer to shift to the new view. On many occasions, producers and directors have changed the direction of a part because of the fresh interpretation the actor brought in.

It seems that mainly stars and name actors were asked to audition for pilots this season. Is that more and more a trend?

Actually, we can take more chances on newcomers in pilots than in anything else. There is always an opportunity to break in actors who don't have a lot of experience but offer an exciting quality. Newcomers are also often hired for financial reasons. The situation changes day to day in regards to the budget of a pilot. One day you can afford a star, the next day you can't, because they moved the dollars budgeted for the cast into other departments.

Do the stars who are series regulars have any clout with the producers regarding the casting of actors that they like?

Yes. There are often people the producer must listen to, but it all depends on who the producers and directors are and what kind of presence and power they have. In my experience, we are always open to seeing people who are recommended by the other actors. We don't necessarily give them the job, but we do give them the chance to come in and compete. If they earn the role, it's theirs.

Do you feel that a good actor is capable of performing in any type of series television show?

I've worked on some shows where I couldn't use a number of very good actors because they were too "real." For example, a show like *Falcon Crest* is glamorous while *NYPD Blue* is gritty. Every show on the air has its own style. The look and quality of the actor has to fit the genre of that show. Producers go through great effort to hire directors and casting directors whose vision matches theirs. In the pressure-filled world of series television, everybody has to be in perfect sync so that constant battles don't erupt over every casting choice.

Also, there are some actors who are incapable of playing smaller roles with the right emphasis. They don't seem to be able to grasp that these smaller parts are not about them, but are there to move everything else along. These small parts are the hardest ones to audition for; they require simplicity and reality in just a few words.

If an actor feels that they are absolutely not right for a role or the part is too small, should they turn down the audition?

I personally think that going in for an interview is never a waste of anyone's time. Even if you are not right, a producer, director and casting director have seen you, and if you're good and interesting, they may bring you back for something else in the future. I know actors have heard this before, but it is important that this truth becomes second nature to them: We make notes on everyone we meet. If we see something we like, we will remember you.

Furthermore, on many occasions, when a part proves difficult to cast, we see many people who, on the surface, don't fit what we are looking for. Then an actor walks in and instantly the role comes into sharp focus. So I would say that it is foolish to turn down any audition. The sole duty of the actor is to do the best job he can whenever he is given an opportunity to perform. Now I'm going to contradict myself and say that if you absolutely cannot connect with a role and choose not to come in, that's okay too.

What missteps have you seen actors repeatedly make during auditions?

A lot of actors don't listen to what's going on in a scene. They are so busy acting, they don't pay attention to what the reader is saying and doing. They just deliver their lines the way they have planned, without being affected by what the other person gives them.

Another problem is the shallow readings that actors sometimes give. When reading with them, I can immediately sense whether anything is going on inside them. Some actors bring a lot of technique but because subtext is missing from their interpretation, the reading remains shallow.

Could this be because of nerves?

I realize that it's not easy but I caution actors not to bring their fear into the room. When you come in, you have to be centered, focused and joyous. You can't be worried about the parking meter or even about your next meal. The people in the room generally don't have time for that. They just want to know if you're good. And it is your responsibility to be good. If you are a wonderful actor then what you need to do is get rid of all the garbage that stands in the way of giving a great audition. That's why you need a discipline such as yoga, meditation or whatever else you can find to center yourself and allow yourself to be present.

Do you feel that casting directors can help certain good actors who are not great at auditioning?
We help those actors by telling the director and producer beforehand that the actor coming in is not a good auditioner but does great film work and perhaps we show them some tape. Actors often forget that casting directors are their best friends. We try to get any ammunition we can to help the actor. Like a mother hen, we want to show you off in the best light.

When the reading goes off in the wrong direction do you think it's okay for the actor to stop and start again?
Yes, but if you have a four-page scene, don't wait until the third page to figure that out. When you realize you are off early on, just say, "Excuse me, I'd like to start again," and go ahead and do it. Don't make a big histrionic scene about it. Do it casually. Or sometimes the casting director, producer or director will stop you and ask you to start it again differently.

What annoys you and what gives you the greatest joy as a casting director?
I get crazy when actors are given the opportunity to read a script beforehand but don't. Some actors come into the room and ask, "Is this a comedy or a drama?" It's your job to find that out before your audition. Otherwise, how can you properly prepare? On the other hand, there are actors who do their homework and come in thoroughly prepared. They begin to read and instantly make the role sing. They own the role. It doesn't happen often, but once in awhile, when the actor owns the part seamlessly, I, as a casting director, feel extremely fulfilled.

. . . .
Melinda Gartzman
11271 Ventura Blvd., #248
Studio City, CA 91604
. . . .

JEFF GERRARD

Jeff Gerrard worked as an actor for over a decade both in New York and Los Angeles, before deciding to shift his focus to commercial casting. As an independent commercial casting director, Gerrard has cast over 1,000 commercials for almost every conceivable product.

You've worked on both coasts; is Los Angeles or New York a better place for an actor to launch a career?

When you're young, it's hard wherever you go. You are cutting the apron-strings for the first time. But you can help yourself if, before you make your choice, you honestly ask yourself what is it that you want from your career. Remember, it's called "show business," and not "show-art." If it's strictly about the art of acting for you, then I'd recommend New York, Seattle, Milwaukee or Chicago. If commercial and financial success are what you seek, then the place to be is probably Los Angeles.

Do you accept unsolicited submissions?

We look at all of them and file them for three months. Then we discard them. That's why I tell actors to do a mailing every three months. What comes in today may not be what I am looking for, but what you send three months later may be exactly what I need.

Often actors freeze when they are asked to improvise or to tell the camera about their favorite hobbies, etc. How can actors overcome that awkwardness?
Think about ten things in your life that excite you. Once you genuinely rehearse it, you will never stammer in front of the camera. Ask yourself, do you like sky-diving? Hiking? Mountain climbing? Are you getting married? Is your sister having a baby? We ask actors to talk about things or people they love because it instantly brings out their sparkle and enthusiasm. In commercials, we want to buy your positive, unique sense of fun, energy and joy. Remember, there is nothing terminal in commercials. By the end of a commercial everything has to work out.

What else can enhance actors' spontaneous expression?
Keep up with your improv and comedy classes and even take a directing course. In this business, the actors who book all the time are the ones who do their homework and come in with several choices. Sometimes, instead of reading alone, we may ask you to do the spot with another actor. The trained actors immediately adjust their intentions to suit the new situation.

How should the actor prepare for the callback?
Don't change your wardrobe, hair or look unless someone asks you to. And don't change your interpretation either. You are called back for a reason, and you never know what that reason is. So stick to what worked. If we don't book you, it doesn't mean we dislike you as an actor. It may just be that we are not interested in your product at that moment. You might be strawberry ice cream, and we may be looking for butter pecan.

Should the actor memorize the copy?
We haven't paid you the session fee yet to memorize. We have cue cards up there. They are the actor's best friend. But don't read them like you're reading a Public Service Announcement (PSA). Speak into the lens as if you are speaking to an individual. The biggest failure of actors is their inability to make us see the off-camera person. Often I ask the actors who they are talking to, and they'll say, "The camera, the masses out there." It's not about that. I want them to talk to a specific person in the camera. I could give you the same dialogue but depending on who you're addressing (e.g., your beer buddy, your father, your teacher) it will always come out differently. When you find that person in the lens, you have personalized your work.

We also want to feel that you are creating the moment for the first time ever. As the commercial goes: "Try it again for the very first time." Acting is the same way. Say the lines again and again, but let me feel that each time you are saying them for the first time.

Can actors break into film work on the strength of a commercial?

The "I love you, man" campaign for Bud Light Beer was phenomenal. Rob Fitzgerald, the actor, appeared on talk shows and has been called in on pilots and movies. Actors often snub their noses at commercials. I can't tell you how many times we get calls here from casting directors saying, "We hear you cast such and such commercial. Who's the guy in it? We want to call him in."

Do you have any final tips?

Be secure in who you are. Enjoy your craft, but realize that it is also a business. I think someone should offer a class to actors on the business aspects of acting. Behaving professionally, being on time, knowing who you're there to see and how the advertiser wants his product represented are all so important. In more basic areas, I recommend that you have a résumé at all times stapled to your picture. Even for commercials, I want to know as much about your background and training as I can. Also make sure the picture is current, presentable and you.

When you audition, you have three minutes or so in that room. Make it your three minutes. Have the presence of mind to be fully there. Don't think about a bad interview you may just have given at another audition. Be committed to the work you are doing now. You have a unique personality, that's what I want to see confidently expressed. I also want to see the commitment that you have made to your choices.

Nothing can replace continued training. And I don't care what you have to do to get to those acting classes. Work the graveyard shift, or for a delivery company, whatever you have to do. The idea is that you have to know your craft before you go on and open those doors. The acting teacher Estelle Harman taught me a very valuable lesson: "Don't open up those doors unless you are ready to walk through them." The first time, maybe you're a little off. The second time, maybe you're having a bad day. By the third time you have to know your business or those doors will stop opening. Once they do, it might take a number of years to open them again. So know your craft and be secure in what you are doing. Don't go out there until you are ready.

. . . .

Jeff Gerrard
Big House Studios
4420 Lankershim Blvd.
North Hollywood, CA 91602
. . . .

DAVID GIELLA, CSA

David Giella has been in casting for the last twenty years. Having begun his career as a New York actor at seventeen, he worked steadily in both theatre and commercials but found himself interested in the production side when he started reading with actors at Hughes-Moss Casting. Within a few months, he was casting for them while continuing his pursuit of an acting career. In 1987, he moved to Los Angeles after realizing that he enjoyed casting more than acting. He began his new career

at Reuben Cannon and Associates where his work included *What's Love Got to Do with It, Geronimo, Blind Justice*, several *Rockford Files* MOWs and the series *Under one Roof.* In 1996 he struck out on his own. He currently casts the hit series *Touched by an Angel* and its spin off, *Promised Land.*

Why did you quit acting?
I had an epiphany. I had just come from a final call-back for the lead in a feature film that I actually got. Walking to my car after the audition, it occurred to me that I'm very good at what I do and yet, if I spend 99 percent of my time acting, I'm only spending one-half a percent of my time doing the kind of acting that really makes me happy or allows me to contribute in the way I want to. At that

moment in my life I was, for the first time, more interested in being happy than in being an actor. I was very good and I am very good. But I didn't make a lot of difference on the planet. And so I went on and it's led me to a place where—through my expertise in acting and directing and coaching—I feel that, on a weekly basis, I can impact 25 million people on a series called *Touched by an Angel*. As a casting director I can make an enormous difference and a huge contribution. I was an actor every second up until the time I wasn't, up until life led me to a point where I realized that the journey was taking a turn. And I've never regretted it for an instant.

What do you advise somebody who suddenly wants to do act?
I tell people that if they wanted to be a doctor, they'd have ten years of training before they cut into anybody. The same goes for acting. I believe you need to learn craft and technique and then practice it for ten years. When I started acting it wasn't until probably ten years into it that it became organic and just how I breathe. Train somewhere; go do theatre and plays; get jobs in student films and finally, in TV and film. Then in ten years you'll know. I'm speaking of having a career that will sustain decades. There are always going to be people who can get off a bus, get a pilot and a TV series and work for a couple of years if they're lucky. But in the course of that time, if they don't learn the craft, then I doubt they can sustain a successful career.

Do you think it's better to start a career in New York or here in Los Angeles?
That depends on where you're more marketable. If you can sing and dance and have lots of energy with a bright personality and a sense of depth, go to New York and get into plays and musicals. Do theatre. Many of our top television actors in the half hour world come from theatre. Christine Baranski is a Tony Award winning actress from the theatre. Jason Alexander, Tony Award winning actor. John Mahoney. Do what you're best at and television will find you. You just need to go to a place where you are strong, good and marketable; a place where you can compete and win. That's where you want to be.

Let's talk a little about your shows. A lot of actors would love to be on them.
I know, it breaks my heart to be working on two shows that are hits but we only cast the big name talent from here. The reality is that these shows shoot in Salt Lake City, so many of the roles that would be open for the majority of the acting pool are just not available because they're cast in Utah. And guest leads on *Touched by an Angel* are tough roles. They attract stars who are not normally interested in a standard guest role on a television series. It's like a lead on an MOW. The actor

not only has to be responsible for his part, but for the whole story. A lead on our show is on fifty-two of fifty-four pages. The angels, the series regulars, most of the time take supporting roles in that lead's story. So you can't just hire a good actor; you need somebody with the charisma and accountability for the whole show. And unless somebody has carried a series or feature film, it's rare that they have the muscle developed to be able to deliver that.

I usually ask casting directors if they go to the theatre, but I know that you do because I've seen you there.

Yes, I do go. But people shouldn't be upset when casting directors come to your play and leave after the first act. It's usually not personal. It's just that we've seen what we need. We've already been working since early in the morning. We've worked on Saturdays. I'm usually in the office until 7:15 or 7:30 P.M. and then I go to see a piece of theatre. By 9:15 P.M., I'm tired of working. I deserve my life.

Do you do generals?

I don't love them but . . .

Why? Because you can't really tell someone's talent from a meeting?

Oh no, you absolutely can. Look, I've been in this active investigation of talent, acting, technique, presence and star quality since I was seventeen. If you walk into a doctor's office they can just look at you and get a sense. A good therapist will sit down with somebody and in two minutes they'll be able to determine if there's been physical abuse or if this is a child of an alcoholic. It's present in the room with you. The actor walks in the room and everything is out there. Your talent, your presence, your nerves, whether you can do a series regular or a guest or recurring role. All of that stuff is present in the room with you. As casting directors, we're aware of that. We know and we're hardly ever wrong. Every once in a while I'm surprised. Somebody who I didn't expect to do very well does. And every once in a while I'm disappointed. Somebody who's just great in the room and in the meeting will read and you think, "What happened?"

Is there anything that annoys you during an audition?

For me there are not a lot of rules. Some casting directors will say never to bring props, for example. When you do, it pisses them off. Reality is that casting directors say never to bring props because nine times out of ten they just don't work. They get in the way, ruin your audition and they make you look amateurish. The casting directors are just trying to help you. If you're using a prop, it had better feed the moment. That's all I have to say. You can come in with your little portable phone if you have to do a phone conversation. But you don't need to bring in food, for instance, unless it's a choice that is going to make a moment brilliant. I'm sure that the casting director who says never, ever bring in a prop will get over it if you actually do bring in a prop and you're brilliant.

Now costumes. From an acting standpoint, clothing can make the character. But if you're auditioning for a nurse, I don't have to see you in a nurse's outfit. It probably would be inappropriate to wear high heels, though. If you're making a choice of clothing to wear because of the character, the feel of the clothing should feed your acting. If it doesn't, don't bother. As a nurse you might want to wear the kind of shoes that make you feel that you've been on your feet all day. Character appropriate attire is fine, but nobody needs to see you in the costume unless you're a six foot two and half inch muscle man and you're coming in for the role of a drag queen.

It is not a good idea to touch the person you're reading with. If there's a scene and somebody kisses you, you don't need to feel the lips to act the meaning of that moment. You just need to know what that moment is, know what that moment means, and then act it. Same thing for hitting or for a gentle touch on the arm or holding hands or anything else. You don't need the physical . . . it's all the meaning of the moment. The audition is always the close-up. I don't need to see you moving around the room. You don't need to do blocking unless movement is vital to the meaning of the scene. Otherwise put your butt in a chair or plant your feet somewhere and stand and just act like it's your close-up.

We've all had experiences where you're being taped and they say, "Well, walk around and do what you want" but what you really want to do is just sit.
As an actor, if you ever come in and do something because you think it's what they want you to do, then shame on you. As an actor, you need to be an expert in human behavior and know the way a human behaves in this given situation. You never want to come in and give us what you think we're looking for. You want to come in and give us your very best acting. I would be interested in practicing my best acting always, regardless of whether I'm gonna get the job I was auditioning for or not. Because if every time I opened my mouth, good acting came out, in five years I'd have a good career. Whereas, if I were constantly second guessing and adjusting my nature and my instincts and my craft to match some casting assistant putting people on tape, I might be compromising my sense of truthful behavior and ultimately, my best acting. I would rather not get this job, but impress you with my work, be remembered and get cast by you in the future.

Any final advice?

Many actors in Hollywood would do better giving up their careers and pursue acting just as a hobby, because most actors don't have a career. If your life is working, if you have an agent and you're happy and content with booking two guest spots or two day player roles a year and your life is filled and creative and happy and you're not complaining about you're career and you're not suffering, then that's great. If, on the other hand, you are booking five day player roles a year and you're not happy and your agent drops you and you can't get another one and you're complaining and miserable and you've been in therapy, maybe it's time for something different. I don't believe in following your heart. But I do believe in letting your life educate you as to the journey that it desires you to take. Maybe there is a different course that actually will bring you a much more fulfilling life that will satisfy you. I went in the direction the world was pushing my life and that is what allowed my dreams to come true.

. . . .

David Giella
12711 Ventura Blvd., Suite 280
Studio City, CA 91604
. . . .

SUSAN GLICKSMAN, CSA AND FERN ORENSTEIN, CSA

Baywatch casting directors Susan Glicksman and Fern Orenstein partnered for more than twelve years before temporarily splitting up, only to happily re-team after Orenstein went to CBS for a stint as a casting executive. Together, they continue to cast *Baywatch* as well as multiple MOWs. Their work has included more than seventy-five TV movies such as *Point Last Seen, Don't Look Down*, Robin Cook's *Lethal Invasion, Murder Line, The West Side Waltz, Beyond Suspicion, The Rescue of Baby Jessica* and the mini-series *Joan of Arc.*

Susan Glicksman (l) and
Fern Orenstein (r)

A lot has happened for you two in the last year. You're back together again!
GLICKSMAN: Yes, thank God.

What happened during the year?
ORENSTEIN: Well, while I was pregnant I went to CBS and was director of movies of the week and mini-series. It was a fabulous job.
GLICKSMAN: I did *Baywatch* by myself for a season and I was lonely.

How long had you been together?

GLICKSMAN: Twelve years.

Wow! That's longer than some marriages. Did you both start out wanting to act?

ORENSTEIN: I never wanted to act. I had no desire. I was at NYU Film School and really, it was the process of casting that I loved. So I decided to be a casting director. I liked meeting all different kinds of people.

GLICKSMAN: I wasn't really sure of what I wanted to do at the beginning of my career. I started out in television publicity.

Fern, tell us the difference between being a casting director and a casting executive?

ORENSTEIN: It's very different. You oversee all the casting directors and you have to deal with a lot of producers at a network level.

GLICKSMAN: Fern would always have to know what the producers were looking for. It wasn't just looking at lists, or making lists.

But you decided to come back to Susan.

ORENSTEIN: Well, I missed the day-to-day casting process and I did miss Susie. That was a big part of coming back.

Can you tell me how the two of you work together?

GLICKSMAN: I can tell you what Fern does. Fern always makes me feel like everything is under control. Now I know that, but for ten years I didn't. From the day we started working together, I've been able to go home and sleep at night knowing that things are taken care of. It's not that one of us needs the other to come up with an idea. We both have the same tastes. It's just a reassurance.

Do you ever argue or fight?

ORENSTEIN: No, we've never had one fight.

In all of those years?

GLICKSMAN: Working in the same room.

ORENSTEIN: Better than any other friendship.

GLICKSMAN You don't have any friends.

Let's talk about _Baywatch_. How often do you look for regulars?
ORENSTEIN: We're always looking. If someone spectacular walks into our office; we're almost always looking. And for a young person with less experience, they've probably got a better chance on _Baywatch_ than they would on another show.

So you're saying that if someone has no credits at all . . .
ORENSTEIN: That will not stop us from seeing them.

What if somebody doesn't even have an agent?
ORENSTEIN: It doesn't stop us.
GLICKSMAN: We open and look at every piece of mail that comes in. When we're looking, I don't even know if a particular picture came from an agent until I turn it over because the envelopes are all opened and the pictures are all stacked up.

Do you look at unsolicited tapes?
GLICKSMAN: Not as much.
ORENSTEIN: For this show, you're better off with a really great picture. It can't be some snapshot your brother-in-law took. It has got to look good because there's too much competition and there are too many good pictures out there.
GLICKSMAN: But its got to look like you, too. It's got to look accurate.

Okay, so let's say I'm seventeen and gorgeous with an incredible body . . .
GLICKSMAN: Call us when you're eighteen.

Why?
ORENSTEIN: Because then we don't have to hire teachers.

Oh. So if they're eighteen and spectacular but they haven't had any experience and they want to get on _Baywatch_, what should they do?
ORENSTEIN: They should start with extra work first. On _Baywatch_ it's not bad to be an extra because you get seen. And you can be upgraded. We upgrade so many extras on the show.

How would someone get to be an extra?
GLICKSMAN: You have to go through Central Casting to be an extra.
ORENSTEIN: You could even become a regular extra. A lifeguard or something. That's not our department, though. But you're on the show and you may be considered for larger roles.

And someone with a little more experience?

ORENSTEIN: Send your pictures here.

GLICKSMAN: And your résumé. And I do think that for *Baywatch*, a full-body shot is appropriate.

ORENSTEIN: But even without a full body, if you're outstandingly gorgeous, your picture will get noticed.

Should actors send a letter?

ORENSTEIN: If you're such a knockout that I've pulled your picture, it's not going to matter. That's why I'm saying a show like this is such a great show, it's not like another show. We are willing to take chances with people.

GLICKSMAN: *Baywatch* is a more visual show than most. Actors who are right for *Baywatch* are not necessarily right for other kinds of shows. Most of the TV movies that we do are just the opposite. They are gritty and real. They would definitely require acting experience from the actors. In those cases, experience and training are the heavy emphasis. *Baywatch* is definitely unique.

When this fabulous eighteen-year-old gets into your office for an audition, what are some of your likes and dislikes?

ORENSTEIN: First of all, they have to be prepared. Our sides and scripts are always available beforehand, so come in knowing them.

Do you do generals?

ORENSTEIN: We're not crazy about generals because you don't get to see the person read. We prefer to meet people through auditions.

Do you use a lot of models?

GLICKSMAN: We do use some.

ORENSTEIN: You wouldn't not be seen because you're a model.

Other than the beauties for *Baywatch*, what do you look for?

ORENSTEIN: It really varies. Don't forget, there are character roles on *Baywatch*, like a teacher or a mom. We'll take pictures from everybody.

GLICKSMAN: I'll tell you, an area that we have a lot of trouble with is doctor roles. We have doctors every three or four episodes. It sounds like it would be easy but good, strong, real looking doctors of either sex who can deliver the material are hard to come by.

Is there any advice that you want to give to actors?

ORENSTEIN: I couldn't do what they do.

GLICKSMAN: Until I went into business for myself, I never really understood what it is that actors go through. In the last fourteen years or so, I've come to understand it. This is going to sound horrible but, in a way, the more easily type-cast you are, the more you'll work.

ORENSTEIN: Sure. Because television writers write for a very visual medium. When the Italian Mama comes on with her two lines, she needs to be cast so that her look says everything. There doesn't have to be a whole lot of history written for the character. Visually, it's all there.

But actors get so upset about being type cast.

ORENSTEIN: We can understand that—but the more quickly we can assess something, the more castable you are. That's where actors make mistakes. They want to play everything. They also tend to ask to read for a larger role during the producer's session and you think, "Well, there goes that person." You forget what they even came in for.

GLICKSMAN: Of course, it's different if the producer wants to try you in another role. That's a totally different situation.

What happens if an actor's on the wrong track during a reading?

GLICKSMAN: We'll stop them.

Can they stop themselves?

ORENSTEIN: Sure.

GLICKSMAN: But don't finish a scene and then ask to do it over. That makes us crazy. They may have given a perfectly fine reading and suddenly, that questioning makes us feel less secure about the actor.

And *Baywatch* is always casting?

ORENSTEIN: Yes. Send us stuff!

. . . .
Susan Glicksman and Fern Orenstein
Glicksman and Orenstein Casting
5433 Beethoven Street
Los Angeles, CA 90066
. . . .

PETER GOLDEN, CSA

Peter Golden, like many casting directors, wanted to act. Unlike most casting directors, however, he gave up that notion by the time he was twelve. He knew then he wanted to work behind the scenes and has done so for years. He began in New York where, for Hughes/Moss Casting, his work included *The Cosby Show*, and the Broadway musical *Sophisticated Ladies*. A move to Los Angeles led him to Universal Studios and a long run with the series *Simon and Simon*. Next came the position of director of casting at NBC before he joined Grant Tinker's GTG Entertainment as head of casting. He then moved on to Steven J. Cannell Productions as vice president of talent and casting, and subsequently as vice president of development. He retained that title at John Landis' St. Clare Entertainment before moving on to CBS where he currently oversees all casting for primetime, daytime, MOWs, mini-series and special projects as senior vice president of talent and casting.

Can you tell us a little about your background?
I grew up in Manhattan as an avid television watcher. I always wanted to be in show business. I thought I wanted to act. Then in sixth grade we did a class film.

Just a 16mm thing. The teacher asked what each person wanted to do and I wanted to be one of the actors. It took place in a classroom and my job was to sit at this desk. I had some dialogue but all day I sat at this desk. My friends who were directing were behind the camera and busy, the writers were busy making changes and I was thinking, "I'd rather do those things, they're more interesting." So from that point on I didn't want to be an actor anymore. However, I always was in awe of actors. I always enjoyed being around them. It's their combination of guts and their ability to communicate to a huge group of people and reveal themselves. I think the genius of acting is somehow being able to reveal who you are while at the same time, adding to it everything that's on the page. That's what we're looking for—someone who takes a piece of paper with lines on it and turns it into something beyond what the writer, director or the network executives expected. It's about bringing uniqueness, humanity, and what makes one person different from every other person in the world.

What is it like to go to network and approximately how many actors come in for each role?

Three or four. The room where we hold network auditions is an intimidating room. I really admire and respect these people for whom this is their livelihood. They have to come in and hope to present themselves in a way that's going to win them a role that can potentially change the course of their career. When an actor walks into the room there are elements that may keep them from showing us their best, and we do take that into account. But there's a point at which you have to take what you see or not. If someone walks in a room and you think they have the right physical look for the role and the voice sounds interesting and their audition is a strong audition, then great. If they come in and totally blow it in the room but the producers feel particularly passionate about them, or one of my colleagues or I knows their work from film, television or theatre, then maybe there can be another chance. It's always tough when producers say, "We saw this actor do a great job in the room and he just didn't do as good a job when he came to you." We understand, but then show us some piece of film or tape that can convince us because, particularly when you're talking about leading roles, there is a huge amount riding on it. It really can be the difference between a project selling or not selling.

Another thing to keep in mind is that when someone's on the set and the sun is going down and hundreds of thousands of dollars are at stake—they have to be able to deliver. You have to think, "If they can't deliver in an audition, how can they be expected to deliver under that kind of pressure?" But the flip side is that some wonderful actors can't audition. Acting is a process and some actors need time to take a character and live with it; granted, in television you don't get a lot of time, but there's still some time to explore a bit. And an audition is, in some cases, just the brush strokes of what that actor's finished character will be.

So we don't look for a complete performance and yet, we do look for elements of a complete performance. There are cases when someone will audition several times because the producers feel that strong about them and we haven't seen it in the room yet. I like to think that the right person ends up in the right role. From an actor's standpoint, I guess the best attitude is if you don't get a certain role, then that wasn't the right role anyway. I know it's hard to go in to an audition and ignore the stakes, ignore the pressure, and just be yourself, but that's why actors get paid a lot of money.

Is there any special protocol for an actor going to network?
It's a very quick process. They come in, they read their scenes and they leave. Usually actors are asked to stay outside while we read other actors. On occasion, we'll want to see something read differently. Les Moonves (the head of CBS) used to be an actor, so he's very conscious and considerate. If he wants one actor to read again, he'll ask them all to read again. Hopefully, the casting director will give the actor a chance to see the room beforehand if they've never been there. As an actor, you should always try to get as much information as you can. In a situation where you are going to read for the network, it can help to see the room so you have a sense of the lay of the land and where the people are going to be. Assume there will be six or seven people there: head of the network, members of the casting department, head of the drama or comedy department, producers, writers, director. There's nothing to chat about. You just come in and take the cue from the room. Some people come in and make a joke and may break the ice a bit. But it's serious business.

I remember John Rubenstein once told a class at NYU about auditioning. He said that he felt so blessed to be able to perform and he so loved performing that he'd do it for free. He considered the salary he received to be compensation for all of the auditions he had to go through. He considered the audition to be a large part of the job.

What is your actual function as senior vice president of talent and casting at CBS?
I oversee the casting of all current programs, all series in development, including movies and daytime, and each of these areas has someone who covers them specifically. On a day to day basis, it is dealing with and being a liaison between all the casting directors on the specific projects and our executives. It's keeping everybody aware of the hundreds of actors who are discussed for every project on a weekly basis and concluding that, in everyone's estimation, these are the best choices—whether it's for an episode of *Diagnosis Murder*, a recurring or new character on *Chicago Hope* or a development deal for actors like John Larroquette, Katie Segall or Tom Selleck.

If you saw a wonderful actor with strong stage credits in the theatre, what could you do for them?
If I think there is something interesting there, I'd have them meet some of the casting directors on our episodic shows like *Chicago Hope* or *L.A. Doctors* to see if they could read for guest roles.

Do you go to a lot of theatre?
I don't go as much as I used to. Now, other people go more often and tell me about actors they saw. I'll tell you one place where I find a lot of interesting people—student films. I would recommend them to any actor who doesn't have a steady acting gig or isn't really making a living as an actor. If you can get into a student film it can be a big benefit, particularly if the director becomes successful. I'm more likely to attend evenings of student films before I attend scene showcase nights. I can't think of a situation, in terms of acting work, where somehow an actor couldn't come away from a student film without having learned something beneficial—even if the director is the worst and it's total chaos.

Do you still look at pictures?
I look at every picture and résumé that comes into my office. But I am less and less likely to be able to do anything with them because each of our shows has its own casting director. Occasionally a picture will come across my desk that'll be interesting and I'll meet that person for a general. But if you're a young actor coming to town, you should try to connect with casting directors who are most likely to use your services. That probably means the large ensemble drama shows because they seem, week after week, to need the most roles.

No one gets "discovered" any more, do they?
An agent called me recently to tell me about a really personable waitress who had waited on him. She had been in Los Angeles since last December and had not had a whole lot of luck getting out on auditions. He and his friend both agreed they would call five people for her to meet. I met her and she's very attractive and has a lot of personality. She did a scene and was really pretty good. It can still be about being in the right place at the right time and coming across the right people.

. . . .

Peter Golden
Sr. VP of Talent and Casting
CBS Entertainment
7800 Beverly Blvd., Suite 284
Los Angeles, CA 90036
Talent Coordinator: Marilyn Fischer
. . . .

Danny Goldman

Danny Goldman was a critically acclaimed actor and director in the theatre before becoming one of the busiest commercial casting directors in Los Angeles. Along with an L.A. Drama Critics' Circle Award for an improvisational play about the Entebbe hijacking, he has won six Drama-Logue Awards—three for directing and three for acting. Though he still acts occasionally, Goldman and his associate, Alan Kaminsky, are most often busy casting three to five commercials a day.

What is the best way for actors to reach you?

Actors are welcome to come to our office and drop off their pictures and résumés. However, when I say bring in your pictures and résumés, I am not saying you can come and crash auditions. It is also a very good idea to mail us postcards and inform us, "I'm doing a show; I recently signed with this person or that, etc." We remember those people. I always go through my postcards.

But the first thing actors should do is get an agent. I work on the phone all day long with agents. I prefer agent recommendations to headshots because I like to hear about the person from the agent's own lips. Commercial agents are more open and receptive than theatrical agents to representing unknown actors because it's a very disposable world. The commercial agents know they need a backlog of people without extensive credits because a lot of directors want actors who've never been on television.

What do you love to see in actors when they come in for an audition?
I want to see them come in and do their business well. I like them to have taken classes, but that depends on who the teacher is. There are some people out there who are teaching an old-fashioned kind of commercial acting that died out in 1969. It's phony, insincere, too big, too fake, too over the top, too cartoony. That's out. Take a look at what's on television now and you'll see that it's more reality based today.

What are some of the annoying things that actors tend to do?
I don't like to see actors degrade themselves. I find it painful when actors try too hard to please. There was a woman who used to come here and she would invent holidays to send us gifts. It was painful and I asked her not to do it anymore. There are people who love to be showered with gifts, but I don't.

Can you talk about what happens after an actor auditions and is taped?
What happens is this: we send a copy of the tape to the director and a copy to the ad agency. Then they duke it out and decide who they are going to call back. Normally they hold in-studio callbacks where the agency, client and the director are present, and they begin to direct the actors.

Do they usually know precisely what they are looking for?
They often don't. They think they want one thing and sometimes part of our job is to make them change their minds. You bring in somebody who's brilliantly talented and they'll change their minds. Therefore, actors shouldn't ask unnecessary questions when they are auditioning. A lot of times the director has not committed himself to a vision of the part yet. When an actor comes in and asks a lot of questions, the director may feel threatened because he doesn't want to commit so early in the process—especially in front of the producers who hired him. An actor should just come in, do the taping and leave. Sometimes there are twelve or so people in the room watching an audition. And sometimes they're grim and won't laugh when the actor is expecting one. I'll go out into the lobby beforehand and say, "It's grim in there. Just go in and do your stuff and don't be hurt if they don't laugh." There could be any number of reasons for their mood. Don't blame yourself; just do your business and leave.

How can an actor really take control of his or her audition?
An actor should just go in there and give an audition that makes them proud. That's it. Do what you want to do rather than imagining what the buyers want. The buyers are looking for their spot to come alive.

Sometimes someone might say to an actor, "Please have a seat." If the actor knows that their energy is going to fall apart if they sit down, for example, it's okay to ask, "Do you mind if I stand?" Remember: it's your audition. You have to please yourself as well as them. Otherwise, you will second guess yourself all the way home, "Why didn't I have the guts to ask to stand up? Why did I freeze? Why didn't I have courage?" What I'm really saying is that actors should own their auditions. Own it! Make it so that you are the part, rather than trying to think, "Well maybe I can slide this little part of myself into this part." Use as much of yourself as possible. Don't think, "Oh, I wonder if they want me to do it this way, or to say it that way." When the actor wonders like that during the audition, their head is not in the moment. If you have all this machinery of wondering going on in your head, you'll become so busy inside that you won't even hear what anybody else is saying.

The reason I feel I am pretty good at this job is because I have made every mistake an actor could possibly make. I have made them time and time again. I've lived them.

Which is harder for an actor to get: a role in a commercial or a part on television or film?
Getting a commercial is much harder. For a theatrical role, casting directors will probably see seven or eight actors. For commercials, we sometimes look at seventy to a hundred people for a single part.

That means that ninety-nine people will have to deal with rejection. Do you have any suggestions to help actors cope?
The minute an actor's audition ends, they should let it go. Forget about it and move on. Don't run an inner dialogue of, "I should have done this, I could have done that." There is no way to predict how one gets a part. There are just too many variables and too many people who are in the decision making process.

What is the key to becoming a successful commercial actor?
An actor has to get his look together and have some sense of himself. This has nothing to do with whether or not you're a good actor. There are some actors who have a brilliant sense of marketing. They know just what to do with themselves. They have an understanding of what they're doing and where they're going and what they're playing. Sometimes, to make it easier on the casting directors, actors consciously stereotype themselves into a certain niche based on what they look like and how people are going to cast them.

There was an actress with a wedge haircut and we used to cast her as a working mom. I saw her with long hair and didn't recognize her. I asked her to get the wedge cut again because she was identifiable; she had such a strong look. It is important to have a command of what it is you look like and how you can turn that to your advantage.

On the other hand, there are actors who don't know what to do with themselves. They have no idea how others perceive them. You need to have a clear idea of how you can be utilized in this universe as an actor. Understand what you have to offer and go after it.

Do you have any final advice for actors?

I recommend that people dress in a way that is suggestive of the part they are auditioning for, but not necessarily in costume. There have been times when we were casting waitresses and the actresses came dressed as waitresses. Sometimes this works and sometimes it doesn't. There are no rules. Follow your instincts. Résumés are very important—they can be conversation pieces. Include details of all the things you can do on your résumé. I mean, if you can drive a big rig, shouldn't you include that on your résumé? There are actually some actors in SAG who are lawyers and doctors. I would be insane if I didn't call them in for those parts. For some reason, somebody out there is giving the wrong information and telling actors not to put extra capabilities on their résumés. There are people out there who can help actors write résumés. They can elicit things from the actor to really beef it up. Even if it's just a great deal of community theatre, it's their work, they did it. A lot of actors think it isn't good enough if it isn't Broadway. Don't walk in the door feeling inadequate. There are enough people out there who will try to make you feel that way. Sitting in the lobby, something can happen to the actor and they begin to lose confidence, lose their sense of self. They start to get intimidated and think of all the reasons why they aren't right for the part. Actors should psych themselves into a certain frame of mind and believe that they are enough.

Please remember that casting directors are just people trying to do a job. We don't have the power to give you work. Our only power is to get the actor in for an audition. It's up to the actor after that. Most actors are passive about their careers. They want somebody to find them. They are in hiding somewhere, and the casting director is supposed to go hunting for them and to discover them. The whole effort to do what needs to be done embarrasses them. To succeed, an actor should always keep growing, working and improving. Actors should believe in themselves. More than anything else, getting a job is a confidence game.

. . . .
Danny Goldman
Danny Goldman & Assoc.
1006 N. Cole Ave.
Los Angeles, CA 90038
. . . .

Jeff Greenberg, CSA

Since 1985, Jeff Greenberg has been happily ensconced on the Paramount lot where he cast *Cheers* for the final seven of its eleven seasons and *Frasier* for the subsequent seven. Like most casting directors, he began as an actor but, unlike most casting directors, Greenberg acted successfully for many years. He gave it up quite unexpectedly when Casting Director Linda Francis, a friend, asked him to fill in assisting her on a film project. Greenberg fell in love with casting and never went back to acting. After assisting Francis for three years and nine features, Greenberg successfully struck out on his own. His work has been made up of stage, including plays at the Mark Taper Forum and the Tiffany, such feature films as *Look Who's Talking, Father of the Bride 2* and *A Night at the Roxbury* and television, including *Nothing Sacred, Wings, My So-Called Life, Newsradio, Early Edition, Dear John,* and, of course, *Cheers* and *Frasier.* Along the way, he's picked up four Artios Awards and three Emmy nominations.

In a recent pilot you cast, you had to let someone go. Can you talk about the reasons that can happen?
Just about every pilot that gets on the air has at least one cast change. Either

someone wasn't right or they feel the chemistry wasn't there or sometimes the look is not quite right. It's just so unfortunate because there's nothing more horrible for me than having to fire an actor. It's a nightmare. But it happens, and ultimately, you have to do what best suits the project. The play is the thing. These are hard decisions that are never made lightly.

When we were shooting the pilot for *Frasier*, the role of Roz was initially played by Lisa Kudrow. She was great and we all loved her but during rehearsals, we found that the show was off-balance. There was all of this conflict in the home scenes but there was very little of it in the radio station scenes. The character that Lisa had created, which is exactly what we wanted her to do, wasn't going to provide enough conflict and Frasier is funniest when he's pushed and conflicted. We had to make a change. It was a dark day for us because we love Lisa, personally and professionally, but we had to go with a personality who would more readily go toe to toe with Frasier. That's a perfect example of a change that had to happen and it wasn't about good acting, it was about good casting.

So sometimes it has nothing to do with the actor or his talent?
Actually, and I hate to say this, but sometimes it is. Sometimes actors are just not good enough. Their best performance is the audition. Sometimes their work on film is different than it is in the office. And sometimes it's our mistake; the work just isn't strong enough.

Elia Kazan talked about rejection and said, "Acting is a career of comebacks."
Yes, yes—you're rejected on some level every time you don't get a part. I think if that's going to be a problem, acting is probably the wrong career for you. I think you have to find a way to know and realize that you weren't the best choice for the role and that's okay. If you can do that, you're ahead of the game. And it's a hard thing to do for an actor at any level, at any age.

So what you're saying is that actors have to have more than talent; they have to have a talent for survival.
It's true. The perseverance factor is hanging in there and not letting the business get you down. And if you hang in there, while you wait you can keep getting better and better at your craft.

And at auditioning, because these days, it seems the whole performance has to be there from the get-go, doesn't it?
Unfortunately, in television, it's more about result. They really want to see the performance in the audition room and at the first rehearsal. On the very first

day of rehearsal, if it doesn't work, something's wrong—either the actor's wrong or the material's wrong. And if they've heard the material work in the audition and it's not working now, they have to figure out why. Sometimes it is the material and they'll fix it or sometimes the actor's not working and they give them an adjustment to try to make it work. If it still doesn't work then they have to make a change. But it's all about results. Fast. It's too fast.

Theatre trained actors aren't used to that. They're process oriented. And yet, you prefer theatre actors.

Well, they're so well suited to this four-camera process. Sitcoms are like doing a twenty-two minute play. They're performed like theatre, in sequence, whereas film is often not. Sitcoms require actors who can make adjustments quickly and then have the chops to recreate the performance time and time again. Sometimes actors without a lot of stage experience have a difficult time completely recreating what they did. Actors need to know that for sitcoms, when something works, retain it. The directors don't want you to keep experimenting with it, they want you to keep experimenting with the things that aren't quite working.

Does that mean that, if you get a role, you should recreate what you did at the audition?

Unless they give you an adjustment, they want you to recreate what you did in the audition. And if that gets laughs at the table reading, they want you to recreate it the next day.

So there's a lot of pressure at the table read.

Yeah. It's a nervous time for me because a lot of the executives and creators who were not a part of the casting process are seeing the actors for the first time as well as hearing the material. And they're always very quick to judge. The beauty of *Frasier* is that the words are everything. It's so beautifully crafted that if you're right for the part and you understand it, you can just say the words and it will be funny. You play the reality. Comedy is, of course, best when it's rooted in reality.

You once said to me that you think actors shouldn't feel the need to sell themselves at auditions. They should just be themselves.

Every actor's asset is that there is no one else quite like them. So rather than make themselves like everyone else, actors need to trust their own special uniqueness. Certainly people have to play a character but the trick is to find a way to tap into something of yourself. That gives it a reality. Use who you are as well as your techniques and skills as an actor to create the character.

There are casting directors who love to chat with actors before a reading and then there are casting directors who want to get down to it with very little conversation. Do you have any preferences?

I really love to chat and get to know someone but sometimes there is simply no time. Often I'm seeing three actors every fifteen minutes for a small role, so there's no time for schmoozing. The actor must learn to always take the cue from the room you walk into. If they want to chat with you first, they'll chat with you. They'll ask you questions about you, about your résumé, about the material, whatever. But, if they say, "Okay, could you begin at the top of page two," you do that. At the end of your audition, you have to take your cues too. If we say, "Thank you very much," that is your cue to leave. I have seen someone be so wonderful in an audition and then we say, "Thank you," and I know they are going to get the part—then they launch into a story about God knows what and you just want them to shut up and let the work stand on its own. I've seen so many actors blow it, not from the work, but from not taking the cues from the room.

Do you go to the theatre?

Yes, often. But I'm tired of walking out of things at intermission so I'm very selective about what I see. I read reviews and I talk to people. I really do a little investigation to make sure it's going to be a good evening of theatre.

And you look at every picture and résumé?

I do. And I meet with people either because I think that they might be right for whatever project I'm working on, or just because there's something about their résumé or photograph that makes me want to meet them. There are probably around one hundred people in my "to meet" folder at any one time and when I have time, I call them in. I also get an enormous number of referrals from people I know who want me to meet someone they know. I never mind that because they're just being talent scouts for me.

. . . .

Jeff Greenberg
Paramount Studios
5555 Melrose Ave.
Marx Brothers Building, #102
Los Angeles, CA 90038
. . . .

Iris Grossman, CSA

Iris Grossman, the senior vice president of talent and casting at Turner Network Television, oversees the casting for all of the original projects at TNT. Originally from New York, Grossman ran a classical theatre company, The Public Player's Theatre, for two and a half years before becoming a talent agent at ICM. She's been with TNT since 1992. During her time there, Grossman has been instrumental in casting stars in TNT's original films including Tommy Lee

Jones in *The Good Old Boys*, Ben Kingsley in *Joseph and Moses*, Diane Keaton in *Amelia Earhart: The Final Flight*, Jamie Lee Curtis and Tom Hulce in *The Heidi Chronicles*, John Malkovich in *Heart of Darkness*, Jack Lemmon and Matthew Broderick in *A Life in the Theatre* and Tom Selleck in *Broken Trust*. Recently, Grossman has worked on *The Hunchback* starring Mandy Patinkin and Richard Harris, *Wallace* starring Gary Sinese, and *The Man Who Captured Eichman* starring Robert Duvall. For the latter two, Grossman was honored with Artios nominations, winning one for *Wallace*.

Grossman has also spent the last three years as the president of Women In Film, and the last two as the mother of her son, Max.

Have you worked on any projects recently that you found particularly rewarding?
Definitely *Wallace* with Gary Sinese. That was directed by John Frankenheimer and it was an incredible experience. John was hiring people at their auditions. Right in the room. I've never seen that before. He is just so right-on and he goes with his instincts. He's just amazing. It was such a wonderful thing to see these actors light up and walk out wanting to jump for joy. And it was very emotional to get the CSA nomination for *The Man Who Captured Eichman* because that movie meant a lot to me.

Why is it that big stars will work on cable but not on network?
The quality. The networks do between fifty and fifty-two MOWs each year. In those fifty to fifty-two, about ten of them are Hallmark type, prestigious movies. What the networks call their MOWs are written and shot really fast. Sometimes they're just a rehash of other movies. At TNT, we only make twelve films a year so each one has to be a jewel. Each one is done like a feature film.

How can actors get to you? Can they send pictures?
Sure they can, but sending a picture and cover letter through an agent will always get my attention more than something unsolicited. Once in a blue moon, I do see a picture that interests me enough to call someone in. You know it when you look at pictures and résumés, you can tell who's going to be a star. There's something a little off. It's not a perfect, smiley, happy picture. There's something behind the eyes and it comes out on the face. It's an intelligence that comes through. After you've seen a thousand pictures, your eyes kind of stop focusing but then there's the one that grabs you. I try to see as many people as I can. I don't go to waiver theatre but I do go to the theatre. The thing that actors have to learn is that there is a way to seek a job and a way not to. There is aggressive, which is good—and obnoxious, which is bad. Actors have to learn the difference. Once an actor crosses to obnoxious, they knock themselves out of the running for the foreseeable future. It's one thing to submit and have an initial conversation but if it ends in "No," and you keep at it, all it does is put a bad taste in the casting director's mouth. These people get in their own way.

The other thing that actors have to learn, and I know it's tough, but after awhile, if you're not working, then maybe it's not the right field for you. Maybe you should be a writer or maybe you'd be a good story editor or director. Maybe you're good at something else. But at a certain point and a certain age, if things aren't going well, you have to say, "This is not working." It's not giving up, it's being smart enough to make a change. And if you're an actor and you go into casting or directing, for example, imagine how much you bring to the table as far as understanding the actors' emotions, the trials and tribulations they go through, the process, the empathy.

You have a reputation of being nice to actors.
When I was an agent, I represented actors who complained about the meanness of some casting people. I go out of my way to make sure that when an actor leaves my office, they leave with a handshake and a smile. I know it's like living in a fantasy world, thinking that I can make everybody feel good. But what's so bad about being nice to people?

What general advice do you have for actors?
My advice is "less is more." When you come in for an audition, don't perform as though you are in a large theatre. We are in a small office. Besides, if you give it all away, there is no mystery left for us to work with later. Holding back makes the actor more interesting.

Young actors should also know that they will be rejected on a daily basis. And that's the hardest thing in the world to endure. Even when you do get a part and you're as high as you can be, when the job ends you will have to start at the bottom again. Furthermore, even if you become a star, you may still have to restart your career time and time again.

Is there anything actors do in auditions that really annoys you?
What turns me off are people who are dressed inappropriately for an interview. I don't like it if someone walks in wearing a tank-top and shorts or if a woman is not wearing any undergarments. You don't have to dress like the character, but dress appropriately. The worst is when actors dress in costumes and bring props. A friend told me that a girl brought a real gun to an audition. He took it away from her and took out the bullets. It was actually loaded! And I know a lot of casting directors who've been in situations with actors who've turned over desks or had inappropriate props. It's not necessary. We do have imaginations. That's why we're in the job we're in.

There's also such a thing as being too prepared for an audition. It's one thing to be prepared, it's another thing to be overprepared. If you're overprepared, there's not going to be any spontaneity. Of course you have to be familiar with the material but there has to be spontaneity. If someone shows me a full performance in the room, it makes me nervous because I don't know if they have anything else other than what they just gave me. It's funny but sometimes the people that are better actors are the people who can't really audition.

Do you have any final tips?

Actors should be serious about their work. They need to study. And I don't just mean acting classes; they need to be aware of the past. A lot of actors have no idea who certain actors were, so if you say, "I'm looking for a Gary Cooper type," they look at you like you're from another planet. Or you say, " A Jimmy Stewart type;" that should translate immediately to them as Tom Hanks, who is our Jimmy Stewart now. You have to know film history to know how Tom Hanks fills a void. You have to have a sense of history in order to have some sense of the present; it's not only knowing your craft, it's knowing the medium and knowing the art form. Sometimes you can learn more from watching the work of the great actors of the past than by taking another acting class. Great acting touches a chord in us and makes us feel, think and experience the flow of life as it really is and what it is to be a human being.

. . . .

Iris Grossman
Sr. VP of Talent and Casting
TNT
1888 Century Park East, 14th floor
Los Angeles, CA 90067
. . . .

Bob Harbin, csa

As senior vice president of talent and casting at the Fox Broadcasting Company, Bob Harbin oversees casting on all current programs as well as those in development. Prior to joining Fox in 1990, he was an independent casting director partnered with Beth Hymson. Together they cast *Doogie Howser, M.D., L.A. Law* and various TV movies.

Harbin has been nominated for six Artios Awards, winning two of them, one for *L.A. Law* and one for *Pee Wee's Playhouse*.

Were you ever an actor?
For about three days. I came to Los Angeles wanting to become an actor, but soon realized that my college acting experience in Small Town, USA hadn't really prepared me for what the business is actually like in Los Angeles.

I've always tried to keep options open and listen to what could happen. As a result, I shifted my focus from acting and got a job working as an assistant at a talent agency. I was an executive assistant and subsequently became a sub-agent. I was lucky to have worked with great people such as Nicole David and Arnold Rifkin, who treated me so well both professionally and personally. From there I went to NBC as a secretary and worked my way up to manager of casting. Joel

Thurm and Lori Openden were instrumental in urging me to go independent with the *L.A. Law* job.

You started working at Fox in 1990. What was it like working for a brand new network?

Scary. We—Wendi Matthews and myself—were establishing a completely new department with no set of rules or regulations; no set ways of doing anything. There was very little money to spend on projects. We therefore had to find actors for our series who had little or no name recognition.

With the help of shows like *Beverly Hills, 90210*, the community began to notice that talented unknowns were becoming name actors. Actors began noticing that they had a shot at Fox, even if they weren't big names.

Your office is so comfortable—do you audition people for the network here?

Yes. We have all network auditions in my office. We try to make it as simple and as easy as we can. Again, I'm lucky to be working for someone who has a great deal of respect for actors and the casting process—Peter Roth. With the help of Bob Huber and Ty Harman in my department we try to make actors as comfortable as possible in a completely uncomfortable situation.

What is the process for a network reading with Fox?

When a project is purchased by the network, the casting process is set in motion. A breakdown goes out, and from that the independent casting director on the project receives submissions. First the actor reads for the casting director. From there, you hopefully get a callback for the producer and/or the director. Then it's a callback for the production company or someone from the studio. And finally, you may get a callback to come and read for the network. Sometimes, when you have a more established career, you can skip stages one, two or even three, and come directly to the network. Hopefully, by then, a test option deal is in place and you don't have to sweat out final deal points while you are trying to prepare for the audition.

Can you describe a "test option deal?"

It is a negotiated deal between a production company and an agent that options the services of an actor for seven years. So when you do get the role, the deal is already set.

Can you give any suggestions to help actors ease the tension as they wait outside the room for their network audition?

If you could find a way to not see the other actors there as competitors, that would release a great deal of tension. You need to believe, and know, that you have something special and different to offer. That belief alone can reduce the competitive nature of auditions. You have already achieved a great level of success by just being there. You can then only hope that what you have to offer is what we're looking for on that day. But you truly have no real control over that. Let it go and just give the best damn audition you can. Then go home and collapse.

What knowledge could help actors nail a role?

If there was a surefire way to nail an audition every time, you and I would write the book and be very wealthy. It's talent, preparation, a good agent, a casting director who believes in you—all of these things. And part of it remains a crap shoot. There are so many variables that cannot be defined. That's why it's important to passionately believe in what it is you do, and clearly know why you're doing it.

Acting is an art, yet it is also a profession, a business. Like the rest of us, actors have to prioritize. You can't make each audition too important to your life. When you do, each disappointment and rejection, and each success and acceptance, will be magnified out of proportion. Most actors experience more defeat than success, but even success, unless it's in perspective, can get out of hand.

Who at Fox makes final casting decisions?

Peter Roth has the ultimate approval. But in most cases, rarely is one person solely responsible for the decision. Casting people have the potential of being very influential in these decisions. I can certainly be influential as to who gets the opportunity to audition here. And when a decision is very close, hopefully, I'm qualified to decide. I have to trust my instincts, filtered through lots of opinions and homework.

What advice would you give to a young actor new in town?

Develop perseverance and have some sense of self. I also think that you need to be seen performing as much as possible. Though a lot of people don't believe in the theatre in Los Angeles, I do. Whether theatre is good or bad, some casting people still go. Agents still go. So never snub your nose at the theatre. Get yourself seen. If I have seen you in a play, and I have noticed something there that interests me, then it is my obligation to get you into my office and meet you.

So you go to the theatre?

Yes, I do. I go to the theatre here, and also in New York, Chicago, Denver and elsewhere, to find new people who are fresh and exciting.

The consensus is, however, that casting directors don't like to go to the theatre in Los Angeles.

Some casting directors might not be able to go, but I'll bet that their assistants might if they were invited. Don't dismiss the value of the assistants. Assistants do a lot of work for very little money, attention or praise, and they can be extremely influential. If an assistant of mine goes to see a play and tells me, "I saw somebody last night; you really have to see him," then I am going to see that person. But if you send the flyer only to me, I may not be able to go. So invite assistants and be glad when they show up. Send your invitation to the whole department. Never forget that the assistants of today may be the heads of casting departments tomorrow. I was an assistant once, and I remember who was kind to me then.

> *Don't dismiss the value of the assistants. Assistants do a lot of work for very little money, attention or praise, and they can be extremely influential.*

What final advice would you want to give actors?

Try to remember that what we are doing is a people sport. We are all people trying to do our best. What makes this business wonderful is that a lot of different egos somehow manage to live together in creative tension and harmony. And if you can be supportive of others trying to achieve their dreams, then maybe they will be supportive of yours and what you are looking for won't be as hard to find.

. . . .

Bob Harbin
Sr. VP of Talent and Casting
Fox Broadcasting Co.
10201 W. Pico Blvd.
Building 100, Room 4010
Los Angeles, CA 90035
. . . .

CATHY HENDERSON, CSA AND DORI ZUCKERMAN, CSA

Cathy Henderson was focused on casting feature films and Dori Zuckerman was an independent casting director for television, when they decided to pool their talents and form Henderson/Zuckerman Casting five years ago. The synergy seems to have the right magic; currently, the duo is casting a full slate of features, having just completed *What's Cooking* with Alfre Woodard and Juliana Margolies. Henderson grew up in

Cathy Henderson (l) and Dori Zuckerman (r)

Hollywood, surrounded by film people. Her father was Production Manager on such shows as *Gunsmoke* and *Rawhide*. She began her career by working for Linda Otto and Joel Thurm but soon shifted gears, becoming an independent casting director on series such as *Charlie's Angels, Hawaii Five-O* and *MacGyver* among others. Her work on movies for television and cable include *Element of Truth, Extreme Justice* and *Criminal Justice*. She has also cast such features as *Weeds,* starring Nick Nolte; *Love Letters, Echo Park* and dozens of action pictures including *Perfect Weapon* and *Stonecold.*

Dori Zuckerman also grew up surrounded by creative people. Her mother was a light-opera singer and actress. Deciding to become a performer herself, she first trained at A.C.T. in San Francisco before continuing her studies at Northridge University in Los Angeles. After graduation, she realized she didn't have the temperament for acting, and shifted her attention to casting. Her first assignment was on the American Playhouse film *It Ain't Bebop*.

Since then, she's worked with Mary Jo Slater on *Babylon 5*, the HBO feature *Running Mates*, and the feature *Knights*. She has collaborated with Fern Champion on such projects as the series *The New WKRP in Cincinnati* and *They Came from Outer Space*, as well as the features *Body Parts* and *Suburban Commando*. Some of her favorite projects include the series *Frank's Place* in conjunction with Deborah Barylski, and the feature *Pretty Woman*, which she cast with Dianne Crittenden.

What is your advice to auditioning actors?

ZUCKERMAN: Relaxation, focus and flexibility are the best things they can bring into the room. Many actors can grasp the essence of a scene in two minutes and give a good reading. Others need coaches and reassurance, and sometimes, it shows that they have worked too hard on it. They have been given extensive notes and have become too settled in their choices.

They shouldn't memorize the text, because the dialogue may change. Scripts are rewritten even during audition sessions. We've noticed that when actors memorize the script, not

> *Actors should realize that within the first two lines that they read, we usually know if they are right for the part or not.*

only do they sometimes get nervous and forget their lines, but often, they can't incorporate new dialogue. In addition, when you are rigidly set in your choices, you may not be able to follow new directions that the director comes up with. So get to know the material, gather as much information as you can before you come to the office, then remain relaxed and flexible. Actors should realize that within the first two lines that they read, we usually know if they are right for the part or not. So it's important to start with a bang. I don't mean really climbing to the ceiling, I mean being there from the beginning.

HENDERSON: Actors are so eager to please and be liked that often they spend too much of the director's and producer's valuable time chatting. Casting comes at a time when the creative team is worrying about every other aspect of the project as well. So don't ask background and relationship questions during a callback. You should have asked your agent or the casting director those questions beforehand. And remember, there is always a script available at the office.

Most producers and directors hope the actor will do the scenes, then ask if there's anything else they'd like to see; ninety-nine percent of the time, they'll say no and the actor can leave. Act professionally, so they are confident that if they give you new lines or choices on the set, you won't be thrown.

Don't come in and yak and yak and put the director on the spot. Directors push those actors out. They realize that this person will be difficult and cost them money on the set.

Talking too much is probably a defense mechanism for actors who are nervous.
HENDERSON: They have to find a way to tone it down. If you know you are a hyper person, act being calm as soon as you walk into the room. If you are too shy, act a little more aggressive. Know your weak points and will yourself to find a happy medium. Then make that a part of your audition.

How important is theatre experience as preparation for film work?
HENDERSON: People with stage experience are the ones who are ready for any situation. They are good at improv, and comfortable working with other actors. When I get a submission, I always read the résumé—not to see how many shows they have done, but to see if they have studied and whether they have done any work on stage.
ZUCKERMAN: An actor blew an audition once because of his negative attitude toward the theatre. The director of the film was from England and loved to read the résumés of the actors to see what plays they'd done. When this actor came in, the director said, "I see you haven't done any stage." The actor reacted with, "And thank God I haven't had to!" He obviously didn't get the part. He was "too TV." Many actors who have been on television for a long time are "too TV." You should be familiar with acting in all media—television, film *and* theatre.

Do you use readers during your sessions?
HENDERSON: We do, and that opportunity is available for actors who want to educate themselves about the whole casting process. They objectively see what works and what doesn't, and they can learn from the mistakes of others. In

addition, they are sometimes given small roles in the show. I highly recommend every actor to read for a session.

What to you are the joys and pains of the casting profession?
HENDERSON: We are liaisons between agents, actors, producers and directors, and sometimes there can be a lot of pressure. Luckily, I have a partner like Dori. Each of us takes on the people that best fit our personalities. I am better with some people, while Dori excels in dealing with others.

I wish actors would realize how difficult it is for casting directors to function in the business. Our credits are often disputed, and many times we don't get paid on time or we aren't given credit for our creative input.

Actors often complain about the audition situation. But everybody, on all levels, auditions in this town. We audition for the directors, the directors audition for the producers, the producers audition for the studios, and even studios audition for their corporate chairmen and their distribution departments. Despite all that, we wouldn't want to be anywhere else; we are in awe of all artistic endeavors and we love talented people.

. . . .
Cathy Henderson and Dori Zuckerman
Henderson/Zuckerman Casting
225 Santa Monica Blvd., Suite 414
Santa Monica, CA 90401
. . . .

Phyllis Huffman, CSA

Phyllis Huffman has cast numerous award-winning films, including over a dozen with Clint Eastwood. She began her career in New York as an assistant to an agent and a casting director. In Los Angeles she worked at Paramount and later at Warner Bros. for casting director Marion Dougherty. From 1982 to 1989, she was vice president of talent and casting at Warner Bros. Television. In 1989, she relocated to New York where she continued casting for Warner Bros. Television until  1991. Her film work includes the Eastwood projects *True Crime, Midnight in the Garden of Good and Evil, Absolute Power, White Hunter, Black Heart, Bird, Tightrope, A Perfect World* and the Academy Award winning *Unforgiven*. Other features include *Private Parts, National Lampoon's Vacation* and *The Stars Fell on Henrietta*. Huffman has also cast her share of Broadway plays, cable projects, the network pilots for *Murphy Brown* and *China Beach*, the mini-series *North and South* (Parts I and II) and *Napoleon and Josephine* and MOWs such as Hallmark's *Breathing Lessons* and *The Piano Lesson*.

What should an actor bring to an audition?

As a casting director, when the door opens, you sort of know who that person is and what qualities they are bringing into the room Great acting happens only when the actor successfully melds who they are with the role they're playing. To do that, you need technique. That's why I believe that everybody has to be in class all the time, even actors who have been in the business for years. Take a dance class, an audition class, or any other class that offers you the opportunity to express yourself on your feet. You are a performing artist and therefore have to perform on a regular basis.

When you are in class, you develop confidence. When that door opens for an audition, you have a limited amount of time to express your personality, to interpret the role and to present yourself confidently. This confidence comes from understanding your art, and gives you the wisdom to know exactly who you are and how to work. There is the part of acting that can be explained—for example, the choices that you make. Then there is the part of acting that cannot be explained. Who can explain charisma? It's almost spiritual.

Is New York or Los Angeles the better place for a young actor to start a career?

You can't compare the volume of work that's available in Los Angeles to New York. Yet, I still think young actors should go to New York. You can't make good money there but you can become a better actor because of all the good theatre you can do. In my opinion, theatre is the basis of becoming a real actor. I think it is hard to become a better actor in Los Angeles when you are young because you can be so seduced by the money and all the other possibilities. An actress who was here told me that she went back to New York because she realized that when she had to choose between going to her acting class or the gym, she was always choosing the gym.

Are you open to unsolicited submissions?

Absolutely. I think young actors should have every opportunity to be seen through their pictures and through their work. We look at every picture that comes in. The best thing an actor can do is have very good pictures that look just like them. It's an investment you have to make. It may be your one chance. My associate, Olivia Harris, does a lot of generals. We've been together for about twelve years. She has an extraordinary gift. She loves to go to all the hole-in-the-wall places downtown. She'll go everywhere. It can be in the dregs, but if there is somebody there with a glimmer of something, she can see it. She has a real talent for that. She brings them to me. We are a great team because we complement each other.

What can you say to actors who might one day audition for Clint Eastwood?

He is very kind to actors, even when it's just the two of us watching the audition tapes. He only casts from tape because he feels the audition process is very difficult for an actor and he likes to make it as low-key as possible. He's got such confidence and instincts. He knows the film business so viscerally. He also knows that film is a visual medium and, as a result, the faces he chooses are very deliberate. We tape all auditions and, when he views them, he always looks for the simplicity of the actor's work. He might choose a persona that may be a little off or more charactery, but the work has to still be simple.

What audition habits annoy you?

I am amazed when actors come in unprepared. I know sometimes you can't get the sides or read the whole script, but many times actors come in and just wing it. Maybe they think it has to be just instinctual. Believe me, there is no substitute for good preparation.

What advice do you have for young people contemplating a career in film and theatre?

What I want to say to the young actor is something that they probably would not want to hear. The competition in the acting world is extraordinary. I don't know why there are so many actors. I work in both New York and Los Angeles and I am absolutely stunned at the volume of people who go into this as a profession. Acting has become too accessible to anyone who wants to do it.

Similarly, I think it can become very confusing for young people going into the business to hear the expression "making it." What that term means these days is that you

> *The truth is if you can make a living as an actor, if you can take care of yourself and your family, then you have made it!*

have to become a star and make a lot of money. The thinking is that if you don't "make it" as a star, you are a total failure. This kind of thinking can have a very debilitating effect on people. The truth is if you can make a living as an actor, if you can take care of yourself and your family, then you have made it!

Another fact the young actor should become aware of is the truth that no actor has the chance to work every day. So how are you going to spend the days that you are not working? Do you have other interests? Can you do volunteer work? Somebody should make young people aware of the reality of life in our business: Know before you go into acting that you are not going to work every day. Know that competition for roles is extremely stiff. Know that you have to keep studying constantly. And finally, know that you can't afford to fall into the trap of being in the business to get rich and famous. If you do, you are going to be disappointed and disillusioned very quickly.

On the other hand, if you are in the business to tell a story and communicate all kinds of emotions, that's great. And if you get paid for it, that's even better. So go into this business for the right reason, which is to be a communicator who stimulates people's emotions, who makes them feel, makes them think and see life in a fresh, new way that they wouldn't have been able to do without your storytelling work.

. . . .
Phyllis Huffman
1325 Sixth Avenue, 31st Floor
New York, NY 10019
. . . .

JULIE HUGHES, CSA AND BARRY MOSS, CSA

Julie Hughes and Barry Moss, who together make up Hughes/Moss Casting Ltd., have been partnered for twenty years. Their awe-inspiring credits include television, film, and over seventy Broadway shows making them one of New York's top casting teams. Their stage work has included *Nine, Torch Song Trilogy, 42nd Street, Crazy for You, Dancing at Lughnasa, The Who's Tommy, The Will Rogers Follies, Jelly's Last Jam, How to Succeed in Business Without*

Barry Moss (l) and
Julie Hughes (r)

Really Trying, The Life, An Inspector Calls, Titanic, Jekyll and Hyde, The Scarlet Pimpernel and *Footloose*. The Hughes/Moss film work includes *The Champ, Purple Rain, A Soldier's Story, Cry Freedom* and *The Cotton Club*. For television, they have cast *As the World Turns, The Cosby Mysteries, A Different World*, and eight seasons of *The Cosby Show*.

Did you want to be actors?
HUGHES: Not me. But I did know that I wanted to be in the theatre. Both of my parents were in the theatre. My father was a stage manager and my mother was a sometime actress. She didn't like to audition, so she didn't work very much.

I just kind of fell into casting. I became a professional twenty or twenty-five years ago when you could almost earn a living.

How about you, Barry?
MOSS: When I was in college I wanted to be an actor but I realized that I wanted to be the kind of actor who gets discovered sipping a soda at Schwab's. I didn't want to work hard. I saw a friend of mine taking voice lessons, fencing and dance. He was working his butt off and I realized that if that's what I had to do, I'd better find something else. I think a lot of people don't realize how hard it is to be an actor. They think it's easy and that all you need is a pretty face.

How did you two get together?
HUGHES: I started casting with a firm called Theatre Now. Barry was an agent at that time. He was one of the few agents who actually accompanied his actors to auditions. That used to happen twenty-five years ago. We met at that point and we had a mutual respect for one another. When I needed a partner, I asked Barry.
MOSS: The first thing we cast together was *The Champ*.

You discovered Ricky Schroeder for that film.
MOSS: Ricky was extraordinarily bright. He also had a wonderful mother. She was a very, very intelligent, caring, supportive, non-stage mother. That helps. I think the biggest mistake stage parents make is to try to act for their kids. They take the material home and tell the kids how to read it. They try to make them into Shirley Temple-y type children. But that wasn't Rick. Actually, Franco [director Franco Zeffirelli] was looking for a kid the total opposite of Ricky. Brown haired, dark eyed. When Franco would meet with these kids, he'd throw them lines from the script and expect them to answer. So, we warned Ricky that that was going to happen and he was prepared. When he went in, Franco said to him, "You're such a chubby little boy. Why are you so fat?" Ricky looked at him and said, "Well, you're not exactly skinny." He had the part at that moment!

You also did *Blood Simple*. Wasn't that Frances McDormand's first role?
HUGHES: I suspect it was.
MOSS: We really fought for her. Obviously, it paid off because she got the role and married one of the Coen brothers. But casting directors often fight for actors and the actor has no idea we're doing it. They have no clue.

If the two of you were young actors, would you begin your careers in New York or Los Angeles?

MOSS: You're asking the wrong person because I don't like Los Angeles. It's too movie oriented for me. I went out to dinner there and somebody said, "Isn't it terrible about Paul Newman, his last three films have been flops." Other than Paul, who cares? I think a better question to ask yourself is, what kind of career do want? If you want to be in film and television, you should be in Los Angeles. If you want to be in the theatre, you should be in New York. I think the best training is in New York, but that doesn't mean you should train here and then go to Los Angeles.

HUGHES: An interesting thing that's been happening in the last five or six years is that more people who went out to the West Coast are coming back here. I think that a lot of people feel isolated and insulated out there and are really happy to be back on the East Coast and outside in life instead of in cars.

What about for older actors? Do you think there is more work in New York than in Los Angeles?

HUGHES: Not a lot, because there's not a lot of television here. For actors of a certain age, if they're not slightly known, they're not likely to get the theatre jobs. There are a lot of actors here in New York and there isn't a lot of theatre work. It's very competitive. I would suggest that the middle-aged actor go west because the chances are better that they'll get episodic and movie roles and at least make some bucks.

MOSS: But even in television, the sad trend is that Carol Burnett plays the mother of Helen Hunt. Not that Carol Burnett isn't an excellent actress, but she gets cast as opposed to a strong character actress who should be getting those roles. They give them to stars and it's a big problem. And there are stars who are working for scale in films. So, it's very difficult. And casting directors are human. We have egos. If we can say, "Wow, I got Rod Steiger to do a four line bit in this movie! Aren't I terrific!" the producers are going to go with Rod Steiger as opposed to a good, lesser known actor who needs the job.

In terms of actors getting in to see you, are you open-door? Do you do generals? Do you look at every picture and résumé?

MOSS: (laughing) Too many questions. Okay. First of all, we are very open. Our doors are never locked. We encourage actors to drop by. We encourage our receptionist to be aware of current projects we're involved with so they can alert us if someone who might be right for something has dropped by. We do not, however, do generals. We don't have time. We do see every picture and résumé that comes in. Do we keep them? No. We keep the ones that are possible for the project at hand. But we do hold on to the pictures of people who we've seen already. If someone comes in and auditions for *Titanic* and we like them, we'll go through that file when we're casting *Jekyll And Hyde*. So it all pays off in the future.

Do you cast straight plays as well or just musicals?
HUGHES: Recently, we've been doing a lot of musicals, but certainly we've cast a lot of straight plays in the past. There are more musicals in New York and we've been very fortunate in that we've had success with them.

Do you think that every actor should learn to sing and dance?
HUGHES: If they can, it's a plus. One of the things we found when we were casting the Broadway company of *Titanic* was interesting. The director, Richard Jones, was very concerned with acting credits. He really wanted *actors* who could sing. We found more actors who sang than we ever dreamed existed. They came out of the woodwork. If you have a voice you can brush up for a musical, that doesn't hurt. Although, you can either sing or you can't and if you can't, brushing up isn't going to help you.
MOSS: But if we're talking about young actors who are starting, it's very wise for them to learn the techniques because you can always get an audition for a musical. They have chorus calls and you can always get seen.

Is there anything you want to say to actors that might empower them before they come in to meet you?
MOSS: I've said this before—and this is the absolute truth but you won't believe me—the fact is, we need you more than you need us. When you walk into an audition, you have to understand that you're there to help us with our problem. We're the ones in trouble. We're the ones that have to solve this problem of putting on a show, casting a movie or getting a television show on the air and you're there to help us do that. Actors need to remember this and have that confidence when they walk in. If you have trouble with that confidence, there's a book I recommend every time I teach: Og Mandino's *The Greatest Salesman in the World*. Basically, it gives you ten tenets of self confidence that use a mantra every day for a month; then they become habit. I recommend the book to everybody.
HUGHES: The other empowering tip I share with actors is that they've got to know they have at least one friend in the room and that's the casting director. I don't know that this is always true, but certainly in our case it is.

MOSS: It has to be true. We don't have time to bring you in otherwise. Every person brought in by the casting director, or the producer or director, should know they have that little cheering section.

What happens when a wonderful actor comes in and really blows it? What do you suggest? Can they ask to try again?
MOSS: First of all, actors can be their own harshest critics.
HUGHES: A lot of times, they think they've made a mess of it and they really haven't.
MOSS: Also, there are so many reasons for not getting a role that have absolutely nothing to do with the audition. You might look like the girl who jilted the producer on his prom night or you might be caught in a battle between the writer and the director and out you go. There are so many reasons that you can't even begin to think about it. But, if an actor doesn't do what we know they can do in an audition, when they're finished we can explain to the producers and fight for a call-back.

Any final tips?
MOSS: Just believe in yourself. Have a lot of joy in what you're doing. People say that they hate to audition. How can they hate to audition? Auditions should be a little performance which will lead to even more performing, which you should love to do. So, remember that sometimes we see thirty or forty people in a day and it's the people who walk in glad to be here, bright and energetic that make us think, "Oh, good!"

. . . .
Julie Hughes and Barry Moss
Hughes/Moss Casting
1600 Broadway, Suite 703
New York, NY 10036
. . . .

DONNA ISAACSON, CSA

Donna Isaacson, senior vice president of feature casting at 20th Century Fox, believes that actors can best build their careers by "getting up every single day and doing something positive for themselves—even if it means taking the day off."

Isaacson came out of the High School of Performing Arts and earned an MFA at NYU's School of the Arts. After graduating, she began her career in New York as an actress. In 1980, she decided to move behind the scenes and thought casting would be a great opportunity. She was subsequently hired as the artistic director of the Manhattan Theatre Club and remained until 1993. During her tenure there, she also cast features such as *Miller's Crossing, Rising Sun, Raising Arizona, Dirty Rotten Scoundrels, Father of the Bride* and *Barton Fink*. After casting the feature *The Hudsucker Proxy* for Warner Bros., in 1993 she joined 20th Century Fox as senior vice president of feature casting and, along with her duties as an executive, cast the features *The Crucible, Broken Arrow* and *A Life Less Ordinary*.

How did your current position come about?

I was here in Los Angeles after a movie I was to cast got postponed. Out of the blue, the phone rang and I was asked if I were interested in starting a department at Fox. I met with them and three weeks later I started.

What are the duties of a senior vice president of casting?

Primarily, a casting executive oversees the casting of the various movies being done at the studio. We generate lists for the key roles and participate in the creative conversations prior to the film getting its green light. I then work with the individual casting directors, producers and directors in whatever capacity they may need me. When I accepted the position at Fox, it was agreed to that I could continue to cast films on my own.

What, in your opinion, is the best way for an actor to deal with rejection?

It's like going on a blind date. They are not rejecting you—they don't know who you are. They're rejecting something silly, like maybe the color of your hair. In the same way, there are so many reasons why a person does or does not get cast. Very often, it has nothing to do with talent so you mustn't take everything personally. I know that's easy to say, but really try not to think of it as rejection. When people turn down certain of my ideas, I don't look at it as rejection. If I did I wouldn't be able to function. It's just a difference of opinion. It's not always a particularly kind or fair business so you have to develop a thick skin, but great things do happen.

What methods would help the actor thrive in this competitive situation?

It's a very frustrating business when you are not a star. The actor has to think of himself as running his own business. If you owned a clothing store you wouldn't just sit there and wait for the phone to ring; you'd wake up every morning and think of ways to advertise and improve sales. The actor has to take charge of his career in the very same way. You have to ask yourself, how many people did you meet today? Did you make a note of your meetings? Do you remember their names? How can you follow up in a positive way? Did you go to the library to find a scene or a play that you could perform brilliantly? Should you try to develop it on your own? As an example, look at performance artists like Anna Devere-Smith or John Leguizamo who were knocking around New York for years, frustrated, until they each created a show for themselves. Similarly, Tim Robbins founded his own theatre company in Chicago, giving him a creative outlet and propelling him into major film roles. More and more actors are starting their own groups and becoming visible. That is one way to turn around an uncontrollable situation—a very dangerous place for an actor to be. It's about keeping hope alive, staying creative and, as a result, making yourself visible.

There is so much theatre space in Los Angeles! There are also a great number of talented writers, directors and actors who are all looking to work. Can you imagine if all of that talent were pooled what it might turn into? I've seen it happen and it's exhilarating!

Do you look at every picture and résumé that comes into your office?

I do when I am casting a movie. Any other time, unsolicited pictures are looked at by myself or by a staff member and many lead to generals—which we try to do every three or four months. I don't think actors realize how much we love to discover new talent. When the pool gets too small it stops being interesting. I love Sundance because I love to find new people. That's a marketplace for new talent, for actors whose first shot it is carrying a movie. The only purpose for going there is to find new talent.

Do you pay more attention to submissions from bigger agencies?

I talk more frequently with the larger agencies because they call me more often. They have designated people who cover the studios. We deal with them constantly because we hire their star clients. But when I am going through the submissions to see who's interesting to meet, I don't necessarily pay too much attention to where the package comes from. I may even be intrigued by a picture from an agency I don't know anything about.

Do you see actors without agents?

When I am doing a movie and I see a submission that is interesting, I'll bring them in. Similarly, if a colleague called and asked me to see someone, I always will. And I will, in turn, call them to set up a meeting for someone I find interesting.

Would you also recommend actors to agents?

On rare occasions I do, but in general it's my policy not to ask agents to see actors. Yet there have been times when I have recommended actors. For example, in New York, I brought in an actor through a submission who gave a brilliant reading from the script. Since I didn't know his previous work, I was a little concerned about bringing him to the director. So I told him it was a good reading but would he mind preparing a monologue and coming back. He did and blew me away. I sent him to two agents and he was signed immediately. He booked seven movies his first year and at the end was signed by CAA.

What, to you, is star material?

Every actor should ask himself the question, "What draws me to a certain actor?" The answer is what star material is about. Also, being movie star material and being a great actor don't necessarily go together. There are movie stars who don't have training and if you give them a character to sustain on the stage for two hours, they will not succeed. But on film, they give such amazing performances. Like children, they are who they are. And you don't know how they do it. There is always something interesting going on behind their eyes. There is a mystery to them, a sense of humor in their very being that gives them more range. There's also a stillness to them. All is done effortlessly. It feels that they are just existing in that world. I think that's what charisma on the screen is all about.

. . . .

Donna Isaacson
Senior VP of Feature Casting
20th Century Fox
10201 West Pico Blvd., Bldg. 12, #201
Los Angeles, CA 90035
. . . .

Jane Jenkins, csa and Janet Hirshenson, csa

Janet Hirshenson and Jane Jenkins, who together make up The Casting Company, are two of the most highly respected casting directors in Los Angeles. Deservedly so. Their résumé reads like a veritable Hollywood blockbuster check-list. Among their films—which number over a hundred—are *Edtv, Tomorrow Never Dies, Air Force One, The Lost World: Jurassic Park, Space Jam, An American President, Apollo 13, Mrs. Doubtfire, In the Line of Fire,*

Jane Jenkins (l) and
Janet Hirshenson (r)

A Few Good Men, Backdraft, Ghost, Home Alone, The Godfather III, When Harry Met Sally, Mystic Pizza, Ferris Bueller's Day Off, Stand by Me and *The Outsiders.* Most recently, the two completed work on Ron Howard's *The Grinch,* starring Jim Carrey; Rob Reiner's new romantic comedy, *The Story of Us,* starring Bruce Willis and Michelle Pfeiffer; and Chris Columbus' *The Bicentennial Man* starring Robin Williams.

How did you two become partners?
HIRSHENSON: I had no intention of going into show business. I just fell into it and started working for Jennifer Shull. A few years later, Jane came along and

the three of us started working together. Three months later, we were hired to be the casting department at Francis Ford Coppola's Zoetrope Films.

JENKINS: The three of us went into partnership. As the studio was beginning to fall apart and there was less and less money, the casting department was the only division generating any money.

HIRSHENSON: They'd loan us out.

JENKINS: We were paid a salary by the studio and if they loaned us out, the studio would get paid. It was like the old studio star system. As the studio was financially disintegrating, and we had less and less to do there, the three of us sat down and added up how many films we had done for other people and how much money we would have made if we had done them ourselves. We figured out that it was enough money for us to live on and maybe . . .

HIRSHENSON: . . . since it was ending there anyway . . .

JENKINS: The handwriting was on the wall. So we figured that maybe a better deal would be for Zoetrope not to pay our salaries but to pay our overhead and we'd continue to work for them for a nominal fee and do outside work independently. We did that for a couple of months and then it was income tax time so we formed a company. Right after that, Jennifer was offered a job at Columbia as vice president in charge of talent. She was going to turn it down and we said, "Jennifer, that's not a good idea. We don't even have our next job. One of us should be employed." So she went off to Columbia and wound up staying. Jennifer had really looked after all of us. Her manner of being kind and generous and thoughtful to actors and other human beings was passed on to us. We feel lucky to have learned from her. Anyway, we opened our little office and hung out our shingle.

And the rest is history. How do you think the two of you compliment each other?

JENKINS: We've never really analyzed it because it works perfectly. It has to do with the people we are. Both of us are basically shy, retiring human beings. Neither one of us has to be the one who's right. It doesn't make any difference as long as the job gets done, and our job has always been to serve the director's vision. I think that we both feel pretty privileged to be part of the process and work with who we've worked with. I don't know that we would be as non-competitive or non-combative if we were both grumpy and grouchy because we were working on a bunch of crappy projects with crappy people that we didn't like. But we have been privileged to work with the crème de la crème.

Who have been some of your favorites?

JENKINS: That's a really hard question to answer because we've been so lucky to work with a lot of directors who were just starting out, who became enormously successful and have remained loyal to us. When you do Rob Reiner's first movie after *Spinal Tap*, when you do Ron Howard's first mainstream feature, when you work with a young Chris Columbus who's just starting out, or John Hughes who's at the top of his form, and these people then hire you over and over again, it's really wonderful. Our careers grow along with their success. It makes the whole working process and casting process a very different experience when you're working with people with whom you have a history. You have a casting short-hand. An actor you saw years before can suddenly become your star. Meg Ryan is, perhaps, the perfect example. Meg Ryan was an actress Rob Reiner and I met when we were doing *The Sure Thing*, which was his first studio film. He thought that she was absolutely adorable but hired Daphne Zuniga instead. Then, when we were doing *The Princess Bride*, he saw Meg Ryan again and he loved her but wound up casting Robin Wright.

Why didn't Meg Ryan get it?

JENKINS: Because Robin Wright was absolutely perfect.

HIRSHENSON: There was no question.

JENKINS: Actually, there was a history there, too. We saw Robin when she was eighteen years old for *The Sure Thing*. She was still a little green. She was breathtakingly beautiful but not quite ready. When we were doing *The Princess Bride*, her agent called to get me to see the twenty-year-old Robin. She said that Robin had been studying really hard and had been working on a soap, which to me is often the kiss of death.

Why?

JENKINS: Because actors can learn a lot of bad habits on soaps. They don't necessarily grow. It doesn't necessarily bring out the best of one's talent. But Robin walked in and she was still breathtakingly beautiful. Around that same time we realized that perhaps the reason we had been having so much trouble casting the role of Buttercup was that all the girls who had come in had spoken in their American accents and it occurred to us that that didn't sound right. We needed something different for this fairy tale. So we started asking people to make up accents, just some sort of Romantic accent. Robin came in and right before she opened her mouth I said, "Oh, and if you can do it, we'd like to try some kind of accent." She said, "Well, my step-father's British so I can do a pretty good English accent." At this point, I had literally met hundreds of women for this role from all over. She opened her mouth, the words came out and I was delirious. I called Rob and said, "This is it." So he met her and then there was a meeting with Bill Goldman, the writer. It was at Rob's house and we opened the door and there she was in the doorway, long blond hair, back-lit by God and Bill said, "Well, that's what I wrote."

So what's the best mind-set for an actor to come into an audition with?
HIRSHENSON: It's good to find out all you can about what the producers are looking for in a role. Maybe there is a specific quality. Then come in and take a stand. You don't want to be so middle of the road that the role loses any interesting quality. What sometimes ends up being more interesting is the actor who throws it away a little bit.
JENKINS: I think the actor's biggest downfall is putting so much importance on whatever the part is. If you're not a star, then you're coming in to audition for a role that is, most likely, a smaller or supporting part. There is this overwhelming expectation, the whole rejection factor, the need for the job, all the stuff that comes in with the actor and practically cripples them from being able to do their best work. I know it's easier said than done, but if you can find a way to leave all of that garbage behind and just come in and bring your humanity to the part, you have a much better chance. You also have to be really aware of the nature of the piece you're reading for. I don't think actors ever ask enough questions about the tone of the piece.

We just did a sitcom pilot which was really interesting since most of our casting is in features. Actors came in and would be so over the top it was as if they were auditioning for *I Love Lucy*. They wouldn't even ask. They'd just be over the top because they assumed that, as a sitcom, that was what the piece was. When you look at what's on the air that's working, even a show like *Drew Carey*, which is heightened, still has a level of reality and that's what we respond to as an audience. The characters' humanity is what we're looking for. The actors who came in and were real were the ones who got callbacks.

Did you tell the actors to perhaps bring their energy down a bit?
HIRSHENSON: There wasn't really a chance.
JENKINS: I find that, unless there is a quality that either the writer or director sees and responds to, frequently nobody says anything. There's no direction. That's the unfortunate thing. Hardly anyone directs at auditions anymore. The whole style of coming in has changed. A lot of directors wait to see the part walk in as opposed to an actor who, with direction, can play it. There were a couple of actors who came in on the sitcom and I know their work and knew they could

do better so I stopped the reading to give them adjustments. But that's rare.

HIRSHENSON: Also, actors really need to remember that if they come in and do a good reading, even if they don't get the part, a good audition ripples out. The casting director likes you, the producers remember you. A good reading unto itself is a nice goal.

JENKINS: Which brings me back to the Meg Ryan story. So, she auditioned for *The Sure Thing* and *The Princess Bride* and didn't get them. In the meantime she moved out here and Janet and I fell in love with her. We tested her five times in one year. Then along came *When Harry Met Sally*. Rob had already decided that he was going to hire Billy Crystal. Meg read with Billy and Rob said, "Well, I think it's her turn now." This was the one she was right for. Seeing a young actor mature and seeing them grow is really part of the joy.

You just described every actor's dream: to be respected by you and repeatedly brought in hoping that . . .

JENKINS: . . . magic happens. Auditions are so funny. People learn all these meditations and relaxation techniques in acting classes and then they come in and that stuff goes right out the window. It's a very hard thing to do, but the fact is that a great deal is riding on every single audition. Your life could change, you could have a job, you could pay the rent, etc. I find that bringing all of that in with you weakens your reading. I don't know how to tell anybody to just relax. Come in and have a good time and enjoy it. Ron Howard always says that he thinks the audition is the actual job and getting the role is just icing on the cake. I think that's true. There is a certain comfort when you have a job. You're secure and there's nothing left to prove. If actors could start at that place, they'd be so tremendously helped. For example, on the sitcom, the people who were real and funny and asked appropriate questions were the people we responded to. The people who didn't seem to invest the weight of their entire life in this one moment were the people who interested us most.

HIRSHENSON: It might take some of the pressure off the actor if they knew that, often, television producers are looking for the right persona. It's almost more important to them than the best actor. Television casting is so much more immediate than for film. You have to know who a person is instantly.

JENKINS: Particularly in sitcoms, persona is what people respond to. A drama show is a different thing altogether. Which is why, by the way, it's so important for actors to know the nature of the piece they're auditioning for. I can't tell you how often people come in and they don't know if they're auditioning for a feature, a drama, a sitcom or a MOW.

HIRSHENSON: Actors need to ask their agents those questions and if they have more questions, they should ask the casting assistant or the receptionist. That's the homework. If auditioning is your job, then you need to do the preparation for your job.

JENKINS: If you're auditioning for a Rob Reiner film, his body of work proves over and over and over again that, when he's finished, the kind of acting on the screen is simple. I frequently tell people, "Do no acting in this room. You're not playing to the balcony." There is a camera very close to the actor's face and the mic is very nearby. I was watching news coverage of Frank Sinatra's funeral and Jack Jones was speaking. He was trying so hard to keep it together that it made me cry. The humanity of watching him try to control the emotion as opposed to bawling hysterically was so moving. The camera is right there and it captures the emotion—what's underneath.

Okay, now a question that most actors who have never met you want the answer to: How can they get to meet you?

JENKINS: We get hundreds of pictures and résumés a day but this is the honest truth: I look at all of these pictures and then we recycle them. If, by some miracle, your picture falls on our desk and you're what we're looking for right then, that can be great. But it's really rare. It's almost like winning the lottery.

HIRSHENSON: It's timing.

JENKINS: We do go to the movies and theatre and watch television. Frequently on television, I'll see an actor I haven't seen before and the credits go by so quickly your own mother wouldn't see your name. I'll call the casting directors to find out who someone is.

Do you ever watch unsolicited tapes?

JENKINS: There's never time. One of the things that drives me crazy is the number of actors who think that their tape is the only tape we get and there is no identifying way to return it to them. No name, no agent, no phone number. What am I supposed to do with that?

HIRSHENSON: And there are actors who send a whole episode of a show they're in for two minutes. Edit!

JENKINS: A five minute tape is enough. And tapes are really important these days. But know that the tape is going to get turned off within the first minute or two. Whether or not we like someone, we only need a minute to tell and, once we know, we don't keep watching.

HIRSHENSON: You want to show your range and show different kinds of things—but keep it short. And put your best work first.

What are some things that you love and hate that actors do in auditions?

HIRSHENSON: When actors come in and say, "I really didn't have a chance to look at this," I think, "Then why are you coming in for the role?" Or they say, "Do you want to tell me about this?" You need to have that information and take that time before you come in. I know there are a million auditions but we don't have time for people who don't take time to do the work. It's especially bad when a director is in the room. Someone once actually said to a director, "Your script isn't bad. Should we read some of it?" They didn't get the job.

JENKINS: So, somewhere between that attitude and being an overly effusive fan or a bundle of nerves is what you're going for. If you come in and you meet a director who has an enormous body of work, you can tell them that you admire it without going overboard. We meet a lot of people on any given day so the level of chit-chat and exchange can be an exhausting part of the process. Go with the flow. Go in with your best self and without all of the problems and desperation.

HIRSHENSON: Even on those two line parts. You have to remember that the scene is not about Cop No. 2. You've really got to throw it away.

JENKINS: Your contribution to Cop No. 2 is that you're going to be interesting. It doesn't mean that you have to be big. Who you are is going to add another layer of the reality to the role, and that's why you'll be cast.

Any final tips?
JENKINS: Well, yes. Be born into a wealthy family.

Jane Jenkins and Janet Hirshenson
The Casting Company
7461 Beverly Blvd., Penthouse
Los Angeles, CA 90036

Lorna Johnson

Lorna Johnson believes that one of the most important things an actor can bring into the room is his or her own unique energy. Johnson, who cast the series *Lois & Clark: The New Adventures of Superman* further explained, "When you are sitting in a room and reading numerous actors and someone walks in with a spark of unique energy, you can't help but notice and respond positively."

Johnson came to casting after getting her degree from Cal State Long Beach and then toiling at various jobs outside of entertainment. Her break into the industry came when she was hired as an assistant by Barbara Miller, the senior vice president, talent and casting at Warner Bros. Television.

As an assistant, Johnson worked on many shows, including the pilots of *Friends*, and *The Drew Carey Show;* and the series *Midnight Caller, Knots Landing* and *I'll Fly Away*. More recently, she has formed a partnership with veteran casting director, Ellie Kanner.

Do you go the theatre often, and do you think that good theatre acting can translate to television?

I don't get to the theatre as much as I'd like to. It's difficult sometimes during the episodic season. I try to make a special effort when our shows are on hiatus. And yes, I think good acting can translate to any medium. When I see someone on stage who moves me, when the right role becomes available, I'll bring that person in.

Are you open to unsolicited submissions?

I look at every submission and if someone looks as though they might be right for a role, I'll bring him in. But for the most part, we work through a combination of breakdown submissions, agent pitches, actors we are familiar with and suggestions from the producer or director.

What path would you suggest for the young actor just starting out?

I don't think there is one single path to success. However, being prepared if an opportunity comes your way is important. Get as much training as you can—school, classes, theatre.

Do you have any tips on dealing with the perpetual hardships of the acting profession?

As we all know, there are a lot of negative things you have to deal with as an actor, especially the rejection, it's part of the package. Best advice I could give is try to keep a sense of balance in your life: friends, family, hobbies, etc. It's so easy for this business to become all consuming. It's hard for me too. When things get especially hectic and stressful, I try to remind myself what we do isn't brain surgery.

But each audition is a big event in an actor's life. It may finally lead to that break that separates the working actor from one who works once or twice a year.

I think every audition is important but you do have to keep it in perspective. And if you put too much pressure on yourself it can affect your audition.

I think it takes great courage to be an actor. You are constantly putting yourself on the line with each audition. That's why I try to create a supportive environment in my office. I think that helps the actor do the best job he or she can do.

Do you have any audition tips on what not to do?

A couple of things come to mind. Don't incorporate the casting director into the physical parts of the scene. There is no need to shake or grab a casting director during an audition. Keep some sense of distance. It doesn't help your audition if the casting director or producers begin to focus more on the fact that the casting director might get hurt than on the actual reading. I also think that it's better not to use props. They seem to get in the way of the actor more than they help. And never bring weapons to an audition!

What are some of the pleasures of being a casting director?
So much of our work is, as is the case with most jobs, stressful and repetitive. But when I bring in an actor and I think they're wonderful and the producers concur and the actor gets the role, I feel very gratified.

During my very first session as a casting director, we had to cast the role of a little boy. I read this child who had absolutely no experience but who knocked me out. He had incredible energy, was so likable and took direction very well. Because this was my first session, I obviously felt a great deal of pressure, and initially thought that there was no way I could bring in a total novice. Then I thought, "Everybody is taking a chance on me here, I should take a chance on him." And I did. I brought him in and he was very good. The producers loved him and he landed the role. Since then he's worked on numerous episodic shows and a feature film. Experiences like that are what I enjoy most about being a casting director.

> *I also think that it's better not to use props . . . And never bring weapons to an audition!*

What sort of protocol should actors follow with casting assistants?
In my opinion, it's a very bad idea to dismiss the assistants. If an actor is rude to them, the casting director is going to hear about it, believe me. I think assistants can be another means for actors to get exposure to casting directors. When you mail flyers for a play you are doing, it would be a good idea to extend the invitation to also include the assistants. If I can't make it to a play but my assistant goes and sees someone wonderful, he'll let me know. And, of course, a lot of assistants end up as casting directors.

Could interning with a casting director help an actor's career?
I think whatever you can do to learn about all the different aspects of the business, you should do. If an opportunity comes where you can watch the casting process from the other side it will demystify the experience. You might find out that a

lot of things you thought really mattered actually don't. I know actors will sometimes be sitting in a casting reception room trying to guess how the other actors are doing and how it's going to effect them. For example, if another actor spends a lot of time in the audition, you might think they are favoring that actor when the reality may be that the actor is just talking a lot. Once you find out how some decisions are made, you can stop psyching yourself out for reasons that are not essential and just concentrate on your work.

. . . .

Lorna Johnson
Kanner/Johnson Casting
c/o CSA
606 N. Larchmont Blvd., Suite 4B
Los Angeles, CA 90004

. . . .

ELLIE KANNER, CSA

At the age of nineteen, Ellie Kanner left Bloomfield, Connecticut for Los Angeles to pursue a life in show business. She worked as an agent with Irvin Arthur and Associates before becoming an assistant to casting directors Fern Champion and Pamela Basker (then partners). After a year there, she went to Lorimar and worked as a casting assistant on *Homefront*, the last season of *Dallas*, and the first season of *Sisters*. Soon after, Barbara Miller, the senior vice president of talent and casting at Warner Bros., promoted her to full-fledged casting director at Lorimar. Since that time, the warm and dynamic Kanner has had amazing success casting pilots that have gone on to become hit series. They include the pilot and first season of *Friends*, for which she was nominated for an Artios, *Lois and Clark; The New Adventures of Superman* (another Artios nomination, this one shared with Geraldine Leder), *The Drew Carey Show; Sabrina, The Teenage Witch* and recently, the pilot for the HBO series, *Sex and the City*, which she shared with Billy Hopkins. Her many other credits include MOWs and the features *Sleep with Me, Kicking and Screaming* and *Eden*. Her book, *NEXT: An Actor's*

Guide to Auditioning, is available from Lone Eagle Publishing. Recently, she joined forces with casting director Lorna Johnson.

Why did you stop casting *Friends*?

I loved casting the pilot and the first season on *Friends*, but I've always wanted to cast features. I had to leave Warner Bros. to pursue that. In addition, leaving allowed me the opportunity to work with my husband, who created and produced his own show.

How did you assemble the cast for *Friends*?

Casting is a collaborative effort. You're only as good as the script, the producers, network and studio behind it. On *Friends* we had producers with impeccable taste, and NBC and Warner Bros. who gave us all the help and support we could have asked for.

Still, putting the cast together wasn't easy. Matt LeBlanc, Courtney Cox and Lisa Kudrow landed their jobs through the usual audition process, while Jennifer Aniston and Matthew Perry took some time to lock in because they had previous pilot commitments. David Schwimmer, on the other hand, did not want to do a series. But when he read the script, spoke with the producers and became interested, we flew him in from Chicago where he was doing a play, and he signed on.

Is it true that a newcomer has a better chance at getting a lead in a series than a guest-star role?

It depends. Most of the time it is very hard for a newcomer to get a guest role, only because of the time constraints on television. We don't have the luxury of auditioning as many actors in episodic as we do when casting a pilot. But it is difficult for newcomers to get either job because producers want tried and true performers whom they can trust to do the job and hit their marks with as few problems or adjustments as possible. Also, stunt-casting (the casting of a star in a guest role), is becoming more and more common. The networks and studios actually look for roles they can stunt so they can heavily promote the show—particularly during sweeps periods. This makes it more difficult for an actor who is not a celebrity to get a guest role because the competition is so great. But it is not impossible—look at Christa Miller, who plays a series-regular role opposite Drew Carey. She had done some work, but didn't have that many credits. I brought her in, she gave a great reading and got it.

What, in an actor's work, makes you take notice?

An actor coming in to read for a part can't possibly know exactly what it is we are looking for. There are a million ways to say one line, let alone a whole scene. So when an actor with the right look comes in, what I look for most is a sparkle that tells me the actor has connected with the character. This intimate connection means a lot. It's better than being the best auditioner of the day. Only when I see these elements in the actor do I bring them to the producers and director.

What preparatory work should the actor do once they are given an audition appointment?

First of all, they should read the whole script. You can usually get the script, unless the final draft isn't written yet. If you can't get it ahead of time, go to the casting office and ask if you can read it there. I appreciate thoroughness.

The second step is to go to an acting coach, your manager, etc., and work on the role with them. Then decide what to wear to help suggest the character. But don't go too far with your costumes. You want to suggest, not distract.

Finally, come to the office a little early and get focused. You may have to wait, so learn to live with it without losing your concentration. If you are running late, please call and say so. I can't tell you how many times I've had to beg my producers to wait another five minutes because an actor was late and didn't call.

Having done all that, go in there and do the best you can; try to have fun!

What's the best audition policy—to give a full, memorized performance or to hold the sides to suggest that it is a work in progress?

It depends on the type of director you are auditioning for. Some want to see the full performance, thinking, "Whatever I am getting here is the same level I am going to get on the set." Then there are others who will direct you if you look the part and show talent.

Actors often complain that casting directors don't go to the theatre and see their work enough. What do you feel actors can do to tempt a casting director to their performance?

Casting directors are often reluctant to go to the theatre because they've wasted too much time and been burned too often by shoddy productions. I've seen many good actors wasted in bad plays, or sabotaged by bad actors. I don't want to sound harsh; I understand that the actor has to do whatever work he can get, especially in the beginning. But he can help his case by following some ground rules: Send flyers two to three weeks in advance. Don't send flyers on a Friday that read, "Come see my show this Saturday! One night only." You also want to be proud of the whole show. If it's a showcase with ten scenes, you don't want each scene to be twenty minutes long. And make sure the scenes are enjoyable and entertaining. Finally, if the theatre has secured parking, note that on your invitation.

Any final thoughts on how best to sculpt an acting career?
Part of doing your homework before you come to an audition is knowing the show you're reading for. Each show has a different style. Look at every show at least once when the season begins. If it's a film, as I said before, do everything you can to get the script and get as much information on the character you're reading for as possible. If you have questions, ask the casting director—especially during the pre-read.

So many actors look at the casting director as the enemy that they have to somehow get through to get to the producers. I don't think that's the healthiest attitude. Keep in mind that we always want you to do well.

When a casting director offers direction, don't dismiss it. We are there to tell you what the directors and producers are looking for; what their vision of the character is. We can help you find what makes a particular scene funnier. When we hear the material a hundred times, believe me, we have a sense of what works and what doesn't.

I know that every casting director says this but the actor must realize how important it is to prepare thoroughly. Some actors come in and say, "I'm ready. I didn't read the sides, but let's just run through it and see what happens." This attitude usually doesn't work. This is a business about working hard. It is about working hard to be brilliant. How else can you shine brighter than your competition?

. . . .
Ellie Kanner
Kanner/Johnson Casting
c/o CSA
606 N. Larchmont Blvd., Suite 4B
Los Angeles, CA 90004
. . . .

DARLENE KAPLAN, CSA

After graduating from Yale, Darlene Kaplan went to New York City to work for the WPA Theatre as literary advisor and casting director. During her tenure there, the theatre produced over a dozen original works that moved on to great acclaim both in the theatre and film including *Nuts, Key Exchange, Little Shop of Horrors* and *Steel Magnolias*.

Kaplan moved to Los Angeles over a decade ago, and went to work as a staff casting director at Universal on such series as *Coach* and *Columbo*.

As an independent casting director, her work on series includes *The Bonnie Hunt Show* and *Ray Bradbury Theatre;* her pilots include *Law and Order, The Antagonists* and *Nineteen.* She has also cast such MOWs as *Gold Rush, We the Jury, Adrift, Vestige of Honor* and *Love Can Be Murder.*

Do you think that moving to New York may help an actor's career?
For young actors, absolutely yes. Go and get your chops. You can freelance with agents, there is a smaller pool of actors and there are fewer casting directors, so you'll be able to get to know everyone more quickly. Plus, there are wonderful, small companies where you can work. You can still walk down the street and

bump into a friend who might say, "I'm doing a reading next week, would you be interested in doing one of the parts?" It's a great place to get experience and build confidence. Some of my friends are working there constantly and they feel no need to move to Los Angeles.

There is also the theory that any move you make brings action. That's why people change agents. Every time you do something different, it wakes people up.

Having said that, I also believe that at a certain point in your career you will have to move to Los Angeles. When I first came here, there was not a single pilot that didn't also cast in New York. Now it has changed. Fewer and fewer Los Angeles-based productions are casting in New York.

How can actors get to meet you?

Most of the actors I see are submitted through agents. But there are a few who submit themselves. One actor recently wrote to me saying he felt he was perfect for a series I was working on. I brought him in and he got a callback.

In general, I pre-read a lot of people for each role. I see the pre-read process as a way to help the right actors get ready for the producers. I feel strongly that my job is to bring in only those actors who are viable candidates for the role. Producers are busy and do not have a lot of time to see everybody.

Do you go to the theatre to find new talent?

Yes, I do. When you're in a play, let me know about it. Even if I can't come, it's important that I know you're doing theatre. You never know what I may be working on.

Recently, on a pilot, I was having a lot of trouble casting one of the roles—we had seen everyone. Out of the blue, an actor sent me a postcard to let me know he was appearing on a television show. I realized we had forgotten him. I brought him and he got the job! Postcards are the best way to communicate with us.

How should an actor prepare for a reading before coming in to see you?

I've seen so many actors second guess what people want. The truth is, people are going to hire you for what you, specifically, bring to the role. You have to know who you are so you can infuse yourself into the character. It's all about how *you* would be in certain situations. If you don't bring to the reading what you would be in the role, and instead bring something different, then we don't see the role or find out who you are.

Do you prefer Method Actors then?

English actors begin from the outside and build inwards. American actors build from the inside out. If you can mesh the two, you can be brilliant. To me, the actor has to get as many different kinds of training as possible. Then, he has to come up with his own method. You can't follow rules. You have to go with your instincts.

And when you're looking for a teacher, don't feel that just because one teacher is great for a friend of yours, that they will be perfect for you. If you don't have trust and a connection with a teacher, if their language is not working for you, there may be another teacher who can reach you. Find the person you connect with.

What works best for you after the actor gets into the room?
It's your fifteen minutes, and whatever works for you is fine with me. If you want to ask questions or talk first that's fine. If you just want to go to work immediately, I respect that too. For a lot of people, they come in prepared and are ready to do the role. They don't want to be diffused. Others want to chat first. This has its disadvantages. I've seen a lot of actors talk themselves out of the audition. They spend so much time talking that by the time they get around to the reading part, the energy is diffused. Just the other day, an actor came in and charmed everyone in the room, but by the time he got to the reading, it went downhill. The minute the reading didn't click the way the meeting did, I watched his face drain and the energy of the room dropped.

Is there any particular audition behavior that annoys you?
The only thing that bothers me is when people come in with an attitude of, "I don't really want to be here." Maybe they're having a bad day. When that happens, I don't mind if agents call and re-schedule. But if you decide to come in anyway, you have to leave your rotten day out in the waiting room. Just like I am not going to sit down and tell you about my difficult day. More and more, producers tell me, "Nobody's worth the baggage." This is especially true for television. On film there's more time and money. But with a series-regular role, for example, you may have to spend seven years with that actor. So you want them to be pleasant and passionate about wanting to do the work.

Other than talent, and fitting the character perfectly, what other qualities are needed to play a series regular role?
You need to have a strong presence. You can be the most brilliant actor in the world but may never be able to carry a single-lead in a television series. A lot of our biggest television stars are also personalities. But, if you have talent and not the presence, it doesn't mean you can't be a lead in an *ensemble* piece. Thank God for shows like *ER* and *NYPD Blue*.

How do you define "presence?"

Some people just walk into the room and have an aura about them that people like. It's not about looks; it's not something you can learn. But I am not saying you have to be born with it. Often, actors gain this weight and presence as they begin to mature. On the other hand, some actors are charismatic when they're young, but as they mature, they lose it. Others, like Gene Hackman, start as young character people who mature into leading men. So you can't think and plan, "I will do such and such in my twenties, and this other thing in my forties." What you have to do instead is to study your craft and your life continuously so you grow in confidence, not only as an actor, but as a human being.

. . . .

Darlene Kaplan
11712 Moorpark Street, Suite #203
Studio City, CA 91604
. . . .

LISA MILLER KATZ, CSA

Lisa Miller Katz grew up in Upland, California and attended Loyola Marymount University, majoring in Communication Arts and Television Production. Having acted in high school, Katz thought briefly about pursuing an acting career, but one visit to the drama society at Loyola convinced her that she didn't have the required pluck. Turning her concentration to television, she learned all facets of television production and interned in several areas of the entertainment

business. A friend of a friend put her in touch with Peter Golden, who was about to head up the casting department of Grant Tinker's new production company, GTG. Golden was looking for an assistant, and although Katz had no experience with casting, Golden hired her along with Cheryl Bayer. They worked at GTG for about two and a half years before the company closed its doors. When Golden moved to Stephen J. Cannell as vice president of casting, he made Katz his associate. While they were there, they did a couple of MOWs, the last season of *Wise Guy,* and a pilot called *The Hundred Lives of Black Joe Savage.* When it went to series, Katz cast the episodes. After one year at Cannell, she felt ready to move on. Cheryl Bayer had gone out independently so she hired Katz to be her associate, and together they cast *Herman's Head, Sibs, A Different World* and *Good Advice,* as well as the feature film *Son-in-Law* with Pauly Shore. Katz then took a job with Francine Maisler for a couple of months, assisting with the casting of the feature *The Usual Suspects.* Eventually, Katz was hired as casting director for *The Fresh Prince of Bel-Air* for its final two seasons. Katz has gone on to cast the pilots *The Last Frontier, Baker Shift* and *Veronica's Video* and the pilots and series *Space: Above and Beyond, Hang Time* and her current projects, the current hit series *Everybody Loves Raymond* and its spin-off, *King of Queens.*

During an audition, what are some of your likes and dislikes?
What strikes me most, when I meet an actor for the first time, is a sense of fun about them. A person who comes in smiling with a lot of energy gives me the feeling that we are going to have a good time. People who take it all too seriously and bring in this weight with them really affect the audition. I know that towards the end of pilot season, actors can get really burned out, what with having lots of auditions and material changing all the time. So it's really easy to lose your sense of humor. I had a moment with an actor on *Baker Shift*, a pilot I was casting. He came in to read and we just got off on the wrong foot. He said, "Well, maybe I should just leave," and I said, "Okay. Fine. Goodbye." We were both at fault and didn't handle it properly. Everyone was in a bad temper, I was running very late, the phone was ringing, I had to talk to a producer, there was a crisis on *Raymond* and I was in the middle of a lot of other things. So he had literally just left when I picked up the phone and called his agent and apologized and asked if we could try it again in a couple of days. I had been really excited to meet this actor, his agent had talked him up, and I was really intrigued by his résumé. I want actors to be great—I want every actor that walks through the door to be the one to hire. When he came back to read for me, we both had a good laugh about our bad day, and then he gave a great reading.

Also, it's important to be perfectly honest about your availability for projects. If you think you may be out of town when the project shoots, tell me beforehand, or have your agent tell me. And if you book the job, are you willing to change your plans? It is frustrating for me to have to tell producers that they can't have the actor they want and that someone we believed was available, really isn't.

How does an actor handle the rather delicate situation of passing on "under-fives" in hopes they can be considered for larger roles?
If you have done roles like that before and are no longer interested, have your

agent pass on your behalf. Have your agent say that you are really trying to focus on the bigger roles. Those small roles are sometimes the hardest to cast. The person who walks in the room and says, "Here's your pizza," is almost harder to cast than a guest lead. The person must be really interesting and on a half-hour show, you hope that when the actor comes in and delivers the pizza, they get a laugh. It's a rare moment when they tell me that there are too many laughs in the show. When I did *Space: Above and Beyond,* there was a small role of a commander on the spaceship. It was for three days and I only had three day's salary to offer. I brought in an actor I had really liked for a long time, and almost as soon as he walked in the room, they hired him. Within a couple of episodes his character became recurring and if the show had gone to a second year, he would have been a series regular. So you never know what a small part will lead to. There are so many actors out there who need the work; if someone passes, I know a hundred other actors who need the money and the work.

Movie stars are now doing television, so everyone else is doing smaller roles. This effects the way I work too. Ninety-nine percent of the shows I cast pay scale plus 10. My budget on *Raymond* is barely enough to pay three guest leads. And they are always after me to stunt cast. Ray plays a sportswriter on the show, so they are always saying, "Wouldn't it be great if he bumped into Barry Bonds or Kristy Yamaguchi." I love this show and am so proud of it, but that is the most difficult part of my job. It's great when I actually have a week when I can sink my teeth into casting a couple of good roles as opposed to booking sports celebrities.

Do you have any final advice for actors?

If you are just starting out in this business, I want you to be studying and flexing those muscles every chance you get. Do as much theatre as you can, get yourself out there so people can see you. I go to as much theatre as I can when I am not working. I know the actors who do a lot of theatre. I read the reviews. I also want you to have a picture that is an actual representation of what you look like today, not three years ago. So many actors in this town have a very airbrushed, fake and dishonest picture. If I respond to something in your picture, I want that person to walk into my office. I also think it's important to find an agent you feel confident with. If you don't think you're going out enough, you need to be able to talk with your agent and find out why they are not sending you. A lot of actors treat their agents very gingerly—they are so afraid they are going to lose them. There are agents in this town who think by just submitting your picture that their job is done. A thousand people can submit pictures to me, but it's the agents who pick up the phone to say, "Lisa, do you know who you should see for this part?" that I respond to. It's great when they call me the morning of the breakdown to pitch someone. Then there are the agents who call me three or four days later looking for appointments and the role was actually cast two days before. I open every submission and yes, I go through them, but it's really great when an agent does their job by calling me and pitching actors they feel passionate about.

Come in having done your homework. I can smell a cold reading a mile away. I really believe auditioning is an actor's job and the reward is getting the part. I am always frustrated by people who fly by the seat of their pants, or think charm and looks can compensate for lack of preparedness. And I think it's really important if you are auditioning for episodic television to make sure you see the show at least once. I have had actors who have come into my office and I'll say, "Have you seen the show?" and they'll say, "No, I don't watch TV," as if TV is beneath them. That's very frustrating to me.

And lastly, whether it's about casting or production or acting, life is too short for it to be about only one thing. Actors are the gutsiest people I know. I admire anyone who has the drive and the desire to do this. However, I think an actor needs to have balance in his life, just as casting directors and producers need to have balance in their lives. If you are doing something twelve to fourteen hours a day, and that's all you do, then your life will suffer. Do good work in this business but balance it with a real life.

· · · · · · · · · · · · · · · · · · ·

Lisa Miller Katz
Warner Bros.
4000 Warner Blvd., Building 131
Burbank, CA 91522
· · · · · · · · · · · · · · · · · · ·

Eileen Mack Knight, csa

Eileen Mack Knight returned to her first love, the world of theatre, after working as a psychiatric head nurse at Bellevue in New York for five years. After a stint as a receptionist to Mary Goldberg, head of casting at the Public Theatre in New York, she became an assistant to Juliet Taylor, who was then running Marion Dougherty and Associates Casting. The first film she was involved with was *Annie Hall*. She then moved to Los Angeles and worked as an assistant to Reuben

Cannon while learning the business of casting for television. She subsequently put her television casting knowledge to good use—first at Lorimar, then at MTM, and currently as an independent.

A nominee for six Artios Awards, Knight won for her outstanding work on the animated feature *Bebe's Kids*. Her other feature work includes *Vampire in Brooklyn, The Great White Hype, New Jack City, House Party* and many more. Her MOWs include *The Cherokee Kid, Perry Mason Returns* and *The Women of Brewster Place*. She's also done extensive work on both pilots and series, including *413 Hope Street, Damon, Happily Ever After, Flamingo Road, Martin* and *Mr. President*, as well as the pilot for *Matlock*. Her work on series includes such hits as *Lou Grant*, *Night Court* and *Mad About You*.

Reuben Cannon is one of the best casting mentors in town. What would you say you learned from him?

When I first got to Los Angeles, there was no Breakdown Services. Agents used to come in, drop off their submissions and sell their clients to the casting director. It was a revolving door, and you got to see who you talked to. In New York, I had great telephone relationships with people but didn't meet them personally. In Los Angeles, working for Reuben, I learned how to do the business face to face. Reuben also taught me about cold readings. I learned to glean, from that five-minute read, the essential things I needed to know and how to tap into my instincts about actors in a short span of time. Everything moves very quickly in television; you have to be able to make snap decisions about an actor's work that prove to be right.

What can casting directors do to make the audition process less traumatic?

It's good to remember that the actor-casting director relationship is symbiotic. When you do your best in front of the producers, we look good, too. To get the best work from actors, we have to make them feel as comfortable as possible. When someone comes in to read for me, I first ask them where they are from. No matter how short a time I have, I like to know a little about the person sitting across from me. After all, a cold reading is just that—cold. All I can glean from the cold reading is what types of role you can play. I also get to know a little about your instincts. So, if you come in to read for a part for which you are not right, I don't make a judgment on your acting ability. I am only focused on whether you are right for the role. To me, this alleviates the trauma of auditioning.

Are there specific things that an actor does in the audition that annoy you?

It bugs me when the actor comes in with a picture in one hand, a résumé in the other and asks for a stapler. Of course, this is a minor thing, but why aren't you prepared?

But what I really don't like is when the actor comes in and starts a long discussion about the part. Some of it can meander into areas that have no direct bearing on the character. Neither the pre-read, nor the producer's session, is the best place to go into involved discussions. Do your homework and be brief with your questions. If you do have questions about the character, then call your agent or my assistant.

In addition, when you are asked to come in to read for a specific role, don't insist on reading for other roles in the script. And when the casting director says, "No," don't go in and ask the producers to read for the other parts!

If an actor feels they have given a bad audition, is it appropriate to ask if they can do it again?

It's your prerogative to ask that question. If you thought the reading went badly in the producer's session, ask the casting director if you can do it again. But wait until you are outside in the lobby. Last week an actress came in, picked up the sides and did the audition without any preparation. She didn't feel good about her reading and asked to do it again. She said, "It doesn't matter to me whether I get the part or not. I just have to do it again." We had a whole afternoon of auditions left, so I asked her to come back the next day. She did and got the role.

What did she do differently the next day?

She got a chance to study the material. But this was a case where I already knew that she was very right for the role. I was also familiar with her work, and felt that she didn't do her best work the first time around. Of course I asked the producers if it was okay for her to come back.

On many occasions actors are asked to audition at the very last minute, just like this actress was. That doesn't seem to be fair to the actor.

I am always casting shows that are shot immediately. Some actors love those spontaneous situations. They enjoy the challenge of creating a role very quickly. But if you need more time, it's your decision whether to go ahead with it or turn it down. I don't offer advice one way or another, except to say, "This is the situation, you make the decision." It is the actor's responsibility to choose. You have to use your instincts.

Do you meet with actors who submit unsolicited pictures and résumés?

I look at every résumé. It's a compulsion on my part. And I guess I am still willing to meet actors who look interesting. I get to do a variety of projects and must therefore keep in close touch with the pulse of new and interesting actors. The picture is important, but more than likely, the résumé is the deciding factor. I respond positively to theatre credits and to graduates from good acting schools.

What tips would you give actors to make them feel more empowered when they come in to read for you?

You just have to be who you are. There is no other way to be in this business. You can't compromise yourself.

The other day an actor, whose work I love, came in to read. Though he is well known and has been a regular on a series, he understood that he still has to audition for people who don't know his work. Although he had prepared for the audition, when it didn't go as well as he thought it should, he stopped and said, "You know what, this isn't going well. I don't want to continue and waste your time." He wasn't accustomed to auditioning. Instead of trying to fumble his way through, he stopped the audition. By doing that, in my opinion, he remained true to who he was. I respect that.

Being true to yourself makes everybody's life easier. Some actors walk in with an acquired attitude that does not ring true. They arbitrarily decide a particular way they want to conduct an interview. For example, even if naturally they are far from being assertive, they decide to act as such. I know it is a defense mechanism. But it does not serve any real purpose. It's best to be yourself and let the chips fall where they may. You know why? I firmly believe that in life everything happens the way it is supposed to. If you go in knowing who you are, you'll have no regrets, no matter what happens in that room. You'll walk out the door knowing you were true to yourself.

. . . .
Eileen Mack Knight
12031 Ventura Blvd., Suite #3
Studio City, CA 91604
. . . .

WENDY KURTZMAN

Wendy Kurtzman received a degree in Theatre from UCLA and worked as an actress in musicals before joining the casting offices of Reuben Cannon as an intern. After working there for two days, she was hired full-time. Her first project as an independent casting director was the television MOW *God Bless the Child* for ABC. Soon after, she was hired by the NBC Network to serve as manager of casting for drama, a position she held from 1987 to 1990. Since then, her work for television includes the mini-series *JFK: Reckless Youth* and *A Woman of Independent Means* with Sally Field (Emmy nomination in casting), among others. She's also done two dozen or so MOWs, among them *Wildflower* and *Lucky Day* (Artios nominations for both), *Sudie and Simpson* and *Twisted Desire*. Her work on features include the mega-hit *Independence Day*, *Stigmata*, *Dangerous Beauty*, *Stephen King's Sleepwalkers*, *Carried Away* with Dennis Hopper, and *Digging to China* starring Kevin Bacon and Mary Stuart Masterson, directed by Timothy Hutton.

How would you define a good casting director?
A good casting director has the talent to take the director's vision of the script and, by incorporating his or her own vision into it, bring a whole new life to the project. The casting director can do this through provocative and unorthodox casting, through the changing of gender or race of the role as written, and generally by going against the grain. Even when these new choices don't pan out, this process helps the director acquire a new perspective towards the role in question.

Do you think training at a college is necessary for a successful acting career?
When I look back at my experience in college, I feel that the UC system wasn't the best place to learn about acting. They get you involved in so many areas of the theatre, building sets, costumes and make-up, etc., when all you want to do

is act and learn the business. All acting schools should teach the actor about the business side of acting (i.e., what agents do, what casting directors do, what producers do, etc.). As an actor, I would have learned more about the real world by interning at a casting office. The university made me well-rounded and gave me a degree to face the world, but it was up to me to find the ropes.

What qualities in actors immediately spark your interest when they enter your office?

The actors who immediately attract attention are those who have something especially appealing about them. Some are strange and intriguing. Some have a great sense of humor or charm. Case in point is Brad Pitt. In the beginning of his career, when he auditioned for me, his charisma and appeal were obvious as soon as he walked in. First of all, he was gorgeous. You couldn't take your eyes off him. And second, he was genuine. Most casting people can really sense when an actor is genuine and when he is not. And when he is, it's a very attractive quality.

Are the qualities needed for television success the same as those for film?

The television actor has to have a certain appealing look. Otherwise viewers will not invite them to come into their homes every week. When you look carefully, you'll see that nobody on television is really bad looking. You find more "character" actors in comedy. In film however, you have the freedom to cast a closer reality to the real world.

Can you talk about the casting of the beautiful mini-series *A Woman of Independent Means*, and about its director?

It had a huge cast which was put together here and in Texas where it was shot. Other than Sally Field, who was already attached to the project, I put together the core leading players such as Ron Silver, Brenda Fricker, Charles Durning and the others, while the rest of the cast came from Texas. Most MOWs and mini-series use local talent when they shoot out of town. As for its director, Robert Greenwald comes from the theatre and genuinely loves actors and enjoys conversing with them. He has a way about him that puts actors at ease. I've never had any feedback from an actor who did not enjoy the process of auditioning for Robert.

Did you enjoy casting the big canvas of *Independence Day*?

Yes! The script was one of the most fun scripts I had ever read. It was like an E-ticket ride at Disneyland. As soon as I read it, I wanted to cast it. It was a huge job. We worked on it for four months and filled over a hundred and twenty speaking roles.

What are your likes and dislikes regarding auditioning?
I don't have a rule book on audition "dos and don'ts" but there are a few things to think about. One is, you should never come in if you are not prepared. It's annoying when actors come in and they have no idea what their character is about, what they are supposed to be doing, and what they are supposed to be saying in the context of the rest of the scene. Before you come in, know what the project is about, who the character is, how the scene or scenes you're doing fit in with the rest of the movie, then make a committed choice.

Another thing the actor should avoid is coming too close to the face of the casting director during a scene, even if the directions require it. If you come really close, how is a casting director supposed to physically see what you are doing? Always, keep a bit of a cushion between the two of you.

During callbacks, I think the actor should hold small-talk with the producers and director to a minimum. It's fine for a little bit, and often the casting director facilitates that. But at other times, you may keep on talking, and what may have been interesting about you when you first walked in, starts getting less and less interesting the more and more you talk. It's best to come in ready to do the work and leave them wanting more.

What would entice you to go to the theatre?
I go to a lot of theatre. If I could make a living casting for theatre, I would do it. That's what I grew up knowing. When in New York, I try to see as many shows as possible. Eating and then going to the theatre is my favorite thing to do in New York. In Los Angeles, I go to the theatre more as a learning experience than for the pure enjoyment of it. If I look at a cast list and see that I know all the actors, I don't really feel that I need to go and see their work on stage. But if I see that a play got very good reviews and I don't know the actors in it, then I go to find out about them. I also go when a star is doing a play with a cast of unknowns. Then it becomes a treat to see that star and to also find out about the others.

How can actors get to meet you?
We deal through agents and managers. And most actors who have some credits usually have representation. Another way to connect with casting directors is to join one of the better waiver theatres around town. I do go to the theatres with good reputations regularly and so do many casting directors.

What's the toughest part of the audition process? Any words of advice?
Auditioning for smaller roles is tough. You have to put everything you are and can do into the span of two lines. It's like asking someone: "Tell me everything about yourself using only two sentences." And some actors can't put in the subtleties and nuances and they fall flat or overact. You have to make it interesting somehow and that takes real talent. I once auditioned an actor for a role of a technician and before he spoke, he sat down and mimed working on a panel. That gave weight and life to his few lines. There is an art to it. A couple of times I've had actors come in for a few lines and they were a little embarrassed. I knew from the start I'd have a problem with them. The role should never be beneath you. If it is, don't come in. You have to bring the same YOU to whatever you are doing.

. . . .
Wendy Kurtzman
10536 Culver Blvd., Suite E
Culver City, CA 90232
. . . .

JASON LA PADURA, CSA AND NATALIE HART, CSA

Asked which coast would be better for a young actor to launch a career, casting director Jason La Padura responded, "New York would definitely be an easier place to start. There are more opportunities for open calls there, and the casting directors do go to many of the showcases." However, according to his partner (and sister) Natalie Hart, that decision, "would depend on whether the actor would rather play Laertes on stage

Jason La Padura (l) and Natalie Hart (r)

or a recurring role for three weeks on a sitcom in Los Angeles."

Before becoming partners, Jason La Padura was an actor and stage manager, while Natalie Hart worked in the management area of rock and roll. Together, they have cast over one-hundred and fifty stage productions and about six dozen film and television projects. Their theatre work includes Broadway productions of *Prelude to a Kiss* and the Tony Award-winning musical, *Big River*. Their regional theatre work includes assignments for The Guthrie, The Arena Stage, Hartford Stage Company, and the La Jolla Playhouse.

For television, they have cast *Muddling Through, Wiseguy* (New York casting), *Empty Nest, 21 Jump Street, War of the Worlds* and the pilots *The Expert* and *Buddy Farrow*. They were nominated for Artios Awards for TNT's *The Good Old Boys* and the Academy Award nominated, Golden Globe winning *Longtime Companion*. Other TV, mini-series and film projects include *Toothless, Prelude to a Kiss, Internal Affairs, For Love and Glory, Tyson* and *Ruby Ridge*.

Your offices are located within the Edgar Scherick Company. Do you cast for him primarily, or are you independent?

LA PADURA: We are independent but have a housekeeping deal here. That is, though we cast all Edgar Scherick's projects, we also work for many other producers. In addition, he has given us the opportunity to bring new ideas to him for development.

HART: Another thing we do here is to generate lists for Edgar before he goes in to the networks or studios to make a pitch. We act as casting consultants.

But what we enjoy most is being casting directors. Casting is like being Santa Claus. It's a wonderful feeling to be creative, to give actors jobs, and to help them move up in their careers.

You know the theatrical scene on both coasts. How do they compare?

HART: Unlike New York, when I go out to the smaller theatres here, I rarely run into anybody I know from the business.

LA PADURA: Los Angeles is a more event-oriented place. People will go to *Angels in America* or *Master Class*—but how many of them went to see *Blade to the Heat* at the Taper?

In contrast, Stanley Sobel, my former partner, once saw an actress in a play in New York at the small 18th Street Theatre and brought her in to meet the people at Witt-Thomas. They put her in three television projects.

Do you see many new people getting breaks here in Los Angeles?

HART: It's so hard for unknowns to get guest-starring roles here, unless you convince the producers, who sometimes may not be so sure of their own power to take a chance. Similarly, when you hand a photo to a director and he doesn't see any credits on the back, he's definitely going to be hesitant. On the other hand, there are people like director Fred Walton who want to discover new talent all the time.

What would you do to help your career it you were actors?

HART: Most of my buddies are actors, and I keep telling them that they have to generate their own momentum. You have to do something yourself so that people take notice. Look at John Leguizamo who did his one-man shows, *Spic-O-Rama*, *Mambo Mouth* and *Freak*; look at Camryn Manheim who did *I'm Fat, Get Over it!* and now has an Emmy for *The Practice*.

LA PADURA: Our own former intern, Jeff Sumner, has made a splash by creating the "Pam Teflon" character. When he first came out here, he couldn't get any work and so became a Tupperware salesperson. His mother told him to develop a character when selling these things. He came up with this character who dresses up in drag, and became the biggest Tupperware salesman in the West. He's now been featured in Los Angeles Times Magazine, and recently was on Public Radio. He is out there!

HART: There's also the story of the actress Claudia Shear, who was at the end of her rope. She was heavy, charactery, was never taken seriously, and couldn't even get an agent. Then, through the suggestion of a friend, she sat down and wrote her experiences in the form of a monologue. The play, *Blown Sideways Through Life*, was first given a reading, and was produced soon after. Within three weeks of the show's run, she was signed by ICM!

LA PADURA: Hers is a phenomenal story, a fairy tale. Her show has now been broadcast on PBS.

Other than one-person shows, do you recommend actors mount full-scale productions?

HART: Definitely, provided that they are not vanity productions. The actor who puts up the money shouldn't be the only one showcased. The whole cast has to be shown in a good light. The play's the thing, not the producer/actor's vanity.

The award-winning film, *Longtime Companion*, had an excellent ensemble of actors in it; can you talk about the casting of that project?

LA PADURA: We had a very hard time casting that film. Though we got Bruce Davison early on—his was the first name on the first list I made—every agency we approached found an excuse for their actors not to do it. We heard absurd excuses like, "A directors' strike is being threatened, so we have to wait." Or, "Our actor is coming out of a bad relationship and can't focus on a new project."

HART: After working on it for six months, we only had Patrick Cassidy and Alec Baldwin but when *The Hunt for Red October* came up, Baldwin had to drop out to do that, of course. Griffin Dunne also wanted to do it, but another project of his was green-lighted.

Why were the agents all so reluctant for their clients?

LA PADURA: This was the first time AIDS was going to be dealt with in a mainstream film. The climate has, of course, changed since. But in 1989 it wasn't cool. Not only was the film about gay characters, but also about gays who were dying of this disease.

HART: At the time, agents were obviously afraid that their clients wouldn't get work because of it.

LA PADURA: Luckily, because of our knowledge of the regional theatre scene, we finally managed to get terrific actors. One day, I got a piece of mail from The Hartford Stage Company, and there was Mark Lamos' picture in it. We immediately thought that he would be great as Sean, one of the leads. I called and asked if he would be interested. He was. But he couldn't leave town. He was (and still is) the artistic director for The Hartford Stage Company. So we all went there to read him and he got the part.

Then you might not have thought of him if you hadn't seen his picture?

HART: I don't know. But I do think actors should definitely send cards to casting directors to remind them what they're up to. Often we may forget actors whose work we admire and who may just be perfect for a role we are casting.

Any final advice to actors?

HART: The most intimidating part of the auditioning process is going into a room and facing a bunch of strangers. But if the actor keeps in mind that the people sitting on the other side of the room are all rooting for him to do well, his anxiety may disappear. We want your reading to work out as much as you do. We know this has been said before, but still actors don't seem to understand the importance of this fact.

LA PADURA: So remember it when you enter a room next time. Other than that, try to be honest about everything; about your résumé, your capabilities and your experience, etc. More than anything else, what we look for in a performance is sheer honesty and integrity. Do that, and the rest will take care of itself.

. . . .

Jason La Padura and Natalie Hart
La Padura/Hart Casting
1950 Sawtelle Blvd., Suite 282
Los Angeles, CA 90025.

. . . .

RUTH LAMBERT, CSA

The time between a film's casting and its release can sometimes be long. The films cast by Ruth Lambert probably set some sort of record. As head of casting, feature animation at Disney, where films take years to produce, the most recent project she cast will be released in 2001. In fact, of the nine films she's cast over the four years she's been there, more than half have yet to be released.

Her stellar résumé boasts *Pocahontas* (for which she won an Artios Award), *The Hunchback of Notre Dame* (another Artios), *Hercules, Mulan, Kingdom of the Sun, A Bug's Life, Tarzan, Dinosaur* and *Atlantis.*

How long does it take to produce a Disney animated feature?
Once they actually start production, about three years.

How long to cast?
Practically all three years. As the animators work, things constantly change. Characters change or, if they're not working, they're replaced. I usually have about six months to do the initial casting, and after that, if they've added a character or changed a character, it can go on for a few additional months. But they can't animate without the voices, so once they start, most of my work is done.

What's the casting process on one of your projects like?

Well, on *A Bug's Life*, for example, I met with the director, John Lassetter, and he gave me the characters and an idea of who he sort of had in mind. I sat with him, the producers, and story people with big, fat shopping lists of actors. We whittled the lists down and then I had them get material together for each character. There was no script yet, so they had to write sides. They didn't even know how big the parts were going to be, so they just wrote material that would help the actors—little monologues and scenes. And they sent me artwork so I could send character sketches to the actor along with the sides. That really helps the actors see where the voices are coming from.

And everybody who reads is pretty much a star?

On *A Bug's Life*, yes, but that's not true of all of our movies. This one has a pretty starry cast: Phyllis Diller, Dave Foley, Julia Louis-Dreyfus, Bonnie Hunt, Roddy McDowall, Kevin Spacey, Edie McClurg and Denis Leary, among others. At one point in auditions, we had Rosemary Harris, Faith Prince, Deborah Rush and Doris Belack all sitting in the waiting room at once. It was pretty amazing.

And the stars audition?

Just like everybody else. Sometimes, if it's someone we really want, we might pitch the project to them a little, but it's the same process. And we've had really incredible people audition. Actors like Carol Burnett and James Woods came in because they were really into doing an animated project. My concern is to try to stagger their auditions. I never like to have people sitting in the lobby, surrounded by a million other people. I feel uncomfortable about that. I feel that people should be treated kindly, stars and otherwise.

What's the process at the audition?

It's exactly the way you audition for a live-action feature or TV show: You get your material, you come in, you sign in, someone comes and gets you, you get taken to a room, you read with me. The only difference is that you read into a microphone instead of a camera. Sometimes it's in a booth, depending on what the directors are most comfortable with. If the project is a musical, you'll sing first and then read. We have you sing the actual music or, if it's not written yet, something similar which is appropriate. You read for me or my associate, Mary Hidalgo. Callbacks work exactly the same way, except that there are directors and a producer there.

What can be hard for the actors is that, because it's animation, the directors and producer tend to put their heads down or turn away. They want to just listen, and it can be confusing for the actors unless they're warned. When you read and you look up from your script and you see producers with their heads on the table, your ego automatically comes into play. It's easy to think that they hate you or that they're not paying attention. Actors sort of panic and I just have to keep them focused on reading with me.

I've heard they often like actors who physically resemble their characters in animation. Why is that?

I don't know. It can be weird. During *Hunchback*, there were some really good-looking guys who came in to read for Quasimodo, and one of the directors said, "Look at them! They can't be Quasimodo!" Sometimes they can't get past the actor's physicality, even though it's voice-over. You sometimes have to give up. Of course, Tom Hulce did the role, and he's very nice-looking. But in general, the actor and the character are very similar. Once the actor has been cast, we videotape them as they record. The animators use that as guidance and that's why the characters in the finished film can ultimately end up looking quite a bit like the actor who voiced them.

Is looping ever done at Disney?

No, never. Everything is recorded first and then animated. Everything. We might add some words or sounds at the end, but that's it. The voice always comes first and the animators work from the voices. All animation in this country is done that way. It's not like in *Mrs. Doubtfire* where Robin Williams looped into that little bird at the beginning of the movie. That just never happens.

I guess one of the nice things about working in animation, for the actor, is that you don't have to worry about how you look. You get to come in, sit down, and do the work.

Yes, but you need *a lot* of energy. More than for live-action, because you can't rely on your face and body. It's also hard because the actors usually record alone. They'll have readers perform the other lines, so the actor isn't working in a vacuum, but the actor will be the only one being recorded. Sometimes, we'll set up two booths and have actors read together because, in something like a love scene, it really helps the actors to have each other. But mostly it's done separately. For purely technical reasons, it's just better to have each actor on a separate, clean voice track.

We give a lot of breaks and we only work people for four or five hours at a time, which is plenty. It's really intensive work. You have a microphone and there are a bunch of people in a booth talking to you. You get through a sequence and then you stop and take a break. They usually do a whole page—four or five lines—again and again, and they keep adjusting and directing. And then they go back and hit each line individually. It seems easy—until you're there in front of the microphone. Plus, we ask people to ad-lib, if they're comfortable doing that, and that's really hard work. That's really encouraged here.

Why?
It helps the character. It also brings some of the actor to the role. We tend to hire people for who they are, not because they can do funny voices or anything like that. For the most part, we really just want people to be themselves. We want them to use their own voice, bring their own personality, and paint a picture for the animator.

And a lot of times, what looks good on the page doesn't necessarily read well out of a mouth. So we encourage people to come in and say, "This is hard to say," or, "If I switch these words around, would that bother you?" When James Woods did *Hercules*, he came in to the audition and ad-libbed the entire thing. I had to wait for him to stop talking to know it was my turn. But if you can't ad-lib, you can't, and that's also fine.

How do you find people when you're not looking for a name?
We put out a breakdown, we pre-read. I look at pictures.

Pictures?
Yes, I like getting pictures. It's really helpful to see someone and get a sense of age and energy. Plus, if we hire that person, the picture ends up with the animator, who uses it. And sometimes I can't remember if I've met someone unless I've seen their picture. The résumé also tells me a lot.

Can people send you voice-over tapes?
Yes, but not commercial tapes. I don't care if you can sell a car. I'd rather hear people reading a poem or telling a kids' story, not longer than three minutes. Stories are worth listening to, whereas a voice-over tape is usually commercial. It's not the sort of acting that we do here. We're much more natural and we like people being themselves. If you're sending a tape, just use your own voice—don't do funny voices.

If people don't have professional tapes, can they send you something they make at home?

Yes, it doesn't have to be professional. Don't spend a lot of money to make a tape.

Any final tips?

The best career advice I can give to actors is, like at any audition, be prepared. Be willing to take direction in a room and be prepared to ask any questions you want to ask. Don't be afraid. Everyone here is so nice, there's no reason not to ask. It's always better to feel silly and ask a question than not to. There isn't always a second chance, and you don't want to walk out wishing you had done something about your question.

. . . .

Ruth Lambert
Head of Casting, Feature Animation
Disney Studios
500 S. Buena Vista Street
Burbank, CA 91521
. . . .

JOHN LEVEY, CSA

John Levey was born in New York City to a scientist (indeed, one of the first women to receive a Ph.D. in the hard sciences from Columbia) and a *New York Times* columnist (a tradition his brother carries on today with a column in the *Washington Post*—providing Levey with what he jokingly calls, "a suspicious relationship with the press"). He started going to the theatre at a fairly young age when his mother forced him to stop playing basketball and sent him to shows

instead. It wasn't long before theatre was the preferred pastime. He began his career as a director, first as a directing fellow at the Center Theatre Group in Los Angeles where he assisted the late, great director José Quintero. While there he helped produce the Taper Literary Cafe at the Itchey Foote Restaurant and directed the Taper Too productions of *Estonia You Fall* and *Cakewalk*. His other directorial work includes *Shades* at South Coast Rep. and *The Dining Room* at the Coronet Theatre. His most notable television casting work includes *China Beach*, *Head of the Class*, *Growing Pains*, the MOWs *Promises to Keep*, *Babe Ruth*, and now, the critically acclaimed *ER* for which both he and Barbara Miller, the senior vice president of casting at Warner Bros., have won two

Emmys and four Artios Awards. Levey was recently named vice president of talent and casting at Warner Bros.

Did you ever want to be an actor?

No, I didn't want to act. I like attention but I don't crave it. I have ambition but it's not at the center of my life. I like to participate rather than be at the center. Casting is being part of the storytelling which I love. That whole aspect of communication is enormously fascinating to me and now, unlike the storytelling of previous generations, you don't have to be the storyteller to participate.

In television, casting is the rehearsal process, casting is the tone meeting, casting is where the director, writer and producer come together about what the quality of the scene ought to be. You can see and like five different actors for a role and each is going to bring more of something than the others. So you ask yourself, "What's at the center of the scene? What do you need to tell the story?"

And you must keep in mind that that story is almost always about the series regular. The guest is there to feed the story about the star. Even if you've got a bravura, virtuoso kind of a part, the scene is really about the regular because that's whose life we're tracking. That little part of you that's you the actor, not you the character, has to think about shining a light on the star. In a comedy, you may have your own jokes but you're probably there to set up the jokes for the star. The stories we're telling on *ER* are the stories of the nine series regulars.

When I was at the Taper, I had the opportunity to work with Steven Berkoff, José Quintero, John Madden, Gordon Davidson and lots of talented and wonderful, charismatic people. It crystallized my feeling that the key to great storytelling is what you can freely, deeply, authentically bring of yourself to the work—your own charismatic nature, the things that are your strengths and your power base. If you can bring that into your task—and probably this is true in the selling of aluminum siding or any other job but certainly in the telling of human stories—then you have something. If you can't bring your own powerful self into the work then you're probably not going to be a great artist.

What do you think makes you such a good casting director?

I grew up surrounded by talent. Later, I had to learn the rules, regulations and procedures. But being around talent was never intimidating to me. I understand the writer, I understand the director, I understand the actor. I understand their processes and their needs; I can foster communication between these groups that don't often understand each other even though they're so intrinsically tied. Directors are so visual and actors are so instinctively emotional and writers are so cerebral. When they combine in a beautiful way, you've got the whole deal. The best part of the work that I do on *ER* isn't the result (although I'm very proud of the result), it's the environment the actors get to audition in. An actor just sent me a thank you note saying that I made it easy for him and allowed him the opportunity to stop thinking about being in a room auditioning and to commit to the work. If I do anything that I'm really proud of, it's that I create an environment for actors to do their best.

What is your advice to actors who have a hard time relaxing into that environment?

The solution to everything is do your work. If you're looking in the hallway and thinking, "She's prettier than I am," or, "It calls for a bald guy and I have more hair," your goose is cooked. Come in, play the scene. Do what you intend. Make a choice, execute your choice and go on with the rest of your day. If you end up punching the steering wheel saying, "Why did I do that?" or, "Why didn't I do that?" then you're watching yourself. Just come in and take a big swing at the ball. It lands where it lands, and go on with your day. How do you cope with your insecurity about a pimple they may or may not notice? Do the work. You can't control the other stuff but you can control the work.

It's about authenticity. That's what I try to bring to my work and the environment I try to create for actors and that's what I expect from actors—that they are going to bring authenticity, not falseness of any kind. No acting, please. Being. If I do anything to help actors achieve that, it's my own authenticity. I'm myself, I fool around, I talk about my problems.

How can an actor get to meet you?

I don't know. I just know when someone hits my receptivity, they hit. Just yesterday we put out a breakdown. I went through enough pictures to fill six U.S. mailboxes. I found one or two who I will bring in and who may be among the six or seven people I bring to the producers for each role. I'm sure it's not fair and I'm sure I'm missing out on a lot of great people, particularly young kids who haven't yet landed.

When I first started working with Barbara Claman many years ago, she said, "I've got a working knowledge of 10,000 actors." I didn't know how that was possible. And now I know. I've been casting for more than a dozen years and I've seen a helluva lot of people. I can't always remember my children's birthdays but I can remember all those people.

I also do go to the theatre, although more and more I go to see somebody who I already know and like. In so doing I will, of course, see the other people. I went to see an old friend in something and there were other people in it who were wonderful. I brought them in and one ended up on the show. I go to the Taper more often than I go to waiver theatre because I like to be a regular guy and just be entertained. I don't like it when people know that I'm there. I get a great many invitations and I go when I can. My assistant, Cheryl, is very diligent and goes to a lot of stuff. I also do look at tapes although I don't accept unsolicited tapes under any circumstances. I send them back, unwatched.

The next thing I want to ask . . .
Do the work. That should be the answer to every question you ask me.

A lot of actors *are* doing their work.
Not all of them are. I think that actors are a singularly lazy group. A lot of them rely on how cute or funny or charming they are. Most of them don't do their work even if they're in class. They must learn to bring their authentic selves to their work. Many of the actors I know are strategizing and hiding—relying on tricks they've had success with in the past and pretending to be the people they're supposed to be inhabiting. That's not doing your work, that's relying on how great your eyes are, how sharp your smile is, how great you look in fashionable clothes. That's not the answer. Those are all wonderful attributes but drawing from the well of the truth and exploring how to get more and more of your authentic self into your work is doing the work. Hiding behind the various successful masks that you've used in the past isn't doing the work, it's faking people out. Most actors fake people out.

What they really need to do is artistically uncover. Gary Shandling was recently talking about the value of terror and harnessing that terror instead of trying to hide it. Terror can overwhelm your ability, but if you can harness your terror then you have an engine. Find a way to roll with what you actually are instead of trying to hide it. After all, if an actor doesn't invest himself, what else does he have? A piano player has eighty-eight keys and each key has its sound and will always have it. As an actor, you are the instrument and the player and you've got to find where G is. All you have is your own uniqueness. If you try to homogenize yourself, you're diluting your uniqueness. If you try to guess what they want and become that, you're strategizing and you're not in the moment. All you can do is what you can do. And that's not a limitation. Your responsibility is to become as interesting a person as you can. If you're going to tell human stories, be as dimensional a human being as you can. Actors spend far too much time at the gym. While it's nice to have a good body, actors should be as interested in developing themselves spiritually, emotionally and intellectually as they do physically. They tend to think that grooming, attire and body—the physical self—is the true self. Truth is exploring your own humanity. Most of us spend time with people who are mirror images of ourselves and it can be pretty boring. It doesn't enhance you as an artist in any way to do that. See if you can spend a third of the time that you are spending in the gym, doing something that you don't have an inclination for, and see if you can develop an inclination for it.

Is there anything that you want to say to actors about auditioning? Anything that drives you crazy?
Don't be late, don't be unprepared and don't blame me if you're unprepared. People come in and say, "Oh, I just got these sides," and I'd like to kill them because I made the sides available at least the day before.

Any final words?
I'll say it again: if you want to do this rather awesome thing—the storytelling of our time—then you have to invest yourself in being part of the archetypes of our time. You have to understand something about the evolution of human nature. Certainly it's fun to get awards and drive in limousines and drink champagne but it's more exhilarating by far to do your work with all of yourself.

John Levey
VP of Talent & Casting
Warner Bros. Television
300 Television Plaza, Bldg 140, Rm 138
Burbank, CA 91505

TERRY LIEBLING

Born and raised in Manhattan, Terry Hamlisch Liebling got her start in show business working as executive secretary to a story editor at 20th Century Fox in New York. While there, Liebling made some contacts in the talent department; when the opportunity arose to get into casting, she jumped at it and for the next two years worked as the assistant to the head of new talent at Fox. Following her passion to be the best casting director she could possibly be, Liebling enrolled in acting classes.

She wanted to learn how to talk to actors, how to speak their language and how to elicit the best performance she could. Studying first at HB Studios with Bill Hickey and later independently with Dustin Hoffman, she came to appreciate how difficult it is to deliver a well crafted performance. Although she took a few independent casting jobs in New York, she didn't work full time again until moving to Los Angeles, when she began casting under Lynn Stalmaster. After four years of working for him, Liebling went on to assist the casting of Coppola's *Apocalypse Now*, and then as the casting director for Rafelson's *The Postman always Rings Twice* and *Black Widow* and later the features *Brubaker, Nine to Five, The Cemetery Club, The Two Jakes* and *Terminal Velocity*, among others.

How can an actor get to you?

Well, demo tapes are a great way for a casting director to see work. Tapes are a good introduction to the actor, but I don't think that casting should be done from a demo tape. I don't like the fact that people are using videotapes only, in certain instances, to cast the smaller roles. You don't know what it took to get that performance from the actor or how responsive they are to direction because you never get a real sense of who that person is. Fortunately, most directors I've worked with want to meet the actors. As for generals, I usually don't have a lot of time for them. I wish I did. When I do generals, I take recommendations from agents, managers or creative people whom I respect. Also, I make notes on people in films that I like and don't know and try to meet them. In terms of auditioning, sometimes some very talented actors don't audition well, so I will talk to the director before the actor comes in and say, "Look, this actor doesn't audition well, but trust me his work is great." That's when a tape comes in handy to prove my point.

I will look at any tape an actor sends me and I will make sure it gets back to them if they provide a self addressed, stamped envelope. I also look at all pictures and résumés that come to me. But an actor should not besiege a casting director with postcards. Don't overdo it. I may not get to your play, but a card does make some kind of impact—even though it might seem like it is being tossed in the big pile in the sky. Also, I want to mention how important your photo is because we have to get a real sense of the person from that one shot. Unfortunately, we can't keep all the pictures—if we did, we'd have to move out of our office. But I really have trouble tearing up pictures or throwing them out. I feel like I'm throwing out a person.

Do you attend theatre and showcases?

I occasionally go. I wish I could say I do it all the time, but I can't. There are just so many films, television shows and actors' tapes to catch up on that my VCR is running constantly. There is so much theatre worth seeing, but it comes down to time and energy. Sometimes I send David Liebling, my assistant, to something I can't go to. I trust him. He has wonderful taste and I will set up general meetings on the basis of his opinion.

Do you believe in casting seminars?

I am very opposed to them if the actor has to pay a lot of money to attend. I don't think the casting director should be charging anything to provide the opportunity for actors to meet them. I think it's important to have free or relatively inexpensive seminars, panels, and workshops where casting directors can communicate with actors. Actors should also not go these seminars thinking they will be discovered. Their intent should only be to meet the casting director and to learn what they can.

Do you have any likes and dislikes during the actual audition that you would like to share with actors?
In an audition, try very hard to hold onto who you are before coming into the office. If that means wearing certain shoes or an outfit that makes you comfortable, then do it. If you are asked to talk about yourself, share some of the interesting things you have been doing or things that have recently happened to you, not your résumé. I am always looking for ways to open up the meeting and you should do the same thing. I know it's a delicate thing, because a lot of casting directors just want to get to the reading.

Some casting directors want you to come dressed sort of like the part, but I don't care about that. I won't even remember. I just want you to have a wonderful, comfortable audition. The most important thing is for the casting director to get a sense of who you are.

Any final thoughts?
You know what the fun in casting is? Finding someone who is not represented by one of the big agencies, someone who is a new talent, a new face. That's really a high for a casting director. I like to read résumés; I want to see how you are building your career. Don't lie on your résumé because I've caught some people who have put themselves in my films. I really do look for the steps the person has taken to enhance their career and their talent. I also look for special things that a person does, like being a stand-up comedian or a carpenter. I might have a part that calls for that particular skill.

Depression can be an actor's greatest enemy. Cultivate an interest outside of acting so you have somewhere to redirect your energy. This way, that energy can become a positive force and not turn against you. Your other interest might be a different facet of show business—writing, for example—but find something that nurtures

> *Cultivate an interest outside of acting so you have somewhere to redirect your energy. This way, that energy can become a positive force and not turn against you.*

you and gives you hope. Also, take care of your body. Go to the gym and keep yourself in shape for when the call does come. I know that's hard to do when you're depressed and all you want to do is stay in bed and watch television but you have to keep yourself whole. Be with people, don't isolate yourself and don't brood.

When I hear a scene I've already heard over a hundred times and suddenly it's alive, the walls are gone, time stands still and it makes me feel that I am hearing it for the first time—that's a great reading because it actually puts me in an altered state of being. When that happens, I rejoice for you *and* me.

. . . .

Terry Liebling
c/o CSA
606 N. Larchmont Blvd., Suite 4B
Los Angeles, CA 90004

. . . .

MICHAEL LIEN

For over twenty years, Michael Lien has
been casting commercials for
everything from Coke to Colgate, Sears
to Sea World, Hallmark to Hershey.
Among the myriad of directors he has
worked with are Penny Marshall, Rob
Pritts, Mark Pellington and Academy
Award winner Caleb Deschanel.
While Lien has done music videos,
CD-ROMs, trailers and industrials,
commercials are clearly his
specialty.

**How would you suggest an actor
deal with an audition that is to be videotaped?**
I think that actors should know that it's a bad idea not to tape your rehearsal. If it's
not good, they'll always tape over it because no casting director is going to submit
a tape that looks bad if they want to keep working with that advertising agency.

Actors to memorize the first and last line. That way, they're looking right at
the camera, at least for the beginning and the end. You don't have to memorize
everything in between. Just concentrate on the first and last.

Do the clients watch the whole tape?
It's judged in the first few seconds and they may or may not watch beyond that.
They're evaluating your look first and your ability second. Therefore, you should
dress closely to the part. Don't try to be exact or wear a uniform but do try to
suggest the role.

So much is about look and type, isn't it?

Yes, but I think more people have a shot now than when I first started. Clients don't like to see people in commercials that they've seen before. Certainly an actor is not going to be punished if they've done other commercials; but generally, if you don't have anything running and you do a good performance and you're up against someone who did a good performance and has a lot on the air, you probably have the better shot.

Do you think actors should list their commercial credits on a separate résumé?

No. Usually, they want to know about your theatrical credits, not your commercial credits. They want to think you're their discovery.

What are some of the things that you're proud of?

Well, I cast the first big music video—Michael Jackson's "Beat It"—and I wrote the Taft-Hartley letter on Robin Williams.

I was working on two jobs at the time. Robin came in for one and was totally wrong for it. The other project was for Illinois Bell. It had a guy talking into the phone and imitating all of these voices. When I came out into the waiting room, Robin was talking to a friend and he was making all of these weird noises the way Robin Williams does. I sent him to the director immediately and they loved him. He had never worked in front of a camera before. I ended up working for that advertising agency *forever* after that. I've always been impressed with the quality of actors who have done commercials and with what the commercials have done for the actors. It really gives people a base and foundation. When I started, people like Chevy Chase and Marsha Mason were coming in.

Do you ever cast non-union actors?

I try my best to stay away from any non-union casting. Really, I would only call in non-union talent for print casting or maybe an independent film for AFI. I always advise my clients to go union because it's really their best option. It's best to do everything above board. I make my living working with SAG actors so I try to support the union anyway I can.

How can an actor get to meet you?

We get a stack of mail everyday and we put a large percentage of our jobs in the Breakdown Service. If you have an agent, I'll eventually end up seeing your picture. If an actor doesn't have representation, unless they have a really obscure talent—a fire-eater, fluency in Gaelic or something that most people aren't— there is almost no reason I would see them. I just get too many submissions. I look at them all, but I can't call all those people in. If we put out a breakdown for ten parts, we usually get anywhere from one to five thousand submissions and we'll call between ten and thirty people for each role.

Do you think that the electronic services will become more widely used?
I think that eventually, it will be all electronic. There's no doubt in my mind. Right now, you have to grab your client and drag them to the computer or print a scanned picture and that image isn't going to be nearly as good as an original. So a good picture and résumé are still key. But the electronic service is a good tool. I saw it in use the other day and that's when I changed my mind about it. An actress with special stunt talents couldn't make the audition but had a picture available to the client via the service. It was after 7:00 P.M. and all the agencies were closed. There was no way to get a picture faxed. The clients were sitting here and all I had to do was turn on the computer to get her picture, résumé and pager number. It was really handy.

Is there anything in particular that you like to see in a headshot?
Anything that shows body language is good. It helps us to see a little bit more of the actor's personality. You just have to remember that your headshot has to be better than the next one. With most casting directors, your shots have less than one second to make an impression. They have to be great. If you're not getting out on auditions, that's probably one of the reasons. Very rarely do actors with bad pictures get in to auditions. Actors shouldn't be sending me their pictures anyway. Their agents should do that and if they don't have agents, they should spend their time trying to get one instead of trying to get to me. When actors send pictures here, it's in an envelope that we have to open and discard. It all takes time. I can't tell you how much we appreciate it when people make it easy and just send a postcard with some information on the back. It's quick and easy. And it's much better for the actor's advertising dollar. Now, if they're looking for an agent, obviously they have to send the whole picture and résumé, but for me, that's not necessary. I know these things seem small but cumulatively, with the stacks of mail that we get, it's not small.

What impresses you on a résumé?
Quality shows. And résumés need to be current. If the last thing you did was ten years ago, I'm going to wonder why. You can include older shows as a representation but they have to be balanced with more recent work. The other thing that is so important on a résumé is the actor's height, weight, and coloring. Let's say I get a picture in the mail and I'm looking for a husband for a specific actress. The picture is of a new face and I like it. But if I don't know what his height or weight is, I can't match them up. What if the characters have kids? I

need to know the coloring. What if the project is a car commercial and they're too big for the car or too small for the car? I have to be able to tell from the résumé. And it's not just for commercial, it's theatrical too. What if they want to put you with Dustin Hoffman? Dustin Hoffman is very small. What if they want to put you with Arnold Schwarzenegger? He's very big. So you only help yourself by telling the truth.

I always like to ask casting directors what their personal likes and dislikes at auditions are.
I hate to keep dwelling on the negative, but generally, if you have a bad attitude on a particular day, don't go on an audition. It won't help you. You'll only make an enemy of the casting director—and if you're in this for the long haul, that's not something you want to do. There are actors, for example, who get uppity when they walk in and see thirty other people waiting to audition. They should be grateful that they're one of the thirty! Three thousand actors who weren't called in submitted for that role. That stuff makes me crazy. Number two, say hello to your friends *after* the audition. Get prepared first. Otherwise, all you'll do is slow things down and hurt your own chances. And when you come in, have your choices and decisions made. You're going to be a much better judge of what's going to work for you than I am. There are actors who come in and ask us which clothes they should wear. That's not up to me.

Any final tips?
You would be shocked at how many times we get pictures that don't have the actor's name or their agent's information on them. A lot of actors assume that their agents will take care of that. Guess again. Another thing, be nice to my assistant, because you never know when he's going to be running the company. There are secretaries who have become vice presidents of networks. So always be nice to everybody you meet. Some actors won't talk to assistants. Even agents can be that way. Well, if they won't talk to my assistant, they are never going to get through to me. It's such a silly thing and it happens a lot. I don't hire people here that I don't trust. He opens the envelopes and don't think he doesn't say to me, "You know, this person was really rude to me." So I avoid that person. Believe me, it's a small circle. None of us need unpleasantness in our lives.

. . . .

Michael Lien
The Casting Co.
7461 Beverly Blvd., Suite 203
Los Angeles, CA 90036
. . . .

Junie Lowry-Johnson, csa

Junie Lowry-Johnson believes that
during auditions, the actors who hang
themselves are those who do too much
and destroy reality. What matters in
life—what matters in our work and
in everything we do—is genuineness.
It has tremendous power. The award-
winning Lowry-Johnson's impressive
résumé includes the features *La
Bamba, The Hand That Rocks the
Cradle, Liar, Liar, Grosse Pointe
Blank* and the *Star Trek* features.
Her television work includes the
MOWs *Gia, The Burning Season,*

By Dawn's Early Light, Roe vs. Wade; the pilots for *Civil Wars* and *Cop Rock* and
the series *Murder One, Brooklyn South, Total Security* and the *Star Trek* series. She
is best known, however, for her extraordinary work casting ABC's *NYPD Blue*
for which she has been honored with two Emmy Awards.

What do you love most about casting?
Casting gives me the opportunity to constantly and continuously study human
nature. I get to sit and observe people all day. People watching is always a
wonderful exercise for casting directors and actors alike. It tunes you into real
life. I also love the creative surprises I encounter while casting. For example, I
get a script, read a scene, and it means one thing to me. Then eight actors can

come in and read the same scene and each do something totally different from one another. I am so in awe of people who can act. What some actors can do is pure magic.

How do you trust that someone is a good actor from a reading?
Through observation and intuition. When I started casting under Jackie Burch, I remember asking her before an important casting session, "How will we know if these people are good?" And she said to me, "Ask me that at the end of the day." I sat with her and, by just watching and observing, began to trust my instincts. As I watched, I slowly realized that the good actors were those who came in and did their scenes comfortably and made wonderful choices. The others were all personality and chit chat. Substance in your craft is ultimately much more important than how smooth you are in the room.

How many actors do you bring in for each role on *NYPD Blue*?
On average, I bring in fifteen to twenty actors. Then the numbers shrink because some of them come in unprepared and blow the audition. Others fail because they are not really right for the role. You end up with six or seven actors who are terrific and give great, but completely different, readings. Each of them has an opinion about the scene and has taken a stand. But even with their talent, they might be rejected because their look or quality isn't what the producer and director are looking for. When we say, "No," you must remember that we are not rejecting your special essence but are merely saying that you don't fit our idea of this character.

How do you help the actor during pre-reads?
I tell them what the producers and director are looking for, but I do not go into the details of the back story. The biggest direction I give is, "Do less. Bring it down. Be more still."

Some people use a lot of hand gestures. As an exercise, I ask them to sit on their hands and do the whole thing again. Often, when they do that, they suddenly get very calm and centered. The emotions begin to play on their faces and their work gets very focused.

Other than talented, what kind of actor do you respond to?
What thrills me is when someone not particularly exciting walks in and, as soon as they begin to do the scene, they captivate me. I am captivated by their honesty, by their full presence at that moment and by their intense focus. Focus means

they are paying total attention to what this moment is all about. Nine out of ten casting people would say that they can tell whether someone will work out or not from the first two sentences the actor utters.

During auditions, what behavior endears actors to you?

The thing that endears me the most is the honesty and realness of the actor. On the other hand, there are some actors who come in and work the room. They love to chat, forgetting that this is all about work. I am more touched by the people who simply come in, do the scene, and, leave quickly when they've finished. If you just do it and exit gracefully, you leave a much better impression. You leave them with the memory of what you just did and not with the awkward feeling of your lingering.

It is also important for actors to know that they should only ask relevant questions. Don't just ask something for the sake of asking a question.

Similarly, if you didn't have time to read the script, just take a stab at it. Don't manipulate the room to take care of you. If you want to take a minute to prepare in the room, okay. But please don't take forever. I guarantee that if you do, that audition is over.

Do you accept unsolicited submissions?

Yes, we do. When submissions come in, we file them according to character and by the various shows. I also have specific banks for each show, category and each ethnic type. The people in the bank are those actors on whom I can depend when I need to bring in a certain type. I know them. I have watched their work and I can go right to them.

In general, after I read a script I am to cast, I start making my own list before the breakdowns go out. Then I take the whole stack of photos that have been submitted and go through all of them. Sometimes you say, "I didn't envision that at all but this person looks interesting." Then I set up appointments with the producers. And, if there are people I am interested in but don't know, I set them up for pre-reads.

Does Steven Bochco participate in the casting sessions?

Mr. Bochco is involved in all the choices for *NYPD Blue*. He is actually very casual and comfortable with actors. He enjoys watching them. When actors come in for a callback, it is much more pressurized for everyone, but he's always the most relaxed and easiest person in the room. He has a wonderful gift for putting people at ease.

Constant rejection is hard for actors to live with on a daily basis. What advice can you offer them?

Actors cannot afford the luxury of trying to figure out why they didn't get a part. You can't figure out the particulars of any single audition. It is much better to prepare well, to give a genuine audition, and then forget all about it. When it's over, let it be over. The more you can distance yourself at that point, the freer you will be from an obsessive relationship with yourself about yourself. To survive as an actor, keep focusing on the work and not on whether you got the job or not. That may not be easy to do, but it does work.

How do you think casting has changed your life?

It has made me more open. It has given me the capability to look at somebody and make assessments without passing judgment. When you look at the various types of people—big, small, ethnic, beautiful, ugly, tough—without prejudice, you start seeing the amazing richness and variety of life. I find this outlook enormously liberating. For example, I bring in actors all the time whom I may not even like personally. But I love their work. To me, casting isn't about liking, it's about finding mentally and emotionally rich people who can bring the scripted characters to life.

. . . .
Junie Lowry-Johnson
20th Century Fox
10201 W. Pico Blvd.
Bochco Bldg., Suite 232
Los Angeles, CA 90035.
. . . .

Linda Lowy, CSA

Linda Lowy studied acting at the American Academy of Dramatic Arts in New York, before going to Northwestern and earning degrees in Drama and Education for the Deaf.

After a few years in Chicago teaching sign language to adults and drama to deaf children, she moved to New York to work for the Theatre Development Fund (TDF). While there, she founded the Theatre Access Project, a program that helps make Broadway and off-Broadway accessible to the disabled theatre-going public.

In addition, she spearheaded a campaign to provide sign language interpreters for stage plays and musicals. After initial rejections, her perseverance paid off and such productions as *A Chorus Line* and *The Elephant Man* began to use sign language interpreters. Signing for the deaf continues in New York theatres today.

Lowy moved to Los Angeles and worked as an assistant to Gretchen Rennell at Disney for three and a half years, before working her way up to director of casting. While there, she oversaw the casting of such features as *Three Men and a Baby, Turner and Hooch* and *Three Fugitives,* among others.

As an independent, she cast *Class Action* and *Rookie of the Year*. With her associate, John Brace, she worked on *Nell, Blink, Extreme Measures* and the Showtime television movie *Bastard Out of Carolina*.

Lowy is married to actor-director Jeff Perry, who is one of the founders of the Steppenwolf Theatre Company in Chicago.

What, in your opinion, are the key duties of a good casting director?
As a casting director, my job is to listen. To listen to what the script requires, to what the director wants, and to what the actor brings to the role. A good casting director works with the actor to help elevate the caliber of the performance before taking him to the director. We are hired for our expertise and not just because we can make lists. It is also our job to have some background knowledge of all the actors that we bring in. The director might not have seen the actor before, so if an actor gives a mediocre audition, I can find tape of the actor doing great work. That often leads to a callback.

You worked on Anjelica Huston's film directorial debut, *Bastard Out of Carolina*. What was the experience like?
I love working with directors who are also actors like Anjelica and Daniel Stern. Initially, both of them were almost wanting to hide behind the curtains during the auditions. They identified with the nervousness of the actors. Two auditions later, Anjelica felt completely comfortable. I loved being there for them; watching them blossom as directors during pre-production. Actors responded to them so well, as their initial approach to the character was from an actor's point of view.

You've worked on many projects with director Michael Apted. What does he look for in actors?
Michael is a brilliant director and documentarian. He looks for naturalism. When he asks an actor to try again his comment is usually "make it crisper." Which means, simplify it. Keep it real. Clean it up. Be yourself. Allow your own personality to come through the character. Through Michael, I have learned that an actor needs to find the character from within himself. I like to see the humanity of the actor coming naturally through the character. Let your unique quality shine through. I love to work with actors. I let them read until they feel satisfied and comfortable with their audition.

Can you talk about auditioning for day player roles and under fives?

Day players are the hardest to cast. What we want is for the actor to come in and just nail it. There's not a lot of background information for a character who has five lines. The actor has to use his own depth and dimension to define the role, as opposed to the role defining the actor. When you come in for these small roles, make a strong choice. It is very hard to direct actors with those one or two lines. Therefore, we need the actors to make a choice. Don't be vague. When you make the right physical impression and say the lines naturally, usually the part will be yours. Ironically, it is harder for some actors to do one or two lines than a bigger part.

How can actors get to meet you?

I occasionally do generals, but I prefer to audition people for something that they may be right for. My memory serves me better that way. But they can send me their pictures and résumés. I love meeting new talent, and I tend to audition many actors for each part.

Any pet peeves?

Well, there are the obvious actors who don't come in to see the casting director because they have done a lot of work and have a name. They only come in to see the director. Then there are the actors in the gray area who also want to go right to the director. I usually call their agents and ask them to send tape. But often the tape doesn't fit the nature of the part we are casting. I want those actors in the gray area to know that it's difficult to be in a director's session. I don't want to sit there with a director and have them look at me with an expression of, "What was that!?!" on their faces. If I pre-read the actor, I can then respond and say, "He had a spark that I thought would work." My advice is, if you are on the fence, see the casting director. I am the nurse before you see the doctor. When you need a prescription, I'm gonna give it to you. I'm gonna tell you what the director wants.

Any final advice to actors?

Don't sabotage yourselves during auditions. When you come in to see the director, don't say things like, "I'm not really right for this part." Similarly, don't go on and on about your private life, what happened to your cousin yesterday, etc. Come in, say a few words and audition. Of course we want to know the actor as a human being, but we prefer to see that humanity shine through their work.

The other advice I would give actors is to be patient with it all. This is a tough and depressing business full of rejections. There are so many actors competing, but if you are talented and work hard, one day it may all happen for you. Don't let yourself get frustrated too quickly.

. . . .

Linda Lowy
Linda Lowy Casting
5225 Wilshire Blvd. Suite 718,
Los Angeles, CA, 90036

. . . .

Marilyn Mandel

In Los Angeles, a town fueled by film and TV production, Marilyn Mandel is a rare entity: a casting director for the theatre. As a casting director at the Pasadena Playhouse, the resident casting director at Joe Sterns' Matrix Theatre Company, and a consultant for many other Los Angeles theatres, Mandel has carved out a niche for herself which allows her to work with great actors but without the constraints of studio pressures and casting dictated by budgets.

Occasionally, Mandel will cross over into casting for Hollywood. Most recently, in addition to casting the Pasadena production of *Present Laughter*, she cast the short film *Love Bites*, the feature *Catalina Trust*, and the HBO children's series *Crashbox*.

How did you become a casting director?
I was writing for television with a few different collaborators. I had always loved comedy writing and felt that was my area. But being locked up in a room was never something I liked. Sitting on my butt for hours was just an impossibility. My energy is such that the magic happens when I get to interact with other people. I wasn't doing that, and I needed to get back to it. As luck would have it, a friend who was assisting a casting director called to see if I could cover for her. That was the beginning.

I was on my own shortly thereafter because I was so opinionated. Then, six years ago, I started working with Joe Stern at the Matrix Theatre. I had no idea what I was stepping into. He was brilliant but so demanding. I had to learn as I went along, but it was really my introduction to understanding great acting. It's been an amazing school for me. Here was a relatively small group of people who all had a body of work behind them and, while they were all doing television and film, in many cases making a really good living at it, their commitment and dedication to theatre was so profound. Actors really get fed and inspired when they're allowed to rehearse, and there is no place other than theatre; no other arena can offer that time.

How can actors audition to be part of the Matrix?
You can audition only if there's a need. The company is somewhat unique in that it's not a company with open auditions. When there is a need that cannot be fulfilled by at least two company members (because there are two actors for every role), then we look. So membership is achieved by having been in a production.

There's a roster of people who have remained very, very active in the company. What Joe looks for are people who can put their energies into the company; people who will show up, who care, who come to see shows, who attend readings, who really want to be a part of it. It's a family, and the only way the double casting can succeed is if people leave their egos at the door. The people who tend to come into the fold and really succeed are the people for whom the work is everything. They are able to say, "Okay, I'll watch you do it for a while and see what I can get from what you do."

And you also work for the Pasadena Playhouse?
Yes. Basically, I do many of the straight plays there, but I don't do the musicals. Occasionally directors bring in their own casting people, but for the most part I am the casting director everyone associates with the Playhouse. Since I'm involved with other things, that works out nicely. But between the Matrix and Pasadena, there are many similarities.

In what way?
The actors at both typically have classical and New York training. I would say that the Matrix actors tend to have a bit more of an edge, if I had to differentiate.

What do you mean by an "edge?"
The Matrix is never about being crowd-pleasing. The intention is to go out on a limb and do good work. It's not polite. The actors don't try to win over the audiences.

When you speak of New York training, a lot of Los Angeles actors get sensitive, because they think they're getting their training out here. They take workshops, or take a class. They don't understand the mentality of New York actors or the difference in training.

Los Angeles will never be New York. But it's boring to talk about; everybody knows that.

No, they don't.

Well, this is the deal: Los Angeles will never be New York. Theatre just doesn't command the same inherent interest or respect here. That doesn't mean that there are not people here who respect theatre, but it's pulling teeth to get people to go, and if a theatre like the Matrix or the Geffen or the Pasadena Playhouse has to pull teeth, you know you're not in a theatre town. Television and film are what make this town go 'round. Theatre here is not an industry as it is in New York. That is the reality, and to think that it's not is a foolish illusion.

Do you think, then, that an actor given the choice should go to New York?

Yes. Any actor who's serious should. They don't necessarily have to move there forever, but they should have the New York experience. There's nothing like what happens to a person, particularly an actor, on the streets of New York. That cannot be replicated in Los Angeles. It's just a different energy. Working in New York is boot camp, and that experience can only feed the actor. Even though there are more than a thousand productions here a year, it's always a struggle to get attention and respect. That's the essential difference.

What can people expect when they come in to audition for you?

A good time. My reputation is that I'm pretty generous with actors. I love actors and I don't have a thing about needing to pigeonhole people. I'm very open to seeing actors do a variety of things at different times. With me, I think they walk into a room and experience somebody who's glad to be there for them. If I can't be that, I shouldn't be in this job. Of course, I can't give them jobs all the time, but I think it is astonishing that they do what they do. When they come in to see me, I feel that it's my job to be there for them and see them each individually.

Any pet peeves?

When they're so into themselves that they can't pay attention to what is obviously going on in the room. I think an actor has to be able to come in and do his thing and also be there to react to whatever is going on in the room. He might actually get a job not because of the reading, but because of something else that happens in that room. It's so important that actors let themselves be people. The humanity needs to come across. And sometimes, the actors don't even know the material. I sit there and think, "How come they don't know it?" They're glued to the damned sides. I mean, do your homework. Don't be off-book, it's a reading, but know it. Have a comfort zone with your material or you won't be able to be playful enough to act spontaneously. In other words, if you're not prepared, don't come in. You're not helping yourself.

And what is it that you really like from an actor?
I like character. The more unique an actor is with his or her material, the more alive I feel. It wakes me up. When somebody has the guts to create his own world in a way that goes beyond the limits of what is obvious or usual, I'm thrilled. I love it when an actor can come in and show me something in the material that I didn't even know was there. Don't give me what I expect. As long as you're going to take the risk of coming into this room, you may as well really risk it all instead of staying in the safety zone.

Of course, auditioning for television is something else entirely. There, you have to deliver what they expect and you have to adhere to the rhythms and cadences of the script. It's a different preparation.

Do you have any final tips for actors?
Crash auditions if you absolutely have to. Take your career into your own hands. I know it's not politically correct to say that, but I don't care. I can afford to be un-P.C. If there's a role that you think is completely right, go out on a limb. The people who succeed are people who go out on a limb. Don't be so polite about your career. I don't want people crashing callbacks, but at auditions, I've had people show up because they're right for a role and for some reason they weren't submitted. That actually happens a lot in theatre, because agents don't always pay attention where theatre is concerned.

I think actors shouldn't depend so much on their agents and their managers to know what's going on. They should make a real effort to find out what's casting and do their own follow-through. If you're really right for a role, forget the rules and just go for it. No one is ever remembered, in the final analysis, for being polite. This profession is fueled by passion.

So your bottom line is guts.
Guts, talent, knowledge and tenacity. And let's not forget luck.

What kind of mark do you want to leave as a casting director?

I'd like to feel that I've been able to make some kind of difference in breaking the stereotype of a casting person that actors feel intimidated by. I don't want to be that. Many casting directors have no sense of humor about their job. It's only entertainment, kids; get over yourselves. All I have to do in the morning is shower and show up. The actor showers, rehearses, chooses wardrobe, rehearses some more, throws up, memorizes in the car, faces a room full of twenty clones vying for the same part, and gets five minutes of my time. There has to be respect for that. They've certainly earned mine.

. . . .

Marilyn Mandel
Marilyn Mandel Casting
P.O. Box 691044
West Hollywood, CA 90069

. . . .

SHEILA MANNING

Sheila Manning is one of the queens of commercial casting, having done everything from finding a young girl with an iguana to some of the most prestigious campaigns ever launched. She was once an actress and occasionally casts features as well.

Let's say an actor has a great face and has been told he ought to be in commercials, but he doesn't have an agent and is not a member of SAG. What would you recommend?

In this office we're not prejudiced against people without agents or who are not in the guild, as long as they fulfill the SAG requirements for membership—which are that you must have studied for a career as an actor. If you have a great face and have trained as an actor, then you have a chance. I always emphasize training, training, training. Acting is different for stage, it's different for film, it's different for TV and it's different for commercials. But it's all acting. The old days of commercial overacting are long gone. Now we are into a reality time, which is great. A strong acting background, with maybe a commercial class that teaches you what's happening in the commercial world, is what will help get you the job. You don't really learn acting from commercial classes—you learn what the current trends are in commercials. And those trends change, so if you study with a good teacher, you will learn what the clients are looking for. You want to know what they're going to talk about after you leave the room.

What are some of the things producers and directors talk about behind closed doors?

They absolutely despise phoniness. The simplest and best thing to learn is how to slate. In life, when you meet somebody brand new, you know in a second whether you want to get to know that person, even if this is an unconscious thought. Just by your stating your first name and your surname, I'll learn more about you than you'll ever know. When you slate, they make an immediate decision about whether they're even going to stay for your performance. I can't tell you how often the producer or the director will hit the fast forward button because someone is just not being themselves.

If you want to learn how to slate, the best thing to do is to practice looking in the mirror and saying your name. If I were slating, I would just state my name and go directly into the audition. I wouldn't slate in character—I think that's obnoxious. Acting for commercials is different because we're in the business of twenty-eight second characterizations. We don't have time for back story or sub-plot. We don't have time for you to establish who you are, which is why, very often, we don't cast against type. We need to recognize you and that character instantly.

How accessible is your casting office to actors?

In my office, you can always drop off a picture; we're always glad to see people. Depending on the mood of the moment, if I'm not busy, I might chat politics with you for five minutes. But you have to be sensitive to the mood of people's offices. If you come in and all hell is breaking loose—as it is frequently—just say, "Hi, nice to see you again," drop off some pictures and leave. If it looks like somebody wants to chat with you, then you can stay around and chat.

One thing that really annoys me is when actors waste their time and money sending me gimmicks to get themselves in the door. Gimmicks make me crazy. Years ago I got a child's toy TV set with an actor's face on the screen and a note saying, "I just wanted you to see how I look on television." The poor guy had spent a fortune doing that, and for what? I care that you can act, not whether or not you can think of clever gimmicks. Those days of mailing yourself to somebody in a big box are over. Somebody actually delivered himself to a producer via UPS. We once got a box of fortune cookies from a dog. The dog wanted a commercial, and all the fortunes said, "Hire Duke!" Just don't do that. Mail only your picture and résumé. Some actors somehow think that commercials are a stepchild so they don't bother to send résumés, as though we're really only looking for a face. Sometimes we are, but 99 percent of the time, even if I'm looking just for a face, I'm looking for a face that can act.

You obviously see a lot of pictures! What are the things that catch your eye and what turns you off?

For starters, I hate composite pictures. I have hated them for years. Composites were for the old days when we didn't need people to act. You had pictures of somebody stirring a bowl, then a guy with a kid on his shoulders, sometimes we got to see a guy both in a work-shirt and a business suit and tie. What does that mean? That we can't figure it out on our own that they can dress differently? I like a nice close up of the face, with living eyes. It is very important that the picture look like you today, not twelve years ago when you were thirty pounds lighter! Yesterday I got a picture of a model, his knees were almost covering his face, and I could see only one eye and the tip of the nose. Now, what can I tell about this actor except that he has a pretty knee and an eye?

Can you talk about other things actors do that you like and dislike?

We have a very hard and fast rule in this office—if you crash an interview here, you'll never walk through our door again. It's a harsh rule, but I get paid to choose the talent and actors have no way of knowing what the director has said to me. The actor may see other people that are similar to them in the waiting room and say, "Hey, I'm a blonde woman, I'm going in." But what if the director wanted a blonde woman who speaks Russian? When the director or the client sees somebody on the tape who is completely wrong, they think, "Sheila doesn't know what she's doing." I'm the one who loses that account, not the actor. This is why I'm so strict about crashing. It is very important for actors to know this because it stops them before they make a mistake. It's my career that I'm protecting. Dropping a picture and résumé and asking for an interview is one thing, but signing your name on the list as if you have an appointment to be seen at the interview is a separate thing. That's what I call crashing.

I also will not tolerate rudeness. If you are nasty to me or those who work for me, you'll certainly be in my bad graces, and it isn't easy to be in my bad graces. There was an actor I refused to see for ten years because he came in drunk. He thought I was the receptionist and was so viciously insulting that I never forgave him.

I like intelligent actors, I like warmth, I like people who come prepared. I like people in general and I think this office is very actor-oriented. The best thing an actor can do at an audition is be memorable. If we are going to see one hundred people, your job is to find a way to read a line that no one else has thought of. If you're in a group, and everyone is slating, don't say, "Hi." Be the first to just state your name. Be different and hopefully better than everyone else. Be yourself no matter what. Don't make up something interesting to say when I ask you to talk about yourself. Dare to bare your soul. It will actually work. Also, there are two tests you are put to at an audition: one is with the dialogue and the other is whether someone wants to spend eight hours a day working with you.

Any final advice for actors?

I think it's a bad idea to list your commercials on your résumé. Just add "Commercials upon request" to your theatrical résumé. Don't let something you did regionally five years ago stand in your way of getting a job today.

I think that actors are the most vulnerable group of people in the business. Actors are required to put themselves on the line every day; that is, if they're lucky and have a good agent. I always say that an actor's job is to go to auditions. That's the job. If you do your job correctly, we reward you by letting you come and play with us on the set and then we give you money. So when people say angrily that an actor worked one day and made fifty thousand dollars, they're wrong. I mean, really, what about the three hundred auditions that they went on before they worked that one day? Those are the days the residuals are for, not the days that he was on the set. It makes me crazy when people say that.

. . . .

Sheila Manning
508 S. San Vicente Blvd.
Los Angeles, CA 90048
. . . .

DEBI MANWILLER, CSA

Although Debi Manwiller went to Cal Arts and graduated with a B.F.A. in Theatre Arts, she calls her career in casting "an accident;" a friend had started in casting and Manwiller was intrigued. She learned that casting was pretty close to her love for acting and theatre so she gave herself a year to see if she could live without acting. Very quickly, she discovered she was "immensely happy" and stayed in casting. She met Rick Pagano in 1989 and by 1990, Pagano and Manwiller were

partnered. They, along with casting director Peggy Kennedy, currently cast the critically acclaimed series *Chicago Hope*, as well as many MOWs and features such as *Very Bad Things* and *The Astronaut's Wife*.

In addition to your work in film and television, do you cast any theatre?
I can't remember the last play we cast, but we used to cast ten or twelve a year. For the right director or for a play that we love, we'd do it again. You have to have an amazing passion to cast theatre in Los Angeles because actors are just so hard to book. They don't want to come in for it. Actors are trying to make a living just like everybody else and theatre doesn't pay very well. It's hard to cast theatre out of Los Angeles because it's sending people to work out of town

for $500 a week when they think they might get a film or TV role. The argument we always made when we were casting theatre was that, even though it's not a lot of money, it's steady for a guaranteed period of time, even if it's out of town. The option is to either take it or wait for a day's episodic work that you may or may not get. It's hard to make an actor understand that maybe the theatre is valuable and valid.

So many actors want to work on *Chicago Hope*—any suggestions?
It's always hard to get into any casting director's office for anything. For *Chicago Hope*, we don't use breakdowns very often because the pace of casting the show is just too fast. By the time I put a breakdown out and I get submissions, I don't even have time to open them all and I'm still getting submissions after the episode is cast. Generally, I have maybe three or four days to cast an episode that may have fifteen or twenty people in it. A lot of those people come out of my head or Peggy's head or Rick's head.

Do you have the time to do generals?
I do when we're not actively casting something. *Chicago Hope* is ongoing so it's hard to find the time. The people I'll meet first are the ones who are recommended to me by producers or actors or agents who I trust. I also go through my mail and keep stacks of pictures that interest me. There's no formula, I just do generals when I can.

How else can people meet you?
Get in a play that gets some good reviews. I don't get to go to the theatre as much as I used to but I do make my staff go! And, between all of us, we see a fair amount of theatre. At our staff meetings, we talk about what people went to see and who was good and what the play was like. So even if I haven't seen three plays in a week myself, between all of us, we usually manage that. If someone on my staff says an actor is good, I'll trust their judgment and bring the actor in for something.

Let's talk about your generals and auditions. What can actors expect when they come in to meet you?
Well, unless I know the person, I like to see monologues. If the actor is right for something specific that we might be casting at the moment, I'll have them read for that. I mean, obviously if it's a lot of material, I send them home for a night, but if it's something small I might have them look it over for an hour and then read it for me. I've seen many actors shoot themselves in the foot during

auditions—hemming and hawing and apologizing about how they didn't have time to look at the script. Or they say that they're not a good reader. They're apologizing and setting themselves up for failure before even opening their mouths to read. That's not good. I mean, I interview for jobs too, and I can't walk in apologizing and say, "You know, I really don't have any good ideas for this script but I'd like you to hire me anyway," or, "I promise I'll be better when you hire me. I really know I can do it." You have to just do the reading. And while there are people who are not good cold readers, unless a casting director really knows your work and will go to bat for you with directors, your reading is all you've got. You have to keep working on those skills and get better at it.

Auditioning for TV is different from film. TV producers tend to be looking more for performance, more for a result, and if you can't produce it in the room, they're less likely to hire you than film producers. In episodic television, they shoot eight pages in a day and they're looking for something pretty close to what they're going to get on the set because they don't have time for anything less. There is no real rehearsal. You hit your mark, you shoot. They need to know, in the audition, that you can get to that place or pretty close to it, whether you're directed or not. Sometimes you get a director who doesn't work with people in auditions for that reason. They just want to see you do it. They may give you an adjustment if you need it or if you're off track but if you can't get the emotion or tears or whatever, they will choose a person who can get to that place. It's hard. The director knows that there isn't going to be time to rehearse or explain and casts accordingly. Some directors will work with people and they'll be able to see through the nerves of an audition or know that it isn't at performance level. But I find, more often than not, that they tend toward the people who don't require too much of their time. It's just more practical. In film, there's rehearsal and a little more time. You may get to do twenty takes. You don't ever get to do twenty takes in television.

Let's talk about pre-reads. I know many actors don't like that step, but I see it as a chance to read with the casting director who can direct you before you have to face producers. It's like a dress rehearsal.

Absolutely. There are times when I will bring someone in for a pre-read even if I know their work quite well. There might be something I know about the material that the actor doesn't. Or maybe I've never seen them do this kind of role and, while I like their work, I'm not sure they can stretch to this other place and I need to see that. Or maybe I'm working with a director who's very particular and I want to prepare the actor as best as I can. If I'm going to bring someone I already know in for a pre-read, I'm not doing it for my health. I have other things to do. And it can only help you. One of two things will happen. Either A) you will get a callback because you were right for the role and in that pre-read you had a chance to ask those questions you might not be able to later and you got a sense from me of what we're looking for and how do the scenes. Then you go to the producers with a leg up. Or, B) I don't give you a callback but I've seen you do good work and I will remember you for next time. It's not a wasted audition just because you didn't get a callback. It's my job to remember the people I've seen, to take notes on every actor I meet, and to call them in when there's something they are right for. One of those two things will happen and neither one of them are bad. All of that said, I try to pre-read as little as possible. Again, there isn't time in television. Usually, I pre-read kids, people whose work I don't know at all or for very specific roles.

When actors come in to audition for you, you want them to be themselves but also confident. How can people find that balance?
You don't have to come on like gangbusters and you don't have to be tap dancing. It's about the work. Not everybody can come in with a mega-watt smile and crack the right joke as they're sitting down and taking off their coat. Nor should they need to. Sometimes, when an actor walks in, he doesn't even want to meet the people in the room. He's ready to work. He'll just say, "Hi," and start. You can talk afterward. Sometimes the scene will require that; some actors just prefer it. As long as they're not being rude, that's fine. I think that more often than not, actors will sabotage themselves by trying to talk too much because they're nervous and trying to make themselves comfortable in the room. So remember, when you come in, while you want to be at ease and you want to be comfortable, you don't have to come in and entertain people before you do the work.

Any final tips?
I think actors need to take more responsibility for their careers as opposed to relying on agents, relying on the casting director's opinion of them, or relying on past auditions. Taking responsibility also means coming to auditions prepared and ready to work. Until you have a job, your work is getting the job. It always surprises me how many people will come in who, it seems, haven't really looked at the scene or even read it carefully. The lack of basic preparation sometimes just amazes me but it happens more often than I would like. Taking responsibility also means keeping yourself well oiled by taking classes or being in a play, and making sure you're working so you keep the wheels turning. It's often said, and it's true, that actors are like athletes. An athlete wouldn't run a marathon or a race without having trained and prepared for it. The athlete's

job is to be physically fit and alert. It's the same for an actor. Unless you keep working at it, you get flabby.

I want to end by saying that both Rick and I want to create a place where actors feel comfortable. Part of our job is to make actors feel free enough and safe enough to do what they need to do, so that they have the best possible shot of doing their strongest work.

. . . .

Debi Manwiller
Pagano/Manwiller Casting
20th Century Fox
10201 West Pico Boulevard, Trailer 776
Los Angeles, CA 90035
. . . .

MELISSA MARTIN

Melissa Martin was born in San Diego and educated in San Luis Obispo before she headed up to San Francisco to pursue her dream of singing. She had studied opera but switched to musical theatre and subsequently performed in over forty musicals. Before pursuing a career in casting, she also spent six years as a singing waitress. She then assisted two commercial casting directors before striking out on her own and moving to Los Angeles. Since relocating, her work has included a wide variety  of products and companies including Nike, IBM, Volkswagen, Energizer, Johnson & Johnson and Saturn, to name just a few of her clients.

Generally speaking, what makes the actor who gets a callback different from the actor who does not?
Well, other than a certain subjective look that you either have or you don't for that particular spot, actors receive the same copy. The person who can take those words and turn them into something special is the one who pops out over all the rest. It's the actor who brings a quirkiness or an interesting behavior—maybe it's how they break up the copy, where everyone else just ran right through it. I look for sincerity and honesty as opposed to being over the top. It's a fine line though,

sometimes actors don't make enough out of what they're saying. It's that funny balance of not going too far with it and not being flat. I think the acting style for commercials is becoming more and more cinematic. Commercials are using much more subtle acting than they used to. I think one of the reasons that's true is because there has been such a swing in the last few years toward hiring non-professional talent from all over the county. Real rodeo riders or real little old ladies from the senior center or real bowlers, etc. Whatever it is that these real people do, they do it without thinking or editing themselves. And quite honestly, the tapes are so much more visually appealing because it's generally not a bunch of actors shoved up against a wall in a casting studio all day.

What's your advice to actors new to Los Angeles, who want to start in commercials?

Well, first of all, they don't have to be in Los Angeles. I know actors who have lived in Florida, Chicago, Atlanta, Nashville and San Francisco, just to name a few places. In San Francisco, from my experience, you can work constantly, get experience and, importantly, get your SAG and/or AFTRA cards. Then, when you come to Los Angeles, you are more prepared because you're familiar with the audition process, so it's not such a big, high tension event. Also, having your card gives you more legitimacy when pursuing an agent. I would say, for a beginner, take acting classes that encourage improv skills so you're quick on your feet. I can't tell you how that training sets actors apart. The reason comedic actors are so in demand is because they can adapt to new situations in a blink. However, sometimes the downside is that while they're funny, they're so "on" that they appear insincere, so be careful there. Also, I would never lock in with one teacher for very long. Actors will study with one teacher for years, and it's not always in their best interest. Move on—even if it feels disloyal. Gain information from as many teachers as you can. Get feedback on bad habits that may be in your way. Quite frankly, it looks better for your résumé if you have taken various types of classes from teachers known in this area.

Another suggestion is to get friends to tape you and do your own self criticism. That can be really useful. When I was first doing commercial acting, I used to go to the grocery store and write down the copy from the back of the product labels; they are often worded very similarly to commercials, so I'd go home and practice using the copy I'd gotten from the labels. Watching, or I should say, studying commercials is another great learning tool. When you're paying attention, you notice that different products use different approaches. Daytime commercials vs. nighttime commercials tend to be very different animals. If you study commercials—the clothing, the makeup, the line delivery—technically, you will know better how to prepare when you get a similar audition. A Clorox audition will be different from a Budweiser or a car spot. If you don't know what to do with your makeup, go to a department store and have them do a makeover. See how they apply it, what colors look best, etc. It's free and you can get a lot of objective input. You have to start thinking about your body and your face as a complete package along with your acting skills. Do your homework so when you walk into the casting room you know exactly what you're doing.

When you really get to know the business, you'll get to know the types certain directors like and look for. I used to literally walk in and ask, "Who's directing this commercial?" Depending on who it was, the earrings would come off, the makeup came down, I'd roll up the sleeves or make the collar crooked, because I knew that this particular director favored a less than perfect look. They thought I was just walking in off of the street that way.

There are two magazines, *Shoot* and *Adweek*, both of which are geared to the production side of commercials. You can get these and they are great. You can learn who just shot what, what they are about to shoot, trends, and so on and that can familiarize you with different directors' styles. I can't tell you how helpful that can be. There are so many things that actors can do to study their business and be prepared.

Any advice on slating?

Overly bright and perky slates are phony and over the top. Back off. Don't be arrogant or cocky. The director will fast-forward right through your audition to the next actor. You should be confident and friendly. If you are asked for profiles after slating, just do it. Don't commentate—"here's my left, here's my right." It is not flattering and comes off as nervous if you talk your way through it. They actually may need to see the side of your face for a particular shot. When you are done slating, just relax. The camera will either cue you or you will just take a beat and go into the audition. Listen for instructions.

Remember, many times the sound is turned down when the directors watch audition tapes. Or they'll fast forward through the tapes, only stopping if someone or something catches their attention. As I mentioned, they are looking for sincerity, interesting behavior, body language, etc. Often it is not what you say, but how you say it that separates you from everyone else.

Can an actor break into commercials without an agent?

There's nothing more frustrating for an actor than feeling as if you're ready to go and not having an agent. You do need one. But if you don't have one, you can submit yourself. You can make the rounds to some of the different casting studios. Many casting directors have some sort of in-basket near the receptionist. Leave your picture. Do it once a week. It makes you feel proactive and you never know what they are casting right then that you might be perfect for. You don't need to write a note; we know what you want. But please, put your phone number on the front and back of your headshot/résumé. I cannot tell you how many pictures I get without contact numbers! But do be aware that when you drop your picture in the casting director's box, there is a pretty good chance it will go right into the trash. Most casting directors can't hold onto pictures due to the sheer volume received. That's why it's not unusual for an actor to do this once a week. This, of course, is in addition to submitting to agents. Get an agency guide at a bookstore. Quite often it will tell you the various agencies' emphasis—kids, TV, film, commercials, whatever. The guide may also indicate whether or not they accept new talent.

Keep all these things in mind as you prepare yourself. Success in this business is nothing but hard work. Believe it.

. . . .

Melissa Martin
Chelsea Studios
4605 Lankershim Blvd., Suite. 500
North Hollywood, CA 91602

. . . .

VALORIE MASSALAS, CSA

Valorie Massalas has been involved in the casting of some of Hollywood's biggest films. Along with Mike Fenton, Jane Feinberg and Judy Taylor, she has cast *Back to the Future II* and *III*, *Indiana Jones: The Last Crusade*, and *Total Recall*. She has also cast *Chaplin, Alive, Honeymoon in Vegas* and *Triumph of the Spirit*. For television she cast Steven Spielberg's *Amazing Stories, Poor Little Rich Girl* and *Serving in Silence*, produced by Barbra Streisand and Glenn Close, for which she won

an Artios Award. More recently, she worked on the films *Twilight of the Golds* and the extraordinary, Academy Award and Golden Globe winning *Gods and Monsters*, both of which she co-produced. She is presently casting the Disney feature *Annie* with Kathy Bates.

What techniques do you suggest actors use to prepare for their interviews and auditions?
One of the things most actors don't like, more than anything else, is the interview. They're not comfortable just being themselves. But the truth is, the most important things are with them all the time. It's what's inside! Of course, it's also important that actors listen and learn and study with good people. They have to

watch the classics and fill themselves up with quality information and performances. But when it's time for you to walk through that door, you have to come from your heart, no matter how much you've exhausted your mind, and how much you've done your research, homework and preparation. And that is the most difficult thing to do today. People are so overwhelmed with the movies they're seeing, the newspapers and magazines they're reading and the television they're watching, that it's made our society hard and mean. So it's difficult in today's world to wear your emotions on your sleeve, but that's what you have to be able to do as an actor.

How would you advise actors to prepare so that they can come from the heart?
You have to be willing to live your life to such a degree that you're able to interpret it as an actor. What is grossly absent in so many of the scripts today is a sense of humanity, some kind of message the world is starving to hear. That's why some smaller movies with messages are so highly acclaimed. The word of mouth is greater than any other publicity or a $40 million budget, because people want to hear that message and they want to believe that there is still good on this planet. If you want to come from your heart, you have to be the one who promotes the goodness, that sense of humanity. You can't sit back and wait for it to find you. Volunteer and do charity work, for example; that will allow you to really see clearly.

Actors should understand that if you're not living your life, you can't express it. You have to be able to get out of your head and into your feelings. You have to really ask yourself, "Am I a good friend? Do I know that every time I do something to someone, it causes a reaction? Do I know that when I speak, when I say something about someone else, it creates karma?" Being good and nourishing creates good effects, while destructive words and actions create destructive effects. This is another way of saying, "Whatever you sow, you shall also reap."

How have some of the movies you've cast impacted your own life?
I was greatly affected by *Alive* and *Triumph of the Spirit*. Even the titles say a lot about what you can get from these movies. For instance, in the film *Alive*—which is about a plane crash in the remote mountains of South America—the leaders within the group believed that they were the ones best suited to survive such a tragedy. But ironically, it was those "leaders" who couldn't survive, while the ones you would not have suspected were ultimately who led the survivors to safety. You have to ask yourself, what role might I have played on that mountain?

Triumph of the Spirit was similar in that respect. We all have walked the halls of Auschwitz in our minds—what it must have been like to hear the voices, to smell the smells, to feel the cold, damp earth. Arnold Koppelson, who produced the film, came back from the Auschwitz location with a piece of barbed wire and a fork he had found in the ground. I remember picking them up and bursting into tears. Even though I didn't have people in my family who lost their lives in Auschwitz, a piece of me feels and understands what happened there.

What is it in an actor that moves you?

An actor has to really understand both his role and life itself to move me. They have to strip their soul, and show us who they really are inside. We revere the actors and actresses who are willing to do that. When I see the body of work Glenn Close has put out there, from *Dangerous Liaisons* to Margarethe Cammermeyer in *Serving In Silence,* I can't help but admire her ability. Every time she embodies a character, she doesn't just learn the dialogue, she changes totally and completely. She can transform every hair on her head, every gesture, every step, every breath, every blink of her eye. Everything about her is totally transformed.

> *There's an old saying in Hollywood: "Ten percent of actors in this town are dying to be discovered and ninety percent are scared to death that they will be."*

What suggestions can you give to actors who are new to Los Angeles, other than finding a great acting class?

To actors who come to town and are not sure what direction to take, I recommend cold-reading workshops. These places are set up to introduce new actors to casting directors. The actor goes in and is given a partner and a scene, which they then perform in front of casting directors. You also get an opportunity to ask questions of the casting director. On many occasions, when I had to cast day players for various projects, I always went to my workshop file. They are a great opportunity for actors to take control, which is not something this town offers readily. Participating in a workshops can help alleviate the frustration that builds when you're sitting around and nothing is happening in your career and your life.

Some actors look at these workshops as opportunities for casting directors to make extra money.

That's not a healthy approach. I think that if you're an actor who's angry about having to pay to meet a casting director and feels ripped off, then you shouldn't go to that class. Don't bring your anger to the workshop. If your first question to the casting director is, "Are you doing this for money?" you will offend them. Realize that they work fourteen hours a day and they are usually doing these workshops to help the actor! Also know that it's their job to remember you and to try to bring you into their world. There's an old saying in Hollywood: "Ten percent of actors in this town are dying to be discovered and ninety percent are scared to death that they will be." I guess you have to ask yourself whether you are part of the ten percent or the ninety percent.

. . . .

Valerie Massalas
c/o CSA
606 N. Larchmont Blvd., Suite 4B
Los Angeles, CA 90004
. . . .

VALERIE McCAFFREY, CSA

After graduating from college, Valerie McCaffrey went to work for game show master Chuck Barris as a contestant coordinator. A few other production jobs followed before an eight year stint at Universal, first assisting Nancy Nayor and later as director of feature casting. She has spent the last five years as the vice president of feature casting at New Line where her projects have included the Academy Award winning *Babe*, *B.A.P.S.*, *The Island of Doctor Moreau* with Marlon Brando,

Now and Then, Money Talks, The Bachelor, Most Wanted and *American History X*.

Can you talk a little about your background?
I was born in Fresno, California and went to school at the University of Hawaii. They had a great theatre department there so I dabbled in acting, but prefered the production end. It's so difficult being in the acting end because I'm the kind of person who has to go to work every day. My personality is more suited for the other side of the camera. I came back to California and finished my schooling at Cal State Long Beach. My first job out of college was working for Chuck Barris; then I went to work for Cheech and Chong and later, for David Gerber. Eventually, I ended up working in advertising which led me to Universal. At the time, jobs were available in both casting and production at Universal, so I decided

on casting. After eight years there I had to decide either to go independent or start a casting department at another studio. New Line was looking for someone, so here I am! What I've enjoyed most about being here has been the opportunity to do the more artsy movies where it's more a labor of love. Actors want to do these parts because the stories are so special.

What is the difference between New Line and Fine Line?
Everybody asks that! New Line basically makes very high concept, highly commercial movies that appeal to the masses. Fine Line, of course, likes to appeal to the masses as well, but they're more genre movies. They're more specialized, more into the art house world.

Let's talk a little about the actor James Cromwell. You cast him in *Babe* which made him a recognized face as well as an Academy Award nominee.
It couldn't have happened to a nicer guy! While I was at Universal, I auditioned him for *The Babe* (the John Goodman movie about Babe Ruth), and he came in and brought tears to my eyes. Very few actors can do that. I can count on one hand the number of times that's happened to me. I was so impressed with him and was such an instant fan that he was the only actor for the part I brought to the producers. He got the job in two seconds. He made my job really easy. When I was given the script for *Babe* and they told me it was a story about a pig who wants to be a sheepdog, I thought, "Oh my God, my career is over." Then I read it and I was blown away. It was a script that left you weeping. James Cromwell was the only person I saw in the farmer's part. When I called to set the audition, there was some talk about the fact that there wasn't very much to do and that there were very few lines. I said, "Listen, he's one of two humans in the movie. If this movie is a hit, he'll be a star." Little did I know that those words would come true. One thing about Jamie Cromwell is that he has so much heart and soul in himself that when he acts, it comes out in his whole persona. It's who he is and that's something very special.

Do you have any advice for actors who aren't great at auditioning for film?
There's the auditioning process where you come in, you read and then you leave. Then there's auditioning where you're auditioning but you're "playing." Those who aren't really good at straight auditioning should come in and discuss the part and play. What I mean by that is that they'll say, "This is the choice I've made, this is what I'm thinking. What do you think?" and then they do some of the scene. Then they get feedback and become a little more comfortable in the audition. Some people need to find the character that way. Improvise, talk in

character, whatever helps you. But to come in fully prepared with a choice is sometimes difficult for actors. That doesn't mean they're incapable of making those choices once they've got the part; they just need some help to start with.

What about the casting directors who don't like to talk at all, who don't allow room for "play"?

It's tough. There is a lot of that in television because of the time constraints. In film, you have a little bit more room to play. But not every actor who comes into my office is going to have that opportunity because then I'd be casting each part forever. It's actually more for producer sessions where there's more discussion going on in the room and there's more of a loose feel. Plus, I don't have fifty people waiting. But if an actor comes into the room and has questions for me, I am always going to be there for them. It's a very hard business, acting. We say "No" more than we say "Yes." The joy is when we can get on the phone and say, "Yes, let's make the deal." That's the joy.

What are some of the ways you find new actors who you may not yet know?

If an actor is in a play and gets a great review, I'll track them down. I go to the theatre and if I can't, my assistant will go and report back to me. Let's say you do a short film or a movie—get me tape of your scene. If you do a TV show and you are proud of your work—get me tape. I'm not saying that I'm going to be able to look at it the second I get it, but I do look at everything. An actor can always send in their material.

What about actors who don't have tape yet? How do you feel about classes where actors do scenes or monologues on film?

I don't like those. They look stagy and they're usually not done very well. It's hard to translate that work. You don't get the full essence of it. Even with soap opera stuff, I can't tell if it's good acting or not. It's a different form of acting. There's a little bit of melodrama that goes into it.

Once someone gets through your door, what are your likes and dislikes?

I don't like it when actors are given the opportunity to read a full script and they don't. Especially for the bigger roles. That really irritates me. Actors will come in and say, "What do you want from this?" and I'll say, "Did you read the script?" "No, I didn't have time because I had four other auditions." That is the worst thing you could say to me. First of all, you're not making this audition important. I am the head of casting and I oversee all the New Line and Fine Line movies, plus I cast individual movies; it's not smart. Do the research. You should always know who you're going in to meet. Actors should spend time working on every audition but they should also learn who the casting directors are. And when you're given the opportunity to read a script, why wouldn't you do it? It amazes me. Maybe actors are used to TV where it can be hard to get a script, but for features you can always get one. Actors are in business for themselves. How you present yourself and how you prepare determines whether or not I want to buy your services. Why would I buy you when I can buy someone out there with a better presentation? If I were an actor, I would have my agent cancel auditions if I had too many to be able to prepare properly. I want them coming in to do their best work. I don't want them coming in and doing mediocre work. If everyone did that, it would take us years to cast a movie.

> *You should always know who you're going in to meet. Actors should spend time working on every audition but they should also learn who the casting directors are.*

What do you recognize as talent?

You can be any shape, size or look as an actor. It's what comes off from inside of you. It's how connected you are to your humanity and your craft. When we say, "He's not right for this part," it has nothing to do with talent. It's the essence of the person. That's what makes them so interesting and that's what makes people stars.

How do you balance work and the rest of your life?

It's so easy to get consumed in this business. I think it's important to have outside interests. If I didn't do something for charity, I don't think I'd feel whole. Right now I work for the World Children's Transplant Fund. I've also taught drama to inner city kids. It really feeds me to know that I'm helping someone. Most actors want to please people and there is a very giving part to what they do. That's why a lot of actors are involved with charities and fund-raising. It gives them a good feeling to give of themselves. You can also use these opportunities to do research and have new life experiences which help you understand more about human nature, and that can make you a better actor.

Any final thoughts?

Acting is a lifetime journey. It is learning and being better at it every single day. That's the journey and the beauty. Each talented person usually has their time in the sun if they're willing to take the steps. And who's to say that it happens at twenty or forty? It can happen any time. Look at Jamie Cromwell. Plus, if you stay with it, there's much less competition as you get older and are doing character roles. People drop out. So my advise is to just hang in there!

. . . .

Valerie McCaffrey
VP of Feature Casting
New Line Cinema
9056 Santa Monica Blvd., Suite 300
Los Angeles, CA 90069

. . . .

Barbara Miller, CSA

The legendary Barbara Miller has been involved in the casting of hit television series and movies for more than two decades. Currently she is the senior vice president of casting and talent for Warner Bros. Television. You've see her name role by in the credits for such shows as *ER, Friends, Lois and Clark*, and such well-remembered series as *Dallas, Knots Landing, Eight is Enough* and *Falcon Crest*.

Miller began her career in the feature division of Warner Bros. with such landmark films as *Alice Doesn't Live Here Anymore, All the President's Men* and *The Exorcist*. She served a stint as casting manager at CBS before going to Lorimar in 1976.

In 1992, Miller was recognized by the CSA with an Artios Award for her work with Melinda Gartzman on the series *I'll Fly Away*. In 1995, she was once again recognized, this time with John Levey for work on *ER*, eventually winning a total of four Artios Awards and two Emmy Awards.

Today, at Warner Bros., Miller supervises over two dozen casting directors and assistants working on as many as twenty different projects.

What do you think makes a good casting director?

Good casting directors genuinely like actors and care for them. They also have the instinct in the pit of their bellies that tells them whether a person can act or not—even without knowing anything about the actor's previous work. Good casting directors always do their homework by going to the theatre and watching a lot of television and films. They constantly bring in new talent and do loads of pre-reads. They put actors at ease and know how to bring out the personalities hidden within. And finally, they know how to direct them toward the essentials of a role.

As senior vice president, are you ever involved in the day-to-day casting sessions?

I oversee the department by putting the right casting director with the right project. And I am very lucky because my casting directors can do both comedy and drama, and they like to mix it up. Once they are set, each casting director basically takes care of the assigned series. And although my job has become a little more administrative lately—doing all the budgets, working closely with the development people, attending production meetings—I still love the creative part of it. I do get more involved during pilot season or when we are adding an actor to a series already on the air. Also, having worked with so many of the network executives who purchase our programs, I have an inkling as to what they like. Therefore, I can suggest choices to my casting directors accordingly. For example, some networks like actors who are little more off-beat, others like names, and still others prefer theatre people.

Do you think the actor is the primary reason a series becomes a hit?

It's the combination of good acting, writing and directing that makes a hit. For example, George Clooney, who was under contract to us for almost three years before *ER*, was put into many unsuccessful pilots. Then *ER* came up and George loved it. In fact, he was offered another pilot at NBC but turned it down because he wanted so much to be a part of *ER*. George always had personality and a great sense of humor. Yet, even with all that, his pilots didn't go. With *ER*, however, he had the chance to work with good writers, good actors and good behind-the-scenes people who know how to run a show. As a result, he is part of a huge hit.

Can you talk about putting actors under contract?

Putting actors under contract guarantees that the studio will have talented people available during pilot season. During pilot time, everybody invariably starts looking for an attractive leading man in his thirties. Similarly, the business is currently saturated with stand-up comics who have the potential to anchor sitcoms. As a result, the competition gets so keen that when another studio hears that you are meeting with someone, they quickly grab them and pay them to be available to their studio exclusively.

How do you search for talent?

I have a huge department and a lot of them go to the clubs and theatres to watch talent. We also have people in development who are into that. Sometimes I will call them and say, "I saw a tape of this stand-up performing live and I think we should set up a meeting." Other times they will get a call from an agent saying, "We have this new stand-up or actor in town and there is a lot of interest. You should meet him." Often we find talent through unsolicited submissions. I look at every picture and postcard that I get. Actors should continue to submit, especially when they don't yet have an agent or manager.

If, after looking at the photo and résumé of an actor, something hits me, I might say to myself, "This person might be good for *ER.*" Then I talk to John Levey, the show's casting director, and ask, "Can you meet this person?" or "Let's meet this actor." On *ER*, you have approximately forty guests or featured players in each episode, so there's a wonderful opportunity to give new people a chance.

What practical advice would you give to an actor who gets on a set for the first time?

Perhaps the area the young actor should be sensitive about is his working relationship with the other actors and the director. Not all the actors you are going to work with are on the same level. Some may be terrific and some are just not going to be. When you work with the better actors, you have to learn to lift yourself up to their levels. And, when working with actors who are on a lower level than you, you have to be able to keep your work from dropping down to their level.

As for directors, be aware that they come in all types. Some directors are technical, others are actor-oriented, while still others are time and budget oriented. So when you get on the set, observe and find out what type your director is. Then, if you're working for a technical-minded director, you won't ask him, "What's my motivation in this scene?" If you do, he'll look at you as if you're crazy.

Some actors are intimidated by casting directors. Can you talk about that?

Why should actors be intimidated by casting directors? Casting directors are your best friends. We really are. Any actor who walks in this door and is good makes us look good. I really think that most actors who come in here are treated very nicely. Often they have to wait, but that's because behind the scenes we are constantly dealing with problems. Please also understand that when we are doing a series, we are under tremendous time pressure. We pay casting directors to come up with five or six good ideas for each role. There is no time to bring in twenty-five people for a guest role.

I personally believe that casting directors are some of the hardest working people in this business. So are their assistants. They are the ones who call the agents, set up the meetings, get the paperwork done. Casting is hard work and long hours don't mean very much. Assistants do whatever needs to be done. They are amazing people.

What mindset might help actors deal with audition trauma?

Actors should know that the producer or director sitting across the room is a human being who may have good or bad days, just like anyone else. So whatever happens during the audition or afterwards, don't take any of it personally. When you come in for a reading, be prepared, be presentable, and give the best you can. Having given your best, tell yourself, "I gave a great reading and I hope my name is on this one." Then forget all about it because you don't know what's really going on in the director's or producer's mind. There are so many reasons that have nothing to do with your talent. So why get upset over things you cannot control?

Have you ever been instrumental in discovering a new talent or launching their career?

I find it really difficult when someone says, "I discovered so and so." I could go on and tell you that Brad Pitt did an arc on *Dallas* for us or that Robin Williams played a crazy English rock manager on *Eight is Enough,* but did I discover them? No. Did I see something in them? Yes. The only credit I can allow myself is that when I met them, I saw talent, personality and charm—so I hired them.

For television, is it more important for an actor to have great talent or great charm and personality?

I've done shows with the best actors in the world that nobody watched. So, often we have to hire certain actors for their pleasant looks, personality and appeal alone. The first thing people sitting in front of their television sets see is a personality. They begin to think, "I like the way this looks. I'll watch it." They make up their minds whether to stay tuned or not, even before they hear the actors talk.

Of course it's best to have both appeal and talent that keep on improving. Most of the actors working on shows like *ER* and *Friends* are constantly learning from each other. These are people who are not only working on projects that they truly believe in and love, but who are also having the opportunity to learn more and improve their craft constantly. It's magical to watch that happen.

. . . .

Barbara Miller
Senior VP of Talent & Casting
Warner Bros. TV
300 Television Plaza, Bldg. 140, 1st Floor.
Burbank, CA 91505
. . . .

RICK MILLIKAN, CSA

While there are several casting directors who regularly work on more than one series, Rick Millikan has the distinction of casting two series, *The X-Files* and *Sabrina, the Teenage Witch*, of completely different genres—both of which are hits. Millikan began his career as an actor but switched to casting and became the director of talent and casting at MGM Television and, later, at Columbia Pictures Television. His work has included the series *Route 66, In the Heat of the Night, The Young Riders*, and the MOW *Christmas on Division Street*. For his outstanding work on *The X-Files*, Millikan was nominated for an Artios Award for Outstanding Achievement in Dramatic Episodic Casting.

Lets talk about the casting of *The X-Files* and *Sabrina, the Teenage Witch*.
On *X-Files* we ship the guest stars to Vancouver for ten days. The smaller roles are generally cast up there. For *Sabrina* I cast all the parts so I'm looking at day players and one line things and three-day players and sort of everything in between. In the case of day players, I tend to pre-read a lot of them because sometimes, the delivery of one line in a half hour show can make or break an entire show. Sometimes one line can be so important and it can also be the hardest thing to deliver. I like to see people do it before I actually bring them to producers.

I've been told that doing a one line role is almost its own art form.

It almost is because, even in the audition process, when somebody reads just one line it can come across as silly. But it can't be silly in the context of the show because it's pushing the show forward to some point and it's an important moment or it wouldn't be there. One line roles can be very difficult to do and a lot of people don't take it seriously. People think, "I'm not going in for one line. Forget it." But it can be a very important thing for new people. We need somebody who brings a uniqueness to that line, who makes it stand out and makes it make sense.

For a one line role, do actors come in and say, "Rick, I've got about five ways to do this. Do you want me to do them for you?" or should they wait for you to say, "That was fine. Can you do it a couple of other ways?"

I think it's always okay to ask those questions, if you truly have five different ways to do it. Don't tell me you do and then it's exactly the same. That drives me crazy because it's wasting my time and your time. A lot of people do that. If you're going to ask to do it again make sure it's different.

You use such interesting types on _The X-Files_. Can you talk about what you look for?

It's all about being real and making it look like "Anybody, USA;" that these things could be happening to any of us. We're looking for people who almost don't even look like actors. I just actually had to produce a session last week where I brought in a very good actress who's very attractive and the note from the producers was, "She looks too much like an actor." And it really struck me how hard we try to stay away from people that are too beautiful or too perfect; we really try to use people that look "real." If you stand at an airport and watch people all day, or you sit at a bus stop—people can be very strange-looking. It's funny, I see people who've spent hours getting ready and looking their best for the audition, but for _The X-Files_ you don't need to do that. You need to just be a raw human being because that's what I'm looking for. It's people who can bring out that raw humanity and not everybody can do that. A lot of people think they can do it, but not everybody can really unzip that outer layer and let us all in. That's what I think good acting is really all about. And actors have to know what they're going in for. Know what the show is.

Let's talk about auditioning for you. Any advice?

If I were an actor, I would try to get myself into a comfortable place in whatever way I do that. Obviously meeting somebody for the first time is an exchange of energy. Sometimes it's difficult, sometimes it's easy, just because people have different chemistries with each other. Sometimes I meet actors and there are immediate little tensions, sometimes I'm completely comfortable with someone right away. But as an actor, you sort of have to blow those feelings off and make yourself comfortable whether you feel that way or not. You need to be able to open up immediately. And how you do that I don't know. If there's something happening here between you and the casting director that's a little uncomfortable maybe you can use it somehow. But, you have to remember that a casting director has a specific job to do and that is to cast a part and other parts you don't even know about. There are plenty of people outside waiting for their chance. Obviously we've got to keep things moving. So, I'd read my sides and say, "Would you like to see anything else? Thank you very much. Nice to meet you. Goodbye." That's the perfect audition for me. If something wonderful happens between the two of you and you strike up a great conversation and the casting director wants to see a little more of you as a person, great. But the actor shouldn't initiate that. I know immediately that I'm bringing you to the producers; maybe you're perfect, I don't need to see anymore and I've got to move on. That could be the case. Maybe I just know immediately that you're not really right and I need to keep looking. That's not a negative thing, it's just the way it is. You can't take it personally as an actor.

Why did you give up acting?

Because I wasn't making any money. It wasn't what I was hoping it would be and I didn't want to keep pushing and going on auditions and wake up ten years later thinking, "Now what am I going to do?" I wanted to develop a career for myself early on. That was my choice. And I'm so glad I did because I've been pretty lucky. I think you really have to be happy with yourself. You have to look at yourself in the mirror and say, "Am I happy? Am I fulfilled? Is this why I'm here on this earth? Is going on auditions fulfilling to me? Is that what I want?" If the answer is yes, then go for it. By all means go for it if that's what you have to do in this lifetime to make your dreams come true and your life happy. If casting ended for me tomorrow, I'd find something else to do. I wouldn't sit back saying, "Now what do I do?" I think every actor needs to accept the possibility that they might not make it. To get a role as a series regular where you make a lot of money is almost like playing the lottery. You still push and you have to do everything possible in your powers to try to make it, but I would also be prepared to have something else—just in case. People say, "I'm going to do it. I'm going to make it. I don't care. I don't care. I'll do anything!" I understand what that dream is about. I respect the dream and the drive and the excitement of getting that role. I'll never forget when I got my first day player role in a movie-of-the-week and I went through the roof. My agent said, "Rick, you're working for one day. Relax." I know when I book an actor for a day player role and it's their first job, I know what that does to somebody and it really thrills me to give them work.

Can an actor get to you without an agent? Can they submit themselves?
Of course they can submit and actors do submit all day long. I think if you don't have an agent and you don't have any connections, I think you have to submit. I think you have to do everything in your power to get yourself out and seen. I don't know what else you do but submit, showcase, do workshops and plays. Let your face get out. It's the only way you're going to get rolling and hopefully something will click. You can get a series regular role tomorrow. It happens that quickly. That's the strange thing about this business. You can walk into a room today, audition, next thing you know you're on a series for five years. Look at Gillian Anderson and David Duchovny. They walked into a room one day, auditioned, and from one audition they are now stars of a major TV series and making a lot of money. They got a call, they went. Boom. Done!

And every actor reading this right now is thinking, "I bet they had really good agents and that's how they got into the audition."
If you're out working and you're doing plays, if you're good, you're going to get a good agent. Gillian Anderson was in plays in New York and Chicago and somebody saw her, picked her up, sent her on a call for this pilot called *The X-Files* and there she went. That was the perfect example of being ready. She was ready to go. But casting directors and agents are all out there. Everyone's out there looking. When the goods are there and somebody's new and fresh and hot—they're going to get snapped up in two seconds because the hype starts. It's like a frenzy. It's a shark feeding frenzy and that's what pilot season is all about. Everyone is looking for that next series star. So do whatever you can do. Hopefully it's quality work and you're surrounded by good people. Not all plays are good and not all work is good but I think you really have to just put yourself out there—because again, it's a hugely competitive business. There are not just ten actors running around in this town. There are ten million now.

Any final words?
Yeah. Hang in there, baby.

. . . .

Rick Millikan
20th Century Fox Studios
10201 W. Pico Blvd., Bldg. 75
Los Angeles, CA 90035
. . . .

BOB MORONES

Artios-winning casting director Bob Morones believes that actors should go into the audition room with an attitude of, "I am here to breathe life into this character—watch me," rather than going in worried sick about whether they're playing it right.

Morones studied filmmaking at UCLA and soon joined Universal Studios as a casting trainee during the Ralph Winters era. He quickly moved from trainee to assistant to casting director on series such as *Night Gallery, Marcus Welby,*

M.D., Owen Marshall, Baretta, McMillan and Wife and *Columbo.* After five-and-a-half years at Universal, he turned independent and cast the features *El Norte, Salvador, American Me, Shadow of the Wolf, Pumpkinhead* and *Scarface* with Alixe Gordon. Morones received the Artios Award for casting Oliver Stone's Oscar winning *Platoon.* In 1995, he was nominated for another Artios Award for KCET's *Story Time,* a series with celebrities sitting and reading stories for young audiences. Morones also has a Drama-Logue Award for directing the play, *Cuba and His Teddy Bear.*

You were at Universal during their heyday of television programming. What was the atmosphere like?

It was hectic and exciting. We would cast two to three shows a week without the benefit of Breakdown Services, which didn't exist then. Instead, SAG insisted we make every screenplay that was to be cast available. Every agent and actor had the right to come in, read the scripts, and make submissions by putting their pictures and résumés in the appropriate boxes for each show.

It was also a time when Black and Latino actors were not well represented in the film industry. I was told that was because there weren't enough seasoned and trained minority actors. Since I was brought up during the Civil Rights days, I wanted to rectify the situation. Luckily, Lew Wasserman, the visionary head of M.C.A., instituted Affirmative Action at Universal and brought in people from Latino groups and from the NAACP to educate the producers and writers. Change is hard to come by, but in light of that, I was assigned to seek new actors with talent. I loved it. I went into every theatre searching out those actors. Eventually I became an expert in that area.

Do you feel that only Latino actors should play Latino roles, etc.?

The best actor should play the role. However, when the role calls for an ethnic actor, we like to see them first. If they don't work out, then we open up the field for everybody.

How can actors overcome audition jitters?

I am a great advocate of meditation. You can gain a great deal of control and confidence if you briefly meditate before facing a pressure-filled situation such as an audition. I am not advocating any specific kind of meditation. Find the one that fits you best.

Another confidence builder is regular physical exercise. Have a passion about a sport. It will keep your body fresh, your breathing deep and your confidence in shape. Confidence also comes when the actor is well-trained, does his homework, knows the material and trusts his skills.

What do you think is the best way to audition for a director?

They are concerned about their performance as a director, and as a result want to hire actors who will make them look good. So when an actor comes in and gives an interesting, confident performance, directors automatically attach themselves to that person. They don't have time to give acting lessons during the shoot. The director further tests the actor by saying, "Let's try this another way," to see if the actor has the ability to take direction.

Many times, I have seen actors come in with such strong portrayals of a character that the director would throw his own thoughts out and go with the actor's vision instead. Case in point is James Woods' audition for *Salvador*. He gave so much enrichment to the character that Oliver Stone was stunned. Woods came in while we had Jim Belushi in the room. They read together and the rapport was dynamic. Their relationship worked so well that Oliver clearly saw that he indeed did have a movie. Before that, he was thinking of shooting *Salvador* as a cinema verite-type film with non-actors.

Other than confidence and talent, what else are directors looking for in the actor?
The key indicator for most directors is to get so sucked into the scene that time becomes suspended. They instantly forget about deadlines, appointments, and other pressing needs. When the magic happens, the part usually goes to that actor.

What's it like to audition for Oliver Stone?
It's tough. On *Platoon* we had actors come back twenty to thirty times. The primary reason was that Oliver wanted to see the platoon together. He wanted to see the chemistry and camaraderie that he had experienced in the service. Through the process of elimination we finally got the guys we wanted. Many actors refused to come back so many times because their agents wouldn't let them. Remember, *Platoon* was a low-budget film which was going to be shot in the Philippines. Many people didn't realize that it was going to end up winning four Academy Awards.

How does casting for features compare with casting for television?
One of the reasons I like casting feature films is that film offers the convenience of time. The way I like to cast is to give the material to the actors a few days in advance of the audition so they can come in with a full performance. If you can also memorize a scene, fine, if not, use the sides. That's your choice. But it's been my experience that when the actor does not have the sides in front of them, the magic immediately comes up. I always tell people, "Don't worry if you forget the words. I want to see what life you bring to this character."

In contrast, when casting for episodic television, you have to have people come in and deliver immediately. The actor has to be able to hit the points within the scene without too much preparation or thinking.

What career tips would you want to give actors?
When aiming for the top, you have to plot your career methodically and wisely.

So design your career in advance the way you might when registering at a college. You have to decide what courses to take a year in advance. Map your career similarly. If you're an entry level actor, you first need to do the basic things like getting pictures and résumés, finding an agent, deciding what workshops to join. You also have to decide on and hone a monologue that will show you in the best light. I would block off three to six months to achieve this portion of the plan.

Then decide what you need to achieve in the next six months or year. After six months, check back and see whether you achieved your goals, or if you floundered. If so, figure out why.

After three or four years, do a major reassessment and see: Have you been getting supporting roles regularly or not? Are you co-starring or guest-starring? Are you still stuck doing bit parts? You have to continuously check back and adopt new strategies to fulfill your goals. If you keep failing at achieving them, then either they are too unrealistic, you're not trying hard enough, or your vocation lies in another field.

This is how careers are developed. If you can't do it alone, then seek out a manager or even a friend to ease the way, You may need a guide who will keep your goals honest and realistic.

If you are a well-organized and well-prepared actor, who sets goals and doubles efforts to achieve them, then with luck and talent on your side, you'll be an actor who's continuously working. When you appear in one guest-starring role after another on successful shows, your name will pop up regularly at the networks, and they will begin to offer you pilots and series-regular roles. It takes a great deal of talent, confidence, planning, reassessing and commitment to make it as an actor.

What is it you love most about casting?

What I especially love about casting is that after you have fought for an actor you believe in, you get to see the proof of your belief on the screen. No reward is more satisfying.

Bob Morones
c/o Sanmar Studios
861 N. Seward Street
Los Angeles, CA 90038

ROBIN NASSIF, CSA

As director of comedy casting at the
ABC Network from 1988-1996, Robin
Nassif supervised the casting on over
two hundred and fifty programs. "I am
responsible for being a sort of network
lookout for the best series-regulars
that we can find for each project,"
she explained.

In 1984, Nassif graduated from
Berkeley with a degree in Theatre
Arts and started out in the casting
offices of Norman Lear on
Fernwood Tonight. Five years later
she landed her first solo casting
gig on *One Day at a Time*. She subsequently cast the hit comedy series *The Facts
of Life, Silver Spoons* and *Square Pegs* and worked on many other pilots before
going to ABC. Other credits as an independent casting director include the
pilots and series *On Sunset, Dads, Couch Potato Video, Vindicators, Dead Man's
Gun, Stargate* and the features *The Basket* and *Deal of a Lifetime*. In 1997 Nassif
teamed with Mary Jo Slater at Slater & Associates.

**How do you interface with the network and the different casting directors for
each show?**
Donna Rosenstein, vice president of casting for the network, supervises three
directors of casting: one supervises the MOWs and dramas, another does daytime,

and I supervise the comedies. My work with casting directors varies. I work with some on a daily basis and give them ideas to help supplement their work. We all work together to get the best possible cast. I am always thrilled to see the people on their lists who I'm not familiar with, and they usually seem happy to learn about new folks from my lists.

Then you have certain projects that are more self-contained. For example, whenever Steven Bochco or Gary David Goldberg does a project, they and their staff casting directors pretty much find the actors they want, so the network casting involvement is minimal.

Where do you search for the talent that might have series-regular potential?
We find new comedians through a number of different avenues. Sometimes a production company will bring us a comedian with an idea. Other times, we find somebody in a club or at a comedy festival and develop a show for that person, or match him with the proper production company and writers. As far as finding actors for all our regular roles, we find them through agent submissions, theatre and showcase performances and general interviews.

In the instance of Roseanne, she was brought to us by Carsey/Warner Production Company. They had this idea for her, we loved it, and that's how that went.

In the case of Mark Curry, my associate, Donesther Dane, brought me a tape that the agent had sent in. We sat and watched it and thought, "This guy is great." We set up a showcase for him at the Improv, our development people liked him and put him together with Jeff Franklin, who developed a show for him.

Can young comedians submit to you directly?
Unsolicited submissions aren't looked at with the same enthusiasm as are the pictures and résumés that are sent through agents and managers we know and trust. That is simply because we know it takes a certain amount of talent and "specialness" to procure an agent or manager.

On the other hand, we do look at everything submitted to us, and once in a while we bring people in from those submissions. You can try it, but it is more advantageous to put your energies toward finding an agent or manager who will be able to send you in the right direction. So go out there and hang out with other actors and comics. Try to get a gig at the Improv or other clubs. Get involved with a theatre group and try to land a good play. There are agents and managers looking for talent everyday in those clubs and theatres.

What types of comedians are you looking for?

If you look at the comedians we have, you will see that they are not just funny people, but they bring a specific point of view to their shows. Tim Allen had the whole "tool-time," male macho thing. Roseanne had the housewife with an attitude point of view. Brett Butler had the point of view of a working single mom coping with daily problems. The performers' acts already had these themes and we built the shows around them.

Auditioning for the network can induce sheer panic in some actors. What do you think could ease this tension?

Network nerves are a huge problem for many actors. The only way to overcome this tension is to have wide ranging experience. We have a theatrical setting for auditions at the network, where the actor is on the stage under theatrical lighting, so the audience isn't really seen. Naturally then, theatre experience is invaluable. The more experience you have on stage and in front of the camera, the more comfortable you will be with the set up. We also show the actors the room prior to their audition, which seems to help.

During network auditions, stand-up comics who have an improv background are more comfortable than actors. They are used to being in front of a crowd, they are used to the fact that anything can happen.

Do you recommend improv training for all actors?

All actors should study a little improv, so they have that on-your-toes readiness for any situation. When an improv-trained actor walks into an audition room, they feel comfortable enough to say something quick and witty, which breaks the ice and makes the executives more open, loose and ready to have a good time.

Who makes final casting decisions?

There is no one voice. We all sit in a room together, the production company, the casting, development and current programming people from the network, the studio, the director and all of us make the final casting decisions together.

What are those decisions primarily based on?

It's such an ephemeral thing. When John Goodman came in to read with Roseanne, he had this wonderful chemistry with her. He was her best friend, he was also her sparring partner. So I would say that more than star quality, we look for chemistry between the actors. We look for people who are going to work well with the actors who are already in place. We put a lot of different combinations of people together to see how their chemistry comes across. Sometimes it is disastrous, other times it is purely magical.

What advice would you want to give young actors to make their path of ascent easier?

Being at the right place at the right time is fine, but having the experience to back it up will help the actor land the role. Therefore, train hard so you are absolutely ready when the opportunity presents itself.

. . . .

Robin Nassif
Slater & Associates Casting
2425 Colorado Ave., Suite 204
Santa Monica, CA 90404
. . . .

NANCY NAYOR, CSA

Nancy Nayor trained to become an actress and performed summer stock for three seasons at the Hampton Playhouse in New Hampshire before gravitating to casting and rising to the top of the profession. As senior vice president of feature casting at Universal from 1982 to 1996, she was responsible for overseeing all feature films at Universal Studios. She also directly cast many features including *The Flintstones, Ghost Dad, White Palace, The Babe, Dark Man* and *Casper.*

Since 1996, she has become an independent casting director and has worked on pilots and features, including the recent *Judas' Kiss* and *The Whole Nine Yards*, starring Bruce Willis.

What are you duties as senior vice president of feature film casting?

For most of the movies, we hire independent casting directors, and I work as a liaison between them and the producers, directors, and studio executives. As they narrow down their casting choices, I may add new choices. There are always passionate battles about creative casting choices. It's hard to get people to agree and often, I get stuck in the middle. Sometimes I might see the logic of the studio, other times I might fight on the side of the director.

Should actors submit to independent casting directors who are doing a Universal picture, or to you directly?

Submit to both of us. I also act as a casting director for a certain number of Universal films per year, so sending to me is a good idea. I look at every picture that comes in. I have met with and have hired many actors who submitted themselves to me directly.

Do you also look at tape?

Yes, I do. That's why I advise young actors to get into AFI or other student films. Sometimes good footage from a strong student film can capture the attention of a casting director on a major feature.

Another way to have tape is to put together a monologue yourself. I know many wonderful actors who got their first break from a monologue on a homemade tape that they had put together themselves. Actor Kevin O'Conner, who played the poet in *Peggy Sue Got Married*, had never done anything on film when he sent a homemade tape to Fred Roos. His self-made monologue tape got him his first role.

A lot of casting directors will not look at a homemade video. In your opinion, what could an actor do to insure that their homemade tape might be seen?

It baffles me that casting directors would pass up the opportunity to see talent. If I can see the actor's talent on the tape, it's a find for me. However, an actor must use his or her best judgment. Obviously, homemade is one thing, but scratchy and overly amateurish is something else. The tape should be somewhat professional. It is best to rent a small studio for an hour or so and have good lighting and camera work. When an actor is first starting out, they may not really have a choice of what they put on their reel because many of their professional roles are small and won't show their range. Putting yourself on tape with a good three minute monologue, done in a professional manner, is an excellent way to demonstrate your abilities to a casting director.

What is the best way for an actor to keep in touch with a casting director?

I would send out postcards, as opposed to calling. Even if you have an agent, send a postcard every couple of months. There are so many actors out there; it helps to have a reminder in front of you. Often, when actors have agents, they think the agent will do all the work. In fact, what they should actually assume is that they themselves have to do most of the work. Agents have a great number of people to take care of. Therefore the actor has to constantly watch out for himself.

If they hear through the grapevine that something is being cast, they should pursue it on their own; submitting a picture and résumé with a personal note.

In your opinion, what is star quality?

Each star is famous for such different reasons. Compare Tom Cruise and Dustin Hoffman, for example—both are stars, but for such very different reasons. Sometimes, actors come in and they don't look interesting at all. But when the camera begins to roll, something happens and they light up on screen. A glow comes out of them and the camera captures their essence in a way the human eye cannot. Perhaps this happens because certain actors have an innate capacity to reach down to their soul, spirit and heart, and to bring out and express vibrant emotions that 99 percent of the population can't find.

What are some of the things you like and dislike actors to do during auditions?

I like the actor to do all their preparation *outside* the room. For example, an actor came in to read for a scene that required a lot of nervous energy. Suddenly, he began to jog around the room to work out the needed energy. Also, if someone feels they need such deep preparation that they can't chat with the director before a reading, I don't have a problem with an actor saying, "Do you mind if we talk after the reading?" But when they chat first and then take a long, noisy preparation, I admit, it annoys me. I remember an actress who came in, went into a corner, and started making barking seal noises! I didn't know how long her preparation was going to go on, but it felt like forever. You have to present yourself as someone who can go in and out of character fast, especially in smaller roles. The director is not going to have time to give you all that preparation on the set.

Another thing actors should be careful to avoid is appearing needy or desperate. Often, actors come in to read and are so desperate for the role, that you get the feeling they will surely die if you don't give them the part. Emotionally, you want to give them the part; but at the same time, I think it's the actors with self confidence who get the roles instead. A needy actor makes you feel claustrophobic. There is passion there, but the need undercuts the passion. Come in and have a great time. It's an opportunity to practice your craft. The odds of getting the part are always so slim because the competition is so strong—you have to try to enjoy the audition process itself. Auditions are a great opportunity to show your talent.

Props and costumes can not only be annoying, but can also detract from the audition itself. Occasionally, someone pulls it off so brilliantly that I forget all the previous times that sort of thing annoyed me. But generally, I find that props and costumes only divert my attention away from the talent.

There is a fine line between self confidence and cockiness. Self confidence does not mean you are so confident in your talent that you only look at the script casually once or twice before you walk in. The actor should treat each audition with respect, and say to himself: "I have this opportunity to audition, and even if I am not in love with the part, I am going to present myself with my best foot forward. I am going in as prepared as I can possibly be, and I will shine brightly in the room. Even if I'm not crazy about this part, I want everyone in the room to remember me as an utterly professional and fantastic actor."

Is it a good idea for actors to come to the audition with more than one firm acting choice?
Absolutely! I like it when the actor, right after finishing a reading, asks us, "Do you want to see me do it another way?" During long audition sessions, directors are often tired, and when they don't like someone's first choice, they think, "It's so off, I don't think I'll ask them to do it again." But when the actor is very ready, willing and interested in doing it a second time in a different way, that can capture the director's attention. But, and this is very important, if they are allowed to do it again, then they had better do it in a truly different way. The worst thing is when they do it the same way again—including scratching their ear in the same spot.

Do you have any final thoughts you'd like to share?
They give an Academy Award to a man who throws a watermelon on the ground to make a squishy sound, but they don't recognize the person who is so integrally involved with the major decisions on a film. I think the "Best Casting Director" category should be added to the Academy Awards. I am hoping that through the efforts of CSA, this category will someday be added. We have to enlighten the whole Academy about what it is that we casting directors do. The same way that a wardrobe person or lighting person gives choices to the director, and fights for choices the director hadn't even thought of, the casting directors also bring inventive colors and shapes and textures that fully impact the quality of a movie. The contributions of casting directors should also be rewarded by the Academy.

. . . .

Nancy Nayor
6320 Commodore Sloat
Los Angeles, CA 90048
. . . .

LORI OPENDEN, CSA

Lori Openden began her career in the entertainment industry as a secretary at the William Morris Agency. She soon found herself interested in casting, however, and when producer Danny Arnold asked her take over the casting of *Barney Miller*, she jumped at the chance. Two years later, she moved to MTM and cast such shows as *Rhoda, The Betty White Show, The White Shadow* and *Hill Street Blues*. After a seven year stint at MTM, she became an independent casting director. Her

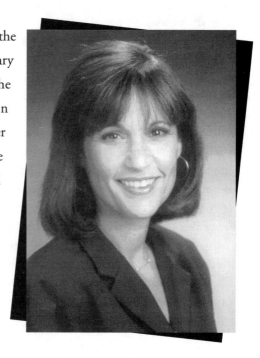

work included several pilots and MOWs as well as the series *Cheers*. In 1985, Joel Thurm invited her to join NBC as vice president of casting. She was subsequently promoted to vice president of talent and casting, and in 1993, she became senior vice president of talent and casting at NBC.

Can actors who don't yet have agents submit themselves directly to you for pilots and MOWs, or should they submit to the individual shows?
I do look at all of the pictures that are sent to me, but I meet very few of the actors who send them. Once in a while I'll see an actor who looks like they might be especially right for something and I'll have them meet somebody associated with that project. But I usually only deal with who's going to star in

the pilots and MOWs rather than the smaller parts. The best thing a new actor can do in Los Angeles is to submit pictures and résumés to the casting directors of the individual shows so they can perhaps get the opportunity to be seen.

How do you find new talent?

I keep track of television movies, because I am so involved in TV movies for NBC that I have to watch the competition to see which actors are doing what movies for the other networks. I also have people within my department who cover the other key areas. They go to clubs and track comedians, they go to the theatre here and in New York, and they see every movie ever made. Although I do not get a chance to go to the theatre as much as I used to before I had children, whenever I do go to a play, I always run into casting directors. I think we all do our homework.

What can an actor expect when they read for the network?

After a casting director and studio representatives have decided that a certain actor is one of three choices for a role in a pilot, we give them a session time to come and test for NBC executives as well as studio executives. We make our decisions after the three actors read in front of all of us. The readings take place in my office. We have coffee and cold drinks, and we try to make the atmosphere as friendly as possible. But of course, the reality is that network readings are always tense situations. Often, through nobody's fault, the actor has to wait for a long time outside. You also sometimes have to sit out there in the waiting room with your competition, which is not always a pleasant situation. But there's no way around it.

Do you have any advice to help actors prepare for these readings?

Always keep in mind that when you test at the network, you've got a roomful of people cheering you on. We're rooting for you to do well. No one is looking for anybody to fail. And if there is any small thing I can do to make it more comfortable, just ask.

Don't bother bringing props; they're totally unnecessary. If it makes you feel better to hold a phone in your hand, that's fine. But don't worry about a suitcase full of props. It actually puts people off. We are looking for a performance, not a staged reading.

Also, make sure to come to the audition early so you can take a little time to chill out. Have a cup of tea and relax as best you can. Also, tell your agent to have your deal done. Very often actors will get to the network and they've got to call their agent, and there's hustling going on back and forth. That's not something actors need to have on their heads right before they audition.

What do you mean when you say, "Tell your agent to have your deal done?" Can you elaborate on that?
The "Test Option Deal" is the agreement between the production company and the actor for their services, and includes items regarding the promised billing, a certain amount of money, etc. A Test Option Deal has to be closed before the actor reads for the network. This is to protect us so that when I show an actor to my superiors and they love that actor, I know a deal can be made—as opposed to finding out later that we can't reach an agreement. When I have the actors in my office, it is understood that the deal is already made. The Test Option Deal is an accepted practice around Hollywood. All the networks do it. We usually have five business days to decide after a test. Very often, we have people read and we want them to come back. Sometimes we have them read with the star. It's not an easy decision, but it's never done haphazardly. A lot of thought goes into it.

Who makes the ultimate network casting decisions for the key roles?
It's a group decision; it's not one person saying yes or no. In many cases, the choice is very obvious. We rarely fight about it. But sometimes we'll say, "Actor number one was pretty good, yet we're just not sure. Bring them back and let's have a couple of other choices also." That's why sometimes an actor has come back to read for the network. Even well established stars are asked to read. When we were preparing *Mad About You,* Paul Reiser brought in Helen Hunt, who was already an established actress. She gladly came and read. We really insist on having even the stars read because we're buying chemistry between actors who will play brothers or lovers. We're buying more than the actor in a vacuum. Of course, there is also a level of talent that refuses to test and sometimes mistakes are made. Sometimes a star is simply miscast. We prefer to read everybody, and we do have a very good track record for picking the right people.

Sometimes actors who appeared in the pilot for a series are replaced if the pilot sells. Why is that?
Very often our focus groups who watch the shows come back and tell us that they didn't like a particular character. However, I don't think we would ever replace a character just from testing. We also have to feel it. The testing is not 100 percent responsible for cast changes, but we do pay close attention to the feedback.

Do you have anything else that you would like to say to actors?

I love casting, I love talent and I so much like television. The pace is much quicker than features. We get a project, we cast it, produce it and air it within a span of a few months. And we get audience feedback right away.

Finally, I want actors to know that NBC is a great place for actors to be because we've made our mark with sophisticated comedies and good, relevant drama. Also, all of us here have a real affection for actors. We're rooting for you. When we find wonderful actors for our projects, it is we, the casting people, who look good.

. . . .

Lori Openden
Senior VP of Talent and Casting
NBC
3000 West Alameda Ave., #231
Burbank, CA 91523
. . . .

Kim Orchen

Cleveland-born Kim Orchen studied
theatre while in college, but went into
the world of business after graduation.
Ultimately, she decided to pursue a
career in casting because she felt it to
be an area that would make use of
both her creative abilities and her
business experience. It would also
serve as a bridge to another interest,
producing.

After working at the Arena Stage
in Washington D.C., she came to
Los Angeles in 1990 and worked
as an casting assistant. She
connected with casting director Heidi Levitt and, in the subsequent two years,
worked as an associate on such projects as *Class Of '96, TV Nation* and the
features *Smoke, Trial By Jury* and *Evita*. On her own, Orchen has cast independent
features, MOWs and theatre, she has also associate-produced and cast an original
hip hop musical called *The Gang's New Threads*.

For the past several years, she has been serving as the west coast casting director
for the La Jolla Playhouse, under the artistic direction of Michael Greif. Most
recently she's been casting features and pilots in association with Liberman/
Hirschfeld Casting.

Do you mainly cast star names at La Jolla?
It isn't the mandate of the Playhouse to have names. We look for good actors. But we are also interested in name talent as much as any other non-profit theatre company trying to draw audiences.

What do you look for in actors who may want to work at La Jolla?
If the actor is just starting out, what interests me most is whether or not they are conservatory-trained (e.g., ACT, Yale, Julliard, NYU, ART, North Carolina School of the Arts). The plays we do often require technical skills of which well-trained actors are the most capable.

How can actors get an audition for the Playhouse?
I keep the submitted pictures for the whole season. I look at all the submissions, both agency and individual alike. And by the way, if you have submitted once, please don't send another a few months later. Save your money. Trust that I am doing my job, as much as I trust that you are doing yours. However, I like it when actors keep in touch by sending postcards for shows they are doing.

What types of pictures do you like?
You're fine as long as your picture looks like you and is current. This is more important to me than the style or pose chosen. If your look changes dramatically (i.e., age, weight, hair color), so should your picture. It's your greatest marketing tool.

What factors do you think go into making a successful actor?
I think it is a combination of things: talent, perseverance and lots of luck. Another factor is your passion. Do it because it's the only thing that gets you out of bed in the morning. When it stops being your passion, find something else. This means you also have to have real talent to survive. I meet many actors who don't have what it takes, but it's not my job to tell them. What I try to do instead, is to help guide them in a direction that will capitalize on their strong points. You have to learn to maximize your chances, and turn your challenges into opportunities.

What do you like to see in an audition?
Preparedness. Auditioning for theatre is not like auditioning for a sitcom, where you get your sides overnight and give a reading the next day. You need to get the play and read the whole thing. You have to know the material and take the time to understand the character. You can't just wing it with Oscar Wilde or

Shakespeare. You've got to know what you are doing. If you're not prepared, not only do you make yourself look bad, you also hurt your chances of coming back for something else.

Another thing I look for is strong choices. It's better to make a "wrong" choice than not to make a choice at all. I appreciate it when an actor takes a risk because it indicates both inventiveness and courage. When you come in to audition, think of it as an opportunity to do something you truly enjoy. When you walk into that room, it's your time and you should use it as wisely as you possibly can. It's very disappointing when actors lose their personalities during a reading. They come in, and often I see that they are likable people I might want to sit down and have a cup of coffee with, but when they open their mouths to read the scene, their uniqueness and their sense of humor disappears. I usually find it to be less of a question of nerves than one of preparation.

If you don't trust yourself enough, it's difficult for the people watching to trust you.

You were talking about keeping your personality in a role. I agree with that for film, but for theatre, don't you think it's better to lose your personality in the role?

You have to start with what's coming from inside your core and radiate it out as you build the character around it. The reason *Rent* has been such a phenomenal success is because, in part, the personalities of the actors come out through the roles. It's all about their own individuality, not about somebody getting an idea who the character is supposed to be, and then becoming that character.

The callbacks for *Rent* were a lot of fun because everyone who walked into the room was somebody we really liked as an individual.

Any parting words?

If you want to work in Los Angeles, there are always theatres doing plays. I have a great appreciation for those actors who juggle three jobs in order to afford to do a play for free.

Don't get discouraged either; overnight success is really an illusion. Even when it looks easy, it often comes after ten years of hard work.

I also recommend travel, if one can afford it. It's one of the best ways to learn about people, to understand how they live and what motivates them. Later, you can always draw on those experiences.

Joining an improv group can be of enormous help. Get together with a group of other people who are in a similar situation and practice your craft. Acting is not something you can do in a vacuum.

Having a hobby you love is another helpful thing. I do ceramics for example, because it's good to have something that allows you to focus on the process and not the end result.

Also, do your best to be open to the people around who need you. That's why I volunteer in the emergency room at Cedars-Sinai Hospital. I was raised with the sense that you have to give back to the community in which you live.

And most importantly, try to live a connected life. It's so easy to be isolated in Los Angeles. You get in your car and you drive. You can spend a whole day without really interacting with anybody. In New York, you have no choice but to constantly be confronted by people every single time you walk out of your house. Here, you have to make an effort to mix. Otherwise, the more you isolate yourself, the more you get too involved with what's going on inside of you—the less you can give outwardly. I am not saying it's not important to know yourself. My point is if you become too strong a self-critic, it's hard not have a lot of negative stuff surrounding you as an actor. It doesn't help to bring a lot of excess baggage into the room every time you audition or meet somebody. Relax, focus, and trust your best self.

. . . .
Kim Orchen
4311 Wilshire, #606
Los Angeles, CA 90010
. . . .

RICHARD PAGANO, CSA

Richard Pagano has cast for studio and independent features, three award-winning television series, and many of the top regional theatres around the country. As a student, Pagano had completed most of his doctoral studies in English and Comparative Literature at Columbia University when he took a one-year sabbatical and found himself studying acting and directing at the National Conservatory of Dramatic Arts in Paris. He changed his focus to modern drama when he returned  to Columbia, and began a career as a playwright, stage and music director, and casting director. As partner of Pagano/Manwiller, an independent casting company, Pagano has cast such feature films as *The Astronaut's Wife, One True Thing, Alien Resurrection, Point Break, Drugstore Cowboy, Strange Days* and, most recently, *The Price of Glory*. He has cast for most of the top theatres in America, including the Old Globe, the Goodman Theatre, The Mark Taper Forum, the La Jolla Playhouse, and the Broadway productions of *Big River* and *A Walk in the Woods*. His television work includes the miniseries *Wild Palms* for Oliver Stone, the Emmy Award-winning *Positively True Adventures of the Alleged Texas Cheerleader Murdering Mom* and *The James Brady Story*. His company also cast the series *Picket Fences, The Marshall,* and currently, the award-winning *Chicago Hope.*

How can one best sculpt one's own career?

To succeed, you have to take charge of your life no matter what you do. There is a pervasive illusion that an agent or manager is supposed to do all the work for the actor. You have to shift your view and clearly realize that you, and only you, have to be in charge of your career. If I were an actor, I would call all the casting directors in the book. Ten of them may get angry. The ones who pick up the phone and talk to you are the ones you want to do business with anyway. You'd be amazed at how many people actually do take your phone calls; how many people do want your picture and résumé. But a lot of actors don't have the follow-through. I've addressed five hundred actors at a time at SAG or Actors Equity and said, "Here's my card. Feel free to call. Or better yet, send me pictures and résumés because I am always looking for new talent. I can't guarantee you that it will work out, but at least you should try." Guess how many of the five hundred actors actually call me? Maybe a handful.

Perhaps they don't really believe that new actors have a chance with you.

When I cast the feature *Strange Days* for director Kathryn Bigelow, we found a number of new faces for the film. She made me work harder than anybody to get her terrific actors who didn't look like actors. She wanted people who were edgy, had interesting faces, and who also could act.

You cast both for the theatre and for film. In your opinion, what differences are there in acting for these two mediums?

This is a complicated subject, but essentially theatre acting is about talking to a person who may be sitting in the back row, while film acting, because of the sensitivity of the camera and sound, is revealing yourself to an intimate, ideal listener. That listener is right there, six inches from your face. As a result, in the theatre an actor has to reveal and project, while in film they have to mask or hide. Very often, a careful observer can see beneath that mask. In fact, the harder a good actor tries to hide, the more they actually reveal to the camera.

Do you find that most stage actors are successful in making the shift to the camera?

In front of the camera, some theatre actors lack trust on two levels: Their acting instrument, and the camera itself. To succeed, you have to trust your instrument and the camera that is recording every flicker of your emotions and thoughts. You can't fake it for the camera; it is a lie detector.

Acting should be similar to playing music effortlessly. While giving a concert, a pianist can't be thinking about where to put their fingers because their mind must be alive on a higher level. Playing has to become instinctual and instantaneous. An actor should be able to act the way a virtuoso plays.

Any final thoughts?

Think of yourself as a salesman. They go and knock at a hundred doors and ninety-five will say, "No," but five just might say, "Yes." Most of the time, when you call a casting office, you might end up talking with an assistant. But remember, in this business, this year's assistant is maybe next year's casting director.

In an audition, base your choices on your own sense of yourself, and what you can uniquely bring to the role. That's the only area you can control. I find that the people we end up casting are those who have a strong sense of who they are. They bring a strong identity into the reading. The audition time is your platform to let us know who you are. So come in and take charge in an assertive but civilized manner. Always be your own cheerleader, your own inspiration and your own secretary. Call people and try to meet agents and casting directors. If we, the casting community, don't know you exist, how are we going to hire you? Thousands of people race through our heads, so we need a reminder. I tell actors to call me once a month. And I try to return their calls. The most successful people in our industry call people back. I think I remember reading a *New York Times* article that quoted Sherry Lansing as saying, "The secret of my success is I return everybody's phone call."

We need your uniqueness. Casting directors need actors more than actors need us. We are always scrambling to cast most roles, and we are desperate for the right person to walk in the door. Good actors are such a valuable commodity and we work hard to find them.

. . . .

Richard Pagano
Pagano/Manwiller Casting
20th Century Fox
10201 West Pico Blvd., Trailer 776
Los Angeles, CA 90035
. . . .

JOEY PAUL, CSA

Joey Paul began her career in Chicago as a child actress in musical theatre. At the age of fourteen, she landed a lead in Benjamin Britten's opera *Turn Of The Screw* at the Chicago Lyric Opera. She stayed with the opera company for four years and then moved to Los Angeles to study at the California Institute of the Arts. After graduation, she pursued a career in regional theatre, television, commercials and animation voice-overs. When an opportunity arose to join the Arthur Company as a casting associate, she decided to take it. A year later she became their staff casting director and worked on such shows as *FBI: The Untold Stories, Adam-12, Dragnet* and *The Munsters Today*. Currently, Joey Paul is an independent casting director. Her features include *Punks, Fallout* and *Evasive Action*. Additionally, she is the casting director in charge of animation projects at Nickelodeon Network. Her work includes the series *Hey Arnold, Angry Beaver* and several animated pilots. Joey has also cast live-action shows for Nickelodeon including the hit series, *The Secret World of Alex Mack*.

What kind of opportunities are there for actors in the animation field?

There is no other area in the business that is exploding quite like the animation market for such various media as interactive, computer-generated products, television and feature films.

Can you tell us about Nickelodeon?

Nickelodeon is a cable network that has been around for seventeen years. Owned by Viacom, it is a sister to MTV, and specializes in children's programming. They produce both animation and live action television programs. They recently began producing feature films also.

What are the trends in animation casting these days?

At one time, animation programs, like sitcoms, used broad characterizations. Now, that's been toned down to a more realistic sound. The complaint most often used in animation is, "We don't want to hire certain actors because they are too cartoony; their voices sound too cliched and not real or believable."

If an actor feels that they have a unique sounding voice, that is, a voice with a distinctive timbre, then they might be right for animation. For example, a gravely tone like Debra Winger's, or a voice with an extremely high pitch or one with lots of texture in its sound can all fit comfortably into our format, as long as the voice belongs to a great actor.

In general, comedic actors do well in animation, because they bring a strong vocal presence to their work and a point-of-view to their acting. Their quick wit and timing also help to create real and interesting characters that can come alive through their voice.

Do the actors watch the animated pictures and try to match the dialogue, or do they perform before the pictures are drawn?

Both systems may be used. Typically, the voice work is done before the cartoons are drawn. First, we begin the pre-reading and callback processes and hire the actors. Then the cast goes in and records the entire script like a theatrical reading. And of course, there is a certain energy created when the cast can work off each other in the studio. As a result, spontaneous ideas flow and they end up providing the director with a variety of takes to choose from. Then they decide, in the editing process, which ones to pick and compile in the final piece.

Once the dialogue is set, the artists begin to animate the pictures. And many times, the way an actor looks is used as a visual inspiration by the animator. Some essence of the actor's look may make it into the actual drawing.

How can an actor get to meet you?

I am very accessible. Everything that comes to me gets opened. I also do generals from time to time. However, if I am not familiar with someone's work, I'd be less likely to consider them. I have a long list of actors whose work I admire, who have come very close to getting booked here, but just haven't so far. I feel an obligation to those actors. If I can't yet help the ones I do know, how can I possibly help the ones I don't know anything about? Having said that, I also want to add that I am still open-minded about bringing in new talent.

Would it help actors if they inform you of their bookings through postcards?

Most definitely. Momentum is very important in this business. If an actor is appearing on television and informs me of it, it becomes easier to persuade my producers to bring him in. It's all sales frenzy and sizzle. That's why actors with no credits have a hard time getting an agent. It's not enough for the agent to call a casting director and say, "I really believe in him, can you please see him?" It is work that gets more work, which then generates more momentum and more sizzle.

Approximately how many submissions do you get for an average-sized project?

Here's an example: if I put in a request for ten characters in the breakdowns, and each of the one hundred or so agencies sends two submissions in for each role, I end up with over two thousand pictures. What would you do if you were faced with over two thousand pictures for only ten parts and a severe time crunch? And that's in addition to the submissions from the management companies. Not to mention that most agencies submit more than two actors per role.

That's why, when actors ask me whether they should send their pictures and résumés to a lot of casting directors, my answer is, "Don't send them to the casting directors, they have no time to deal with that kind of volume. Instead, submit to producers and directors." Why? Because a director or producer I am working with may come to me and say, "I got this picture in the mail and it looks really interesting, I want to meet them." I immediately respond positively and bring the person in.

So read the trades, do your homework and submit to the producer and director of a project.

Could changing one's agent regenerate a stalled career?

Getting a new agent is not necessarily the right answer, particularly if it's a lateral move. That is, when you move to an agency that has a similar status to the one you are leaving. Unless of course, the new agency shows phenomenal enthusiasm for your talent and promises to push you on a regular basis. If you don't inherently feel that, then the lateral move may actually set you back. For example, if I call your old agent to get you in on an audition, they may not know who your agent is. Of course I would then call SAG to find out where you are. But ironically most actors forget to inform SAG of their changes of address.

What can actors do to accelerate their careers?
The only way to ultimately achieve success in this business is to take charge of your career. For instance, develop your writing abilities or find people who can write. Then bring together a group of actors, director, etc., whom you trust, pool your money and resources, rent a space and mount a show. It can even be a showcase of one-acts or original material.

When you take control, not only can you gain visibility, you also show people that you have leadership qualities. And it's a known human fact that people are attracted to leadership. It is infectious. Producers and directors respond to actors who exude success and confidence in what they do. It makes it easier for them to want to buy you.

. . . .

Joey Paul
c/o Nickelodeon Casting
231 West Olive Street
Burbank, CA 91502
. . . .

Donald Paul Pemrick and Dean E. Fronk

Donald Paul Pemrick and Dean E. Fronk, of Pemrick/Fronk Casting, have been partnered since 1995. They started working together at I.R.S. Media, an independent film company, which allowed them the opportunity to cast as well as to occasionally produce. Their vast résumés of independent features includes the Academy Award-nominated film *Tom & Viv, Shakes the Clown, One False Move, Fakin' Da Funk, Ground Control,*

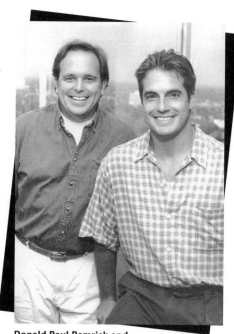

Donald Paul Pemrick and Dean E. Fronk

Monsters, Justice, My Brother the Pig, Rudyard Kipling's The Second Jungle Book and *Young at Heart.*

Tell us a little about your backgrounds and how you got started in casting.
PEMRICK: I was born in upstate New York and was raised to be a doctor. I was also a secret movie fanatic. I never thought of film as a career since Hollywood was 100,000 miles away. I got my degree, which everyone should do—

Why do you think so?
PEMRICK: I think it makes you a more well-rounded person. It allows you to know about things other than the industry.

Do you think actors should get their degrees even though it takes four years of their youth?

PEMRICK: Yes. And I think you can pursue both simultaneously. We just completed casting a movie called *Monsters* for which we were looking at seventeen and eighteen-year-olds for the leads. A lot of them were in school and had to go home to study. Look at all of the people who were child stars who took time to get their degrees: Claire Danes, Fred Savage, Jodie Foster, Brooke Shields. I think it's really important.

Anyway, when I graduated, I decided to take six months off to figure out what I wanted to do. I came to Los Angeles and knocked on some doors but I had no clue as to what I thought I might do here. I got a job in the mailroom at Marble Arch Productions, and very quickly learned how to sneak onto movie lots. Of course, security is tighter now. But one day I ended up on the CBS Radford lot, at Marble Arch, in front of the receptionist's face on the day that there happened to be a job available. Casting came very quickly after that.

I was drawn to casting from the get-go. It seemed like the hub of things to me. One day I started chatting with a publicist who was there for a meeting. He asked me what I did and out of nowhere I said, "casting." He told me that his next picture was *Annie*, and that he'd throw my hat into the ring. I never thought anything would come of it, but a week later I got a call from Ray Stark's office. They met with me and offered me the job of assisting on *Annie*.

I had to learn everything very quickly. It was sink or swim. And so much happened during the nine-month search for that little girl. We did a national search, and I had to go around with that huge stuffed dog, Sandy. He had his own seat on the plane. I'm not kidding.

The mothers would track me down. We had seventeen open calls and, without exaggeration, I'd be awakened at night hearing tap dancing above me. I'd go into the bathroom and above me, there'd be a girl tap dancing. The mother had rented the room above me. I'd hear singing in the hallway and I'd open the door and there'd be a little girl singing! The mom would be at the end of the hall yelling, "Sing, sing, sing!" But the ultimate story was in Texas. I had two thousand girls lined up and there was a little boy in line. I went up to the mother and said, "Excuse me, we're only casting Annie right now." And the mother said, "He can play a girl!" It was frightening. It was a real learning experience.

After *Annie*, I went to Barbara Claman and Mark Schwartz, and learned about day-to-day casting and television. I was with them and then on my own at Universal where I did the series *Charles In Charge* and the pilot for *The Equalizer*. I left Los Angeles in 1988, just to feel out New York, and I partnered with Deborah Aquila for two years. We were at NBC and it was a blast. I was brought back to Los Angeles by I.R.S. Media. They wanted a non-exclusive in-house casting director. So in 1989, I came back to Los Angeles.

What about your background, Dean?

FRONK: Mine is much shorter because I've only been out of college for six years. I grew up in Ohio. My first job when I got out here was with Gary Marsh at Breakdown Services. Breakdown is about as excellent a job as you can possibly get to start off because you meet everyone. I was fortunate to meet a ton of producers and casting directors while working there, and had the opportunity to learn about the process. Don was, more than anyone else, incredibly giving in terms of providing knowledge and information. Then one day I got an offer from him to come to I.R.S. Media in casting.

PEMRICK: What had impressed me about Dean was that I had been raised with the belief that you've got to get out and make your career happen, whether you're behind the camera or in front of it. And Dean was doing that. Even down to the tie. You know, for the first five months I was out here, I used to be kidded all the time for delivering the mail wearing a coat and tie. But to this day, I know for a fact that the only reason that Annie publicist spoke to me was because I was wearing a coat and tie and he thought I was there for a more important job.

How did you become partners?

PEMRICK: He is one of the only people who can read my handwriting.

FRONK: He's a much more creative individual, whereas I'm more hands-on with the business.

PEMRICK: But at the same time, creatively, he's able to tweak a role. He'll make casting choices that aren't as obvious as the role might seem to call for. He'll think of switching genders or types, and that kind of thing can really enliven a film and make it pop.

As partners we bring a unique dynamic to the casting process because we're not just a casting company. We have also found the financing for little films, and we are co-producers on a number of projects. With so many people putting out a shingle as casting directors, it made sense for us to diversify. Not that we find financing for everything that's sent to us. We have to actually fall in love with a script, because it all takes a lot of time. But Dean and I also love to work, so last year we did two SAG modified films.

Can you explain what a SAG modified film is?

PEMRICK: A SAG modified film pays about half what a SAG low-budget would pay. The entire budget has to be under $250,000, so they're difficult films to cast. SAG realized that they had too many members who weren't working, so they created new categories to open up work. First was SAG scale, then SAG low-budget. That classification means that SAG cuts its rates depending on the budget of the film. It allows a lot more actors to get work and a lot more films to be made. Then there's SAG deferred where actors are paid nothing up front, but should the film ever get exhibited for pay, the actors get paid before anyone else. And there's SAG experimental, where there is no pay at all. These are all just pay scales. They have nothing to do with the script or with the quality of the work. It just depends on the budget the producer has. But it creates five different venues for a producer to still hire SAG actors, which is fantastic. That did not exist ten years ago.

Do you look at unsolicited pictures that come in and will you meet with actors who don't necessarily have agents?
PEMRICK: We have permanent offices, which is a real plus in casting because we meet people for one project and, if for whatever reason it doesn't work out on that one, we can file their pictures and have them available for the next one. So we're able to roll submissions over from project to project. If you're sending unsolicited pictures, that's fine, but please do your research. Sending us a picture and résumé is no different than an accountant seeking employment at a corporation. It's seeking a job. So be professional and write us a letter. We, potentially, are going to hire you, so give us the courtesy and the respect that you would give if you were seeking employment in any other venue.
FRONK: We get letters written in crayon.

What would you recommend actors do to get your attention in a submission?
PEMRICK: Start with research. Find out what movies we have done recently, know who we are and what we've done.
FRONK: My younger brother is a great example. He recently graduated from Ohio State and moved here. He got a job within a week at *Dennis Miller Live*, because when he went into his interview, he knew who he was meeting with; he knew her résumé and was able to talk to her about previous shows she'd worked on. Why wouldn't you do that as an actor? If you're given the opportunity to read for a film, you've got to take it one step further and do your homework. Getting the interview is only fifty percent of it; that's getting you in. But what's going to impress the director once you're in? Other than your talent, of course. Being able to say that you've enjoyed certain films they've done will make you stand out. Do your research.

It's the same with mailing submissions. Don't waste time and postage blanketing the town with pictures. Instead, target a dozen or even twenty casting directors whose work you know. Maybe you saw a movie of theirs and realized that there were three lead roles and none of them were played by actors you had heard of. That means the casting director is open to hiring unknowns for larger roles. Target them with a nice letter. You have to be proactive. If you're sitting at home with a beer and watching TV instead of out working in a play, maybe you're not doing enough.

PEMRICK: And while we can't see every play, we read every review. And if somebody is singled out, we'll bring them in for a general.

FRONK: We believe in working with new people. Everyone deserves a chance. And the success stories are half of the fun.

PEMRICK: As Dean mentioned, for every actor sitting around complaining about their career, for every one of them, there are ten actors who can play the same type and who are being more productive. If you are not doing something to better yourself as an actor on a daily basis, you're going to be left behind.

Is there anything actors do that makes you crazy at auditions?

FRONK: The most important thing to remember is that, while acting may be your passion, it's still a profession. This is an industry that takes many, many brilliant and creative people but the bottom line is still the ever powerful dollar. It's a business. No matter how creative you are, you're still under scrutiny by the business and, as an actor, you've got to remember to keep your level of professionalism, no matter what. That's being on time, being prepared, not making excuses, having a picture with you.

Any other final tips?

FRONK: So much of it is timing. You never know when your performance is going to be done in front of the right people, at the right time. But always remember that your career is in your hands. That's what it all comes down to. If you're lucky enough to have found that acting is your true passion, then you've got a give it a one hundred and ten percent effort that's going to push you ahead of the pack if you're going to succeed.

. . . .
Donald Paul Pemrick and Dean E. Fronk
Pemrick/Fronk Casting
14724 Ventura Blvd., Penthouse Suite
Sherman Oaks, CA 91403
. . . .

PENNY PERRY

Penny Perry has cast over one hundred television and feature films. For Carl Reiner she cast *All of Me, Dead Men Don't Wear Plaid* and *The Jerk*. She also cast Robert Redford's Academy Award-winning *Ordinary People* and Alan Parker's *Midnight Express*. Other prominent credits include *Cocoon, *batteries not included, Shoot to Kill, Local Hero, Time Cop, Stranger in the Kingdom, Breastmen, The Relic* and *Reuben, Reuben*. For television, Perry cast the series *Brimstone, Kojak* and *Heartbeat*

and the movies *Zelda* and *The Man with Three Wives* among many others. She has held executive positions at various studios and production companies, including a stint as vice president of talent for Columbia Pictures. During her tenure there, she was instrumental in shaping the casting of such projects as *Boyz N the Hood* and *My Girl*.

What is your philosophy of casting?
During pre-reads, I take the time to talk to the actors in order to get to know who they are as people. When you make somebody comfortable and get to know a little about them, they become more relaxed when they read for you. As a result, the whole process becomes much less tense. I also try not to make the

actors wait too long; and I don't schedule actors back to back for the same role because I do not want awkwardness in the waiting room. Actors are sensitive and fragile beings, and I try my best to make them comfortable when they come to my office.

Once, without divulging my profession as a casting director, I went in for an audition as an actress. I wanted to do it to personally experience what it is like to be on the other side. My daughter drove me to the audition. While I was waiting to go in, another actress came in. I leaned over to my daughter and said, "She's more right for this role." My daughter said, "Mom, get yourself together, don't sabotage yourself before you go in." So finally I went in and my hands were shaking. I was a nervous wreck. As a casting director, I have read with actors thousands of times, but in this situation, my naturalness went down the drain. I started reading with this casting director, and after I finished, this person said, "Do it bigger." So I did it a lot bigger and I was awful. I felt so uncomfortable being put on the spot. And the person reading with me didn't give me a lot. All of a sudden I realized how difficult it is to audition. The actor is actually selling who he is as a human being. Now, when someone comes to read for me and is nervous and uptight, I generally will read with them again and again, until they feel more comfortable. Perhaps every casting director should go through the experience of auditioning.

So after that experience, you will allow an actor to stop and begin again if the reading is going poorly?

I will always allow it, but if you have a producer and director in the room, they may not allow it for a multitude of reasons. In any case, they have probably made up their mind four lines into the reading and already decided if you are right for the role. Unless they are interested in you, they don't want to see you do it again. So I suggest that if you start a reading and it is not going well, stop early on and start the whole scene again. If you read the whole thing, it may be too late.

Can you explain how you work with Breakdown Services?

We send them the script, which they break down by doing a story synopsis and role analysis. Then they send their analysis to us to see if we want any changes. I generally give that report to the director to see if he wants to make changes. Then the report goes back to Breakdown Services and from there is released to the agencies who read it and submit clients appropriately. Often, however, the description in the Breakdown pigeon-holes a character by saying they look a certain way, for example, describing a woman as "a forty-five year old housewife." You can go many different ways with a forty-five year old housewife. Actors shouldn't be afraid to have their agents ask if we could go a different way on a role. Always ask, unless the description is explicit.

What are your thoughts concerning acting schools?

I believe that competitiveness in a place where you are learning is not a good thing. Everybody has to grow at his or her own pace. You have to be validated for what you can do, and not be compared to what someone else can do. Often, when you get into a class and you are at ground zero, you are torn down. I don't believe you have to tear down in order to build up. I don't think an actor can be ripped apart by certain teachers and leave the class feeling good about themselves. Many actors go directly from class to therapy. When actors ask me about teachers, I am very careful about the names I give out. I try to recommend acting teachers who don't mess with the psyche. I have audited many acting classes, and I find some of them to be very destructive. They mean well but the human soul is very delicate. Therefore, when you teach, it has to be done in a very, very loving way. Acting class should be a sanctuary, a haven for growth and creativity.

> *When actors ask me about teachers, I am very careful about the names I give out. I try to recommend acting teachers who don't mess with the psyche . . . Acting class should be a sanctuary, a haven for growth and creativity.*

You have worked with director Carl Reiner on several films and with Robert Redford on *Ordinary People*. What was it like working with these great directors?

I loved working with them both. Carl Reiner trusted my judgment as a casting director, and naturally, you do your best work when somebody trusts you. Sometimes, I showed him just a few actors for each role and he made his decisions quickly. Reiner is very generous to actors; he laughs with them and he has fun with them.

With Redford, the actors who came in initially were intimidated because of who he is. But he makes people very much at home. He knows the whole process. Before readings, he talked to each actor and made them comfortable. After readings, he gave specific adjustments. He is very articulate. He knew what he wanted and was extremely decisive. With some directors, you bring in ten good people but they still can't make up their minds. Mostly because they don't know what they want and they are waiting for it to walk in through the door. But Redford always knew, both intellectually and in his guts. So when Elizabeth McGovern came in—BAM! He knew she was the one. She had the right quality.

In closing, do you have anything you would like to say to actors?
You have to let yourself come out when you do your work. I find that the biggest mistake actors make is that they prepare and come in and try to "be" the part. They forget who they are and lose their own unique personality and perspective. Another thing, as you get older, the parts may start to dwindle—especially for women. Have some other avenue you can pursue in the arts; whether it's painting, sculpting or writing. Something that really fulfills your need to create. Actors are extremely sensitive and need an emotional outlet. Many find audition rejections a difficult thing to handle. Actors must remember that the reason people do not get parts has very little to do with their talent. It's a look, it's how they fit in with another actor who has already been cast. Or a producer might like a certain look and not another. There is no rhyme or reason as to why people get parts. So you do your best and you just keep on going.

. . . .

Penny Perry
PO Box 57677
Sherman Oaks, CA 91413
. . . .

ROBI REED-HUMES

Robi Reed-Humes has, it seems, a
magic touch; she's won awards and
nominations for practically everything
she's cast in recent years. For the
MOW *The Tuskegee Airmen*, she won
a 1996 Emmy Award. Spike Lee's
Malcolm X brought in an Artios
Award, while *Don King: Only in
America* garnered another Emmy
nomination. She was nominated for
another Artios Award for the series
Roc and won a 1990 Ace Award
for *Heatwave*. Other notable
credits include *Soul Food, Clockers,*

Crooklyn, Poetic Justice, Jungle Fever, Do the Right Thing and *School Daze.*

Did you ever want to act?
Well, not as of late, but I did study theatre in college. I went to Hampton
University in Virginia and I did a lot of plays there. I'd been in high school
productions and community theatre but I never wanted to pursue it for a living.
I wanted something with a little more stability. And I wanted to have a bit more
control over what I do. Ironically, being a freelance casting director is a lot like
being an actor in that you're never really sure where your next job is coming
from. Go figure. But I have done a couple of cameos in films I have cast. Eddie
Murphy thought it would be fun to have me in *Harlem Nights* and John Singleton
put me in *Poetic Justice*. But mostly, I stay on this side of the camera.

You've worked with some great directors. What can actors expect when they audition for a director like Spike Lee?

Spike leaves a lot of room for the actors to be creative. If he likes you, he will definitely ask you to improvise and give you the room to explore. Then again, he may just give you a barely audible, "Thank you," and you could still get four or five callbacks and ultimately, the role. He's very hard to read, so if he doesn't have a lot to say to you in the room, you shouldn't take that to mean anything. He's not overt in that way, but he has a really clear vision. He's got a great eye for talent. We've made a good team on everything we've done together.

It's interesting that you say that he can be quiet and it doesn't mean anything. Actors always assume that if a director is quiet, it's the kiss of death.

Actors shouldn't judge by the feedback they get in the room. Each director or casting director is different. I've heard that actors think I don't like them because I'm hard to read. But what am I supposed to do? I'm nice. I try to make people feel comfortable. Actors have to just trust themselves and feel that they're putting their best efforts forward. And then they should just leave it alone and move on.

In situations where a film is being cast on location, if an actor can provide their own housing in the city in question, does it make sense for them to submit to you and indicate that fact?

Absolutely! On a film I just completed, for example, we hired some Los Angeles actors who we couldn't have hired if they didn't have family in New York. For budgetary reasons they had to be local hires. But actors have to specify in the submission that they can be local hires. Otherwise I have no way of knowing.

You do so many projects. How do you do it all?

Well first, I want to make it clear: my *company* is doing a lot. It's not just me. Cydney McCurdy, Doran Reed and Yolanda Hunt also make up Robi Reed Associates.

What would you say to empower actors who are coming in to meet with you?

I think it's important that actors have as much information about the project they're coming in for as possible. They need to know the format; they should try to read the script. That will help them to be prepared. So often actors make the mistake of waiting until the last minute to get the material and they kind of wing it. I don't understand why. If I'm trying to get a casting job, I do my homework before meeting with the producers. I get the script, I break it down, I try to know as much as I can know before I go in so that I'm presenting myself in the best possible way. I take what I do very seriously. If an actor isn't prepared, that says to me that they aren't serious about what they're doing. I understand that there can be extenuating circumstances, but if you aren't prepared you should reschedule. And if you know you're going to be put on tape, don't have paper in your hand. Memorize it!

Really? Because a lot of casting directors advise actors not to.

If you're going on tape, you are already at a disadvantage because you're not in the same room as the people watching you. When you have a paper in your hand, even if you know the material, you're looking down and if you're on video the lighting is probably not good. You're probably washed out from the backdrop. The odds are already against you. So you should make it easiest for them to focus on you, not what's in your hand.

I did an interview with Denise Chamian who cast *Saving Private Ryan*. She said that some of the guys who were cast did some improvising and took some liberties with the script on the tape for Spielberg. Do you think it's okay to improvise?

Well, it depends on what it is that you're doing. Certainly it's not okay with half-hour TV. Nine times out of ten the producers are in the room and they've written it. They want to hear their lines and they want to hear if you can deliver their joke. In film, you usually have some room to improvise a bit. Sometimes the director will want to hear what's written and then they may give you the opportunity to improvise.

Is there anything that actors do that really makes you crazy?

When they don't know how to leave the room! It just happened today. This woman practically had a job and lost it within three minutes. They loved her after her first reading but then she kept offering to do the lines differently. When the producer finally said that she had done enough, she still wanted to do more. She just buried herself. It made them nervous because in half-hour, you need actors who are going to show up and just do it. They were afraid that she would always want to do more. After you audition, if they don't ask for an alternate version, just leave. I'd much rather have to come running after you if we need more than have to squirm because you won't leave the room.

Do you have any final audition tips for actors?

Simple things, like when you have an audition, do your research. Know who's going to be there and try to remember who you're meeting. Remember the names of the casting directors. Lots of actors don't do that. Write it down. And then, as we said, when you audition, it's in and out because it is time and time is precious. Try to keep your pictures updated. Look like your picture. Same with résumés. If you're working a lot, I know it's hard to keep it up-to-the-minute but try. And most importantly, if I provide the material—and the material is almost always very available—it's just inexcusable to me if you come in and you're not prepared. Apologizing in the room does not help.

Are there agents with whom you work more closely than others?
We work with all of them, but there are some agents who are just stronger than others. And there are agents who I know I can count on to send me their best people for any role at a moment's notice. And sometimes with sitcoms, that's what you need.

What do you think of managers?
I think that good management can definitely help. If you have a manager, they can help you get an agent. If you've got an agent and decide on a manager, it should probably be something you and your agent decide on together because you need to have someone your agent feels they can work with and vice versa. They have got to get along.

You have received so many awards. It's really impressive.
Yeah, I guess I have. But I've turned a lot down because, if I have to make an acceptance speech, forget it.

Are you shy?
I just get really nervous. I belong to this organization, The Black Women's Network; each year they have a big breakfast and for the past three years they've asked me to be the guest speaker. I almost did the last one but then I chickened out. It's just shyness.

The funny thing is, a lot of actors are really shy.
I know. Isn't that interesting? I don't know how they do it. I really admire their courage.

. . . .
Robi Reed-Humes
1635 North Cahuenga Blvd., 5th floor
Los Angeles, CA 90028
. . . .

DONNA ROSENSTEIN, CSA

Donna Rosenstein refers to herself as a hopeless optimist—a delightful and useful quality in a woman responsible for casting all of ABC's primetime programs including *NYPD Blue, Home Improvement, The Practice, Spin City* and *Dharma and Greg.* Rosenstein was promoted to senior vice president of casting, ABC Entertainment in September 1993, having been with the network since 1984. Prior to joining ABC, she worked on such projects as *Rambo, Rocky IV, Staying Alive,*

Mama's Family and *It's a Living.* Before that she worked in Hanna-Barbera's live-action division and at ICM in Los Angeles and New York. She began her career as a production assistant at WBNG-TV in Binghampton, New York. A native of New York, Rosenstein holds a B.A. in Mass Communications from State University of New York at Binghampton.

Do you think that the networks can stay competitive with cable programming and how will that impact actors?
While the competition from cable and syndication and other venues make it harder for the networks, that competition can create opportunities for more actors because there are just more shows and more places for their work. That

competition has also led to a lot of stunt casting (the casting of a star in a guest role). But I still think that the good actors are going to work and are going to continue to work. With syndication and all the shows out there, there are tremendous opportunities.

Does comedy seem to be the safer element?
There was a time when the networks were developing shows for so many stand-up comedians and a lot of those shows were not successful. So I think producers are being pickier and choosier and are not doing those shows until the talent is ready. About three years back I read a profile on Jerry Seinfeld and he said that until the time he did his show, he didn't feel he was ready. If you look at all the successful shows on the networks driven by comedians—*Home Improvement, Roseanne, Seinfeld*—those performers had been on the road for years and had very clearly established and defined their personas.

Can you talk a little about going to network and how an actor might be able to ease some of that pressure?
I read all of these articles and people talk about network as "men in suits with cigars," but if we did the audition in a park and we were all dressed in tie dye it would be the same. As soon as you sign that test option deal and you see the potential that might exist if you get this role and the show gets picked up, it's going to be tense. We try to make it as comfortable as possible. We want it to work as much as or more than the actors do. We want somebody to walk in the door and blow us away; even if they are brand new.

Would you take a chance on somebody who just got off the bus if they blew you away?
Absolutely!

Do you screen test actors?
Yes, and I think it's great if that happens for an actor. They get to audition without an audience, they get to be in makeup and wardrobe, they get to work with a director, and they get to do a few takes. There are situations where an actor will come in and the producers will want to do a screen test, then the actor's agent will say they're not interested. I think it should be looked at as an opportunity. If I were in their shoes, I'd be willing to do a screen test.

What can actors expect when they come in for the network? Can they come in before and check out the space?

Sure. You come in and whoever greets you or signs you in can show the space. You wait in the lobby. The producers will usually be there. Some producers demand that their actors be shown the space and then they will work with the actor in the room, which is a great thing to do. All of that is helpful. Anything to dissuade the myth and make things easier. The responsibility is on everyone—the network, the production company, and the actor—to make it the best experience and most productive experience it can be.

I've been in situations where an actor will walk in and not give a good audition and I'll say, "Wait a minute, did you really understand the character?" And I'll bring them back. Some people just don't audition well. That's where an experienced and knowledgeable casting director really makes a difference. They can say, "This actor auditioned for me three months ago and didn't give a good audition, but we brought him back and he was great. He comes through." Tape or film can help.

Then there are the actors who don't want to read or whose agents tell them not to. There are a lot of actors who are at a place in their lives—they've done a series, they've done a certain amount of work, and they don't feel they should read. I understand that but they should consider it. Particularly if it's a different genre than we're used to seeing them in or if it's a chemistry thing with another actor. Plus, not every producer and director knows everyone's work that well. Many established actors read to show that they're proficient in different genres.

Do you go to theatre?

Absolutely. There are only so many hours in the day and in the week but between all of us in the department, we see a lot of stuff. We have two assistants here who are at comedy clubs and theatre every night.

What are some of your likes and dislikes when you meet actors?

When I do a general with someone, I just like them to be themselves. I'm very comfortable talking with people and it helps me to get to know who they are. Sometimes when actors come in, they end up telling me the weirdest things. That feeling they get is one of comfort. That's the feedback I get.

Why do you do generals if you don't actually audition actors?

Because what I do has a very broad impact. I can think of somebody for a role in a series, a hosting opportunity or a guest spot. They become part of my consciousness.

As senior vice president of casting, what is your actual job?

It's difficult. Sometimes I feel that I'm a fireman, putting out fires. Sometimes I feel there is an expectation that I can do what nobody else can, so if a casting director has been working on something for two months and hasn't found what they need, they turn to me. I can keep actors in my memory bank and recommend them to a wide variety of casting directors or projects. Or, if I meet someone extraordinary and there isn't a role for them right now but I think that there will be, I can put them under a holding deal where, for a period, ABC will pay them not to take work elsewhere.

Do you have any fianl tips or words of advice?

Relax, be yourself. Balance is very important. Have other interests. Your life experience is reflected in your ability. And I suggest that actors take one action to advance their careers every day. Ultimately, actors are lucky because they have an emotional outlet when they work that the rest of us do not.

. . . .

Donna Rosenstein
Sr. VP of Casting
ABC
2040 Avenue of the Stars, Fifth Floor
Los Angeles, CA 90067
. . . .

PATRICK RUSH, CSA

Patrick Rush is the seventh of eight children and, like many of his siblings, was a child actor, though, in his case, only briefly. Following two commercials and the subsequent teasing from his classmates, he gave up acting at the age of six and never wanted to do it again. After high school, he took a job in the mail room at Universal and was quickly promoted to a production assistant position for Peter Macgregor-Scott on the film *Gotcha*. He went with Macgregor-Scott to Paramount to

work on two more features and it was there that his relationship with casting directors Julie Selzer and Sally Dennison began. His association with them lasted eight years and began with assisting on such films as *The Accused, Throw Momma from the Train* (for which Rush was responsible for bringing in Oscar nominee Anne Ramsey after an exhaustive search), *Heathers* and the *Robocop* films. He eventually became an associate and then a partner. Subsequently, he spent three years at Liberman/Hirschfeld where, with Meg Liberman, he cast the highly acclaimed *Party of Five*. Rush's other work includes the films *X-Files: The Movie, Look Who's Talking Now, Suture* and *Lawnmower Man*. He was nominated, with Meg Liberman and Marc Hirschfeld, for the Artios Award for his work on the nighttime special *National Lampoon's Favorite Deadly Sins*, and won the award, along with Julie Selzer, for Outstanding Achievement in Mini-series Casting for Truman Capote's *In Cold Blood*. He is now partnered with casting director Sharon Klein.

I recognize the Artios Award but what are all of these other awards on your desk?
Well, they're actually bowling trophies. I'm on a league and my team, Alley of the Dolls, has won seven trophies. I think it's important to have something you do outside of the office to make your life real. I love what I do but I am not what I do for a living. I think that's why I continue to enjoy and love casting. It should be the same for actors. Sometimes you'll see an actress who went off and had a baby, for example, and now there's something about her that's different; her auditions are more relaxed because she realizes that there's something more important. This isn't the biggest deal in the world. This is Hollywood; it's make believe.

What kind of actors do you respond to?
I'm always looking for people who have the gift and I truly think that you either have it or you don't. I don't believe that Meryl Streep knows what she knows from an acting class. I think that's a gift she has exercised and honed. You do have to go to class and you do have to train, but I really believe you have to start with a God-given gift.

You have a reputation for being one of those casting directors who makes people really comfortable.
As a casting director, I can never lose sight of the fact that my side of the desk is so much easier than the other side. My job is hard and stressful sometimes but if I do it right, it shouldn't be too difficult. It's so much harder for the actors. So I try as best I can not to forget that and to read well with them, to give them direction, to be friendly and polite, and to create an atmosphere of comfort. What can I expect to get from an actor if I'm not looking up from the page or if I'm not watching what they're doing? The actor's job is hard enough, they don't need me making things miserable. It can be different in a producers' session, though. Those rooms can be quick and cold so I think it's important for actors to gauge the room. If you walk in and you feel that it's cold, don't try to warm it up. Say your lines and go home. Callbacks can be stickier than reading for me alone. It won't be as friendly because the producers and director have a million

other departments to worry about, not just casting. So I need to get in there, show them the best people I can, and get out. There's not a lot of time for the room to be chatty and warm when you're lining up an hour's worth of actors. Don't try to change the feel of the room because you end up hanging yourself. And you'll realize you're hanging yourself as you do it and then you're so self conscious, you're not even in the reading anymore.

How can actors meet you?

I have found really good actors at cold-reading workshops. Doing them is a chance for me to see as many as twenty-two actors in two hours. That's something I probably couldn't do in my normal work day. At a workshop, I can meet you, spend a little time with you, give you some sides and see you read. I have hired fifteen or sixteen people each season from workshops. They're not coming in for the big guest star or recurring parts, but they're coming in. Sometimes they payoff when they get into the office and sometimes they don't. But I get such a nice feeling when I'm able to hire someone from the workshops because I know that I'm not just attending them for the buck. I see good people there. People often say that they don't think it's right because workshops are paid auditions. I understand that thinking but my response is, if an actor does a mass mailing and sends out a hundred pictures and résumés—which, once you add envelopes and postage, cost about two dollars each—how many casting directors are they actually going to meet? If the actor takes the same $200 they would spend on a mailing and applies it to workshops, they can actually meet people and hand them a picture in person. I think that's much more valuable than a mailing. Although actors should be careful to pick workshops that are reputable and offer casting directors who work on shows the actor could conceivably be right for. Another thing about workshops: they're called workshops for a reason. You work, I shop. I'm not there to teach an acting class. That's not what I do. I can give direction— and I do—but I'm there to see your work.

I noticed a lithograph headshot on your desk. Is it okay to send lithos to you?

When I see a fax of a headshot it usually means that the agent is out of pictures and I would never penalize an actor because the agent is out of pictures. But if you're doing a mailing or submitting yourself, you should never be out of pictures. You must send your best shot, not a copy or a lithograph. If you're going to spend your time and your energy on your craft, which you must love if you're going to do this, why bother if you're not going to give it your all? You don't look as good in a litho.

Furthermore, for actors who do submit themselves, I want to say that things move so quickly in television that by the time an actor gets a breakdown and sends a picture, the role is often cast. Make sure, if you're going to submit yourself, that you check the start date. Submit yourself for features or plays or MOWs, where you know that there is time for the casting people to receive and go through the mail. I think it's a waste for actors to submit themselves on episodic television. It just moves too fast.

Do you have any advice for actors once they get into your office?
Do not be rude to anyone—the assistant, the receptionist—no one. It is not their fault if I'm running late, that we don't validate, or that your beeper's going off and there isn't an available phone. I've had people who've come in and read and whom I planned to call back until I heard that they were rude out front. If you're rude in an office, how much of a nightmare are you going to be when you get on a set? I don't want to hear back from producers that we've hired a problem. There is no excuse for rudeness. Ever. I also don't like actors who ask, "When are callbacks?" No one who's ever asked has been even remotely close to getting one. If you are going to get a callback, you'll find out, don't worry. Do ask questions regarding the material. If you're not sure how to pronounce a word, you should have looked it up before you got here. Don't butcher a word and make yourself look stupid. Do the homework or ask. Otherwise, a great audition can end up in the toilet. I don't ever want to be unapproachable to an actor. I'd rather you ask me all of that stuff before we get started so you can focus on what it is that you need to do. And know what you're auditioning for. Some people came in to audition for *Party of Five* thinking it was a sitcom. A good hint on that is, on the page, television sitcoms are double spaced, dramas are single spaced. Always. If you're auditioning for a show you've never seen, call your friends and ask if they've seen it. Trusting the words on the page of a script that's well written will help you immeasurably. And trust your instincts. Your instincts are what got you into the room. Sometimes I'll be sitting with someone and we'll be chatting before we read and I'll think, "Oh, this is the person." And then they start to read and they become these horrible, robotic monsters. I say, "Let's do it again and do it the way we were chatting. Stop acting!" It's amazing how many people can't be themselves as soon as they start reading other people's words. Whatever you're auditioning for, read it as many times as you can so the words become your own. Give them your rhythms. You're going to be either right or wrong for the role but if you're wrong for the part and you audition well, it is my job to remember you for parts you are right for.

For some actors, their difficulty in being themselves is what led them to acting.
I think there's nothing harder than trying to be yourself and I don't think actors have the market cornered there. I'm trying on a daily basis to be my authentic self. I'm trying right now, so people who are reading this won't think I'm an idiot. Actors who have self-esteem issues—it's not all about them all of the time. We as humans have a lot of those feelings. I'm nervous going to a session wondering if my actors are going to get cast. I'm gunning for the actors to be great. Why would I want them to fail? If I have a session that doesn't go well and my people don't get cast, I'm just like an actor on the way home from a bad audition. I feel like I'm not good at what I do. Actors are not alone.

Any final tips?
Sometimes you have to audition to be the waiter who says, "More pepper?" and those can be the hardest roles to audition for because you've studied and trained your whole life and then you have to come in and say, "More pepper?" That's so hard. There's the desperation of trying to be so good at those two words and really, the scene is not about you. You need to know when the scene's about you and when it's not. I know it's hard and I don't envy that. But again, it's about not acting. It's about the actor who is comfortable enough with who they are that they allow their true self to show. That is what I am always looking for.

. . . .

Patrick Rush
Rush/Klein Casting
6250 Canoga Ave.
Woodland Hills, CA 91367
. . . .

Julie Selzer, csa

Julie Selzer was born in San Antonio, Texas but raised in California. As a young actress, she attended Cal State Northridge, studying theatre and journalism. It was there that she realized that she didn't, in fact, want to be in front of the camera but behind it. When she got her first industry job, interning with Casting Director Sally Dennison, she dropped out of school and began a career in casting where she has happily spent the last seventeen years. Her path to her current

independent status included several jobs assisting and a five year partnership with Dennison who retired in 1992. Her work along the way has included a wide spectrum of films including *Throw Momma from the Train, The Accused, Heathers, Bad Girls* (in conjunction with Mike Fenton), *Robocop, Love Field* and *Nobody's Fool.* Selzer also cast the Showtime anthology *Picture Windows* and won an Artios Award (With Patrick Rush) for the mini-series *In Cold Blood.* She is partnered with Lauris Freeman and continues to work frequently with a favorite director, Jonathan Kaplan, who also happens to be her husband.

What advice would you give your daughter if she decided that she wanted to become an actress?

Realize this is a business and understand the business end of it as well as the artistic end of it. If you could be happy making a nice life for yourself in theatre—and you don't have dreams of super-stardom, but are creatively fulfilled doing theatre—do that. If you can make a living, great. If you can't, get another job that can help you do the theatre. Don't take rejection personally. Know how to sell yourself and know who you are without unrealistic expectations. Know that the look is what's often going to get the job and not the talent. Ninety percent is knowing what you can't do. Try to be objective. Realize that getting the job has nothing to do with who you are or how wonderful a person you are or even how good an actor you are.

Do you have any advice for those beautiful people who have the looks that always seem to get them jobs?

It's even more important for those people to pay their dues in the theatre and to try to get some respectable theatre credits under their belts. Michelle Pfeiffer is a good example. She's someone who's really challenged herself and is really beautiful but is also stretching and, because of that, she is taken seriously. Gwyneth Paltrow is another one. Of course it helps to be that beautiful but they're stretching and they love theatre. It's not just modeling and knowing that you have the right look and can make a gazillion dollars on a night-time soap. Remember, no one's looks last forever, but your training will last a lifetime.

What do you think the atmosphere is like for minority actors?

There have been a lot of inroads with certain ethnic minority groups. Certain others are incredibly underrepresented, like Asians and Latinos. I'm always trying to diversify casts with suggestions of minorities. Of course, it's always ultimately who is best for the part, but if you can go with a minority then why not try to make it happen? My husband's a big believer in that too.

Can you talk about the different styles of acting for the different mediums?

In simple terms for me, comedy acting for television is about delivering the joke. Dramas are about bringing who you are and the reality to a role.

I've found that I don't particularly enjoy television casting because I don't like all the decision-by-committee and what the actors have to go through. I like answering to only a few people. Too many cooks, otherwise. It's like that old joke, "What's a casting director's worst fear? A producer's secretary with a Player's

Guide!" There is also a big difference between theatre acting and screen acting and knowing that both are art forms.

For screen acting you need to let them see you think, while for theatre acting you need to let them see you do. You're much more in control in the theatre. It's a living organic experience and you can take the audience along for the ride and experience it with them

Can you talk about the audition process from your point of view?

I can normally tell right in the beginning if someone's got the chops or not. That's not too tough. There's a confidence there and when an actor knows what they're doing, it's in their choices and I respond to that. Those are the people I know will be able to collaborate with the director and let the director guide them. The director is like a living tool to help the actor create this new world. The casting director should be able to do that too—to help bring the right stuff out of the actor—so that, hopefully, the actor will get the role.

Everyone brings something to the party. That's what makes one actor different from the next. There can be five perfectly valid, wonderful choices for a role. Each actor can be great but ultimately the director is going to go with the actor who helps serve his vision of his movie. It doesn't mean the other four weren't as special and couldn't have been as wonderful. That's the hardest thing for an actor to accept because it feels so personal—but really, it's not.

You work a lot with your husband, Jonathan Kaplan. What are some of the things that he might look for in an audition?

Well, we tape a lot. Jonathan will always have an actor do their take on a character first. He won't give any direction. It's, "Let's see what you've got," and then he'll work with it from there. Any director I've ever worked with will hire the person they feel the most comfortable with—that they feel will deliver the goods. A director has so many things to think about on the set that they want the actor they feel confident about, who will give them what they need. So you should make a strong choice and go with it.

Do you have any real annoyances?

It always annoys me if an actor shows up and isn't prepared or makes some excuse about not getting the sides or not having the material. I'm organized, so you should be organized. I'll work with people; if someone's had a bad day and they want to try to come back another time I'll try to accommodate that. But don't give me lame excuses. A lot of times, through no fault of the casting director, we get material that we have to hand to the actor with no notice and it's, "I'm really sorry to do this, but this is the deal and if you don't read right now, that's it. So take twenty minutes and you're on." Sometimes that happens and it's no one's fault. But usually there's time for preparation and lack of it really annoys me. That's really my only annoyance. I've been doing this long enough that I love almost all of the actors I meet and if I can help them get jobs, that's a great satisfaction.

. . . .

Julie Selzer
Selzer/Freeman Casting
Sunset Gower Studios
1438 N. Gower Street, Bldg. 5, Suite 301
Los Angeles, CA 90028
. . . .

MERYL LIND SHAW

Born in New York City and raised in
Manhattan, Meryl Lind Shaw has spent
her entire professional life in the San
Francisco Bay Area. She began as a
stage manager at the Berkeley
Shakespeare Festival, then at the
Berkeley Stage Company and, finally,
at the Berkeley Repertory Theatre,
where she was ensconced for twelve
years. A temporary casting position
at San Francisco's prestigious
American Conservatory Theatre
(A.C.T.) in 1992 quickly led to a
full time career there. Now, as

their resident casting director, Shaw casts their eight show season and teaches at
A.C.T.'s Conservatory.

**Hollywood can be a real battleground; do you have any advice for the actor to
help them avoid burning out?**
I really believe there are times in your life when the best thing you can do is just
stop and breathe. Take a time-out. Focus on other things, either creative or
personal endeavors, feed them and, on some level, feed your soul. Doing that
can give people a greater sense of who they are and help to recharge their spiritual
batteries. Actors need to remember that they are more than what they do. They
can rediscover what it is that makes them who they are. After all, good acting is
being who you are and then using that to interpret work. Young actors just out

of school often feel as though the world dictates, "Here are the types we're looking for. Mold yourself to become this." The truth is that, for a casting director, what we want to see is who you uniquely are. So a time-out would be to reconnect with whatever it is that makes an actor "them."

A.C.T. was a repertory acting company at one time, wasn't it?
It was, but that ended prior to my coming here. Now we're a company that cultivates an extended family of actors who come and go, as extended families do. So you may see familiar faces popping up again and again. I think very few theatres are in a position to arrange season-long work for actors. And I think there are very few actors who are interested in committing for that length of time and taking themselves out of Los Angeles or New York for so much of the year.

How do you find actors?
I see a lot of shows in San Francisco. I really stay up on the local talent that way. I attend the regional auditions and the Equity LORT (League of Regional Theaters) auditions in Los Angeles, and we hold our own generals, once a year, which we publicize in the Callboard (a Bay Area trade publication) and through the Equity hot-line. We are a LORT A Theatre so all our roles are filled by Equity actors. I also read the Los Angeles and New York reviews just to see who's doing what. Primarily I find out about Los Angeles actors through casting directors and agents. I use casting directors to prepare lists of Los Angeles actors for me to see. And casting directors from all of the theatres talk to each other. I talk to Joanne DeNaut from South Coast Rep. and Stanley Soble from the Taper so there is a certain amount of connection there. And there are several Los Angeles agents with whom I have relationships, who I know understand the requirements of the Geary Theatre [where A.C.T. is housed] and would only send me actors who can handle that theatre in terms of training and experience. An actor can't do contemporary plays in a ninety-nine seat theatre and then expect to take on classical roles in our thousand seat house. Most actors aren't trained for that. So rather than put out a breakdown and open myself up to everybody and be inundated with actors who don't have the qualifications, I reach out to particular agencies. This doesn't happen when I go to New York but, in Los Angeles, the number of actors who would submit themselves or who would be submitted by agents and just have no theatre background or training is overwhelming. I cast eight shows a year and I teach; I don't have time to open myself up to having to screen eight hundred résumés when really, eighty will do. Occasionally, people will see our season listings and write to me expressing interest in a project. I read all of those letters and résumés and I file them appropriately if I think they

might possibly be right for something. Anyone can send me a résumé anytime they want. But we don't do open auditions for each show. Our auditions are by invitation only. So basically, the general auditions are the only place that I get to see people in an open situation.

What do you look for in actors?
If you look at the kind of material A.C.T. produces, we don't do many conversational living room plays. We do elevated language. We do Williams, Shaw, Pinter. It's not conversational, contemporary playwriting. So what I look for on a résumé is someone who's worked on classical language. The Greeks, Moliere, Shakespeare, something that you have to work hard to wrap yourself around and requires training.

At the audition itself, what can you do in three minutes? You can't show me everything in your range. There's no way. I always advise actors to hit me with their best shot and whatever you do best, do that first. Hit me with your strength. The work you feel most strongly about will get you off to your best start. And I want to see what's uniquely you. You can't show me everything you do but I want to get a glimpse of who you are. Who are you? That's really the question that I'm asking myself. What is the essence of this person? What is at least one thing they can do well? I can extrapolate from there. I really advise actors to stay close to home in terms of age and type when choosing monologues for general auditions. Classes are a wonderful time to stretch and do things out of your range; auditions are not an appropriate time to do that. Reveal yourself to me. Let me see the unique thing that you bring to the table.

Is there anything that actors do that you really like or don't like at auditions?
I definitely don't like direct eye contact. It more than annoys me. I feel that it makes me responsible for the actor's success because I've now become their scene partner. If I turn down my eyes to write the notes I need to write to do my job, I feel that I am compromising the actor's concentration and I really resent having that pressure put upon me.

There's nothing more contagious than an actor walking in with a mixture of relaxation and confidence and a joy of performing. The important thing for any actor to remember at any audition is that we're rooting for you. Who doesn't want to see the next great discovery? Or to cast a show well and be finished so that I can move on to my next project? We're rooting for you from the moment you walk in the door. So bring that sense of collaborative joy for the love of the art. I know it's hard. But if an actor walks in with baggage or resentment, that's also contagious. You feel like the actor is blaming you for their hard day or whatever problems they're having. And actors have to be available as human beings. Sometimes actors walk into a room, already so into their first beat that they're kind of glazed over. You can't access the human being there. The audition is a getting-to-know-you moment. Be available.

I also don't think it's a particularly good idea to choose a piece that's too high in emotional content because I don't know that you can go from zero to sixty in a minute and a half. You shouldn't attempt it. It isn't fair to you or the material. You should choose material that takes you on a journey but doesn't ask you to scale heights that really need an hour and a half of performance. You can still find pieces that will give you a nice arc, but avoid pieces that are really emotionally high or are really angry for a sustained period. They set up too difficult a challenge for the actor. What am I looking for? I'm looking for a variety of things. Vocal chops. Speech. How actors deal with language. How they use their body as an instrument. Skills that I'm checking on. But past that, I'm looking for moment to moment. Are they going moment by moment through the piece and do I believe them.

Do you have any final words for actors?

I love actors. I've spent my entire professional life taking care of actors, but I could never be one. It's a hard, hard, hard, hard life to choose and there's only one reason to choose it: because you *have* to act. Given that, I think the best way for actors to come to terms with being actors is to empower themselves as much as possible. They need to create work for themselves, to keep recharging their batteries in any way they can that is outside of acting, to constantly revisit the essence of who they are and keep that strong because that is their most important asset, to fully flesh out their own being and discover who they are, and to be clear about what their strengths are and how those strengths are marketable and how they might be perceived. There are phases when you're someone for whom there will be a lot of work and there are phases when you won't be. Actors need to use those phases creatively, productively and positively and not get caught up in believing that there is some ideal to which they need to mold themselves, but instead, cultivate the wonderful individuals that they are. And especially, they need to know that if they are gifted and persevere, their time will come.

. . . .

Meryl Lind Shaw
A.C.T.
30 Grant Avenue, 6th floor
San Francisco, CA 94108

. . . .

CHRISTINE SHEAKS, CSA

Born in Indiana, Christine Sheaks moved to California as a baby and has been in Los Angeles ever since, with the exception of one five-year stint in New York. A fascination with entertainment led her to 20th Century Fox; luck led her to casting. As an associate to Donna Isaacson and John Lyons, she was immersed in film casting. Later, with Lyons—whom Sheaks counts as her mentor—she worked on several films until he went into production, leaving her to continue casting on her own.

Boogie Nights followed, and with it an Artios Award and a reputation that has studios knocking on Sheaks' door. Her subsequent credits include the features *The Mod Squad*, *In Defense of Sleeping Beauty* and *S'all Good*.

Let's start with how you got into casting.
As a child, my mom would make me watch great old movies. She was a film fanatic and I really loved them as well. Then in my mid-twenties, I reached a point where I loved movies so much that I had to make it my work, not just my hobby. I thought—Okay, I'm going to pick a TV show that I adore and start at the bottom. *Moonlighting* had just aired as a mid-season replacement. I snuck

onto the lot at 20th Century Fox, knocked on the door and asked for a job. They told me there was an opening in casting and, if I interned for a few months, they would help me get a job. I think God played a hand because casting was perfect for me. Everything I was interested in doing was right there. I have this amazing memory—I have always remembered actors and directors, even when I was watching those old movies with my mom. It just felt, for the first time in my life, like I had found my calling. So I was Karen Vice's assistant on *Moonlighting* for four years before moving to New York to work as an associate with John Lyons and Donna Isaacson. I stayed with them for a year until they split up their partnership. Then I was with John for another four years. We worked on Joel and Ethan Coen's movies. We did *Barton Fink, Fargo* and *The Hudsucker Proxy* as well as *Lorenzo's Oil* and the PBS mini-series *Tales of the City*. It was great. Then, John started producing and he asked me to cast. *A Walk in the Clouds* was the first time I got credit in the main titles. John went on to produce *Boogie Nights* and asked me to cast it. That has been one of the high points of my entire career. John has just exquisite taste and I felt so lucky to be working for him.

Is there a difference between casting an independent film like *Boogie Nights* and a big studio film like *Mod Squad*?
I think a casting director has to walk a line; I want the best person, the most interesting person for a role but, if you're doing a big budget movie, you have to weigh in your mind that you need someone with name recognition. I do believe that at the end of the day, if you cast a movie well and it's a good movie, it will prevail. And I will always work hard to get the people I think are the best. I've been known to beg people to do roles that they might not normally do because they thought they were too small. But every role matters. They're all pieces in the puzzle and I want the whole thing to be fantastic.

Of course, everyone wants talented actors, but is there a specific kind of actor you prefer? Has anyone made a contribution to your taste?
It depends entirely on the project and the character. I really like straightforward performances. I like someone to be very real. I'm a fan of not seeing the acting. Acting has changed since the days I grew up watching *Funny Girl*. Everything is more real. The material is more real and the casting is more real. This is a different world from the one thirty or forty years ago and that change has spilled over to affect film-making. My taste is actually directly influenced by John Lyons. He came from Playwright's Horizons in New York, from an amazing theatre background. John has been my guardian angel. He's taught me so much and really looked out for me.

Is there anything that you'd like to say to actors about auditioning?

I think that having someone come in prepared, being themselves, doing their work and talking to me on a real human level is what I'm most looking for. I always remember interesting actors and I use them.

So when people come in to audition, you have a conversation with them? A lot of casting directors hate to chat—especially in television where there are so many time constraints.

I cannot do it any other way. How can anybody? I understand that people are busy, but you know what? We all are. If you're casting a movie, you probably have a bit more time than in television, but there is never a lot. It doesn't help any of us to rush through an audition just for the sake of hurrying. What difference do a couple of minutes make if that's what it takes to make the actor comfortable and able to do their best work?

Do you do generals?

Absolutely.

How can an actor get a general with you?

If I'm looking for something specific on a project and I see an actor's picture, I'll bring them in if they look like they might be right. Often, agents I know will say, "This person is really special." But even if I don't have a relationship with that agent, I will sometimes go on a hunch. Every day is different. Sometimes you don't have time and sometimes you take a chance.

Will you see someone without an agent?

Yes! If a picture catches my eye and I think it's interesting, I will bring in that actor in three seconds. That's something I learned from John Lyons. He never cared one iota if someone was with SAG or whether or not they had an agent. If you're interesting and you're right for a role and you're a good actor, we'll pull you off a street corner. He also taught me to take chances and not go with the obvious but with the most interesting. He taught me to go with actors people wouldn't normally expect to see in certain roles—like Burt Reynolds in *Boogie Nights*.

We did a lot of research for that movie. Seventies porn was very different from what is being made today. People didn't work out then. And, as corny as they were, those movies actually had a story. Paul Thomas Anderson really wanted me to get a feel for the porn people so I would have that feel when I was casting the actors. We made a lot of calls to people in the porn world and several of them were quite good and made it into the film.

Possibly one of the most successful elements of *Boogie Nights* was the casting of Mark Wahlberg. He was such an interesting choice.

When I came aboard the film, there was actually already an offer out to Leonardo DiCaprio. He took a long time deciding because he was also considering *Titanic*. When he finally passed, I was relieved because, as wonderful as I think he is, I didn't see him as Dirk Diggler. I scoured New York and Los Angeles looking for people, but in the end I really think there are only a couple of people who could have done that role. Whenever I cast, I get very specific and I rely a lot on instinct. Mark Wahlberg had a lot of the qualities that I was looking for to make up Dirk Diggler. It took me a long time to get Mark and Paul Thomas Anderson in a room together but once I did, the meeting went very well. I've seen the movie three times now and each time he surprises me. He totally surpassed even my expectations.

What's it like for you to suddenly be in a position to turn work down?

It's wonderful. *Boogie Nights* helped so tremendously. And we never knew how it was going to be received. When Siskel and Ebert mentioned me on their show I was so honored. They never mention casting directors. It meant the world to me because casting directors never get recognition. A costume designer can get an Academy Award but not a casting director. I think that will change soon.

Do you believe in acting classes?

Oh, absolutely. I believe the difference between Los Angeles actors and New York actors is the training. Almost everyone in New York is so well trained. In Los Angeles, I think the history of the city is people just coming here because they have a dream. They want to be a movie star so they get pictures and résumés together and they come here. In New York there seems to be a different mind-set. Perhaps because of the influence of theatre, training is the priority; it's the foundation. That's not always the case in Los Angeles.

So, do you think it's wise for a young actor to go to New York?

Definitely. There is just something that New York gives you, a certain work ethic. It's about being part of an ensemble as opposed to looking at a TV or film script and turning it down because there are only two speeches for your character. When I meet New York actors I breathe a sigh of relief because I know that they're probably well trained. Not that you can't get training here, but not everyone does, and that's really too bad.

· · · · · · · · · · · · · · · · · · · ·

Christine Sheaks
c/o CSA
606 N. Larchmont Blvd., Suite 4B
Los Angeles, CA 90004

· · · · · · · · · · · · · · · · · · · ·

MELISSA SKOFF, CSA

Melissa Skoff trained for the theatre at UCLA and worked in various capacities for producers and directors before joining the casting department at Warner Bros. as a receptionist. Under the guidance of then casting head, Diane Crittenden, she learned the casting process from the bottom up. She was soon promoted to the position of casting director, and later became the associate director of casting at Warner Bros.

After striking out on her own, she spent five years casting the series *The Dukes of Hazzard*. In 1990, she became senior executive in charge of talent for FNM (Fox Night at the Movies) and cast such TV movies as *Bonnie & Clyde: The True Story* and *The Hunted*. Skoff has also cast the features *Nowhere Land, Dream For An Insomniac, The Emerald Forest, Black Rain* (U.S. casting), *The Golden Child* (overseas casting), *Sioux City*, and many others. For television, she has cast the Showtime movie *Last Light*, the NBC mini-series *The Great Escape*, ABC's *Divorce Wars*, and many series, such as *Quantum Leap* and the current *JAG*.

It is so important for actors auditioning for television or film to be able to cold-read well. What advice would you offer them?

A lot of actors find cold reading a mystery. If you give a roomful of actors a choice between doing a cold reading or having root canal work done, some would choose the root canal—to them, it would be less painful. But it shouldn't be. There is an art to cold reading. There's a method to explore the subtext of a scene and understand what it is precisely that you're trying to get across. If you're going to be an actor, you must know how to cold read well, because most actors are not going to get the opportunity to get a role without first auditioning for it.

It has been said that there are a number of great actors, such as Brando and James Dean, who were notoriously bad cold-readers.

A lot of actors can't cold-read but do manage to create brilliant performances. I've convinced many producers and directors to hire an actor despite a bad reading. However, the competition is so stiff that if you can't read well, chances are you won't get the part. Cold-reading is not just reading words, but expressing emotion and subtext through them. If you can't cold-read, then you can't bring emotion and sub-text to your audition. If that's missing, it's very hard for the casting director to say to the director, "This is the best person for the job."

I can't tell you how many times I've had people audition in my office who did very well, but changed everything for the producers and failed miserably. I can't risk bringing in people who don't make me look good. It's embarrassing to bring people in who are mediocre at best, who are unprepared and disorganized, who hand me a picture in one hand and a résumé with the other, who chew gum, who come in looking like they just rolled out of bed or who show up an hour late without a just cause.

How can actors best handle nervousness before an audition?

Nervousness is displaced energy. The actor has to corral that energy and use it in a positive way. If you're going to go out and audition, you have to have all your energy ready. You have to have all your juices flowing and ready to be used. What I like people to do is to channel their nervous energy. Instead of nervously letting it flow through the tips of their fingers, or the tapping of their feet, actors have to take all that energy and use it from within. The actor has to be revved up during an audition, but they have to channel it constructively. Otherwise, when an actor comes in and their hand is shaking or their lip quivering, it's a big strike against them. Nobody wants to hire somebody who is inexperienced. Shaking and quivering are the classic signs of an inexperienced actor. Of course, everybody is nervous when they go in for something important—it could be the project that can finally launch their career. My advice is to put all of that speculation away; it's premature. All you have to do for the moment is go in, experience the moment and make it your best possible work.

What are the current trends in casting?

The whole emphasis of the industry has changed. It used to be an adult industry, now kids are fashionable. All the pilots and series have a lot of kids in them. The kids we have been hiring go anywhere from nine years old to eighteen and up. What we are always craving are eighteen-year-olds who can play younger, or kids who are emancipated and have their high school equivalency.

What do you mean by "emancipated?"

To be emancipated, you have to pass certain high school proficiency tests. After that, the kids are treated by the state as adults. For example, if they get into trouble with the law, they are treated as adults. But I don't necessarily advise emancipation. Kids grow up fast enough. I've seen children who are emancipated who don't have spectacular careers *and* they miss out on a normal high school life. I think it is more important that kids allow themselves the time to mature and experience that part of their life. In the future there will be plenty of time to work.

Of course, you can work as a kid and not be emancipated. But it's hard when we have a child as the lead in an afternoon special or a two-hour TV movie because we don't have a lot of money and a lot of time to spend shooting. On a big feature, you work around the kid.

Do you have advice for kids who want to act?

The thing with kids is to be natural. Nobody wants precocious children anymore. And nobody wants to see them trying to be adults. You want kids to be kids because the whole flavor of the actor these days is the common man, as opposed to the elegant Cary Grants of the world. Kids can work with good coaches, but should not over-work. The idea is to keep it fun. I say to them, "Every time you go on an interview, write down everything in a diary. The last thing you should write down is, 'Did I have fun?'" First of all, I want them to have a record of what they have done and secondly, if acting stops being fun, they shouldn't do it.

Another problem with child actors is that they can feel very pushed by their parents. There is a competitiveness among parents to get their kids jobs. It's got to be handled in such a way that doesn't make the child manic or neurotic.

Do you interview kids in the presence of their parents?

No, the kids come in alone. I want to see what they can do without their parents, especially the little ones. How do they handle adult situations—even if mom is sitting five feet off the set? I want to see how the child responds and how comfortable they are. If I ask a question, I don't want the child to look at his mother for guidance. I want to see what the kid thinks. And these days, everybody's kids are so gorgeous and smart, it's a whole different ballpark. They are so advanced.

How would you define talent?

Talent is the power that reaches out and grabs the audience. In comedy it's great timing; in serious pieces, it's the emotional capacity to elicit tears from the audience.

Talent alone is not enough, however. It's important to work out like an athlete. If you are an athlete, you have to train everyday to keep your muscles in tone. If you are in a good acting class, you are exercising your muscles and learning from your mistakes. It is imperative that people study. It polishes and sensitizes the actor. You have got to have feedback, and the best place for that is a good acting class.

What joy do you get from the casting process?

I love to watch people emerge. I love to uncover new talent. It's very exciting to have the chance to watch someone new do something extraordinary.

Another joy of casting is when the pieces fall together easily. For example, I cast the feature *Sioux City* in only three sessions. Director Lou Diamond Philips loved everybody I brought in. It's very rewarding when you bring two actors for a role, and your producers can't decide between them because they like them both so much.

Luckily, there are a number of actors I trust who are always right on mark, and whose careers I have promoted because they do consistently excellent work. When you look into their eyes, you can see them think. With them, you feel confident that whatever role you call them in for, they're going to give their best. Even if they don't get the role, they're not going to fail you. And that's all we ask for.

. . . .

Melissa Skoff
11684 Ventura Blvd., Suite 5141
Studio City, 91604

. . . .

Mary Jo Slater, CSA

Mary Jo Slater has brought her extraordinary eye for casting to over fifty television productions, dozens of Broadway and off-Broadway shows, and over twenty-five features including *The Gingerbread Man, Spawn, The Grass Harp, Murder in the First, Mother, The Wings of Courage* and *Ace Ventura: Pet Detective*. Originally she trained as an actress, then worked as an assistant agent, an agent, and finally as a casting director when she put together the cast for Neil  Simon's *Chapter Two*. While in New York, she continued casting theatre, as well as the daytime drama *One Life to Live*, for which she won an Artios Award. Relocating to Los Angeles, she was made vice president of talent at MGM in 1986 and held the position for four years, supervising the casting of *Thirtysomething, Dark Shadows, Baby Boom* and over two dozen MOWs, series and pilots. She currently works independently under the banner of Slater & Associates Casting. Slater is the mother of two film actors, Christian Slater and his brother, Ryan.

You have cast on both coasts. Do you recommend that actors experience New York before coming to Los Angeles?

I absolutely do. Look at my son, Christian. He was raised in New York, and at thirteen his agent was Sam Cohn at ICM (a very powerful agent who spotted Christian in an off-Broadway play). Sam used to say that he was so glad Christian was raised in New York, because it made him much savvier and grainier than other young actors. He had acting sophistication at a young age because there is so much diversity in New York theatre. In New York, people would work for $40 a week and be grateful to be part of a production. Here, it's, "What's the bottom line? Do I get a percentage? What's my back end?" The creative attitude of, "Let's put on a great show," does not exist anymore and this saddens me greatly.

How important do you think it is to have connections in the business?

Being related is very helpful but not essential. For example, because of my work, Christian grew up backstage in theatre. When I cast for Broadway shows, he would come along and watch the other actors audition. He was like a sponge. He learned through observation. But his chance to appear in *The Music Man* on Broadway at an early age was a fluke. It had nothing to do with being connected. Stars such as Robert De Niro and Jim Carrey had no connections when they started out. They had something special and someone caught on to it and here they are.

Would you agree that even if you have that something special, it might take many years for people to finally recognize it?

Absolutely. When I came to Los Angeles in 1986, Jim Carrey was one of the first actors I met. At MGM, we were doing a pilot for NBC, and Jim came in and read for the network. He was astonishing! Not only was he brilliantly funny, but he blew me away with his real and sensitive moments. So I turned around to the network folks, full of excitement . . . and they were bored. They didn't give him the role! Here was an actor with limitless ability, who had to pay his dues for many years before the community recognized his talent.

How can newcomers get to meet you? Do you accept unsolicited submissions?

Regrettably, no. There is so little time. We work twelve hours a day. In my free time I go to movies. I see everything. That is where I find new faces for the films I am casting.

Do you use actors' tapes to persuade directors to hire them?

Yes. There is no better way to exhibit your talent to directors than a good tape. In fact, lately my job has become salesman. I have to sell actors and end up renting the videos because the actor's agent does not have a demo of the actor I am trying to sell. In features especially, you often get a role only through a tape. Some directors don't even want to read people—they don't want to talk, they just want to see tape.

In your view, what are the key qualities for success?

Obviously talent does help. Looks also help. And so does perseverance. Sprinkle a little luck into the mixture and perhaps one can become a working actor. I have great respect and admiration for anyone who wants to be an actor. I discourage them and yet I encourage them, because you've got to do what you've got to do. Don't let anyone tell you any differently. You've got to believe in yourself and you've got to go for it. But remember, there are other avenues you can pursue in the business—writing, directing, casting, editing, etc. You do have other options to become a part of the business.

Any final advice on how to best sculpt a career?

I wish there was just one simple plan and I could say, "Take these steps and you will be successful." Early in my career, I was determined to move ahead and not remain an agent. I wanted to go on to the next level and into casting. So I called everybody I knew who might in any way be connected to producers. I put the word out in Los Angeles and in New York. When you open your mouth, things do happen. It happened for me.

Ken Harper, who produced *The Wiz* on Broadway, has said *The Wiz* got produced because he talked to absolutely everyone he met everywhere about his idea of doing a black version of *The Wizard Of Oz*. If you really want something, you will find a way to get it. You can get what you need by putting it out there. I believe you can actually will it and bring it to you. So radiate positive energy, hone your fundamental skills, do your groundwork. If you've got the chops, you're inevitably going to rise. Cream will always rise.

. . . .

Mary Jo Slater
Slater & Associates Casting
2425 Colorado Avenue., Suite 204
Santa Monica, CA 90404

. . . .

STANLEY SOBLE, CSA

Stanley Soble, casting director extraordinaire for the Center Theatre Group, spent his early years exactly where one would expect him to—in the theatre. From 1962 to 1970 he worked steadily as an actor at the American Shakespeare Festival, in the first national tour of *Fiddler on the Roof* and in many off-Broadway shows. In 1970, he switched over to the production side of the theatre, taking a job as a production associate on the Broadway show, *Hair*. Subsequently, he spent time

as an agent and in 1978 he took his first job as a casting director on the New York based CBS daytime drama *Search for Tomorrow*. In 1980, he began the first of four years casting at Joseph Papp's New York Shakespeare Festival. He also cast several Broadway, off-Broadway and national productions including *The Pirates of Penzance, Moon for the Misbegotten* (with casting director Jason LaPadura), *Big River* (1985's Best Musical Tony winner), and the epics *Angels in America* (with casting director Meg Simon) and *The Kentucky Cycle*. The latter two were done in conjunction with his most recent position as casting director for the Center Theatre Group/Mark Taper Forum/Ahmanson Theatre, a position he held for over ten years, making him the longest running casting director in the Taper's history.

Soble's work in film and television included *After Hours* (with casting director Mary Colquhoun), *Lean on Me*, New York casting for *Blind Fury*, the mini-series *Ellis Island*, and numerous MOWs including *Joshua's Heart, David* and *An Early Frost*.

Stanley Soble passed away in July 1999. He will be sorely missed by all who knew and loved him.

It's so wonderful that in this city of film and television you maintain your passion for the theatre.

A lot of film actors are afraid of the theatre because they don't have the chance to change their make-up or do twelve takes. I'm really talking about Los Angeles because, let's face it, this town is all about that kind of thing. The film actor doesn't get the sense of the arc of starting at 8:00 P.M., finishing at 10:30 P.M., and creating a character along the way. A lot of people can't understand the thrill of doing a play for two months or a year because they get used to doing a quick film job, getting paid a lot of money and moving on. A lot of people lose their ability to perform on stage. They've worked on television or film for a long time and they've gotten used to the habit of doing it instantly—and that's not meant to be pejorative. For film, it's really important to be able to take a direction and do it instantly because there's no time. It's about a shooting schedule and things like that. But when people come back to the theatre, they have trouble adjusting to all of the technical aspects— primarily the vocal part. I have to tell actors, "Make this a stage audition." Even though it's a small room, I don't need that little thing actors do for film and TV, I need the expansiveness that theatre is all about.

How can actors you don't know get to meet you?

There are a couple of ways. If you're non-union, there are auditions on the first Monday of every month for the first twenty people in line. They start at 10:00 A.M., so it's recommended that you be here by 8:30 A.M. to sign up. We don't see more than twenty people. It's done by my assistant, who recommends people to me and then I will meet them at a later date. Non-Equity actors may call 213/972-7235 for additional information on these auditions. The other way is to send in pictures. I try, when I'm not busy, to do an hour or two a day of seeing people whom I don't know. It's recommended that the people who do send in a picture be in the union since we open our doors to non-union actors at those Monday calls. I also see a lot of union people at the Equity LORT lottery that is a two-tiered audition for regional theatres. Equity actors are invited to put their names into a pool for the LORT lottery. They pull the names and those people whose names are pulled get a chance to audition for casting directors from theatres from Southern California and sometimes from the East Coast. From that group of actors, those casting directors select the next batch of actors to be seen by the next set of casting directors. The first tier of casting directors see all the actors, the second tier only sees the recommended actors. That's a lot of actors.

Agents also call me to see actors I don't know. We ask them to do two pieces that are contrasting, no longer than three minutes total. Any experienced casting director can see what they need to see in two or three minutes; there isn't any need to do a five minute scene. We're really looking for the quality and the talent of the person and if, after doing this for all of these years, I can't tell after three minutes, then something is wrong.

What do you look for?
Talent. And I look for training on the résumé. I get a little suspicious when I get a résumé and the actor has two movies but no theatre credits. Then I don't know if they have the ability to do what I'm looking for. It doesn't mean that I don't eventually see people like that if they ask for an audition, but I look for a theatre background. A television casting director recently said that she doesn't pay any attention to the theatre credits and I was amazed.

Some television casting directors worry that a theatre actor won't be able to "bring it down" for the small screen.
That's why you do pre-screens. It's sad to think that I've reached a time where, to some people, what used to be thought of as the most important thing on the résumé doesn't count anymore. I say, when you look at that résumé and you see that they have an extensive theatre background, you pre-screen them. Don't write them off! My difficulty is that, out here, agents don't want their actors to put theatre on a résumé. They put film and TV and maybe an obligatory couple of theatre things but they don't really want to put more than that. It's a battle. Then there are those who don't want their clients to do television because they want them to be thought of as film actors. People who have had leads in series don't want to do more TV because they're afraid to be stigmatized. Everybody out here wants to be a movie star. I can remember when people wanted run of the play contracts. They don't even have those anymore.

How do you feel about New York as a place to start a career?
I still believe New York is the one place where you can make a career without having an agent. That's really difficult out here. There's so much off and

off-off-Broadway stuff that doesn't require an agent and the quality can be really good. I very strongly recommend that anyone who wants to learn about what it is to be an actor, especially in the theatre, go to New York. In New York, you use the theatre as the main source for finding people. People will go to an off-off-off-Broadway thing. A lot of the mainstream reviewers will even go. So many people in New York love going to the theatre and will go anywhere to see it.

Can you talk a little about your teaching?

I don't approach the class as if it's high art, but I do try to instill enthusiasm about the theatre. I do tell the actors that they are a marketable product and they need to see that as the nature of the business. They have themselves to sell and they should be doing things that they could be cast in. I also advise. I tell them, for example, not to do wasteful things. If a director asks you a question about your résumé, answer it but don't give him a pageant about the history of your production. If you fall into the trap of whether or not they like you, you're dead in the water. I recently had an experience with an actress where, midway through the audition, I realized that she wasn't doing the work anymore. Afterwards I followed her in the hall and I asked, "Why did you do that?" and she said, "Because I could tell that they didn't like me." You don't know that. You don't know any such thing. How many times have actors come in or you've gone in and you don't think you've done well and then you get hired for the role? There is no way for you to know and if there is a way, I want somebody to call me up and tell me what it is. I try really hard to be a friend to the actors so that when they go into the room they feel someone is there for them. Someone has to instill faith or tell them the truth about this business, about the ugliness, the unfairness, the disappointment and the upset. In my class I give them my knowledge of what goes on in the audition room.

Any final thoughts practically and philosophically?

Remember that you cannot predict the future. You have to go with the punches and if you're talented, things have a way of working out. There will be work. It may not be the job you thought you wanted, but there will be something. Stick with it and don't expect anything to happen overnight. Philosophically? Well, my mind is freed and opened by music and art and things of great beauty. I look at a painting in a museum and it strikes me and I feel something much more than the fact that I'm standing there looking at a painting. The same is true of the theatre. Going to the theatre and being moved by a performance, great acting . . . that's incredible and spiritual.

Dawn Steinberg, CSA

Dawn Steinberg, senior vice president of talent and casting for Big Ticket Television, feels that one of the best ways to sculpt a successful acting career is to connect with those agents and managers who look at the big picture, tell you how and where they can take you in five years, and who have the clout to do so. Steinberg was studying acting at the High School of Performing Arts in Manhattan when director Alan Parker asked her to cast extras and small roles for the feature film *Fame*. During  her summer vacations from Emerson College, she interned in the movie industry and after graduation she became an independent casting director. Her work in the theatre has included *Body Builder's Book of Love* off-Broadway and she was the managing director of the West Bank Cafe Theatre Bar in Manhattan. On the feature film front, she has worked on *The Zone, Pet Sematary* and *Ayn Rand: A Sense of Life*. Her work in television includes such MOWs as *The President's Child* and *Separated by Murder*, and many pilots including *The Big Five, Reality Check* and *Saturday Night in America*. Before leaving New York, she worked at CBS in both the prime time and daytime casting departments. Currently, she oversees casting at Big Ticket Television; she has cast the pilots and first six episodes for their hit series *Moesha* and *Night Stand*. She is also the director for the Los Angeles Stage and Film Company.

What is your favorite medium to work in as a casting director?
I'm a child of the '70s; growing up, television was one of my friends. Also, I like to work fast so I like the pace of television. In TV, you work quickly on ten roles and then collapse. In film, you can work three weeks to six months to cast one or two roles.

How can actors get to you?
My assistant and I go out three nights a week, so send us flyers. It's always easier if a show has six or more people in the cast. That way, we get to see the work of several actors in one night. Similarly, we like to go to the comedy clubs because we can catch the work of ten or more comics. You can also submit pictures and résumés to us with a cover letter. I go through my mail and when I see interesting people, I bring them in for a general. But before submitting themselves to any casting director, actors have to do their research and make sure the show they want to audition for is the kind of thing they're right for. For example, if an actor has no sense of humor, they're not going to get on a show like *Night Stand*. Similarly, comics who haven't trained dramatically will probably not get on *Law and Order*. So target yourself for the appropriate show.

Are you open to new actors who want to do monologues in your office?
Yes, we are. But when we ask an actor to come in, you should have already experimented in an acting class and found a monologue that best represents who you are and highlights your special talents. We cast for television and therefore doing a Shakespearean monologue, for example, is not the best idea. And one more thing—if you choose a piece from a monologue book, please read the whole play. You can't really know a character until you've read the complete script.

What impresses you on a résumé?
I always respond to people who have good training and have done a lot of theatre. Too many people want to be actors but don't put in the time to really learn and explore the craft. Find a class full of actors whose skills are as good or better than yours, not a class where you are the only one who can shine. Acting is hard work and requires great discipline and dedication. You have to push yourself.

An actor can develop an amazing range through theatre work, but when it comes to television or films they still seem to be typecast. Do you have any thoughts about that?

Everybody runs into the typecasting problem—including casting directors. When I show a résumé to a producer and say, "I want this casting director to work for us," they'll say, "But she doesn't cast comedy." It amazes me but that is the reality of the business. Jerry Orbach once told me, "It's not just typecasting—it's the last role you played!" But the actor shouldn't worry about such factors. Just be the best actor you can be. We remember good actors like we remember great art. They stand out. Even when you don't fit a part perfectly, if you're good, we'll remember you and call you back in again.

What can an actor do when he realizes his reading is going in the wrong direction?

The smart actor will stop and go back if his reading starts going south. Don't worry about wasting other people's time. It's your four minutes in the sun. You have to go for it because you may never get that chance again. If you don't end up doing it the way you wanted to, you're not going to be happy. But stop early in the reading and not five pages into it. Otherwise they might not let you do it again. Even in network situations, I am happy when an actor asks to stop and start again.

Do you ever recommend actors to agents?

I have, but it's so hard in Los Angeles for a casting director to get an agent for an actor. In New York, all I had to do was call any agent under the sun and they would see, and often sign, actors that I recommended. In Los Angeles, when I call, they tell me, "Well, we're not looking for anyone right now." And even when they agree to see an actor, they only sign them when all of the agents in the agency approve it. You can't find ten agents who love the same pasta dish at a restaurant so how are they going to like the same actor? It's frustrating. I guess the only way to combat it is to work as often as you can and get as much exposure as possible.

Any thoughts on how to overcome nervousness?

Different people have different methods to channel their nervous energy constructively. Some actors come in already in character. They ask to chat later. This works better for dramatic scenes; if you're about to read a character who's been raped, you don't want to come in and talk with the casting director. Instead, you channel your nervous energy into the circumstances of the character. On the other hand, for comedy auditions, you can chat with the casting director and gradually relax into the scene.

For a year I worked with Dustin Hoffman as his assistant. He had a different way to deal with anxiety. During rehearsals for *Death of a Salesman*, it was my job everyday to work on it with him. We would walk the streets of New York as he learned his lines. That seemed to concentrate and relax him. It would amaze me that he wanted to respect every comma, every word. He didn't want to digress from that text for even one moment. He wanted to get it exactly as Arthur Miller had written it. Precision was his anchor; it focused him. Ironically, some people brand artists like Hoffman, who is a perfectionist, as "difficult." Yet throughout history, when you study the lives of geniuses, you'll find that they were all a little left of center, a little strange. Thank God for that. If everybody was middle of the road, we'd all be living in an awfully boring world.

Dawn Steinberg
Sr. VP of Talent & Casting
Big Ticket Television
Sunset/Gower Studios
1438 North Gower Street,
Bldg. 35, Box 45
Los Angeles, CA 90028

SALLY STINER, CSA

After graduating from Kent State University, Sally Stiner moved to New York knowing that she wanted a career in entertainment, but unsure of where. On the advice of an employment agency, she learned to type, and landed a job temping at ICM. Initially with their music department, Stiner moved into commercials and, when she decided to leave New York, was brought out to Los Angeles as an assistant in ICM's television department. It was there that she realized her love for actors would be best served in casting.

She went to work assisting the late Dodie McLean and later, Tim Flack, with whom she cast the pilot of *The Cosby Show*. The two of them went to NBC together, he as vice president of casting, she as manager of casting, both in comedy. Eventually, Stiner decided to turn independent. Her subsequent work has included features, television movies and countless series. *Empty Nest*, *The Fresh Prince of Bel-Air*, *Boy Meets World*, *The Jeff Foxworthy Show*, *Venus on the Hard Drive* and *Two Guys, a Girl and a Pizza Place* are only a few of her credits.

In the beginning of your casting career, you went from ICM to Dodie McLean to Tim Flack. What were some of the things you learned from those experiences?
At ICM I fell in love with actors and the theatre. In fact, when I read a résumé, I read from the bottom up so I can start with the theatre. I want to know where actors trained and what they did in the theatre. If there isn't any theatre on a résumé, I lose interest quickly. I really believe that it's an important training ground. That's your schooling; it tells me how dedicated an actor is to the job of acting. There's a ton of headshots in this town but not a lot of actors. People say to me, "Look at all those headshots!" I say, "Don't worry, we'll weed through and find the actors."

I believe that theatre training is major and at ICM I was trained to look for that. Dodie McLean was a feisty, wonderful, love of a woman and the best teacher anyone could have in casting. I feel very privileged to have learned from her. She was a great lady.

One of the greatest things Dodie taught me was that, as a casting director, you are a service to your producer. You have to be there with them, guide them, be flexible and available to them creatively. It's about being part of the production as opposed to separate from it.

That's why I won't take on a ton of projects all at once. If I can't handle it, I'm not gonna do it. That would take the enjoyment out of the process for me. Dodie also taught me to respect actors without putting up with any bull. She never stood for actors saying things like, "Oh, I don't have my picture and résumé." She would tell people that this is their career and their business and they'd better pay attention to it.

Tim Flack was the king of comedy casting. He was wonderful. He got me into comedy and gave me my love of half-hour comedies. And half-hour is very close to theatre because you're right there in front of a live audience. Of course, on television, you get a few more shots.

Do you do generals?
Yes, but I never just meet with someone. I always ask them to read something. Someone can be just lovely but if they can't read, I need to know that right away.

Can you talk about what it's like to audition for you specifically?
When people come in and read for me, I won't give them any direction. I want to see what the actor has to offer and what their creativity is. It might be much more interesting than what we've planned for the role.

In the pre-read the actor can stop and say, "I don't understand this," or ask questions. That's not to say that you don't need to do your homework. I've had people come in and do a dramatic scene for a comedy, not realizing the genre of the show they were reading for. They didn't check with me first and they didn't do their research. If you want to do television, watch TV! I believe actors should watch every show at least once a season. That way, if they get called in for a show, they know the style. It's part of your business.

Don't be afraid to ask the casting director questions. Or, if the audition isn't going your way, feel free to say, "I just stank in that reading. Can I try it again?" Hopefully there will be time. Sometimes actors think that they blew a reading, and maybe they did, but people crash and burn on readings all the time and they may still get the role because we can see the talent.

Back from my days at ICM, I remember when actors would call and say, "Oh, I gave a great reading, I know I'm gonna get this role!" and they almost always didn't. When they'd call to say, "Oh, the reading was a disaster," many times they would get the role. It happens all the time and it shows that you never know what they're looking for. People get upset because they missed a word or dropped a line, but it's the whole package that we're looking at. It is so important to me that a person come in here and be alive! I see so many performances without any feeling or passion. What I look for is someone I want to watch, who interest me. Actors are hard on themselves in readings. Harder than casting directors, for the most part. I'll never forget this story: an actress came in to read and, in this particular room, there was a window and the actors could see me before they came in. Well, she had seen me laughing at all of these actors and having a good time, and then she came in and I didn't laugh at all. I didn't do anything. And she left and was devastated. She cried and told her agents that I hated her! Actually, what happened was that I had seen some funny people and had some good readings but nobody was really right for the role. She came in and she was perfect. I was watching her very carefully because I was taken aback by her. She was so right for the role. I actually asked for tape at the end of her reading—something I never would have done if I weren't interested—but she didn't get that. All she knew was that I didn't laugh.

Well, she got the role, a series regular. I loved and supported her from the moment she walked in. So you see, there's a lot going on in a casting director's mind that you just don't know.

Do you have any tips you'd like to share?
You should always be practicing your craft. If an actor comes in and says, "Oh, this is really difficult, I haven't read in a long time," well, join a theatre group or create a new one of your own. Read with your friends. If I didn't pay attention for a couple of months I'd be behind in my business. Even when we go on

hiatus, we get back and day one I'm on the phone with agents and managers asking, "Who's new? Who's doing what?" It's a constantly changing business and you have to be fresh and ready for it. Working on your craft is so important. You have to stretch those muscles!

Are there any particular likes and dislikes you want to make actors aware of?
You know, at least once a day I attack some poor actor who doesn't have a picture and résumé with them. It's such a simple thing. Often I don't have one on hand and I need it. It tells me so much and you never know when I'm gonna see something or someone you worked with that might spark something about you in my memory later. During pilot season, that's particularly important.

And to those who do bring résumés, please have them stapled. I hate it when people come in and start looking for my stapler. I know it sounds petty but I get sick of stapling pictures all day. When you join SAG, you should buy a stapler. And have your name and agent on your picture and résumé. It's shocking, but there are people who don't. Just recently there was a guy I really wanted to call in—but there was no contact information at all.

I also hate it when actors ask me what to wear. I cast talent, I don't do wardrobe. Wardrobe and props make me crazy. Once I had a hatchet pulled on me—that's still my scariest prop incident. I don't remember the actress but I remember the hatchet quite well.

I like people who've done their homework and are professional. I like people who don't make excuses, who just try to do the best job they can. They don't have to do the best job in the world but they have to try. And take risks! Go out there and try it. I get a lot of people just reading. Have emotion, have passion. Let me feel something. I'm looking for life.

. . . .

Sally Stiner
Sally Stiner Casting
CBS
4024 Radford Ave., Big Trailer
Studio City, CA 91604
. . . .

Ron Surma

In the business of casting, it is not unusual for casting directors to have a new job or position each year. It is therefore somewhat amazing to realize that Ron Surma has been in Junie Lowry-Johnson's office for more than ten years. While there, he and Lowry-Johnson have cast several mini-series, MOWs, and features including *Liar, Liar, Powder* and *Grosse Pointe Blank*. Most notably, however, Surma has focused on the *Star Trek* series, including *Voyager* and *Deep Space Nine*, and its features.

Were you ever an actor?

Not really. I did some acting in college and at a few dinner theatres. I had no desire to do it beyond that. You've got to love it to pursue it. I got into casting when a friend called to tell me that she knew of an opening as a casting assistant. I interviewed thinking, "Sure, why not?" I figured all of those years in college (University of Denver and The Goodman School) would finally pay off. I got the job, and started to learn what casting was about. I ended up in Junie's office after I had actually left casting. I had quit almost a year prior because I was just burned out. But I had met her husband, who was in production for a film on which I had been an associate. When Junie needed some help, he recommended me and I came in to meet with her even though I didn't really want the job. We agreed that I would help her out for a few weeks and we would decide from there. We both had an out. That was ten years ago and I still love it.

What do you love about it?
I love reading with actors. Finding the right actor for the part is fun and creative. Getting an actor his first job is probably the biggest pleasure. Or getting someone a better part than they've ever had before.

On the *Star Trek* projects, is there a particular kind of actor you look for?
Generally speaking, actors with theatre experience are a big plus for *Star Trek*. The show itself has a classical feel to it and, for an actor to get out of current time and to be four hundred years in the future, it helps to have a theatrical background. In speech, it's having the crisp diction that you need on stage so the entire audience can understand what you're saying. Many of the actors on most of television today tend to sound a bit slurred. It's a more contemporary sound. Better speech takes your phrasing out of today. If you suddenly pronounce everything the way it's supposed to be pronounced, you fall into a different rhythm. There are fabulous actors who, because of regional accents, I can't use on *Star Trek*; you can pinpoint where they're from on Earth and we're looking for an alien from a planet we've never seen before. So stage training can be very helpful for our needs.

Have you had any casting problems because of all of the make-up required for your shows?
Occasionally we've had to recast after an actor has gone into make-up, having their first fitting with their whole face covered and they realize that they just can't do it. The latex is too confining. It doesn't happen often, though. The important thing to remember about dealing with all the make-up is, when you audition for the show, if it's going to be a full make-up part, you have to go a bit bigger than normal in your acting. It's a very fine line. You can't go too far with it, but you've got to be able to tweak it just a little bit. If you don't give a little extra, once all of the make-up is on, you're not going to come through. But if you go too far, you're going to come off like a cartoon. Alice Krige, who played the Borg Queen in the last movie, in full make-up that took forever, still did a job that was sensual and intelligent and very real. She made it come through the latex.

Have you ever cast people who've never done television but have strong theatre training?

Yes, but training isn't just schooling. It's more about performing and where the performances are. Every theatre school in the country gives training in Shakespeare and sometimes it can be really bad. On a résumé, I look at what performances they've done and at what companies. Some little Shakespeare company in Iowa is not going to tell me anything, whereas if I see A.C.T., Oregon Shakespeare, The Old Globe [San Diego], South Coast Rep., or something like that, then I know I want to meet that actor.

Do you see actors without agents?

Sometimes. But that's rare. I can't keep all the pictures on file, but if I'm looking for a role and during that week an interesting picture comes across my desk, if it's a fit for the role, there's a good chance I'll see the actor. But if a picture comes in when I don't have anything, it's unfortunately going to get tossed with a couple of thousand others. But sending an unsolicited picture can sometimes get results.

Do you have any pet peeves in auditions?

Not much annoys me. It really doesn't. When I'm reading an actor, I want to get to the reading. I don't chat a whole lot, so when an actor comes in, I'll just say, "Hello." I might see something on the résumé that I'll ask about, but chances are good that I'll just ask them if they have any questions about the role. On *Star Trek*, I try to give out the whole script because otherwise it's very hard to understand what's going on without it. If I've figured out exactly what I'm looking for, I'll give them a couple of hints about the quality of the character. This is a tough show; the roles aren't the kind of thing you can research. You can't go out on the street and observe Klingons. So I'm an important resource. And you have to watch the show. Every actor should be sampling every show on the air to get an idea of each show's style.

One thing that does annoy me, and this is not so much the case on a pre-read but in a producers' session, is when people come in and hand out flyers or talk about the show they're doing. That's not what they're there for. When you're with producers, you're there for that show. Period. The best way to come in for any session is to say, "Hello," and do the work. The producers have a lot more to do than casting; they don't have a lot of time. One show is shooting right now, one show is in post production and they're writing the next show while we're casting the current one.

Do you have any final tips for the actor?

First and foremost, actors have to know who they are and bring that knowledge into the audition. Being who you are, through the material, is the only choice to make. Discover who you are in life, and bring that in. I've brought in wonderful actors who didn't connect to the material because they didn't know who they were. I can always tell in the first few lines if the actor is connected to himself. So, preparation at home is making that connection and figuring out how to convey who you are through the script.

· · · · · · · · · · · · · · · · · · · ·

Ron Surma
Junie Lowry-Johnson Casting
Paramount Studios
5555 Melrose Ave.
Von Sternberg Building, # 104
Los Angeles, CA 90038
· · · · · · · · · · · · · · · · · · · ·

MARK TESCHNER, CSA

Mark Teschner has spent the last ten years casting the daytime drama *General Hospital* and, more recently its new spin-off, *Port Charles*. A graduate of Connecticut College, Teschner fell into casting very quickly after realizing that acting wasn't for him. He's been an independent casting director for the last fifteen years. The first seven were spent in New York before ABC brought him to Los Angeles for *General Hospital*. He also casts independent features, and is most recently represented

by *Always Say Goodbye*, which won the Hollywood Film Festival award for best new feature. Until recently, Teschner was on the Board of Governors of the Academy of Television Arts and Sciences and, for the past three years has been vice president of the Casting Society of America.

Teschner has been nominated for six Artios Awards for casting *General Hospital*, winning in 1997.

How many roles, approximately, including the day players, new regulars and principals do you cast each year?
Between the two shows, we literally cast hundreds and hundreds of parts a year. We're looking for people every day.

Do you look at all the submissions personally?

Despite how busy we are, I look at every submission and every piece of mail that comes in the door. I always feel that if I don't, I'm not doing my job and I may miss the one person I'm looking for. We get between three hundred to three hundred and fifty unsolicited photos a week, separate from when we're actively casting a specific role. When we're very busy, I'll come in earlier to accommodate the work load. Casting isn't a nine to five job; casting is a lifestyle where your office hours may be nine to six but what you do is ongoing. I can't go to a movie or watch television without, on some level, working. So, the work gets done. Between myself, my terrific associate, Gwen Hillier, and our casting assistants, everything gets done.

No matter how busy we get, we work very hard at being actor and agent friendly. I feel that it's important to have a dialogue with the talent community. It's a very symbiotic relationship and we're all working together. Agents and managers want their clients on the show and I want the best actors on the show. It's a joint venture. The flip side is that we're all under a lot of pressure and there are a lot of time constraints.

Do you ever use readers?

No. I am the reader. I enjoy working with the actors, I give a lot to them. I don't want to have a reader work with the actors and then, in the callback, have to switch. This way, they read with me and have worked with me so there's a familiarity there. Auditioning is a very hard process for the actor. They have a tough time because they're not necessarily given a lot back from the other side of the table. I tell actors that if they feel they aren't being given enough in an audition, their job is to somehow make that work because the casting director is still going to hire someone and it might as well be them. You just have to go in and find a way to make it work.

How would you describe a General Hospital actor or a *Port Charles* actor?

I like to think that a *General Hospital* or *Port Charles* actor is a really good actor. I don't like to label beyond that because, to me, a good actor is an actor who can transcend all mediums and styles. Some people think that daytime actors require a certain look. but we have many roles where we're not really concerned with the look. Particularly with our recurring roles. Of course, the majority of the contract roles are played by very attractive people because, oftentimes, that is part of the requirement. But that's only one part of it. *General Hospital* has won the Emmy for outstanding daytime drama three years in a row. If we were casting exclusively on looks, we wouldn't have an Emmy in our bag. We're looking for people who bring intelligence, skill, nuance, soul, and a lot of other elements to the roles. If I sound somewhat defensive about the "look question," it's because I think it's a myth that daytime is exclusive to the concept of an actor's looks going into the equation. Every television show and every movie has several people in them who are stars, partly because of the way they look. And daytime is an incredibly tough medium to act in because you're acting new material every day. We've recently dealt with breast cancer, a character dying of AIDS, a character living with HIV, and a physically challenged actor dealing with trying to compete to be a doctor. If we didn't have wonderful actors on our show, we couldn't tell those kinds of stories.

We also have an on-set acting coach to help our actors meet the demands of the script. That's particularly helpful for our younger actors who are thrown into a situation where they probably haven't had a lot of experience and suddenly we're asking them to do twenty or twenty-five pages of material a day. Since one of things we do, for our younger roles, is find and develop raw talent, we want to help the actors that way and really be there, giving them the opportunity to grow and develop.

Do you have any words of wisdom you want to share with actors?
Acting can be a very solitary profession. The actor's community has to come from their own personal life and the community they create either through class or a group of peers who make up a support system. Actors should also create a situation where they're getting together with other actors for readings. I always tell actors not to make your acting career about waiting for the job. If you're not acting and getting paid for it, find another way to act. Either showcase yourself or get together with your peers every week and create an opportunity—even if you're doing a reading in your living room. The craft of acting is a skill and you have to use that acting muscle. If you don't, it atrophies.

I have great empathy for actors. It's hard enough acting, let alone getting a job. And actors only have two things: their talent and their dignity. Those are the two things you can control. Not every audition experience is going to be pleasant or painless, but if actors can come out knowing they did their best work that day, then they can be proud of what they've accomplished. So many factors go into someone getting a job—you can come in and give an incredibly great reading and not get the role. That doesn't mean you haven't left your mark, it doesn't mean you won't get a job down the road. It does mean you were not deemed the right person for that role at that time. For example, for a contract role, I might read anywhere from two hundred to three hundred people. Does that mean that the one hundred and ninety-nine who didn't get the job weren't talented? Of course not. There might have been some wonderful actors who didn't get the job and we may use them later. Good work leads to opportunity, if not at that audition, maybe at the next.

How can actors get to meet you?

Having an agent is crucial in terms of getting you access, but you don't have to have an agent to get here. I will read actors without agents either because I get an unsolicited photo and résumé that captures my attention or because I see them in something and like them. An actor has to showcase himself and create the opportunity to be seen. I go to many showcases, both waiver theatre and scene showcases. I try to cover as much as I can. Many of the actors I see in those circumstances are without representation. Not only have I brought many of them in, I've hired them. I hire a lot of my day players from people I've seen in showcases. In fact, it's one of my favorite things about the job. I love going to the theatre and the next day calling and offering parts to the actors I've seen the night before. Some of those actors may be without representation but they're out there honing their craft and showing their stuff. Here's the reality: in this day and age there are so many actors, it's almost impossible to meet someone just from a photo and résumé in the mail. And it's very hard to get the attention of an agent or a manager through a mailing. I'm not saying don't do mailings; I am saying don't rely on them. Get in the trenches and create the opportunity to be seen. You never know who's going to be there. It's about creating your own chances rather than waiting for them.

. . . .

Mark Teschner
General Hospital
ABC Television Center
4151 Prospect Ave.
General Hospital Building, Stage 54
Los Angeles, CA 90027

. . . .

Joy Todd, CSA

Veteran casting director Joy Todd has cast over one hundred films including *Moscow on the Hudson, The Verdict, Punchline, Prince of the City*, and *Once Upon a Time in America*. Her television work includes such series as *Fame* and the mini-series *Gettysburg*.

Todd came to casting from the world of acting and stand-up comedy. She started by casting extras for such films as *Network* and the television series *Kojak* before moving to principal casting

when Sidney Lumet asked her to work with him on the film *Just Tell Me What You Want*. She subsequently cast thirteen of his films. As she put it, "Because of Sidney, I went from, 'Joy Todd who?' To, 'Joy Todd, baby! Let's have lunch!'"

What would you say makes a good casting director?
You have to be creative. You have to be able to say, "Wouldn't it be interesting if this role were played by an Asian or an African-American man or maybe by a woman," instead of whatever they might have originally conceived. Casting is not about putting together lists. Anybody can make a list.

We are called casting directors, therefore we have to be able to direct. Of course, you cannot direct every actor who comes in. But if I see somebody who has something, I will give them direction. Recently, a very hot-looking actor came to read for a series and was perfect for the part. He read well for me but when I brought him to the director, he just blew it. The next day, I worked with him and he succeeded in incorporating the suggestions. He came back, he did it, and he got the part. He worked for twenty-five weeks. I don't want to take credit because the actor himself got the role. It was simply a matter of steering him in the right direction. That is what I think a casting director should do.

You've worked with the great director Sidney Lumet many times. Can you tell us about his working methods?

Sidney is marvelously sweet and kind to everybody on the set, and in response, everyone breaks their backs for him. As a result, he is always either on or ahead of schedule. Before filming begins, he always rehearses the actors for two weeks. Everything is blocked. Everyone knows what they're doing. And if you do have talent, he doesn't care whether you have credits or not. For example, he cast Eric Thal, who had never done a film in his life, opposite Melanie Griffith in the film *A Stranger Among Us*.

You are a great advocate of positive thinking and positive action. Can you discuss that?

The story of Eric Thal landing the lead in *A Stranger Among Us* is a perfect example. He came to me for direction before the final callback. He gave an excellent reading, which brought him to the next stage, a screen test. He took the positive action to come to my office to rehearse in front of the camera. He wanted to find out everything about make-up, costume and what scenes were going to be taped. He walked through the scenes until he felt totally at ease. He also made a trip to the studio a day before the screen test to find the best route to take, where to park, etc. Through his positive actions, he not only landed the lead but also signed a three picture deal with Disney.

Is there anything in particular that actors do that annoys you?

Attitude. I am generally very kind to and respectful of actors, and I expect the same courtesy from them. To illustrate: we had a young actress who was supposed to come in at four o'clock for an audition, but her agent called and said she would make it at six because she was having car trouble. Six o'clock came and went and still, she hadn't shown up. Our day had come to a close, and as I was ready to leave, she finally arrived. I told her I would see her the next day. She didn't like that and stormed out haughtily. You just can't function in this business with that kind of attitude.

Do you think there is a difference between New York and Los Angeles actors?

Yes, the actors in Los Angeles usually want you to validate their parking! Actually, at one time there was the following difference: if I brought in twelve actors for a role in New York, four of them would get callbacks while in Los Angeles, I would have to see eighteen actors before I would find one for a callback. But now that ratio has vastly improved. The only difference, perhaps, is the fact that New York actors have more opportunity to study, and they are doing Broadway, off-Broadway, off-off-Broadway, cabaret, and Sunday readings. They are constantly working at their craft.

Actors are always told to come into an audition with strong choices. Can you talk about that?

Many actors come in and vacillate because they have taken a middle of the road choice. A wrong choice is better than no choice at all. So make a strong choice and stick to it. If a casting director sees that you are a good actor who is capable of giving a performance, they will generally give you adjustments. They might even say, "You are not right for this role, but you might be fabulous for this other one."

The life of the actor is a roller-coaster ride. Do you have any advice on balance?

It's really simple. Actors are happy when working and unhappy when not working. So keep busy. If you are not working, you should be working on your craft. Do your homework. Read the trades. Find out who just signed who to do what. Is there a role you might be right for in that project? If there is a book on the market that is to be made into a movie, read it to see if there is anything in it for you. Keep at it. If you know somebody and they know somebody, your contacts grow. Move from negative thinking to positive thinking and from there move to positive action. The results will be inevitable.

. . . .
Joy Todd
c/o CSA
606 N. Larchmont Blvd., Suite 4B
Los Angeles, CA 90004
. . . .

PAUL WEBER, CSA

Connecticut born Paul Weber began his
career as an actor. He received a full
acting scholarship to Arizona State
University and later trained at London
University and The American
Academy of Dramatic Arts. Working
at such theatres as the Seattle
Repertory, Weber performed in the
regional theatre circuit until he
moved to Los Angeles in 1986.
Although still acting, he moved
here with a desire to work in the
other side of the business. His first
casting job came in 1990, as an

assistant at Stephen J. Cannell Productions. There he assisted on such shows as
Wiseguy and *21 Jump Street*. Weber also pursued other paths in the business such
as producing and developing game shows for USA Cable, and as a staff writer,
which earned him entrance to the Writer's Guild. Though clearly talented in
many areas of the business, Weber continued casting, working as an associate on
such projects for television as *Tales from the Crypt* for HBO, *McKenna* and
Lifestories. He served as casting director on such feature films as *Downtown Rooms,
Silent Cradle, Let There be Light, Reasonable Force* and Randal Kleiser's *Reasonable
Doubt* starring Melanie Griffith. Since 1994, Weber has been a casting director
with Slater & Associates Casting. Currently, he casts television series and

independent feature films. Along with Mary Jo Slater, he casts three Showtime series, *The Outer Limits*, *Poltergeist: The Legacy* and *Stargate*.

Why did you become a casting director?

I found I didn't have the passion for acting that I had earlier. It had become about the business of being an actor rather than the craft of doing wonderful roles in regional theatre. Not to sound negative, but it had become more about making my insurance and getting the job rather than the work itself. So, faced with the decision of whether or not to continue on as a regional theatre actor in my thirties, I decided to simply transfer my passion to something else.

One of the reasons I got into casting was because of several experiences I (and other actors) had with a few casting directors. They weren't necessarily "actor-friendly." I want to make auditions as comfortable an environment as possible for actors. That's the point I really want to make. Having been an actor, I understand the mentality, the process and the vulnerability of an actor. My goal as a casting director is to bring out an actor's best work.

When you look at a résumé, do you look for stage training, having those roots yourself, or do you find that film credits are the most important thing to you?

Certainly film and TV credits are important; however, I often read a résumé from the bottom up—that is, I look for actors with as much stage training as possible. The theatre training and credits, rather than an under-five on a popular show, tell me more about you. The television credit may tell me that you know how to hustle the business, but you may not be as comfortable in your craft as stage trained actors. Untrained actors with limited TV and film experience will often come in and give a decent, natural reading. Ninety percent of actors can give decent, natural readings, but that isn't good enough. A relatively green actor will come in and try to underplay a scene, and usually that means they have made a less interesting choice. They think that doing less is more, but more often than not their less is less because they don't fill up the moments of a scene enough to make small choices interesting and watchable. Those with formal training tend to make a greater investment in the part, based on all the information they have been able to gather and that makes them more interesting. Theatre actors know how to work, they know the technique of acting, they know the discipline of acting and how to creatively reveal the character they are working on. When they come in, they bring their stage experience with them, and this often scares producers and directors. It strikes them as "too big." And often, they're right. So my advice would be to think in terms of scale. The choices should be just as important, just as powerful, but the scale is different. For example, if you are playing Cyrano on stage and you thrust with your sword to take out your opponent, that is a very theatrical moment. However, the same action in a De Niro movie might appear ridiculous. On film, an actor might make the choice to stand nose to nose with his opponent and stab him in one short, violent movement. That is also a theatrical moment. So you're looking at the same result, the same intention, the same force of motivation, but the scale is different.

Is there anything else that, in your mind, sets an actor apart?
It is so important for an actor to know what their essence is as a human being. An essence is a sense of self-understanding, confidence, focus and grounding that actors bring to a reading, a role and their lives. Every interesting actor has something special that sets him or her apart from someone else. That personal essence makes it easier for me to see where an actor might fit, what types of roles they might be right for. That's what actors need to find within themselves. The only way to get that is to experiment, to study, to travel and to have as many diverse experiences and meet as many people as you can, and do it all with an open mind. Then you have a foundation from which to build. Now, many actors may feel they can play many different roles outside themselves, but I think it is important to know your range. It is important to be aware of how you are perceived based on your own personality. Then, when you get to a certain point in your career, producers, directors and casting directors will be more inclined to allow you to try anything.

How can the actor bring that essence to a role with just a few lines?
Just bring in who you are, not what you think the director. You can have a blast with one line if the show encourages it. But most shows aren't looking for that. They are looking for someone who has an interesting visual look about them and can deliver the material. It's tough. You don't have the arc a guest star role has. You pretty much come in, do it, and leave. Very simple. It's something that the producer will see and just say, "That's it!"

Why is it that producers and directors don't often work with actors or give them adjustments in auditions anymore?
It's very unfortunate that they don't. Many times the producer or director doesn't really want to work with the actor because they would prefer the actor just come in with "it." The "it" is a crapshoot sometimes. You are either "the guy" or you're not. Many times, as we discussed, it's based on the actor's personal essence. The producer just needs to feel in his gut that this guy can play the role when he

walks in the door. It's just who you are, your personality. When an actor tries to put on that personality, unless they are really good at covering who they are, it's a little scary because they are "acting" what they think we want rather than just being who they are.

What are some of your likes and dislikes at auditions?
I love an actor who is comfortable in his own skin, has a great sense of humor, is likable and accessible. I like someone who has done the homework. You don't know how many actors, who have had the material overnight, come in and say they haven't had the material long enough. Where were they all night? That shows me they don't prepare or they are riding on their looks or their last role that put them on the map. Come in on time. If you are running behind, have your agent call. And if you have to wait, practice focus and concentration. Don't put so much importance on this one audition that you shut yourself down emotionally or physically. Develop the tools you need to stay focused—breathing, visualization—so the spontaneity and freshness are not compromised. So many times between the pre-read and the producer's session, the material gets over-rehearsed and the life is siphoned out of it. In pre-reads, we give actors adjustments; take the adjustment, go home, get comfortable with it and the words in the script. It doesn't bother me if you don't memorize because the scripts are out of frame when we tape anyway. Don't wear a funny hat or a mustache or do something drastically different when you go to a producer's session. If the role has changed, I'll come out and give you the adjustment. Otherwise, come in and do the same thing you did in the pre-read, just be a little more familiar with the words and your choices.

Do you have final tips for actors?
Being an actor is such a wonderful, terrifying, unpredictable life, but it gives you such an incredible opportunity to be a Renaissance human being. I would like to encourage every actor to experience life as deeply as possible, because whatever you do, whether you move from acting to another area, whether it's in the business or outside the business, everything you've learned can be utilized. To be able to have that opportunity is a wonderful testament to this business.

. . . .
Paul Weber
Slater & Associates Casting
2425 Colorado Ave., Suite 204
Santa Monica, CA 90404
. . . .

APRIL WEBSTER, CSA

April Webster began as an actress in New York before moving to Los Angeles to work at the Mark Taper Forum, first as an assistant director to the improv company, then eventually as a casting director. Her first break as an independent casting director came when she was hired to cast Alan Parker's *Shoot the Moon*. Since then, she has cast countless hit television series, such as *Night Court, Hill Street Blues* and *The Nanny*. Her MOWs include *Tonya and Nancy: The Inside Story*, and

the monumental *The Day After*. She was nominated for both an Emmy and an Artios for the HBO mini series, *Grand Avenue*. On the feature film front, she has cast *Stargate, Five Corners, Bob Roberts, Godzilla* and has just completed casting *Patriot*, starring Mel Gibson. As busy as she is, Ms. Webster still finds the time to teach and direct for the theatre.

How can an actor get to be known by you?
If they have done a couple of Equity Waiver projects in town, I may have already seen their work. I go to a lot of theatre, but my choices depend on what I am looking for, or the kind of show I am doing at the time. For example, when I was working on the film *Stargate*, we needed a young Egyptian woman. So I went to

all kinds of ethnic plays with the hope that I would find an actress who looked like a young Egyptian woman. The best way for an actor to invite me to his or her play is by writing me a short personal note. It's not enough to just send a flyer, because I get hundreds of flyers every week. I look at every single piece of mail that comes into this office, so if it's a personal note and the actor has done his homework, it can open doors. Send a picture and a résumé, along with press reviews, and a note explaining the type of character you're playing. They should also include the nights that are available for me to come.

One of the most important things for actors to know is that although the creative side of this business is your passion, you can put that passion into how you pursue it as well. For example, understanding how you connect with other people is also about whether or not people will want to work with you. The impression you make when you come into a room is very important; you have to be as present as you can possibly be.

What does it mean to you to be "present?"
To be present is the ability to leave outside whatever was going on with you during the day and to go into your inner, focused center—regardless of all the stuff going on around you. The question is how do you control and channel that energy. I am not saying don't be nervous. I'm saying take that nervousness and put it into the energy of the scene, as opposed to allowing it to distract you.

Actors must develop a method to get out of their heads and allow their instincts to inform them what the part is about. Their instincts know more about the part than they think. Actors should not show me what they think I want to see, but what they can show me from their essence. I don't know what I'm looking for until somebody goes BOOM and I think, "Wow." Suppose I'm doing a pilot and I've read two hundred and fifty people for the same part. When I hear an actor read it and make it sound different I think, "Oh, it's like hearing this material for the first time!"

If an actor is very nervous when they come in to read for you, do you recommend that they share what is going on with them?
I don't need to know the history of what's going on with them. My feeling is, if an actor is having a problem, they should reschedule. This is not a contest to see if they can trick me into thinking they did a good reading. I want to give actors the best possible opportunity I can. But if you are always very nervous, develop your own way of focusing and relaxing.

I want actors who come in to read for me to remember that they are part of the production and this is a collaboration. I am not the job; I am a person doing a job. There is no table between myself and the actors because I want there to be a sort of direct connection. I always seat actors in the harder of the two chairs because I feel it is more comfortable for their work. I am not higher than or superior to the actor—it's a collaboration. If actors know that this is what is going to happen in their reading, then it might make it a little more comfortable for them.

Do you have any advice as to how an actor can find that focused center?
That's the challenge—some people do it through therapy, some people do it through yoga. You have to find that place in yourself that you can go to anytime. I myself have a ten-second meditation that I use to focus myself before meetings. I can now enter that inner place by just breathing, simply because I have practiced it for a long time and am in the habit of experiencing that place in myself.

Do you recommend acting classes?
There are a lot of ways to keep up your acting chops, a lot of ways to keep your body and emotions oiled. If acting class can give you a lot of practice working with other actors, an understanding of how to listen, how to witness and how to be present in a room, then I am all for it.

I recommend that actors join theatre companies or play-reading groups so they have an ongoing community. One of the hardest things for an actor to do is to be comfortable doing a cold reading when they haven't done any acting or play-reading in three months.

During auditions, what are some of the ways that actors sabotage themselves?
I don't like people bringing in props unless they are absolutely essential; generally, they just get hung up in them. It's better to just fake the props. I have also seen actors talk themselves out of jobs. They come in and get into this whole detailed conversation. I'm not saying don't have a conversation, especially if someone has asked you about yourself, but don't get too chatty. Also, by all means ask questions regarding the script at hand. Part of your job as an actor is to get the script ahead of time if you can, and to get as many of your questions answered as possible before you come in to read. After the audition, I have had actors who sat in the room for another five or ten minutes chatting away because they were so nervous, they couldn't stop. I am notorious for spending a lot of time talking to actors, but in certain circumstances, you have to be aware of the climate of the room. If, for instance, you come in and I am frantic and crazed, then you need to just be solid and present. Then you could have a positive effect on me and the whole room.

Any final words of wisdom?

This may sound corny, but basically it's to really honor yourself, to honor the jewel that you are, in the truest possible way, because that's where everything comes from. It's a hard job to do what actors do. It means to become vulnerable and expose your soul in a certain way. If you don't love and honor yourself, then it's even harder. Sometimes self-loathing pops up; the ego is very strong and has a very loud voice. That's why actors have to trust their instincts. Those instincts are such a gift. When I come from that place, everything begins to shift around me.

If you are in this profession because you think you're going to become a big star and make a lot of money, you are probably setting yourself up for a disappointment. If you are doing this for the love of it, the true passionate love of it, then that's where your commitment should lie. To yourself and to your work.

. . . .

April Webster
513 Wilshire Blvd., Suite 196
Santa Monica, CA 90401

. . . .

GERI WINDSOR-FISCHER, CSA

Veteran Casting Director Geri
Windsor-Fischer studied acting at the
Academy of Dramatic Arts in New
York before becoming Broadway
producer David Merrick's casting
director. During her tenure with him,
she cast the Broadway productions
of *Hello, Dolly!* with Pearl Bailey;
*Promises, Promises; Moonchildren;
Play it Again, Sam* and others. In
1972, she joined forces with *Hair*
casting director, Linda Otto.
Together, they cast such landmark
Broadway shows as *Equus, Grease,*

That Championship Season, The Sunshine Boys and *The Wiz.* After coming to Los
Angeles, Windsor-Fischer served as senior vice president talent and casting for
MTM Enterprises from 1980 to 1989. While there, her work included casting
Hill Street Blues, St. Elsewhere, Rhoda, Newhart and *Remington Steele.* Now, as an
independent casting director, she has cast the pilots and series *The Trials of Rosie
O'Neill; Dr. Quinn, Medicine Woman* and various MOWs and mini-series. On
the feature front, she has cast *The Great Gatsby, Leadbelly, The Midnight Man,
Something in Common* and cult favorite, *The Rocky Horror Picture Show.*

In your opinion, which city is the best place to launch an actor's career?

If I were a young actor, I would go to the city that would offer me the most opportunities for work. Right now, that happens to be Los Angeles. When I was in New York, it was the place because there were so many shows like *Grease* where actors could be seen and move on to bright careers in TV and film. Chicago, which is a cross between New York and Los Angeles and has a slightly slower pace, is also a good place to start out. But coming to Los Angeles can easily overwhelm someone just entering the field. People can make many promises they don't keep and disillusion the young actor.

Other than the obvious, sending a picture and résumé, can you think of a way for actors to get an agent?

A very interesting way to get an agent might be to tape your audition pieces on video and to send them to those agencies that represent actors of your age and type. I don't know why more people don't do that. There is no better way to find out whether an actor has talent or not. It's one thing to meet an actor and have a nice chat. It's something altogether different when you see them on tape, acting. I'd pick two scenes that show a broad spectrum of possibilities—one comedic and one dramatic piece—and tape them against a simple background. Keep the scenes short, simple, and understandable. Stay away from elaborate sets, props or make up. Then make copies and send them to agents with a cover letter.

I look at every tape that comes in. Anybody who goes through all the trouble of preparing a tape deserves the attention of agents and casting directors.

How can actors keep communication lines open with casting directors?

Get into a play and send those flyers out. At MTM Television we looked at all the flyers, and if something caught our eyes, we went. Some really good casting people in this town respond to interesting flyers.

Similarly, when you are doing a part on television that you're proud of, send a card to the casting people. Chances are, someone will take a look at it. It's a really good way to keep things moving. Even if they don't watch it, you have nudged their memory in your direction. We are in a business. The town is too big and there are too many actors who are going after the same small number of roles. So you must make yourself visible in any legitimate way you can.

Is there any behavior by actors that annoys or endears you?

I don't like actors with attitudes. It is such a waste of time. Casting directors go through a lot of planning before selecting which actors out of thousands will be called in to read. The actors have to be equally serious and professional about the process. Their duty, from the moment they come into the room, is to be totally prepared and to do their job the best way they can. Be yourself, be natural, be totally focused on the work and nothing else. Have a really good idea of what you want to say through the scene and say it. Don't waffle, but make a choice and stick to it. Then, when you're done, just walk away from it. It is hard, yet you have to learn to detach yourself from the result. If you don't get the job, it doesn't really matter why you didn't get it. It could be for a number of reasons. It could be that the part was changed to that of a short person or a bald person or the opposite sex. So do your best and then forget about it.

What kind of preparation should an actor do at a callback?

Sometimes someone knocks you out during a reading, and you always want to see if they will come close to recreating that during the callback. Often they don't; they've overworked the material. Remember, the reason you are back is because we liked what you did the first time. We wouldn't have you back if we wanted you to change it, unless we specifically told you to change it. So when you come to the callback, do exactly what you did the last time. Don't make it any bigger, don't make it any smaller. Even wear the same clothes.

What attitudes can make the actor's journey a less painful one?

Don't be a victim. Be passionate about committing yourself to this work. Know that success isn't going to happen overnight. But it can happen if you are persistent, if you've got talent, and if you've got the follow-through to stay on top of your own career. Ultimately, you alone are responsible for your own career. Be true to yourself, about what you believe in, what you care about, and constantly work hard. When you get rejected, resolve to work even harder. And never forget to thoroughly enjoy the whole process of preparing, auditioning, callbacks and actual performance. Once you learn to cope with difficulties and persevere, your dreams can come true. And your dreams are our dreams. Casting directors are like gardeners. You get the soil prepared. You weed out. You plant the seeds, water them, keep the bugs away. You tell them you love them. You hope that the sun will shine nicely on them. And you continue to watch their growth until they finally bloom and bear fruit.

. . . .

Geri Windsor-Fischer
c/o CSA
606 N. Larchmont Blvd., Suite 4B
Los Angeles, CA 90004
. . . .

RONNIE YESKEL, CSA

Before she such a fine became a casting director, New Jersey born Ronnie Yeskel held a variety of jobs—teacher, airline employee, bartender, window dresser, waitress, theatrical prop and costume designer, box office clerk, set constructor, stage manager and actor. It wasn't until 1980, while she was a struggling actor in New York, that Yeskel began to seriously consider a career in casting. Her initiation came when she worked with casting director Bonnie Timmerman. A year later, she

went out on her own until she partnered with Jack Kelly. She was casting by day, going to the theatre by night, and proof-reading at a law firm in the early morning. During that phase, she cast for a great number of regional theatres and some Broadway shows. In early 1987 she came to Los Angeles; two weeks after her arrival, she landed the position of casting director for the Los Angeles Theatre Center. From there she moved to CastleRock and cast the features *The Marrying Man* and *After Dark, My Sweet*. In 1990 Yeskel was offered a job casting the hit series *L.A. Law*, then in its fifth season. Though she had never worked on a TV series before and knew the pace could be relentless, she took a leap and never regretted her choice. Yeskel remained with *L.A. Law* for three years, during which time she also cast features. Notable among them was Quentin Tarantino's debut film, *Reservoir Dogs*, in which she cast Tim Roth, Michael Madsen and Steve Buscemi. In 1994, she and Tarantino were reunited when she cast his Academy Award nominated *Pulp Fiction* (with Gary Zuckerbrod) for which she won an Artios Award. Recent work has included *Walking the Dead, Hope Floats, The Long Kiss Goodnight* and *Bean.* She has just completed casting *Four Dogs Playing Poker* and *Bread and Roses.* She is partnered with Richard Hicks.

How can an actor get to meet you?
The fastest way is perhaps to send a note with a picture and résumé through someone we know in common. I do look at unsolicited tapes, but the actor needs to follow up a month or so after sending one. I get a lot of submissions and go through every piece of mail myself for particular projects I am casting, but I can't look at every unsolicited picture and résumé that comes through the mail. There is just not enough time in the day, unfortunately.

What makes you stop and take a second look at a picture and résumé that crosses your desk?
First of all, I look at the picture, I look at the eyes and what's going on inside them. Then, when I am looking at the résumé, the first thing I look for is theatre credits: where you have worked, what roles you've done, what regional credits you have, who you studied with. *Then* I look at the film and television credits.

Why do you look at theatre credits first?
Theatre is where you learn to create a subtext for your character, and it's where you learn how to use your body and voice. An actor has to know how to break down the script and create a life for his character. They have to know how to listen and respond honestly. That's what acting is all about. You have to learn to rely on yourself and know how to make choices. Theatre teaches you all of that.

Sometimes you'll have directors who are technicians, who do not know how to talk to actors, and that's why actors have to know how to do their own homework. That's why an actor has to be trained. An actor needs to be constantly working on his craft so that when he or she works with a director who can't articulate what they want from the actor, the actor can rely on their own abilities, their own instincts. Directors don't all know how to talk the actor's language to get you where they want you to go. Sometimes they don't even know where they want you to go; they're waiting for the actor to come in and show them. You really have to be right on when you go into a television audition, because the pace is very quick. You have to go in there with a pretty finished product because they often don't have the time, the skill or the inclination to give you direction. It seems that more and more there are directors out there who don't know how to talk to actors.

What are some of the things you look for in an actor?
I definitely like a sense of humor. I think if you are funny, you can go very, very far. I like an actor who is really natural. And I also love actors who take risks, who are dangerous, spontaneous, and who are not afraid of making fools of themselves. I really love people who have lots of colors and levels to them. That's exciting to me. Actors should not be afraid to take chances. When things are played safely, it's boring. Star quality is more than just a presence or beauty; sometimes it's an eccentricity, or maybe an offbeat look.

Are there things that you do to help make auditioning easier for actors?
I try to assist actors in every way possible. I hire readers for the callbacks who can really help the actor give their best reading. I encourage the actor to ask questions. The time to find out about the character is when they're with me in the pre-read. I never require an actor to memorize a scene unless it is being taped. If they are in the middle of a reading and it's not going well, I encourage them to stop, and if need be, leave the room for a few minutes. I realize that this is their shot and I don't want them to throw it away needlessly. A casting director should be intuitive enough to know, when an actor comes into the room, if they're off or if they're ready to go. I give them the opportunity to get it together, make another choice or come back another time. We're human. We have our good days and we have our bad days.

How do you feel about actors improvising during the audition?
It's usually difficult when you have the writer in the room. Some writer-directors don't mind, but others do. Their words may already be wonderful so you don't have to improvise. On balance, I don't recommend it. Here and there, a word or two perhaps. But, for the most part, don't do it.

Any final words of advice?
I encourage actors to take their careers into their own hands. Don't wait for agents to find you work. Create your own. Produce a play and maybe it will get the attention of people. Always be in tune with your body and your voice— take dance classes and voice lessons. Keep studying. And if, after a certain

amount of time you don't succeed as an actor, go do something else. Actors should create their own lives outside of acting. It's very competitive out there. It's very, very difficult to get work. If acting is not the most important thing in your life, if it's not what you want to do more than anything else in the world, go do something else.

I love actors. I love the chances they take, I love their risk taking. I was an actor for about five minutes, so I know how hard it is to audition and what it means to try to land a job. I know the high that you get when you're totally in the moment. You are not aware of anything going on except what's happening from your heart. But if you're not serious about doing the work and you're just in it for the money or the fame, then you're in it for the wrong reason. If an actor really wants to act, they should act. I encourage young actors getting out of school to go and do theatre for a few years. Go out and build up your résumé; work in the regional theatres. The majority of good directors and casting directors look for that experience. It's good and wonderful and nourishing. You can't beat it!

. . . .

Ronnie Yeskel
Yeskel/Hicks Casting
225 Santa Monica Blvd., Suite 310
Santa Monica, 90401
. . . .

BONNIE ZANE, CSA

Bonnie Zane began her career in
television and video production. She
was dissatisfied, however, and sought
out casting positions. She began as a
temporary receptionist for Liberman/
Hirschfeld and, in what can only be
described as a meteoric rise, within
four years had her own casting office
and both *Newsradio* and *Mad About
You* under contract. She has received
two Artios nominations for her
work—one for *The Larry Sanders
Show* (with Marc Hirschfeld),
and one for *Mad About You*. Along

with *Newsradio*, she currently casts the series *Sports Night* (with Paula Rosenberg).

**I know there isn't time for you to use breakdowns on a half-hour show. So how
do you cast your shows and how do you meet new actors?**
You're right, there just isn't enough time for breakdowns. And, unfortunately, I
don't usually have time to meet people unless they're referred to me by agents or
industry people I trust. I'm not selective when it comes to the agents. I try to talk
to everyone. And I have many, many, many files that I go through constantly. I
don't save everything that comes through the mail but I do look through
everything. I meet a lot of people through casting workshops, but now that I'm
by myself, it's much harder to find the time to do those kinds of things. I do go
to the theatre and to a lot of comedy showcases.

And you pretty much only do comedy.

Having worked with Marc Hirschfeld—who has been and always will be, my mentor—I am much more drawn to the half- hour format. And it's a crazy way to cast. Yesterday, for instance, I got a script at noon and I had to cast ten roles by five-thirty. Ten. Then I have to call agents at home. It's nuts, but it's because sitcom scripts change so much day-by-day. You'll get a script on Monday and by Friday it's drastically different. There just isn't anytime for pre-reads when I have that kind of crunch. I really have to rely on my mental files.

So under that kind of pressure, people you don't know are probably not going to get a shot.

If it's a substantial role, not at that point. But not every day is like that; not even every week is like that. I would say that 50 percent of the time I have a day to cast, or I have a weekend to set up a session.

Any advice on pre-reads and producers sessions?

When actors come in for their audition with me, I read with them once to get their take on the scene and then I give them notes. I think it's really important to listen to what the casting director is saying because most of the time, we know what the producers are looking for. Most of the time you'll go to producers as soon as half an hour later. I'll usually bring in six to eight people per role.

My advice during producers' sessions is not to try to chat up the room. It's nice to say, "Hello," and tell a brief anecdote if you have to but the producers' time is so limited—they don't need to hear about your cat at the vet or what happened on *Oprah* last week. The producers are really single-mindedly concerned about how you deliver the sides and getting to their editing session because they have an editor's clock ticking, waiting for them. The producers are involved in every aspect of the show, not just picking out next week's cast. Each producer makes notes and then, unless one actor really just outshines everybody else, they sit and discuss. Sometimes they say, "No, we don't have it. Let's try again. See you in a few hours." Or, if they find someone, there are times when that person will go straight from the session to the stage. That is, I think, every casting director's worst nightmare because you have to make all of the actors stay and then say, "Thank you all for coming and oh, by the way, this person has got the role." I hate that. Everyone hates that. But someone ends up going to the set to work while I call their agent and negotiate the deal.

Sitcoms usually have the first work day as the table-read, then they rehearse for two more days, camera-block the fourth and fifth day and then sometimes Fridays are block and shoot. On shooting day, they may do some shooting in the afternoon without the audience. Pre-shooting. On *Mad About You* we would pre-shoot our babies.

On *Newsradio*, they were really great about re-using actors they liked. There was an actress, for example, who, as a favor to me, played a waitress. It was just a two-line role and she's a fabulous actress. The producer just loved her so much and I said, "It's really beneath her to play a role this small," so the producer said, "Well, we'll use her again." And they did.

Do you look at people's tapes?

The ones I ask for. I don't appreciate unsolicited tapes. There's no reason for it. If an agent calls me and says, "You really should take a look at . . ." then I will. But to get a random tape in the mail is just not helpful.

Is there a difference between the kinds of actors you look for pilots and the actors you use for guest-stars?

Series regulars need to have a certain star quality. For me, it's an inherent feeling. During pilot season you see three hundred people for a series regular role. While many of them are fine actors, there are very few who can carry a whole show.

So many casting directors complain that people don't look anything like their pictures and that most of the photos are too glamorous.

Yes. But there are also those cases where we're looking for a leading lady type or a beautiful girl type and when the actress comes in from three or four auditions, she's in her jeans and a T-shirt because she's been running around all day and she doesn't look so great. Then the glamorous picture helps because you realize her potential to be stunning. So it goes both ways.

Do you have any words of wisdom?

I think it's so important for actors to keep working on their craft. Don't think that you've reached a point where you no longer need to or where you've gotten good enough. Being on a series does not mean that you stop going to class or stop working on your art. Just like I have to keep growing. I'm not going to say, "'Well, I already have a full file of thirty year-old leading ladies. I don't need to meet any more." Your whole life, you have to keep growing with your art.

. . . .

Bonnie Zane
c/o CSA
606 N. Larchmont Blvd., Suite 4B
Los Angeles, CA 90004
. . . .

DEBRA ZANE, CSA

Debra Zane studied acting in New York before coming to Los Angeles and joining casting directors David Rubin and Lisa Beach as an assistant. In 1990 she became an Associate in David Rubin's company and helped to cast a string of very successful films including *The Firm, The Addams Family, My Cousin Vinny* and *Fried Green Tomatoes.*

As an independent casting director, she has cast the Showtime Cable series *Fallen Angels* for such directors as Steven Soderbergh and Peter Bogdanovich, and the films *The Truth About Cats and Dogs, Get Shorty, The Last Seduction, Men in Black* (with David Rubin), *Washington Square, Wag the Dog* (with Ellen Chenoweth), *Pleasantville* (with Ellen Lewis), *A Cool Dry Place, Patch Adams, American Beauty, Stuart Little, The Limey* and the award-winning cable series, *Tracey Takes on . . . .*

What do you look for most in actors during readings?

I look for truth and reality. Actors often feel that they have to do something extra to make an impression, when in reality they don't even have to act! I'm always telling actors, "Be much simpler, much smaller. Really bring it down." I can't tell you how many times, when we're videotaping auditions, an actor's first take is so huge. And I always think, when does anybody ever do something so big in real life? To me, an audition is so much more interesting, and often funnier, when it comes out of reality as we know it.

Do you videotape every audition?

If the director is on location, I absolutely rely on the video camera. I can't tell you how many jobs I have helped actors get from taping them at the audition and showing their reading to the director. Or how many jobs I have helped them get from their demo tapes. When an actor has an adequate demo tape, I can show it to the director and say, "I have this guy in mind." When the director agrees, I just call the agent and basically say, "Would your client like to do it?" On tape, an actor's work speaks for itself. Demo tapes are invaluable. Every actor must have a good tape.

How should actors approach an audition which is being taped?

It is always safe to ask the casting director whether to play to them or to the camera. Nine out of ten times, they may ask you to play it to them, unless you are supposed to talk directly to the camera as specified in the script. Before you come in, do your homework and be as familiar with the material as possible. Memorize as much of the scene as you can. And even though you should come in with strong choices, listen to the suggestions of the casting director. They know what the director is expecting in the scene and can help you shape the taped reading. I later edit the tapes and show the director only the actor's best take. I don't want to do you a disservice. I want you to get the part.

Is it okay for an actor to ask to do another take?

I don't see why not. If you think that you did not give your best in a take, ask to do it one more time. Similarly, when an actor comes in and reads badly, and the director says, "I don't think he'll work out," I may ask the director to bring the actor back, because I know that they are capable of doing better. To me, part of the job of a casting director is to educate the director about actors.

Should the actor put on appropriate clothes and make-up for a taping?

You need to do all you can to lend yourself to the role. And so you do have to suggest the character in your clothes and make-up. Don't make it even harder for people to imagine you in that part by dressing completely differently than what the role calls for.

During readings, what do you think about improvisation?

I prefer that actors stay close to the script. You have to show the director that you can play the material as written. The actor isn't hired to come in and do a rewrite. If you want to ad lib before the beginning of a scene to better propel yourself into the rhythm and mood of the piece, then that may be interesting. But when you are in it, particularly when the writer of the words is in the room, I don't recommend that you change anything. If you do, you may upset the rhythm of the lines and the writer.

However, the opposite can also be true. Sometimes, when the writer is present and an actor turns around a line and makes it funnier, the writer will sometimes take the new reading and incorporate it in the script. But that's no guarantee that you will be hired; they may hire someone else but keep your line.

Do you accept unsolicited submissions?

Yes, I do. I look at every piece of mail that comes my way. I'll also watch all the tapes that are sent to me. We're always looking for new actors. If you're interesting, and I don't have a role for you in the project I am currently casting, I'll hang on to the photo and remember it for a later project.

Any final words to help actors better sculpt their careers?

Actors are the bravest folks around. I always hope they understand that when the part doesn't happen for them, it is never a reflection on them or their talent. It's just that the role fit someone else even better. Actors should not worry about why they didn't get the part, but work on techniques to remain positive and relaxed during the audition process. Even if they are extremely nervous, actors must learn not to broadcast it. Remove desperation from your thoughts, and only think about what needs to happen in the scene you are reading. Auditioning should be a joyous process—just think about how lucky you are to even audition! If I am reading people for a part, there may be 2,000 people who might be right for the role, but you are one of the eight people I asked to come in. So, celebrate!

The actors who continuously get the jobs are those who know how to project their vulnerability. When they leave the room, whether they are kids or senior citizens, you wonder about them for the rest of the day.

· ·

Debra Zane
c/o CSA
606 N. Larchmont Blvd., Suite 4B
Los Angeles, CA 90004
· ·

GARY M. ZUCKERBROD, CSA

Gary M. Zuckerbrod started out as an intern for New York casting director Bonnie Timmermann and subsequently became her casting assistant. His first solo assignment in Los Angeles was on the television series *The Twilight Zone*. Since then, he has cast such features as *Beverly Hills Ninja, That Darn Cat, Johnny Be Good* and most notably, *Pulp Fiction* (with Ronnie Yeskel) for which he received an Artios Award. For television, he has cast the pilots for series such as *Touched by an Angel* and *Nightmare Cafe*, and various television movies and miniseries including *Titanic, Heart Full of Rain* and *Bella Mafia*. In 1994, as director of casting, movies and mini-series at CBS, he oversaw the casting on such films as *A Streetcar Named Desire, Buffalo Girls, The Piano Lesson* and *The Thorn Birds III*.

What general attitude would help the actor in the audition room?
You have to judge each situation individually. When you enter the room, be consciously aware of what's going on in there. When they say, "Have a seat and let's read," then just read. If you come into a room and they say, "Hi, how are you?" then you can chat a little if you want. Or you can say, "I am fine, may I start the reading?" You have to do what feels most comfortable for you. Often an

actor will walk in and says, "Do you mind if I just read first and talk afterwards?" I have never heard anybody say anything other than, "Fine, sure."

In your opinion, is it easier for an unknown to break into television or films?
It is easier for an unknown to get a major role in a film, because a film is shot, released, and that's it. The audience walks into a movie theatre to see a film once. In a television series, however, you're asking for the audience to come back week after week for hopefully five seasons or more. So naturally, producers and networks feel more comfortable hiring actors they know or who have been previously well received by viewers.

However, today the crossover between the two mediums is at a peak. For example, everybody wants to make movies with the actors in the television series *Friends*. Similarly, a while back when we were doing an MOW at CBS, we offered the lead to two actresses who had starred in television series, and they both passed. We then went to a major movie actress, and she accepted.

How did you get involved with the casting of *Pulp Fiction*?
It was an amazing gift from Ronnie Yeskel. She was doing another project at the time, and didn't want to give up the opportunity to work with Tarantino again. So she asked if they would allow her to bring in somebody she thought had basically the same background and taste she did. It was fine with them, and we ended up casting it together.

What should actors expect when they read for Quentin Tarantino?
I hope that everybody in the business will someday have the opportunity to work with him, because he is a dream. He is polite, kind, and has more respect for actors than 90 percent of the people in the business. Being an actor himself, he thoroughly understands the process of being an actor better than most directors.

He loves to read with actors. He uses a reader, but often, in order to get a gut feeling, he gets up and reads himself. He sat down with John Travolta and read the script with him from cover to cover before he gave him the job. He tortures himself and agonizes over casting decisions. And in the end, his choices are spectacular.

What is your opinion concerning actors memorizing their lines for auditions?
You have to do what's best for you. If you're an actor who can walk into an audition and get your choices and points across without having memorized your lines, then do that. If you need to memorize in order to be believable, then do that. It doesn't make any difference to me.

It's been said that some stars like Brando, James Dean, and Geraldine Page never learned how to audition well.

That's not true—at least of Geraldine Page. She was a wonderful auditioner. I sat with her on an audition for a role for which she subsequently was nominated for an Academy Award. During the audition, I couldn't even look through the video camera because I was in tears. It was probably one of the most believable things I have seen an actor do. She came in, mesmerized us, and when she left, all of us in the room were in tears. It was staggering. She was brilliant.

Of course, some actors really don't audition well. If an actor has that problem, then hopefully they can get some films under their belt and make it to a level where they can say to the director, "I don't audition well, but you have to trust me. I know I can play this part well." That's how some people do get parts.

How can actors get to meet you?

The best way is to contact me through the mail. I've got a great staff who advise me on all the submissions. And though I'd like to go to the theatre to see talent more frequently, it is impossible to do so when I am working on a project. Frequently though, when I read a good review, I call in the person and read them.

When you receive a submission from an actor without an agent, do you take it seriously?

It depends on whether I am casting a role that person might be right for. If they look right and have a nice résumé, I don't care if they have an agent or not. My job is to cast.

Do you have a prescription for actors to better deal with constant rejection?

Everybody in this business goes through constant rejection. It is not only an actor's problem. Hollywood is full of directors, producers, and writers who cannot get their projects off the ground. We casting directors have to go and tap dance for our jobs too. You can either get really depressed about rejection and allow it to run your life, or you insist on running your life yourself. Some actors have the wonderful ability to say to themselves, "It wasn't meant to be. I'll get something else!"

. . . .

Gary M. Zuckerbrod
c/o CSA
606 N. Larchmont Blvd., Suite 4B
Los Angeles, CA 90004
. . . .

From another P.O.V.

JEFF COREY, ACTING COACH

Brooklyn-born Jeff Corey was a working actor in New York and Los Angeles in the 1940s before World War II took him to Europe. There, he worked as a motion picture photographer and was awarded three citations for his work. Ironically, after being lauded for his national triumphs during the war, Corey found his patriotism questioned when he was blacklisted during the infamous McCarthy hearings. Forced to give up acting, Corey began to teach and continued to

do so even after he was able to act again in the sixties. A vital, ageless man, he has helped create and inspire many of Hollywood's most gifted actors, writers, directors and producers. The impressive list includes Jack Nicholson, Steven Spielberg, Rob Reiner, Jane Fonda, Penny Marshall, Candice Bergen, Carol Burnett, Robin Williams, Paul Reiser, Jennifer Jason-Leigh, Ellen Burstyn, Shirley Knight, Ann-Margaret and the writer Robert Towne.

How did you get into teaching?
I got into teaching because I was blacklisted and unable to work as an actor. I used to go to Michael Chechov's Monday night lectures. He'd have people like Anthony Quinn, Mildred Natwick and me demonstrate the exercises he was

talking about. I loved him. Misha, we called him. Although I do think he was a little stuck in mysticism. Since I was unemployable, they asked if I would teach a class. Although I wasn't paid for it, I had never taught before so I decided to give it a go. I was thirty-seven years old with three kids to support and enrolled at UCLA as a freshman under the G.I. bill. So I started to teach. I had a good class. Gary Cooper and Patricia Neal came. I didn't go through a lot of theories, it was always a hands-on situation. I would say "Let's fool around with this. We'll make some adjustments." And it worked. Cooper and Pat kept coming. He was particularly supportive. He even sent his daughter who said, "Daddy told me that if I ever wanted to learn about acting I should come to you," which touched me very much.

You worked with The Stage Society in Los Angeles. Can you talk a little about the history of that company and about your classes?

The Stage Society's purpose was to do plays in Los Angeles and to maintain classes. It was very prestigious and had been designed really to replace The Actors' Lab which had been Red-baited out of existence. The Lab had done the plays of Sean O'Casey, George Bernard Shaw and Anton Chekov; and the state of mind of the country was such that those people were thought to be Communists. It was all out of ignorance. As The Stage Society became more and more prestigious, it began to get rid of some of its actors who were less important. One of them came to me and asked me to start a class. So I made a go of it while I was getting an education at UCLA After all, I couldn't act. But I never felt defeated. I hated when people would say, "Oh Jeff, you're such a survivor." I did more than survive, I lived a life. Word of mouth for my classes became really wonderful and that's when kids like Jack Nicholson, Sally Kellerman, Rita Moreno, Dean Stockwell, Dick [Richard] Chamberlain and Corey Allen came. Jimmy Dean even came to sit in. It became an "in" thing for actors. In a recent book on Jack Nicholson, it said that the nature of those classes affected a whole generation of actors. When Jack was at AFI recently, he was talking about the classes and said some wonderful things about the improvisations I did and how I would tell people to only work on the implications of the plot and the thematic content. He also talked about an idea he loved, which I actually got from Michael Chechov, which was that when you play a part, you must use 95 percent of yourself in it and then "play" the difference. Ninety-five percent of the role is you and the other five percent is what you act. The personality of the human being doing the acting is of primary importance to a successful performance. There should be a hook, something about an actor, that gets you and allows the audience to be able to imagine themselves in the same circumstances. Saint Augustine said, "The artist is the man." If you see a Michelangelo fresco, you think of Michelangelo, the man. When you see a Botticelli, you think of Botticelli. But if you see a run-of-the-mill painting, the artist doesn't emanate from it.

When Jack Nicholson was in your class did he show great potential?
I never played that prognostication game with my actors. Once in a while when a talented actor just couldn't get started in the industry, I'd take them aside and say, "You'll get work." I did that with Gerald McRaney. He was driving a cab and things were not going well for him. I told him he'd get work and then I felt responsible—so when I started directing, I gave him his first three jobs!

What was James Dean like as a student?
Jimmy used to come to class to watch. He was already a star at that point. And he was very generous. There was a young kid in class who wasn't really up to par and he just couldn't get a certain improvisation exercise. Jimmy took him outside and did the improvisation exercise with him out on the handball court. I worked with Jimmy on physicality because he didn't like what he did physically. So I demonstrated an exercise that requires the actor to do five unconnected physical tasks. You concentrate on the physical tasks and when you've got that all done, then you recite something. Before we could finish the work, he had his accident and was gone.

How does an exercise like that assist an actor?
Stanislavsky said working too excessively on a psychological truth is not as important as finding a physical truth. If you know where you are, if you're aware of your body in a room or in a castle or in a farmyard and if your body is alive and you know what the body wants to do, that's a large piece of the work. If you're in charge of what your body wants, you establish a pattern of physical truths and only then can you get a psychological truth. Brecht said the decision to do something also involves the decision not to do anything else. For example, if I choose to be quiet but I really feel like breaking things, the audience will sense, in my quietude, the possibility of other things. So this underscores the importance of physical truths over psychological truths. It's been said that an inordinate search for psychological truths always leads to a psychological hernia. When you really understand the purpose of playing an action, it becomes habitual. You don't have to stop and say, "What's my action?" You just tend to act with purpose because that's the way you trained yourself. The point is, and I quote the American actor and painter, Joseph Jefferson, "every artist must be the head of his or her academy." Matisse said there are no laws outside of the artist, so

when people ask if I teach [Sanford] Meisner I say "No, Sandy taught Meisner." Do you teach Stanislavsky? No, for better or worse, I teach Jeff Corey. And Jeff Corey says you become the head of your own academy. I don't dwell on sensory exercises. I'd rather see actors do scenes and if they don't show a lot of sensory awareness, I've got a million devices to work with them. But I don't say you start with exercises and you can't do anything else unless you get beyond that. That's not the way I work. As a student I used to go crazy because I wanted to get up and act. I didn't want to hear a whole lot of theory. That's the way I teach too. It's a hands-on experience.

Since you worked directly with the great teacher Michael Chechov, can you share some of the theories you came away with?
Michael said that a great performance had to be the confluence of the right actor and the right part at the right time. He also said, there are things the actor will know about a character that no one else does and the actor has to reveal them.

Many actors put their lives on hold and say they'll start a family when things are secure for them. You've been married for sixty years and have kids and a strong family life. What is your secret?
We've been very, very fortunate. While the kids were growing up, during the fifteen years I was blacklisted, we would go camping. Now, our children and grandchildren go on hikes and we all go camping. We started a strong tradition—all thanks to the blacklist! We endured the war and my family endured the blacklist. We always landed on our feet. We didn't go around beating our breasts and saying, "Oh God, what's happened to us? What kind of life is this?" We didn't let that happen. Practically all of my blacklisted friends showed a great deal of courage. The funny thing is, I don't think anyone was in love with whatever the Communist party was involved with at the time. We were not defending it. We all left political activity years before, but they wanted names of people from way back because that was the currency. Actors are what got headlines, not communist tinsmiths. Our industry was where there was publicity and money. October 19, 1997, on the fiftieth anniversary of the first Hollywood blacklist, it was really redemptive to have that wonderful occasion at the Motion Picture Academy where the four unions admitted that they were culpable and had supported the blacklist. They profoundly apologized that evening. It was very meaningful.

What was your first acting experience in Hollywood like?
When I got here from New York, I walked up Sunset Blvd. and naïvely went

from agent to agent—which you don't do in Hollywood. The first agent was interested and the third hired me. I was working a few days later. And then I was lucky enough to do *The Devil and Daniel Webster* where I met Walter Huston and learned a lot about life and acting from him.

What are some of the things you learned from him?

There was a guy in the Group Theater who was sort of a pill and every time I did a play, I'd freeze when he was in the audience. Walter laughed and said, "Oh kid, don't you know if you're in a 500 seat house or a 200 seat house, there's always gonna be someone who just doesn't like you? What the hell difference does it make? You just go out there, get excited about what you know about the part and play the damned thing and don't worry about some guy's opinion." He also told me about how when he was in *Othello* in New York, he thought his career was over and then he recovered the next year. So if you're in a flop, get up, brush the dirt off your pants and go to work.

What were some of your more memorable acting jobs?

Well, we're so happy anytime we're working, it's hard to say. But after the blacklist was over, I had a great period where I did *True Grit, Little Big Man, Butch Cassidy, In Cold Blood*. I've had the opportunity to do some wonderful things. I've done precisely one hundred features and I'm ready for more. But in my life, I've been on base and I've scored. I can look back with a great deal of pride.

Are you still teaching?

I teach one weekly class. Some of the books about acting classes offer a phone number to my service but, other than word of mouth, that's the only way I meet new students. I don't advertise. Frankly, I just don't feel good about inviting anyone to take on the career of acting. If people do get in touch with me, I do some work with them and if I like them and think they'll fit into the class, I'll allow them to join. You know, I'm pretty modest about my teaching capabilities and my acting capabilities but I'm absolutely vain about the chili I make. It's all in the ingredients. Chili is no good unless you get four or five tastes with each bite.

Sounds like what good acting should be.

Yes. It's the synthesis of ingredients and the penetration of opposites.

· ·

Jeff Corey
Answering Service: 310-456-2033
· ·

MILTON KATSELAS, ACTING COACH

I studied acting with Milton Katselas in the 1980s at the Beverly Hills Playhouse, so it was good to catch up with this charismatic teacher and director in an interview at his Hollywood home, which he also helped to design.

During his long and distinguished career, Katselas has taught and/or directed many of the top acting talents in this country. He directed Blythe Danner in her Tony-winning performance in *Butterflies Are Free,* Eileen Heckart in her Academy Award-winning film performance of the same play, and Bette Davis in *Strangers: The Story of a Mother and Daughter,* for which Davis won an Emmy. Some of his students have included Anne Archer, Tom Selleck, Robert Urich, Jenna Elfman, Patrick Swayze, Michelle Pfeiffer and George Clooney, among many others.

Katselas himself was nominated for a Tony, and his three Los Angeles stage productions have all won L.A. Drama Critics Circle Awards for best direction. Katselas founded the Beverly Hills Playhouse, the site of his teaching, twenty years ago. In 1996 he wrote the best-selling book, *Dreams into Action,* published by Dove Books. He is also active as a playwright, painter, sculptor, and architect.

When you were a child, what did you envision yourself doing with your life?

I wanted to be a basketball player. I was running my father's poolroom—I loved playing pool. Then when I went to college at Carnegie-Mellon, I tried acting. Right away, by the end of freshman year, I knew I wanted to be a director. The acting was wonderful and I enjoyed it—I continued acting all the way through college—but directing took me into the spheres of costuming, architecture, design and visual concepts. In my second year, I took the directing course and I was hooked.

That same year I went to New York for the first time on a visit, and I met Elia Kazan. I was walking in the street with a friend who pointed him out to me. I ran after him, caught him, and spoke to him in Greek. He told me that when I finished college I should come to see him. I did, and he gave me a job as an assistant. So if you see someone you respect walking in the street, chase 'em down and talk to them. Don't be afraid. Kazan and I are friends to this day.

How did you start teaching?

On that visit to New York, I sat in on Strasberg's classes at the Actors' Studio; I just sort of wheedled my way in. Then when I went back to Carnegie, we formed a group. We would meet, I would teach, and eventually we did plays. And I've taught all through the movies and plays I've done. I teach because I enjoy teaching. It's always been a part of my life.

You direct, teach, write, paint, sculpt, and now I hear you're doing some architecture.

I associated with an architect in doing my house, and now we have a small firm and we've done an extensive renovation or two.

So you're a Renaissance man?

Don't say that so loud—the guys from the poolroom might hear.

In everything you do, what theme or truth are you trying to communicate?

Well, the main thing I try to do is have fun. But I guess one of the big themes, if you want to call it that, is rehabilitation. As a painter, besides doing work on canvas, I will take old doors and old wood and all kinds of things, and rehabilitate them, bring them to a new life. I do the same thing, hopefully, with actors. Often I take actors who have lost their zest or their push or their passion and try to rehabilitate them. (Please don't tell them that's what I'm doing!) And I will take young actors who haven't gotten that passion yet and try to instill it in them.

What about your personal search?

Well, when I was nine years old, my father said to me in Greek, "Know thyself." So that's been a kind of search for me all my life: Discovering yourself through your work. But I think the other thing is passion. And risk. Joe Stern said to me once, "You're not happy unless you're on a high wire somewhere." So: risk, the danger of it, taking a chance, passion, rehabilitation, self-discovery. Those are the kinds of things that I'm always looking for in my work.

Other than rehabilitation, do these themes manifest themselves in your teaching?

Absolutely. Just take self-discovery: I try to teach that attitude monitors talent, so your attitude about yourself as an actor and the way you feel about yourself in relation to the business is very important. It monitors whatever talent you have. That's why sometimes you have actors who are less talented than others but have a greater attitude, so more of their talent comes to their work. Whereas another actor who has greater talent might have an attitude that isn't great and therefore he minimizes his own talent. He shipwrecks himself, puts himself on the rocks. It's very important that actors believe in themselves. Confidence releases the juices, releases the life, releases the passion.

I tell actors, "I'm not out to destroy you. I may be out to destroy some part of the bullshit that you have, or some part of your negativity, but I want to build confidence in you. That negativity isn't going to bring you work and money and creativity."

How would you work with someone who might come into your class with great charm, great personality, good looks, but no talent?

Charm, personality, good looks? I'd marry them. Look, I don't believe there is anyone without talent. And above and beyond that, it's not my job as a teacher to judge. As a director, that's something else. In that case I'm casting them, so I have to judge their talent, their personality and physical presence to fulfill a role. But in teaching, time and time again people surprise you with their abilities. I love it when the underdog wins.

What about actors who feel uncomfortable with their looks?

Part of my job is to remove the prejudice they might have about themselves. There is as much prejudice against beautiful people as there is against the so-called unattractive. People think that if actors are beautiful they can't act. And the actor himself may think, "It's all about tits and ass and not about my talent." Or you have the person who thinks they are not attractive and so can't get the romantic leading parts. You have to teach them and show them that attractiveness has to do with attitude as much as anything else. We have some wonderful actors who are not conventionally beautiful, but who convey sex, attractiveness and romance with their attitude and talent. You have to get the person to really see themselves, deal with themselves, and stop making up all these phony stories about their limitations.

I mean, Bogart was not a conventionally handsome guy, but because of his attitude and manliness and talent, the unique way he handled himself and his voice, he was gorgeous. And one has to be careful what to change with an actor, because it may be the clue to their power. So maybe Bogie comes into an acting class and the first thing the teacher might tell him is, "Work on your voice." One has to be very careful when you start advising people.

How do you work with good actors who don't audition well?
In Stanislavsky, there was nothing to do with auditioning. It is something I have always dealt with, however, because I want actors to work. There is no substitute for work. You can study and study, but you must work.

I think the audition process should be worked on with the actors in a class, not just in a cold reading class but as part of their acting journey, as part of their acting work. It is very, very important. One guy in my class was not doing well at auditions at all. I got him up in the class one time and I said, "Dance. And as you dance, I want you to say some of these lines." And he did. And he suddenly got free. So I said, "The next audition you go to, even though it's not a dancing one, I want you to dance." So he went and he did it and he got a callback.

So every actor has his own creative trigger.
Yes. It's something different for everyone, but there is a key for each actor that releases him, and helps him with his auditions. Some like to rehearse a lot. Some like to improvise a little. Some like to be caught off guard—almost not prepared. You have to find what works for you. I have told actors that when you audition and you don't feel good about it, go back that very moment. Don't get in your car and go home sadly. Go back. Say you'd like another three-minute shot. But you had better make sure that the second time is definitely better, because otherwise it's for the birds. You've got to come back with something fresh and new.

One other tip: They want you to give them the confidence that you can do this part, so get off the notion of doing a "reading" for the part—you're doing an acting. And use the script. When they hire you and pay you, then you can put it down. Let them feel, "If he's this good with the script, then he'll be great without it." But remember, it's not a "reading," it's an "acting."

So the attitude is very important in the audition. And the feeling that you have something to offer. You're unique, you see. There is nobody like you. No one. In my book, I have a chapter about "unlikely winners." There are no likely winners. I mean, to think that Ronald Reagan would go from being an actor to being president! Or Mugsy Bogues, the five-foot-three-inch professional basketball player— a likely winner?

In New York, my gang and I thought Robert Redford was low on the totem pole because he was so handsome, we didn't believe he could act. He's handsome as hell, but also a fabulous actor and director. What schmucks my gang and I were! Is Linda Hunt someone you'd ever pick for a winner? She's a small person, but when she acts, she's a giant. When you examine it, people have to work on themselves. And there's a uniqueness. If you turn your back on that uniqueness you have lost the game.

What can you tell me about the actor's personal connection with a role?
Bobby De Niro spoke in my class once, and somebody asked him, "What's your career concept?" He said, "Self-expression." That's very personal to him. He's done everything from gaining weight to shaving his head to express more of himself as an actor and as a person, and I think that's part of his thing. Actors have to learn to understand that the work of the actor has to be personal. Why did this script come to you at this time? What's the personal connection? An obvious example is, while in the middle of a divorce, I received a script for a four-part miniseries called *The Rules of Marriage*. Needless to say, I felt compelled to do it.

What do you say to an actor who might wonder whether they should study acting or not?
Classes not only get you ready for the moment, acting-wise, but as Gurgiev, an Eastern philosopher, says, "The job of the teacher is to wake up the student. Make him aware he is asleep, then wake him up." Many people want to be actors, but they're asleep—sitting in cafes and badmouthing the industry or their agent or something. Badmouthing themselves. So don't just stay in slumberland, get into a class and do. Do, do, do. It is very hard without a teacher. You can do it, but it's very hard.

The director George C. Wolfe said that theatre is "people sitting in the dark watching people in the light showing us what it means to be human. Actors give us feelings of being alive, and if we can't do it in our relationships and our

work, we'll do it in the darkness of a theatre. We dearly hope that they will entertain us and give us light and show us the way." Do you agree with that?
That's beautiful. What he says is hot. The world is going to be saved, if it is saved, by artists. Not by scientists, not by politicians, not by doctors. Those people extend our life, they affect it, no doubt, and we owe them a debt. But what we're interested in is the quality of our life. Theatre and movies bring us understanding; that is the bottom line. To love and understand one another no matter what differences there seem to be.

In Ancient Greece, farmers walked for miles and miles to come to the theatre, to look and see and experience and have this catharsis, as they called it, which brought them understanding. So study life; it's the key to being the best actor you can be. Actors don't go out and study life enough. Don't be caught up in money. Get into the real craft and understanding of the acting. Observe all the time. Life is right there looking at us, square in the face, ready to teach us what we are trying to convey. When you sit in a car and a person walks by, you can see their whole life. You see their economic position. You see their sexuality. You see their political views, You see everything by observing their behavior, manner and clothing. Study all this. As artists we have to convey an understanding of behavior and life. Theatre and film are very powerful, but they need life to inform them.

Do you have any final tips, any last comments for actors?
Be an artist in your life. Make your life work. Make your life sing. Don't be downtrodden. This is your time to learn. This is your time to celebrate. Have fun. Enjoy!

· · · · · · · · · · · · · · · · · · ·
Milton Katselas
Beverly Hills Playhouse
310-855-1556
· · · · · · · · · · · · · · · · · · ·

James Cameron, Director

After interviewing James Cameron in his sun-drenched offices in Santa Monica, I drove away realizing that this boyish, unassuming guy who walks tightropes in his art, has an incredible desire to communicate—whether it be with his actors, his audience or with his own muses and demons. This man, who technically can "part the sea" in his film-making, yearns, it seems, to make us all feel what it is to be alive.

Cameron grew up in Niagara Falls and moved to Brea, California in 1971 to study physics at Fullerton College. In the early 1980s, he got a break with Roger Corman's New World Pictures, moving his way up from building miniatures and painting mattes to working as a production designer and second unit director. His first major film, *The Terminator*, was made in 1984 for $6 million, and ended up grossing $80 million worldwide. He went on to write *Rambo: First Blood Part II* and *Aliens*, the sequel to *Alien*, which he later directed and was released in 1986. Next was the underrated underwater epic *The Abyss*, shot in 1988-1989, followed by the megahit *Terminator II* (grossing $500 million worldwide) and the spy romp *True Lies*.

His films have been distinguished by trailblazing special effects, strong, often passionate writing, and striking economical performances (especially by women actors), but none has approached the narrative ambition, budget or acclaim of *Titanic*, which set a record in worldwide grosses and tied 1950's *All About Eve* for a record number of fourteen Academy Award nominations. *Titanic* went on to win a total of eleven Oscars, including Best Picture and Best Director.

Tell us about your beginnings in the business. Were you ever an actor?
No, I never did any acting. I was in the founding group of the Theatre Arts program at my high school but I went straight into the writing, directing, art direction roles. I was petrified to be on stage. I hated it. I hated getting up in front of the class to do a speech. Terrified. I still am. I don't think I ever made the cognitive leap, at that age, that you get to hide within or behind a character so you think it's not really you out there. A lot of actors can make that kind of dissociative step. I never could, so I never acted. But I wrote plays and I directed them. It's strange, my career was really a confluence of many things. It took me a long time to sort it all out. I was a figurative artist when I was young. I drew comic books and painted pictures. I thought I might be an artist. Then I got interested in writing and I thought I'd be a writer. Or maybe I'd write some sort of illustrated thing. I was trying to tell a story, provide the narrative function, and use imagery at the same time. I didn't quite know how to do that. I was doing theatre and then video production which, at that time— 1969, 1970—was brand new technology. To actually have a video camera and recorder in a school was really something. We had no editing equipment so it almost had to be shot like live TV was, back in the fifties. So I was coming at film from all different directions but it was all related to a narrative sense and wanting to tell stories.

What influenced you to decide on directing?
Well, there was a big time lapse in there. For the first year of college, I continued with literature and video production but then I sort of thought, "I can't get there. I can't get to Hollywood." I was living in Orange County. It sounds close but it isn't. No one there was involved in the film business; it might as well have been another state. I gave up on it and decided I was going to be a scientist. I studied physics and engineering. Eventually, I got married, dropped out of school and drove a truck for a few years. I figured I'd probably be a writer and I should experience life and see some of the world. When I was twenty-four or twenty-

five some friends of mine got in touch with a group of people who wanted to put up some money to do a very low budget feature. They asked me if I had any ideas. I got involved with their project and promptly took it over. From that point on I was very single-mindedly on the film making track. I realized that was where I belonged. It was no problem staying up all night, every night, for as long as it took. It was that young perspective where you're willing to sacrifice everything.

You're still doing that.

Yeah, it gets that way. But I think your ability and willingness to pull seven consecutive all nighters is reduced somewhat when you get into your forties. But there were some times like that on *Titanic*, especially toward the end. There was a period where I got four hours of sleep over the course of seventy-five hours. It's fun doing that stuff every once in awhile, just not too often.

The thing that probably held me back, in a way, was that I didn't really understand the acting process. I had been doing a lot of writing so I approached everything from a character's perspective. You can know it all in your head but if you can't give it to the actors in a way and at a rate that they can assimilate then it doesn't matter. That came with time, I think. Even on *Terminator*, I still wasn't very good at that, I don't think. But I must have been good enough, because I look at that film and I think the performances are quite good, I just think it was a longer process. There was a lot more time spent in rehearsal. I spent a great deal of time working with the actors before we ever got on the set. I don't tend to do that as much, now.

Some people think a lot of rehearsal kills spontaneity on film. You know, those surprises that can happen.

I agree with that wholeheartedly. There's the Sidney Lumet school of thought—which is to tape up the floor, mock up the set on a sound-stage, and rehearse like hell for four or five weeks. Like a play. If you're not willing to go that far, where people have it so at their command that they can experiment from a position of strength, which is difficult on most film production schedules, then don't go halfway because you'll just stop in the middle of what I feel is the stale phase of rehearsal. What I do is I spend a couple of weeks on rehearsal and it's usually pretty exploratory, character wise. We'll do a read-through and have everybody just say the scene the way it's written, just to see if there's anything that's just not going to work out loud. It also gives the actors the time to ask questions for a few days. Then we get to a much more creative level where we do basic representations of the set and break the scenes down into an improv version. On *Titanic*, it was particularly interesting to try doing the scenes in a contemporary idiom. That was really helpful for Leonardo DiCaprio who hadn't done any period work at all. It was a little tricky for him to make the dialogue real. He had to think it in 1996 street-speak first, and then play it.

All the rehearsal time made for a really good process because, when we went into it, we weren't trying to find it on set. We would have wasted a tremendous amount of time and energy and Leo would have always been insecure about his earlier work if the character hadn't already developed. Because on a film, there's no going back.

Do your films have a common emotional thread?
I've always tried, in every film that I've made, to celebrate positive aspects of human nature within an environment where there is either a natural adversity or the negative aspects of human nature threaten to overwhelm. I've been criticized for being sappy, maudlin, or melodramatic on every film I've made for that reason. But it's easy to be hip. It's much easier to be hip than it is to be earnest and emotionally honest in a film.

The audiences went to see *Titanic* again and again. What do you think that was all about?
Once the audience knows the story and you know where it's going, it's not about what's going to happen next. The intellectual part of your brain shuts down a little bit and—I'm guessing now—but I know how I feel when I see a film a second time and I know what's coming, I look at those scenes differently. There's a poignancy to it that reaches another level. I think that anybody who's seeing the film for the first time gets that anyway because you know the ship's going to sink. They don't know who's going to die and who's going to live, but they know that tragedy is coming, and that it's inevitable. It's grinding toward them relentlessly. That's the thing that appealed to me most about making the film. People have talked to me about all of the symbolism and metaphors and metaphor for technology and all of those things. For me it's very simple; the ship is just a metaphor for mortality. Life is a situation where you know the end is coming but you're not dead yet. What do you do in the meantime and how do you respond?

Elia Kazan once said that three-fourths of great directing is in the casting. Do you agree?
Oh, casting is critical. There are ninety-two speaking roles in *Titanic* and it's through the casting that they all seem so unique and have a past. Casting is critical and writing is critical and if you've done those two things properly, you

only have to go the last 20 percent of the way and get the best performance possible from the person saying those words. It occurred to me after going through this huge casting project on this film, that what I wound up selecting—out of all of the various possibilities—were people who had something inherently interesting about them, which gives you an illusion of back-story. It's an indefinable thing and a very subjective thing. An actor should never feel rejected when they're not cast. The subjective process going on in the mind of the director or producer finally making that decision is so particular to that individual.

You use video in your auditions, don't you?
I do a lot on tape first. I've been moving in that direction for the last couple of years, because film is a visual medium. I would never do it that way for theatre. But for film, it's about how that person comes across on screen. Before I know them and talk to them about who they are, I want to have some initial impulse in my mind about how they come across on film. Then I can go to the other levels that I have to get to with any actor. First, who are they as a person? All of my films are long hauls and I always feel like I'm crewing up an expedition. I need to know if we're going to get along. Then it's, who are they as an actor? Can we communicate, are we easy together and will we be able to work together? The reason I don't audition everybody right away is because I like to take a lot of time. I like to do a scene five, six, seven or eight times; whatever it takes. Actors think it's strange because they're used to doing a scene once and you're gone. What can you learn from once? I have to give you the first three takes just so you're comfortable and feel creative. That's why I use the video process—I have to have some way of narrowing the field so that I can spend the time with the people I think might be right for the role. I think actors spend too much time trying to second guess what a particular filmmaker wants based on what they might know about them, or what they've seen in their work. You have to get past that. An actor should show you what they've prepared, but let's not necessarily stick to just that. I want to see a sense of balance and flexibility. Who knows what's going to happen when they go into the mix with other actors? A scene can have its own dynamic. Currents will start to flow through a scene and you've got to be ready to go with it. Sometimes, in an audition, you can sense when an actor's coming in over-prepared and is too insecure to get past what they've already worked out. They've memorized the lines and their choices and they don't hear the direction. It's like they think if they move off of it, they won't know what to do. What I'm looking for is someone who, if I throw them a bone, can catch it in their left hand or right hand. Emotionally speaking.

Now that I have a reputation—an incorrect reputation—for being a taskmaster, a lot of actors come to me with some trepidation and are usually amazed that it's not that way. There's been so much written about the making of my films, which are all hard and grueling films, that there's a misinterpretation about the difficulty factor of the shooting. The physicality of the work gets mixed up with a kind of emotional domination of the cast. Actors are always coming to me with this sense of foreboding and then they're surprised when they discover that I'm not a dictator.

Do you let the actors find their own way in the work or do you bring your vision and say, "Here's what I want, find a way to do it."

It depends upon the individual. The way the human immune system works is that there are antibodies which will key into any organism that comes into the body. They will shape themselves to that organism. I think of directing as being an antibody; I have to reshape myself for each person on the set. The relationship is going to be different for every single actor on the set. Some are going to be most comfortable when you tell them exactly how you want them to play the scene and exactly what you want them to do. They'll throw all of their willpower and all of their creativity into doing the best of that version. Others want to have time to explore a bit. Billy Zane, for example, is an explorer. He'd go to all points on the compass. I didn't find that to be problematic at all. Even though I had written the script, I cast him because I thought he'd bring some dimensionality to the role. I thought he did and, unfortunately, he didn't get as much credit for it as I thought he deserved. It was tough for him because his character never had a chance to be liked. His character represented a time and a set of values that don't really exist anymore which is why, I think, he got criticized for being a mustache twirler. But he was playing a vulnerability and imbalance that was created by his character's inability to deal with his own feelings. Billy understood exactly what he was doing.

What do you do when an actor's in trouble and can't find his way?

I throw new ideas at them. And there are different levels. There are times when an actor may never be satisfied with a scene. I remember working with Ed Harris in *The Abyss*. Ed was never satisfied with a scene and after the first few weeks I realized that was because there was a continual hunger there. His approach is to stay hungry. There's always something better, something more. He'd be on take ten and have done on take eight 200 percent of what I ever expected, and he'd be saying, "I'm floundering, help me, help me." That relationship was about working toward a goal, getting there, refining it, and then—in my mind and separate from my communication with Ed—realizing that I'd gotten it, and then for the next few takes working on Ed to get him to relax and know he had done something worthwhile. A lot of times I'd have to show him the monitor so he could see for himself. There is always a sense, in his mind, that he hasn't gone far enough in the work. Leo and Kate are also like that, but they always knew when they'd gotten it.

Actors who come from the theatre are used to a response from the audience. In film, of course, it's just the director, so they really need the feedback.
Yeah, it took me a long time to realize that you have to give the "Atta boys" but you can't go too far because if you do, no one will believe what you're saying. The second I say, "Cut," is when my work begins. We've just done a take, now what worked and what didn't work? The first thing to say to the actor is, "What did you think about that?" never, "Oh baby, that was great!" because after a week of that, nobody's going to believe a damned thing you say.

What qualities do you think make a great film actor?
There are the God given qualities—the instrument, the eyes, the face, the voice, the body, a certain connection between the brain and the body, how you move your hands, how you act with your whole being. I think a lot of those things are innate. There needs to be a psychological constellation of things at your disposal; the ability to work hard, to concentrate and not be distracted, to focus. The most important thing, regardless of all of those other things—and certainly there are a lot of actors who are missing certain elements—the one thing you can't get away without, is the ability to summon to the surface an emotional state which we as a population are conditioned against from our earliest childhood. We're conditioned not to cry, to be strong, not to show our feelings in public, and actors have to break through all of that conditioning and be in control of it at the same time. That's what I find to be the great magic—to be able to summon the demon and then control it directly. It can't just be wild and out of control because then you might get takes that may be at an inappropriate level. You're acting over a period of time and all of the little pieces of the jigsaw need to go together to create a performance that will have a modulation to it that is perceived by the audience over the course of two or three hours. You're doing this over the course of a six month period. Film acting really diverges from stage acting at that point. You're not building up energy over time to a peak, you're having to dissect it into slices and know what slice you're doing at any given moment in the shoot. The director has to help, in a way, by knowing what slice the actor is in so they don't do too much or too little; so the slices all form the big picture. That's where

rehearsals are helpful—you have to know how far the actor can go and what they can create—to know what you're going to look for when you get to that big cathartic scene. Otherwise you might end up holding back too much.

Great acting is not the release of emotion; it's the repression of the emotion, and it's what leaks around the edges that is most powerful. Sometimes I think that so much of the process is instinctive. Actors just do it. I don't mean to take away from their training, but there's a certain quality of acting that cannot be taught. At least for the best of them. For the great actors, it has to be there and it has to be instinctive.

How did you learn to communicate with actors?
I've never taken classes in directing, I just found my own way of doing it. For me it's a learning experience every time I do a scene with a new actor. I'm always learning something. I can't articulate it into a set of rules. There's an instinctive psychological thing that happens. If I'm not feeling that emotion myself, I can't articulate it. If I'm on the set as the director, I know why the characters are doing and saying what they're doing. They have to be emotions that I've experienced at some point. I'm not saying that I could jump in front of the lens and recreate them visually for the world, but I can recreate them enough that I can somehow articulate or get across the feeling of what's needed.

How do you deal with neurotic actors with issues that might interfere with the work?
It's insecurity. I think there's an inherent insecurity on the part of actors and there's an inherent confidence. They wouldn't want to do it or be drawn to do it, otherwise. They wouldn't be drawn to the act of standing up in front of other humans and trying to express something. Ray Bradbury calls it "the sublime ego," which means that it is the beautiful thing in an artist that allows them to believe, however fleetingly, that they have something to say. It applies to painting, it applies to writing, to everything. If you don't have some aspect of that sublime ego than you're not going to be an artist. You're not going to think that what you have to say is any more important than what anybody else says. I find that most actors have that and also a great insecurity. That insecurity fuels their greatness. I think it is those insecurities that create the great performances. If they didn't have that, they'd be hacks. There's nothing worse than an actor who's so confident that they know exactly what they're doing. Those actors are going to stay at a certain level and never go beyond it.

What is a typical day of shooting like with you?

You might come in to shoot a scene four or five months after we've initially rehearsed it. For me, this is where the creative work really starts because now you're in wardrobe, you're on set, you have the environment. Especially on *Titanic*, but in all my films, the physical environment of the scene forms the staging of it, and the staging is such a critical aspect of how people are going to react to each other emotionally and how they're going to express themselves. So what I usually do is ask everybody to come in before they're dressed, I get some really basic lights on, and I send the crew out. Depending on the complexity of the scene, it may be only a couple of minutes or three or four hours, but there's no other way to do it. I let the actors take the space. I'm not going to tell the actors where to go, although I may give them a rough idea. If you're doing a dinner scene, for instance, somebody's going to have to do the seating. Logistical stuff gets discussed, but I try not to impose what it might look like at this point. So we just play the scene a little bit and see what happens. You'll see how people move, how they might relate to furniture, to each other, and you see interesting things. You have to learn that about a scene before you decide where someone might stand. You've got to start getting the scene on it's feet and things will either happen by instinct or a process of exploration. What an actor chooses may completely change, from a director's standpoint, how you set up the scene, but you don't want to impose that stuff to start with, you just find what works best, unless there are physical limitations. You keep it very amorphous for awhile until things start to feel good, discoveries are made and people start to feel pretty confident. Then I say, "Okay, everybody go get dressed." They usually leave the set with some bounce in their step because they know that they've got some definition as to where they're going with it.

I think you have to keep the excitement level up. I used to sit outside the scenes and watch, but now I'm more involved with them. Sometimes I can also sense that I've taken the actors in a wrong direction and I tell myself to back off and let them find it. There are some directors who just sit back and let the actors work but I can't do that. I trust them and if I screw up, I'll know it. Like with Bernard Hill, who played the captain in *Titanic*. I eventually had to start operating the camera myself because he was doing stuff that was very subtle and I wasn't seeing it on video. I kept thinking, "He's like a stone, he's not doing it." So I'd go in and try to juice him up a little and he'd resist. He'd do it, but there was a sense that he didn't think it was right. I wouldn't see it until the dailies—because what he had done on the takes before I directed him were just the right level, but it was too subtle for the video to see. A lot of stuff in *Titanic* was like that and I wound up jumping on and operating the camera a lot more than I normally do, because there were nuances of performance and a sense of connection that I'd get with the performer doing it that way that I didn't necessarily get watching the video monitor. My operator was a better operator than I am, but I would rather sacrifice perfect operating in order to see what was going on. It's just being able to see really, really clearly what's in the eyes and what's in the nuances. I found that, with Gloria Stuart, I also wanted to get on the camera and operate because she was just so able to modulate the level of her emotions.

Is there anything actors do that makes you crazy?
There are individual things with individual people that upset me and I just grit my teeth, but I try never to shout. It's hard, because actors are probably the people who are most attuned to the states of other people. But there are times when I try to just grit my teeth when someone goes off to craft services for twenty minutes while the rest of the entire unit is standing around. For me, there's a certain work ethic that I have that I know some actors don't have. But I let the A.D.s [assistant directors] deal with that. It would compromise my artistic relationship with the actors to deal on that level. Sometimes I'll deal with it jokingly, but there's nothing that makes me really crazy. I can forgive just about anything. I think I have a good sense of how hard it is to get up in front of that cold, glass eye and be real, be truthful, be human—all of those things. To put yourself in that stripped down, vulnerable state over and over again. I think whatever it takes to get you there is worth it.

Have you decided what you'll be working on next?
I'm tempted, now that I've got a little bit of down time, to join a workshop and do some acting myself. I know I'd be bad, but that's not the point. It would improve my work as a director. I think by doing that, I can learn more about what actors need. The director's job is to serve. With actors, it's, "What can I do to help?" What can I do to be useful to you? What information do you need, what guidance do you need?" Sometimes it can be like throwing a ball back and forth really quickly. It's not as intellectual a process as some people think. Not for me. It's totally instinctive. Film running through the camera is the cheapest thing on the set so, if an actor wants to try something, I'm game. Journalists get it all wrong. They think that a director who goes through a lot of takes is inherently hard on actors. That's backwards. When I walk on a set, I say, "Let's just start shooting, we'll use it as rehearsal," we may be on take five before we even really start shooting. I make film the cheapest resource.

That's so great because actors are taught from working in television that they're in trouble if they do more than a few takes.

I try to get that out of the way from the beginning. And I've never had an actor say to me, "Why do we need to do that again? What didn't I do?" I've also been fortunate in that I've never had a scene where one actor peaked in three takes and the other one didn't get warmed up until take ten. Then you're really messed up. Maybe that's part of the audition process and seeing if they can build. I like actors who can make a discovery in take three, keep it and build on it. There's always the sense of holding out for magic. Sometimes it comes. And sometimes it comes on take twelve. It probably took five hours to light the shot so what's three minutes for another take? The only person who suffers is the person in the next scene who's waiting to go on.

This film was so big. There was so much technical stuff, so much organizational stuff and so many people; I kept having to remind myself why I did this film. I did this film because I thought that event, that story, offered an opportunity as a filmmaker to deal with the full spectrum of human emotion in a way I'd never really gotten to do before. Everyday, I'd be driving up to this giant ship and I'd have to say, "It's not about the ship." On this film we made it our goal to make the emotions first, the performances first and everything else was second. On the top of this massive, technical mountain were the people, their emotions— the simplest things.

John Woo, Director

It is always a temptation for critics to draw parallels between an artist's life and the work he creates. With John Woo, it's almost irresistible. Raised in Hong Kong in the 1950s, having fled communist South China with his family, Woo grew up around gangland violence comparable to 1920s Chicago, as communists and nationalists fought for control of the burgeoning metropolis and the easy money to be made there. Woo's escape from the streets was the Alliance Franchise, which

showed foreign films like *The Wizard of Oz*, a movie the director fell in love with along with many other of the great American musicals. It is not surprising, then, that Woo's greatest action films—*The Killer, Hard-Boiled, Bullet in the Head, Face/Off*—are a combination of bullets and ballet, violent in the extreme, but choreographed beautifully and often set to lyrical music.

It was laughter, not lacerations, which first earned Woo his reputation as a director. His late 1970s comedies, most notably the Asian box-office explosion *Pilferer's Progress*, set Woo up as the Hong Kong comedy king. However, Woo felt limited by the genre and with the backing of producer Tsui Hark and the talent of a young actor named Chow Yun-Fat, Woo made the gangster epic,

A Better Tomorrow which went on to break all box-office records and invented, or rather re-invented, the Hong Kong action film.

Unlike the reigning trends in the genre at the time, defined by the successful Shaw brothers, for whom the director once worked, Woo preferred the gun to the hand—or the foot. Audiences seemed to prefer it, too. The string of successes that followed *A Better Tomorrow* revealed some definite thematic trends in the director's works. Woo's heroes were marked by their extreme self-sacrifice, and the ensuing trend which swept through Hong Kong filmmaking was dubbed the "heroic bloodshed" craze. Again, it might be too easy to point to Woo's Lutheran upbringing—he once considered the priesthood as a young man—as the root of all the selfless blood sacrifice imagery in his films. But it many ways, it's a valid connection, and one Woo himself has admitted to.

Despite his success in China, Woo, like Jackie Chan (who, coincidentally, served as fight choreographer for Woo's first film, *The Young Dragons*) and Woo's alter ego Chow Yun-Fat, found some difficulty locating the right U.S. project to introduce his artistry to Americans. *Hard Target* was a hard learning experience for Woo, who found that the directors in the states are often at the mercy of producers. Next up was *Broken Arrow*, a traditional American action film. While devoid of Woo's poetry in movement, it was a big hit and demonstrated to Hollywood that Woo could be left on his own and still come across with the goods. And that's exactly what he did with *Face/Off*, a truly bloody and beautiful John Woo classic and an American box-office hit. Woo is now at the top of his game in the states, and is currently in production on the Tom Cruise film, *Mission Impossible 2*.

Sitting with Woo in his office on the Sony Studios lot was not the experience I'd expected. All of his action work hadn't prepared me for the warm, gentle man I spoke to. We talked of filmmaking, acting, and the love it takes to be an artist.

Did you ever want to be an actor?
I started as an actor when I was in high school. I did about ten or eleven plays, both acting and directing. When I was a kid I was so shy. I couldn't speak well; it was hard to express myself in words. So I started doing plays to try to overcome

the weakness and to train myself not to be shy. I wanted to try to find a way to communicate with people. It also helped me to learn a lot more about life and about people. Being an actor can really help with self confidence.

Why didn't you continue acting?

I had so many things that I wanted to say. I wanted to be a painter, a musician, a poet, a choreographer. I had so many roads. So only doing performance was not enough. I wanted to use many ways to express myself. I was so much stronger as a painter and I realized that I had a good visual sense. I realized I could use a camera to tell a story and it was worth more to me. I could get more magic. Plus, the actors were tall, handsome and charming—I didn't have any of that; I just have a common look. So I gave it up. I think great actors also have to be really focused and always concentrating on their characters. I couldn't do that. I do too much thinking. Being an actor, you have to live with a character and it's hard to notice anything else. Being a director is much more broad. You can go anywhere, see the world and other people, observe other lives.

Fellini once said, "Even if I set out to make a film about a filet of sole, it would be about me." Is that true for you?

Yes, it is. I always put myself into the movie and use actors to represent me. For example, in *A Better Tomorrow* the main character is part of a gang. I used that as a metaphor for how I struggle, how I see family and friendship, and to send a message of honor, loyalty and chivalry. The movie was also how man cannot be without dignity. Before I made that film, I was a failure for quite a few years. My movies didn't work anymore and I was looked down on by quite a few people. It was quite discouraging. Some people even thought I should retire. I was sad and hurt for a year. But I still had a very strong drive and I told myself that I was a good director and I wouldn't give up. So I put this experience into the film and used it to speak for me. In the story, it's a fight against evil. And I showed that I had my own dignity; I wouldn't give up. It worked very well because all of the feelings came from my heart and the audience got it. They were touched by the story and it was a huge hit in all of Asia. It changed my life.

Is there a difference between directing American actors and Chinese actors?

Well, in general, Chinese actors can be very stage-y. Some of the actors trained on stage and some on television. There are no real acting training schools in Hong Kong. Another group has been trained in the Peking Opera. They're trained in singing, acting, dancing, action and fighting. Sometimes those actors can be a little bit too big for film.

Some of the great Chinese actors also learn from American movies. Some of their idols are Paul Newman, Al Pacino, Robert De Niro, Steve McQueen and Marlon Brando. Chinese actors have been really influenced by them. By imitating the American performers, they'd find techniques for themselves and create their own methods They know their stories, how they started, how they worked, their acting philosophy. For example, when they find out that Robert De Niro worked as a taxi driver to study for *Taxi Driver*, that makes them understand what a real actor is. That wasn't from school or from any acting class. They were learning from life. That gave them heart and a lot of improvement.

I learned the Western way. I believe in and love actors. They are the soul of the movies. I always like to work with a real person. There are two kinds of actor. One is an entertainer who can put on a really good show and try to amuse the audience. Another kind of actor is believable and has a great heart, like Brando or Newman. They came from the heart. That's what I mean by real people. I never know how to demonstrate or teach actors what to do. I wouldn't dare to teach them; the actor is the artist. I usually give them a lot of freedom. I want them to put themselves into the character.

Do you let them improvise?

I let them improvise and I let them change dialogue.

Do you rehearse much?

I don't think much of rehearsing on a set. I like happenings, surprise and instincts. The most important thing is for actors to trust their own instincts and believe in what they are doing. The great actors have great instincts. But some actors, especially American actors, care too much about acting. They work too hard. I think you can work too much and then it's not natural. That's why I don't like to do too many takes. Some actors like to do twenty or thirty takes and try so many different things. I only want one or two. John Travolta, Nick Cage and Joan Allen all wanted to do more. They wanted to work more. I don't like perfect. The first couple of takes are very real and natural because the actors are unprepared and just warming up. Sometimes, a little flaw may be a good thing. When they do something wrong, I think they're more interesting. I've got a nickname in the business. They call me "One-shot John." I know what I like and no matter how many times the actors do it I always like the first few takes. If you do it more, it's no longer coming from instinct. It becomes methodical.

In Hong Kong, I worked pretty much the same way I do here. I like to use actors who are real.

In general, before I start shooting, I like to make friends with the actors and have several conversations with them. I like to see how they feel about everything. I like to hear their story, how they feel about the world, what they love, what they're happy about, and I like to put their experience into the scene and into the character. I write the scene around the actor. Then, they are doing levels of themselves. That's why I like to spend so much time with my actors. I even know their habits. On the set, I like to say, "Okay, forget about the script, forget about the dialogue. Is there any similar experience in your life?" I like to improvise the dialogue. I don't like the typical way of doing things.

I enjoy performers, so while I'm working I forget about story, I forget about other scenes. I only enjoy that particular moment and what the actors are forming in front of the camera. I have no worries about how it's going to fit. If that moment doesn't touch me, then the scene doesn't work. I see myself as one of the audience. I know how people feel. So when that moment really touches me, I know that other people will be touched and that they will like it. They will get the same kind of feeling.

What is the experience like for an actor when they come in to audition for you?
First, I like to meet the actors. The personal impression I get is the most important thing. Sometimes I watch tape but I like to meet people face-to-face and see how I feel with that person. And I like to listen. I don't so much care about their reading. Every actor can read. I just like to listen to them talk to the casting director. I like to see how they interact. And I like to know a little of their background and their story.

What makes you ultimately choose someone over someone else?
Personal impressions. Or I'm convinced by the casting directors. I usually trust them. They select some good people to help me make a final decision. The most important thing is I like to find an actor who really cares about the others. I don't want to work with selfish actors. Some actors only care about themselves or their own image. They can give a performance, but not from the heart. John, Nick, and Joan, they really care. They are good human beings.

Is there anything else that you'd like to say to actors?
They need to be themselves and trust their own instincts. Great actors do that. Great performers think of real life and what comes from their own hearts. I think the director should help the actor to do this. That's very important and that's why I think the director should know the actors well. Actors should believe

in the director and trust them. Everything is about love, especially if you are an actor. Actors should have great love for the character they're playing. Believe in the character, and you will give a great performance.

I see my actors as part of my family. They are my heart. And since I love my actors as my own children, I give them the freedom to do what they want. They have freedom of speech, freedom to create, freedom of thinking. I let them improvise everything and then I will shape it. Sometimes the actors have some ideas but they have a problem with expressing them. A good director will give the guidelines to help the performance. Everything that shows on the screen is their acting, not the directing. I've got to keep a very close and good relationship with the actors. That's how I work. And that's how they end up with self confidence. There is a relationship between an actor and a director that is like a friendship. When an actor has a problem, or they are struck by some personal things, I always like to hear their story and try to help. No matter what the problem, I have time for them; that's the way I work. Or I'll change a scene to use what they're feeling. Sometimes I'll give them some time to work things out and I'll work on something else until they are more comfortable.

It's so wonderful that you care so much. From your heart, as you say.
I believe that we have to know how to respect each other. I respect the actors, they respect me, I respect my crew. I know people need respect. Acting is an insecure business. Most of the people feel insecure. So you have to make them feel comfortable and make them believe in themselves and in their own charm. Every human being has charm They sometimes just don't know how to show it. So my duty is to find the charm. The charm of acting, of the face, of philosophy. If I can help a little bit, I feel happy. A director is not a dictator. A director gives people direction and is there to guide. And the actors sometimes will teach me about life. Sometimes people are built in a different way but deep inside, basically everyone is the same. All of mankind has the same kind of heart.

Author KAREN KONDAZIAN's career as an actor, writer and producer is as diverse as it is long. At the age of eight Karen was chosen to be one of the infamous children on Art Linkletter's "Kids Say the Darndest Things". The opportunity to miss school during tapings was all it took for Karen to abandon her life's goal of becoming a CIA spy and focus on acting. After training at San Francisco State College, The University of Vienna and The London Academy of Music and Dramatic Arts (LAMDA), she began her career in New

York, in Michael Cacoyannis' *Trojan Women* (Circle in the Square). For her stage work, Kondazian has been awarded five Drama-Logues, an L.A. Weekly and a Los Angeles Drama Critics Circle Award and been nominated for a San Francisco Drama Critics Circle Award and an Ovation Award for performances in such productions as *Who's Afraid of Virginia Woolf?* (Berkeley Rep.); *Lady House Blues* (South Coast Rep.); *Sweet Bird of Youth* with Ed Harris; *Tamara* (Los Angeles production); *Orpheus Descending, Freedomland* (South Coast Rep., World Premiere), *Hamlet* with Stacy Keach (Mark Taper Forum), *Richard II* with Richard Chamberlain (Ahmanson), *Night of the Iguana* (Old Globe), the West Coast premiere of Tennessee Williams' *Vieux Carre*, with Ray Stricklyn, and *The Rose Tattoo* (in which her work, both as actor and producer, so impressed Tennessee Williams that he offered her carte blanche to produce any of his works in his lifetime). Her television credits include a series-regular role on *Shannon*; a recurring role on *The Gangster Chronicles*; and guest-starring on a slew of series including *Tracey Takes On..., Ellen, Murder She Wrote, Moonlighting, Cagney & Lacey* and *Hill Street Blues*. Her film work includes the Andy Garcia vehicle *Steal Big, Steal Little; Yes, Giorgio* with Luciano Pavorotti and the forthcoming *My Brother Jack*, starring with Marco Leonardi (*Cinema Paradiso*).

As a writer, her column, "The Actor's Way" appears in *Back Stage West/Drama-Logue*. She is a member of The Actors Studio, The Television Academy of Arts and Sciences, Women in Film, and The Hollywood Women Press Club.

Though co-author EDDIE SHAPIRO's writing and theatre criticism has been published in several magazines and newspapers across the country. He spends the bulk of his time performing; touring the country in five separate one-man musicals for Educational Events Inc. Eddie's other stage work includes off-Broadway, regional productions and more children's theatre productions than he can remember, but chances are, he's scared your kid. On film, you can blink and miss him in several pieces, including anything that features Andy Warhol as a character. Eddie has worked extensively for AIDS Walk, both in Los Angeles and New York, and is a graduate of NYU's Tisch School of the Arts and Circle in the Square Theatre School.

Photographer ED KRIEGER has been a busy actor as well as photographer for over thirty years. His professional acting career began in Chicago, with credits that include *Hot L Baltimore, The Sunshine Boys, Steambath, Robert and Elizabeth* (U.S. premiere), *Company, The Fantasticks, Godspell, Man of La Mancha* and over 1,000 performances of *Fiddler on the Roof.* Since moving to Los Angeles in 1979, he has appeared in local theatre productions of *42nd Street, Evita, Annie, God Bless You Mr. Rosewater* and *Working*. His on-camera credits include *Melrose Place, The Client, Young and the Restless, Against the Grain, Sisters, L.A. Law, General Hospital, The Twilight Zone,* and feature films *Chameleon, Childs Play 2* and *Alien Nation.*

Ed's photo hobby developed into a second career as fellow actors asked him to take headshots for them. He soon had a large clientele which included many actors and major theatres in Chicago. Today, Ed's photos are published in major publications across the country. In Los Angeles, he has photographed for Music Theatre of Southern California, Theatre League, Santa Barbara CLO, Civic Light Opera of South Bay Cities, Cabrillo Music Theatre, The Cast, Theatre 40, Actors Alley, The Fountain Theatre, Deaf West, Actors Co-op, KCET TV, and Screen Actors Guild. He is currently contributing photographer for *Back Stage West/Drama-Logue.*